# THE DICTATOR
# NEXT DOOR

A book in the series

AMERICAN ENCOUNTERS / GLOBAL INTERACTIONS

A series edited by Gilbert M. Joseph

and Emily S. Rosenberg

# THE DICTATOR NEXT DOOR

The Good Neighbor Policy and
the Trujillo Regime in the
Dominican Republic,
1930–1945

ERIC PAUL ROORDA

DUKE UNIVERSITY PRESS

DURHAM AND LONDON, 1998

5th printing, 2006
© 1998 Duke University Press
All rights reserved
Printed in the United States
of America on acid-free paper ∞
Typeset in Bembo by Tseng Information Systems, Inc.
Library of Congress Cataloging-in-Publication Data appear
on the last printed page of this book.

AMERICAN ENCOUNTERS / GLOBAL INTERACTIONS

A series edited by Gilbert M. Joseph
and Emily S. Rosenberg

This series aims to stimulate critical perspectives and fresh interpretive frameworks for scholarship on the history of the imposing global presence of the United States. Its primary concerns include the deployment and contestation of power, the construction and deconstruction of cultural and political borders, the fluid meanings of intercultural encounters, and the complex interplay between the global and the local. *American Encounters* seeks to strengthen dialogue and collaboration between historians of U.S. international relations and area studies specialists.

The series encourages scholarship based on multiarchival historical research. At the same time, it supports a recognition of the representational character of all stories about the past and promotes critical inquiry into issues of subjectivity and narrative. In the process, *American Encounters* strives to understand the context in which meanings related to nations, cultures, and political economy are continually produced, challenged, and reshaped.

TO PEARL ELAINE AND WILLIAM SIMON ROORDA

AND

TO A. E. DOYLE

# CONTENTS

Acknowledgments    ix

Introduction    1

ONE ✦ Dominican History, the United States in the Caribbean,
and the Origins of the Good Neighbor Policy    6

TWO ✦ The Dominican Revolution of 1930 and the Policy
of Nonintervention    31

THREE ✦ The Bankrupt Neighbor Policy: Depression Diplomacy
and the Foreign Bondholders Protective Council    63

FOUR ✦ What Will the Neighbors Think? Dictatorship and
Diplomacy in the Public Eye    88

FIVE ✦ Genocide Next Door: The Haitian Massacre of 1937
and the Sosua Jewish Refugee Settlement    127

SIX ✦ Gold Braid and Striped Pants: The Culture of Foreign
Relations in the Dominican Republic    149

SEVEN ✦ Fortress America, Fortaleza Trujillo: The Hull-Trujillo
Treaty and the Second World War    192

EIGHT ✦ The Good Neighbor Policy and Dictatorship    230

Notes    245
Bibliography    307
Index    327

## ACKNOWLEDGMENTS

◆

The process that produced this book began on a snowy afternoon in Baltimore in 1983, much like this one in Louisville in 1997, listening to Milton S. Eisenhower's views on the U.S. invasion of the Dominican Republic in 1965. After four hours of conversation and a big manhattan in a Disney cartoon tumbler, he suggested I apply to Johns Hopkins for graduate school. My interest in the Dominican Republic and my association with the Johns Hopkins University began with Dr. Eisenhower, and so does this attempt to thank as many of the people who have helped me write this book as I can remember. The first who comes to mind is my friend Paul Haspel, who initiated the chain of introductions that led to my interview with Milton Eisenhower, and who drove me through the snow to see him. Since then, there have been hundreds of people who have given me introductions and rides, among a thousand other kinds of assistance, from my mentors to the people who picked me up hitchhiking on the way to the Hoover Library in Iowa.

Edward Crapol's classes at William and Mary motivated me to study diplomatic history, and he directed the thesis that involved my interview with Milton Eisenhower, among other Eisenhower administration officials. At Johns Hopkins, Louis Galambos, editor of the Dwight Eisenhower Papers (and strayed disciple of Samuel Flagg Bemis), guided me through my dissertation; Franklin W. Knight directed my Latin American studies and assisted me in receiving a Fulbright Fellowship to do research in the Dominican Republic; and Francis E. Rourke schooled me in the perspectives of political science and bureaucracy studies. Professors Galambos, Knight, and Rourke constituted my dissertation committee, which was hard service at low pay. Johns Hopkins also supported my research with graduate fellowships and a grant to go to the Hoover Institute in Palo Alto, California.

Research at the Hoover and Roosevelt presidential libraries has been a joy because of the helpful archivists in West Branch, Iowa, and Hyde Park, New York, inspiring places both. Dwight Miller at the Hoover Library was especially considerate to point me in the right direction. A Vigortone Scholarship from the Hoover Foundation and Beeke-Levy Fellowship from the Eleanor and Franklin Roosevelt Library Foundation made possible the weeks I spent among the papers of the presidents who figure in this study.

I encountered memorable settings, rich information, and affable experts in the many places (twelve towns and three countries) where research for this book took place. A list of all the people who boosted me along the way would run as long as the closing credits of a cinema epic, because they include staff members at the National Archives, old and new, especially the Motion Picture Branch; the Library of Congress, especially the Manuscripts Room and the Hispanics Branch; the Navy and Marine Corps Historical Centers; the Columbus Library of the Organization of American States; the National Air and Space Museum Archive; the Milton Eisenhower Library; the Sterling Memorial Library; the Hoover Institute on War and Peace; the Naval War College; the Pioneer Records Service; the Public Record Office; the Universidad Autónoma de Santo Domingo; the Biblioteca Nacional and the Archivo General de la Nación.

Many scholars have been generous with their knowledge and time, suggesting approaches, sharing sources, collaborating on conference panels, reading drafts, and providing friendship and encouragement. Lauren "Robin" Derby has been especially motivational, beginning when we visited Rafael Trujillo's ruined estate with Julie Franks, another I have to thank. The National Endowment for the Humanities funded the 1993 visit when I met them, support I gratefully acknowledge. The sessions the three of us put together for the Latin American Studies Association and American Historical Association meetings in 1994 triggered many fortunate events for me. These panel presentations assisted me in deepening the study, and I thank Catherine LeGrand, Bruce Calder, and Louis Pérez Jr. for their participation. Panel presentations at two meetings of the Society for Historians of American Foreign Relations also helped me a great deal, with the help of Douglas Little, Judith Ewell, and Michael Weis. Anonymous reviewers at *Diplomatic History* and Howard Wiarda helped me to improve the chapter on the Haitian massacre (Chapter 5), which appeared as an article in that journal. Thanks especially to Gil Joseph and Catherine LeGrand for inviting me to the conference they organized at Yale University with Ricardo Salvatore in 1995, "Rethinking the Post-Colonial Encounter," and for steering me to Duke University Press, which published parts of this study in a volume generated by the conference: *Close Encounters of Empire: Writing the Cultural History of United States Latin American Relations* (1998).

Some of the most captivating information and images in the present volume were kindly provided to me by Scott R. Schoenfeld, whose cooperation was instrumental in the completion of this project.

The Williams College–Mystic Seaport Museum Maritime Studies Program financed my conference travel for three years, supplemented my NEH grant for research in Santo Domingo, and provided student research assistants among whom John Bohannon and Katherine Paculba were especially helpful. John Lewis Gaddis found merit in this approach and offered me the chance to work at the Contemporary History Institute of Ohio University, where I learned a great deal and met Michael Hall, who brought his knowledge of the Dominican Republic to bear on an earlier draft of the manuscript. Bellarmine College, where I teach, supported the last stage of this research with a grant and provides an atmosphere of collegiality that I appreciate.

Many friends helped me during my research travels, especially Barbara Harrick, who puts me up (and puts up with me) every year when I visit Washington to rifle the files, and Mark Welsh, who hosted us during my research at the Public Record Office in Kew, England.

One individual stands out as emblematic of my fourteen-year pursuit of U.S.-Dominican relations. Every time I went to the Dominican Republic, Julio Santana showed up without prior arrangement to add serendipity to the quest. He was there from the first hour I spent in the country in 1985, when he offered to acquaint me with the use of the informal *carro público* system. He was a homeless *tiguere,* a clever young man of the streets of the Las Américas barrio, and although I was distrustful of him, I needed to know how to get downtown. Beginning with that first ride with seven other people in a compact car across the Ozama River to Parque Central, Julio led me to the places I wanted to go, and many other places I knew nothing about, and broke down the fear I had of the sprawling city and its people. He guided me with complete confidence from the office of the director of the National Library to the exclusive interiors of the Casa de Campo resort, gaining access anywhere he wanted to go by being powerfully suave, *suave,* like a smooth *merengue*. This attitude seems to me now to be characteristically Dominican, a lesson in the rise of Rafael Trujillo, and also in the Aristotelian metaphysic that underlies part of the following study: sometimes, form does determine substance. Julio tutored my bad Spanish, speaking in English he learned from U.S. airborne troops in 1965–66, and refused to accept more than a token 100-peso note for many days of help. When I returned in 1988, this time to the north coast, I met Julio on the highway after my first visit to the town of Sosua, which plays a dramatic role in this history and became my base for Fulbright work in 1989. I was waiting for a *guagua* to cling to for the ride back to Puerto Plata; he drove up in a rental car and commented offhandedly, "I knew I would see you again." No longer living on the streets of the capital, he had gotten a job as a translator—of German! I met him last in 1991, when our respective tour groups of German and U.S. visitors met in front of the palace of Diego Columbus in the heart of the ancient colonial zone in Santo Domingo. On that occasion, as in 1988, I had sailed to the country aboard the schooner *Spirit of Massachusetts* with the Long Island University–Southampton SEAmester program. Among many other reasons, I thank the program founder Douglas Hardy, the most durable, indomitable, and energetic man I have ever met, for bringing about these encounters, and for giving me the chance to explore so much of the land and waters of Hispaniola.

Saving the best for last, my most profound appreciation is reserved for those to whom this book is dedicated. My parents have supported my passion to be a historian since I was a little kid, and encouraged me at every turn of the circuitous path of getting an education, competing for a job, and publishing a book. My spouse, A. E. Doyle, has been an editor, researcher, computer consultant, and travel buddy whose spirit and humor have made this odyssey enjoyable. Our daughter Alida has already charmed librarians here and abroad on my behalf, and her sister Frances shows equal promise as a research assistant.

The two subjects of this book help to define each other: the Good Neighbor policy, the initiative to improve Latin American relations through nonintervention and friendship that developed during the Hoover and Roosevelt administrations; and the Generalísimo Rafael Trujillo regime, the dictatorship that consolidated in the Dominican Republic at the same time and lasted thirty-one years. Trujillo's seizure of power in 1930 and his repressive military rule thereafter tested U.S. resolve to quit meddling in the internal affairs of its neighbors and to preserve amiable relationships with all Latin American leaders, regardless of their path to power or political stripe. The formation of the Trujillo regime showed that a foreign policy based on the principles of national sovereignty and self-determination, the *Geist* of the Good Neighbor policy, meant having to accept as gracefully as possible the nearby existence of regimes antithetical to the principles of peace and democracy. The Good Neighbor policy demonstrated to a generation of Caribbean dictators that they were free to run their countries however they pleased, so long as they maintained common enemies with the United States: first the fascists, then the communists.

The combination of nonintervention on the part of the United States and a powerful dictatorship in the Dominican Republic imposed new limits on the hegemony Washington had long exercised over that country. The connection between the Good Neighbor policy and the Trujillo regime offers a revealing perspective on the debate over how democratic states should treat authoritarian governments. It also calls into question the ability of any single individual, group, or branch of government in the United States to control or even to consistently influence the forces of nationalism and personalism that intertwine in the figure of a dictator, whatever he is called: Führer, Duce, Chairman, First Secretary, or Generalísimo.

Dictatorship has been the greatest problem of the twentieth century, rising up after the Great War to fuse the worst aspects of the old autocracies to new ways of thinking and of mobilizing the masses. Gaining momentum with the global depression in the late 1920s and 1930s, the formation of dictatorships in Europe, Asia, and Latin America was a central challenge to the Hoover and Roosevelt administrations. The behavior of these states was menacing, with their single-party political systems; enormous public rallies; ethnic, racial, and anti-intellectual violence; military buildups; and territorial aggression. It was also impossible to ignore, as the proliferation of communications technology—electronic, cinematic, and print—brought these disturbing scenes home to the public in the United States and gave such media greater prominence in society, politics, and foreign relations than they had ever had before. It also increased the importance of public relations, because henceforth diplomacy would be carried out with the cameras rolling, the microphones on, and the bulbs popping. Publicity sometimes made it difficult to discern who really spoke and acted for the United States, as different individuals with claims to represent the country (generals, senators, and secretaries of state) said different things about the various new tyrannies, near and far.

Trujillo's control of the Dominican military assured that stability would prevail under his rule, but sometimes stability did not live up to its billing. Although imposing order with devastating force, the regime's foreign and domestic policies did not coincide with U.S. interests in several important regards. The Dominican Republic became a difficult place to do business, a querulous participant in negotiations, and a major cause of Caribbean disquiet, including genocide, war scares, and assassinations. The regime cooperated with U.S. defense efforts but also made overtures to the Axis governments, which it strongly resembled in style and ideology. Trujillo's dictatorship, directly attributable to the U.S. Marine occupation of the Dominican Republic in 1916–24, rebuked the democratic principles the United States espoused in its foreign policy. The Dominican intervention was supposed to establish a representative system supported by an apolitical police force, but instead it created a military dictatorship with a single-party state organized on the principles not of democracy but of hero worship. Although Trujillo's military mentors prided themselves on the achievements of the occupation and their seeming continuation under the

Trujillo regime, the fact that his rule was sustained by violence and driven by vanity became common knowledge. For this reason, Trujillo's bombastic cooperation with the Good Neighbor policy was unwelcome to many policy makers in the Roosevelt administration who did not want to associate with everyone in the Latin American neighborhood on equal terms, preferring to shun the dictators. The threat of war with much more powerful dictators overseas in the late 1930s removed such discrimination as an option. Overall, Trujillo directed his government's foreign and domestic affairs with self-conscious autonomy and brutal efficiency, giving the lie to the prevailing notion that he was a pliable client of the United States.

Upon close examination of "bilateral" relations between the countries, the appearance of a unified "policy" on the part of the United States begins to blur, and multiple sources of influence instead come into focus. All of these together constitute the full relationship, and it is confusing and contradictory. The picture of the Good Neighbor policy that emerges from this case study shows Trujillo himself at the center of a crowded stage of international actors: diplomats, Navy and Marine officers, bankers, members of the foreign "colonies" in Santo Domingo/Ciudad Trujillo, journalists, lobbyists, and legislators. These individuals disagreed about the merits of Trujillo, and their actions and rhetoric toward the regime communicated conflicting messages to its leader. Trujillo was seen as an embarrassment to the United States by many in the State Department, the news media, and Congress, who opposed close ties with him. But Trujillo's supporters in the U.S. military and the members of a growing "Dominican lobby," especially Franklin Roosevelt's close friend Joseph E. Davies and several powerful congressmen, pressed Trujillo's interests in the United States and accepted his hospitality in the Dominican Republic. The official "policy" had to be sorted out of this muddle, and it was often not easy to find. Those who went looking for it were likely to emerge with different versions of what it meant to be neighborly.

The "Good Neighbor policy" also had to adapt to different environments everywhere. In the case of the Dominican Republic, some of the important factors influencing policy implementation were Trujillo's sweeping megalomania; the conflation of personal, social, and political considerations in the culture of his regime; the committed opposition to his rule by important officials at the State Department, especially Sumner Welles; and the assistance of his circle of military comrades in buying arms and gaining favor in the United States. Every set of bilateral relations is the product of a unique environment of circumstances and individuals, thus preventing broad policy from evolving in identical forms in all places. In the case of the Good Neighbor policy, as the first half of the Trujillo regime demonstrates, the genus mutated into very dissimilar species in the individual nations of Latin America.

The domestic debate over the proper role of the United States in the world shifted against costly military involvement abroad in the 1920s, although the rise of authoritarianism around the world was similarly disfavored in the United States. Nonintervention and dictatorship were particularly difficult to reconcile in the Caribbean, where the U.S. presence had been very invasive, and where its responsibility for political developments was widely discerned. The Good Neighbor policy developed as an effort to encourage order, solvency, cooperation, and liberalism in Latin America through persuasion and benefits, rather than by force, but it would be put to a variety of unforeseen uses by Latin American leaders, especially those with autocratic power like Trujillo. To strenuously oppose dictatorships within the zone of U.S. hegemony, however, would not enhance the country's strategic or economic interests and would invite charges of imperialism from the increasingly anti-interventionist community of Latin American nations. So the debate over dictatorship broke along regional lines: to oppose European and Asian fascism, the United States required a bloc of allies to the south, especially in the region of the Panama Canal, which happened to include several dictatorships. The authoritarian regimes of the Caribbean were integral to U.S. war planning and preparedness against the authoritarian regimes of Europe and Asia, a fact that significantly altered the role of "good neighbor."

The urgency to erect a "Fortress America" against European and Asian fascism came to dominate the Good Neighbor policy in the late 1930s, and the antidictatorial scruples of Roosevelt's diplomats were set aside. Subsequently, the agenda of Trujillo and his U.S. military allies prevailed in relations between the two countries. The Navy and Marines fêted Trujillo on visits to Washington, and he concluded a series of agreements with the United States that removed its objectionable customs receivership from the Dominican Republic (the Hull-Trujillo Treaty of 1940) and established a military alliance in its place. Trujillo's skillful handling of Dominican foreign relations allowed him to perpetrate his genocide of Haitians resident in the Dominican Republic in 1937 without serious diplomatic damage, and to profit from the onset of another crisis, the Second World War, which brought loans from the Export-Import Bank and an air force from the Lend-Lease Act. Although diplomats would temporarily halt the flow of U.S. arms to the Trujillo regime after the war ended, the military culture Trujillo shared with ranking U.S. admirals and generals assured his later place as a Cold War ally of the United States.

◆

# CHAPTER ONE

# Dominican History, the United States in the Caribbean, and the Origins of the Good Neighbor Policy

The western Atlantic Ocean washes a wide arc of land formed by the coast of North America and the archipelago of the Greater Antilles, five thousand miles of shoreline rarely viewed from the sea before the sixteenth century. The native inhabitants of the small (and often seasonal) settlements on the shore built only small craft for fishing and local travel, and only infrequently did they navigate around the stormy capes that lay between the populated estuaries in the north or cross the windy passages between the large islands in the south, called Siboney (Cuba), Quisqueya (Hispaniola), and Borinquen (Puerto Rico) by the Taino people living there.[1] Visitors from the eastern edge of the Atlantic came very rarely, and the ocean remained a virtually insurmountable barrier until the Spanish invasion initiated by Columbus. The admiral's beachhead was the island he named Hispaniola, and the city of Santo Domingo on the south coast became the capital of Spanish colonization in the region and the base from which armies of warriors conquered the neighboring islands and the mainland along the Gulf of Mexico and the Caribbean Sea.

## COLONIZATION

Santo Domingo's years as the center of Spanish expansion were few, however, partly owing to the devastation of the native Taino population from disease and slavery in mines that held little gold or silver. Also, the mineral booty of Mexico and Perú far outstripped the profits of sugar and tobacco cultivation on Hispaniola, and the geographical advantages of the port of Havana, situated near the Gulf Stream on the north coast of Cuba, exceeded those of Santo Domingo, which lay at the mouth of the flood-prone Ozama River far from the transatlantic sea-lanes. As a result, the colony stagnated on the margin of the Spanish empire, which continued to spread southward across South America into the seventeenth century. And although the traffic of ships between Spain and the principal ports of the Caribbean increased and gained importance as the Spanish empire grew, the connections between Spain's Antillean outposts and the landmass to the north, which Spain claimed but did not occupy, remained few.

The seventeenth century brought settlers defiant of Spanish authority to the North American coast and the Lesser Antilles, the chain of small islands running south from Puerto Rico to the coast of South America. English, Dutch, and French colonists from Canada to Curaçao produced food crops, tobacco, cotton, and sugar, often using the labor of slaves taken from West Africa, and gathered furs, timber, and fish, all on land and water claimed by the Spanish. Spain's imperial control of the region slipped further as networks of exchange developed among the new settlements in the western Atlantic and spread to the insular fringe of the Spanish New World empire. Spain's violent opposition to incursions on its mercantile border was ineffective, and the northern European colonies gained a firm purchase and began to expand.

In addition to these rival colonies, which were conceived and underwritten by organizations in London, Amsterdam, and Paris, an international population of "freebooters," mainly former sailors seeking less arduous lives, found a niche for settlement in northwestern Hispaniola. There they hunted wild pigs and cattle, descendants of the conquistadores' livestock, and smoked the meat as the Tainos did on *boucans*. These "buccaneers" traded the product to passing ships, which they also occasionally attacked in small boats from shore. Spain attempted to exterminate the buccaneers on Hispaniola in seaborne assaults launched from Santo Domingo, but the brutal raids gave that heterogeneous lot a common cause: revenge on the Spanish. The buccaneers' damaging piracy against the empire, and their de facto control of the western third of Hispaniola, provided an opening for France to establish the colony of Saint Domingue there in 1697; Spain ceded the territory and recognized French control in return for the suppression of the buccaneers.

French Saint Domingue became the most prosperous colony in the region, while Spanish Santo Domingo on the eastern side of the island remained an imperial backwater. The small population there continued to rely on cattle ranching on open land and subsistence cultivation on small plots, still isolated from the commercial activity of the Atlantic world. But colonists in Saint Domingue turned to agriculture and slave labor during the eighteenth century, importing more than nine hundred thousand unwilling Africans to cultivate cash crops, especially sugar, on large plantations. The tremendous wealth produced by slaves in Saint Domingue made it one of the richest of all the European colonial possessions in the world during that imperial age. The sugar boom drew the ports of Cap François and Port-au-Prince into a closer orbit with metropolitan France and oriented Santo Domingo toward its western border in a paradoxical relationship of trade and aggression that in some respects has not changed even today. But the vicious system of gang labor and the demographic imbalance between the free population (mostly white and mulatto) and the black slave population, which was ten times larger, combined to destabilize the plantation society. The outbreak of the French Revolution in 1789 further confused race and class relations among free colonists, and in 1790 a revolt led by fugitive slaves grew into a general bloodletting that lasted fourteen years and killed legions of French, Spanish, British, African, and creole fighters of every shade of skin color. In 1801, the most celebrated of the African generals, Toussaint L'Ouverture, invaded the eastern half of the island, which had changed hands among the European powers several times since the uprising began eleven years earlier. Although Spain eventually regained control over Santo Domingo, France could not wrest Saint Domingue from the native armies, who won its independence in 1804 under the command of Jean-Jacques Dessalines; he chose the pre-Conquest Taino word for the region, Haiti, as the new country's name.

Changes of a different nature took place in the British colonies of North America during the eighteenth century. The mainland colonies were spared a large measure of the conflict that swept back and forth across the Caribbean islands, but prospered from an active commerce with them, even in time of war, when prices rose to offset the added risks of doing business. In fact, the system of plantation agriculture that developed in the British West Indies was dependent on the northern colonies for food, livestock, timber, shipping, and markets for sugar and molasses. North American merchants also traded with the non-British colonies of the western Atlantic, although the Navigation Acts governing British commerce reduced the legal options for lucrative trade outside the empire. The mercantile regulations of Britain notwithstanding, Yankee entrepreneurs sought sugar wherever it could be purchased at a good price, developing trade connections in the Caribbean wherever the "sugar frontier" of plantation agriculture moved. One of the measures that precipitated the revolt of the North American colonies against Britain was the Sugar Act, which sought to enforce the long-ignored duty on cane products from foreign colonies like Saint Domingue. Success in the American Revolution gave citizens of the United States the right to pursue trade outside the British empire, but they lost the profitable privilege of trading within it. The economy of the new republic was further imperiled by the manifold upheaval of the French Revolution, the Napoleonic Wars, and the Haitian Revolution, which obstructed its commercial relations both in continental Europe and the Caribbean.

Although George Washington dabbled with enterprises in support of L'Ouverture's rebellion in Haiti, the "black republic" was mainly shunned politically by American leaders, especially those in the South, who feared the contagion of slave revolt. But the wars of colonial independence that broke out in Spanish America, where new nations declared their sovereignty one by one in the first quarter of the nineteenth century, were welcomed by the United States. The colony of Santo Domingo proclaimed itself to be the independent Dominican Republic in 1821, but Haiti invaded soon after and began a unification of the island that lasted more than two decades. Haitian rule brought the abolition of Dominican slavery and caused many of the landowning Dominican elite to leave the island. The "Dominican" portion of Hispaniola now became a region of Haiti, whose national sovereignty was not recognized by its former occupiers, Spain, France, and Britain, or by the rising power in the western Atlantic, the United States. Haiti did not share significantly in the growing commerce between North and South America, while neighboring Cuba and Puerto Rico (the last vestiges of Spain's New World empire) expanded the system of sugar and slaves to supply the booming markets in New York and Boston, among other growing cities.[2]

## DOMINICAN INDEPENDENCE AND U.S. EXPANSION

When the Dominican Republic won independence from Haiti in 1844, it reentered the arena of imperial rivalry. The liberal "trinity" of the Dominican independence movement—Juan Pablo Duarte, José del Rosario Sánchez, and Ramón Mella—quickly lost power to the leader of the Dominican military forces, Pedro Santana, who alternated rule with his personal rival,

Buenaventura Báez, for most of the next thirty years. The United States, Spain, France, and Britain competed with one another for advantage with Santana and Báez, who maneuvered among the powers for advantages of their own, especially for protection against Haiti. The European empires and the United States all appointed agents to scout the situation in the Dominican Republic, report on its economic and strategic potential, and sound out the Dominicans on the possibility of annexing a part or all of the republic. Both Santana and Báez proposed annexation to each of the foreign powers at one time or another, and such plans received serious consideration in Washington during that expansionist era. Despite several near misses between 1844 and 1860, the four powers prevented any one of their number from gaining territory in the Dominican Republic, with the European states gradually uniting behind Báez, who raised the specter of U.S. encroachment at every opportunity, against Santana, who had U.S. support. The American Civil War ended the stalemate, providing an opening for Spain to reannex the Dominican Republic in 1861 to prevent it from becoming "Haitian or Yankee," and for Santana to secure the foreign military assistance he desired to combat threats both external and internal.[3]

The sectional conflict in the United States temporarily delayed the steady increase of the nation's influence in the Caribbean region that had begun with the acquisition of Louisiana in 1803. The new American port of New Orleans had boomed with trade since then, an increasing amount of it with Cuba. The Spanish cession of the Floridas in 1819 and the Mexican War settlement of 1848 added two more coasts to the United States: the Gulf Coast and the coast of California. The transportation systems that developed between these new destinations for settlement and trade and the cities of the East Coast brought the Caribbean more closely into the dynamic of U.S. economic development. The extension of the coastal sea-lanes of the United States around Florida to the Gulf Coast increased traffic to Havana and western Cuba, which supplied correspondingly greater amounts of sugar and tobacco to the United States in the decades before the Civil War. Those who wanted to try their luck in California could go there overland across plains and mountains, around brutal Cape Horn on at least a three-month voyage, or across Central America on one of two routes connecting Atlantic and Pacific steamship lines. The first route was a coach road across the Colombian province of Panama that was inaugurated just in time to catch the first wave of the 1849 California Gold Rush; a railroad along the route opened in 1855. The second route was across Nicaragua, using small steamers on the San Juan River and Lake Managua on the way from sea to sea.[4]

After the establishment of these intracoastal enterprises, the United States closely monitored affairs in Panama and Nicaragua, sending gunboats to maintain order along the Panama Railroad and to back up Cornelius Vanderbilt in his squabbles with the Nicaraguan government.[5] The sea-lanes between the East Coast and the two isthmian routes, both of which were imagined as sites for an interoceanic canal, were important in the strategic calculations of the U.S. government.[6] Ships on their way into the Caribbean Sea most often navigated through the Windward and Mona passages flanking the island of Hispaniola, which would have to be defended in the event of war. For this reason, the acquisition of a naval base, or "coaling station," at Samaná Bay in the northeast Dominican Republic was one of the main objects sought by a succession of American envoys to Santo Domingo beginning in 1854.[7] The Spanish Annexation of 1861 interrupted these plans, but they quickly reemerged after the Dominicans expelled the Spanish in the War of Restoration, which ended four months after the American Civil War in 1865.

The Andrew Johnson and Ulysses S. Grant administrations in the United States and the administration of Buenaventura Báez in the Dominican Republic came close to concluding agreements for Samaná Bay on several occasions, with negotiations often in the hands of prominent American military men: Admiral David Dixon Porter for Johnson and General Orville E. Babcock for Grant. The U.S. Navy under Grant also intervened against the enemies of Báez under the command of Gregorio Luperón, who planned an attack from Haiti by sea. But the Báez regime proved to be too shaky, and anti-imperialist sentiment in the U.S. Congress too strong, for territorial deals to solidify, despite a very close call in 1870. On that occasion, the abolitionist Senator Charles Sumner denounced the proposed annexation treaty by comparing it to the murderous acquisition of Naboth's vineyard by the biblical Ahab, who incurred God's wrath and was eaten by dogs. Also working against annexation during the 1870s was the nationalist war hero Luperón, leader of the powerful Azul Party after the Restoration. The strategic potential of Samaná Bay continued to be one of the dominant motifs in relations between the Dominican Republic and the United States, however, even after the Spanish-American War provided the U.S. Navy with prime anchorages in Cuba and Puerto Rico.

Luperón's protégé, Ulisis Heureaux, came to power in 1883 and, break-

ing with his mentor, established a dictatorship in 1888 that lasted eleven
years. Also in 1888, Heureaux took out a loan of three-quarters of a million pounds sterling from the Dutch banking house Westendorp, money
intended to stabilize the existing debt (contracted by Báez) and to finance
the infrastructural development of the Dominican Republic, especially railroad construction. Heureaux used impressive uniforms and military spectacle "to underscore visually the importance of authority" and reduce the
fragmentation of armed forces around the country, where up to a thousand local leaders called themselves "generals" in 1880.[8] He also conducted
his foreign policy personally from a power base of unprecedented internal
stability, although the expanded foreign debt posed new threats of external
interference by the governments of European creditors. The Westendorp
Company collected all Dominican customs through an office set up under
the terms of the Dutch loan, subtracting what was owed to the bondholders from the country's external revenues and providing operating expenses
to the Dominican government from the remaining funds. The Westendorp
Company went bankrupt in 1892 after its agent revealed fraud in the Customs Service, where Heureaux had arranged preferential tariff treatment
for certain of his domestic creditors.

A consortium of U.S. businessmen calling themselves the San Domingo
Improvement Company bought out Westendorp soon after its failure and
took over its railroad contracts and European bondholders. The American
takeover precipitated a dispute with the Dominican National Bank, which
had been chartered by the French banking house Crédit Mobilier. A French
warship called at Santo Domingo in 1892 to protect the interests of Crédit Mobilier and its investors, and two more came in 1895 to investigate
the treatment of French nationals. The second time, three U.S. Navy ships
were on hand as well to observe the dispute, which was settled when the
San Domingo Improvement Company purchased the National Bank from
Crédit Mobilier and paid an indemnity to the French, putting off for the
moment European intervention on the grounds of Dominican insolvency.
In the meantime, the U.S.-owned Clyde Line established regular steamship
service between New York and the principal Dominican ports, increasing
the frequency and regularity of contacts between the countries and forming "part of the advance wave of American economic penetration into the
West Indies."[9] American steamships and investments also fueled the growth
of the Dominican sugar industry during the last twenty years of the century.[10] When Heureaux was assassinated in 1899, he left the foreign debt

intact and the Central Dominican Railroad unfinished; the American investors of the San Domingo Improvement Company controlled both.[11]

## THE ROOSEVELT COROLLARY

The defaulted Westendorp loan dogged Heureaux's successors in the turbulent years following his death, as the European governments whose nationals held the bonds on the Dominican debt—France, Germany, Italy, and the Netherlands—increased their pressure for payment on a series of warring Dominican political leaders. This pressure culminated in an international crisis in 1904, when warships of each of those nations sailed to Santo Domingo to press the creditors' claims on a prostrate Dominican Republic. Coming on the heels of the German and British bombardment of Venezuela to extract debt payments the year before, the multinational convoy was seen as a further threat to U.S. stewardship of the region by Theodore Roosevelt. Roosevelt had recently concluded treaties with the new Republic of Cuba (which had gained putative independence with Yankee help) for the lease of Guantánamo Bay and with the new Republic of Panama (also putatively independent after Yankee intervention) for a Canal Zone along the route of the Panama Railroad line, recently the site of a failed French effort to dig across the isthmus. Moreover, Roosevelt had asserted American rights to arm the canal he proposed to build, leaving little doubt that the United States would exercise strategic control of the region, in addition to its growing economic and cultural influence there.[12]

The combined European threat to the Dominican Republic in 1904 was a direct challenge to Roosevelt's vision of U.S. hegemony in the waters and republics to the south. To preempt intervention in the western Atlantic by any nation other than the United States, Roosevelt added a new dimension to the Monroe Doctrine (1823), which pledged security for the Latin American republics against European imperialism. In his interpretation, the Monroe Doctrine implied a responsibility for the United States to correct the problems that provoked European intervention in Latin America. He announced what became known as the Roosevelt Corollary to the Monroe Doctrine in messages to Congress, asserting that it was the duty of the United States to play the role of an "international police power" when the "impotence" or "wrongdoing" of regional governments attracted the attention of European warships. To ward off the European creditors from the bankrupt Dominican Republic, Roosevelt took control of the Dominican Customs Service in 1904 and enforced a lien on the nation's external revenue, its primary source of income.[13]

The San Domingo Improvement Company had operated the Dominican Customs Service, the Caja General, with some success during Heureaux's rule, but the brief prosperity of the 1890s ended with his death. The ensuing government upheaval made a bad economic situation worse, prolonging the Dominican Republic's transportation problems: shallow ports with poor facilities, short rail lines, and bad roads with few bridges. The political turbulence of the early twentieth century made the country an even less attractive place to trade than it already was, and customs revenues shrank as the internecine warfare dragged on. Despite the beginnings of centralized, industrialized sugar production east of Santo Domingo, the volume of trade did not provide sufficient revenue to pay the debts run up by Heureaux. But the island was central to the Caribbean zone of hegemony that the United States had been projecting with increasing energy for most of its history, an expansion of power in which Theodore Roosevelt had played a significant personal role. When anti-imperialists in Congress balked at his takeover of Dominican customs houses, Roosevelt used executive power to conclude a "modus vivendi" with the Dominican Republic in 1905 which legitimized U.S. control of Dominican finances. He then gained legislative support to formalize the arrangement with a treaty, or "convention," in 1907. Under its terms, the Bureau of Insular Affairs of the War Department staffed and operated the General Receivership of Dominican Customs, which subtracted 55 percent of the duties paid on imports to service the Dominican debt, giving the rest to the Dominican government. The treaty also set the terms of a $20 million loan to the new administration of Ramón Cáceres through National City Bank of New York, a prominent institution in the evolution of "dollar diplomacy" in the Caribbean area. The loan paid off the bonds held in Europe and floated new bonds in the United States.

Two American citizens now had tremendous influence in Dominican affairs: the U.S. minister to the Dominican Republic and the general receiver of dominican customs. Previously, the U.S. minister had been accredited to both nations on Hispaniola, but he lived in the Haitian capital of Port-au-Prince. When the War Department moved into Dominican customs houses in 1904, the State Department upgraded its diplomatic representation, assigning a minister full-time to Santo Domingo. The general receiver, an official of the War Department, became both the steward of the Dominican foreign debt (now owed to U.S. investors) and the supervisor of Dominican ports and foreign trade (increasingly dominated by U.S. businesses). The men who held these positions lived in the capital and came into contact mainly with members of the Dominican upper class, which "consolidated" in the late nineteenth and early twentieth centuries through matrimonial alliances between the elite "old families" of the Dominican Republic and moneyed, light-skinned immigrants from Europe and the neighboring Antilles. These *gente de primera,* or "first-class people," profited from the growing sugar economy and dominated the republic's commercial ties, which were also the main concerns of the resident representatives of the United States.[14] From the perspective of Washington, the hiatus of stability in the Dominican Republic that followed the Convention of 1907 seemed to prove the efficacy of financial intervention, and President William Howard Taft's subsequent "dollar diplomacy" in the Caribbean followed the Dominican model. But such a view underestimated the importance of President Ramón Cáceres in controlling the competition among rivals in the Dominican elite and regional *caudillos* who commanded the allegiance of their local populations. When Cáceres, who had conspired to kill Heureaux in 1899, was himself assassinated in 1911, the momentary political equilibrium lost its fulcrum and five years of unprofitable disorder ensued.[15]

U.S. diplomats moved from a position of influence to one of decisive authority during this period in the Dominican Republic and around the Caribbean. The United States minister in Santo Domingo, like his counterparts in the other regional capitals, had vessels of the growing U.S. Navy at his disposal when local events ran counter to his wishes. Warships visited Dominican shores at State Department behest on dozens of occasions between 1911 and 1916, for a variety of reasons that were also becoming familiar to other Antilleans and Central Americans: to protect "American lives and property," to have a "moral effect" on troublemakers, and to enforce the dictates of commissions sent from Washington. Both Taft and Woodrow Wilson dispatched such commissions to Santo Domingo, in the company of naval forces and Marine Corps guards, whose visits resulted in the removal of two presidents, the cutoff of government revenues by the general receiver, U.S. supervision of a Dominican election, and then a nationalist crisis. The latter crisis was precipitated by the insistent demands of the Wilson administration that the Dominican government turn over control of its budget, public works, and armed forces to the United States.[16]

## THE MARINE OCCUPATION

President Juan Isidro Jiménez, whose victory in the 1914 election had been monitored by U.S. representatives, refused to accept Wilson's terms, which were also presented to Haiti. Jiménez's Haitian counterpart, Vilbrun Guillaume Sam, was killed by a mob in July 1915, prompting the U.S. Navy and Marines to take control of the country and to impose Wilson's plans for supervision of the government, economy, and infrastructure of the country. The Marine occupation of Haiti lasted nineteen years.[17]

In the Dominican Republic, Jiménez was also beleaguered by revolutionaries during 1915, but a pledge from the United States to intervene on his behalf propped up his government until early the next year, when the leader of the Dominican military, General Desiderio Arias, led a revolt against him. The U.S. Navy landed a force in Santo Domingo in May 1916, prompting Jiménez to resign, and demanded the surrender of Arias, prompting him to withdraw and leave the city to the Marines. Navy warships steamed into every major Dominican port, and Marines drove overland to take Santiago, capital of the fertile Cibao Valley region in the north, in early July.[18] The only significant loss for U.S. forces was the wreck of the cruiser *Memphis,* driven by a tidal wave in August onto the jagged coral shoreline of Santo Domingo, where it remained for twenty years as a reminder of the intervention. As in Haiti, the military and diplomatic representatives of the United States pressed the nation's political leaders to accept without compromise Wilson's demands for control of important government functions. When they refused, U.S. Minister William Russell cut off funds from the customs receivership, which supplied 90 percent of government revenues, and denied recognition to the provisional president chosen by the Dominican Congress, Francisco Henríquez y Carvajal. Henríquez ordered new elections for December 1916, but before they could be held the Navy officer commanding the intervention, Captain Harry S. Knapp, announced that he was taking over instead.[19]

Knapp's first orders as military governor of the Dominican Republic were to outlaw gun ownership and impose censorship of speech and the press, and within weeks he had canceled elections and suspended the Dominican Congress. Although Knapp proposed a dual government for the country, with U.S. military administration and courts overseeing matters of their choosing, Henríquez and every member of his cabinet resigned within days of Knapp's announcement, and U.S. Navy officers took their places.

The "Military Occupation of the Dominican Republic," as the intervention was officially termed, extended and formalized U.S. hegemony there, already made manifest by frequent naval visits and a 90 percent share of total Dominican imports. It lasted until 1924.

The onset of World War I had virtually removed European competition for commercial ascendancy in the Caribbean, and the military occupations of Haiti and the Dominican Republic supplanted the remaining German interests in those countries. Having removed both domestic and foreign political actors from their positions of power, the occupation government of the Dominican Republic proceeded unilaterally to restructure the country's social, economic, and military institutions.[20] They carried out an agenda of infrastructural and organizational programs that, along with similar Wilsonian colonial projects in Haiti and Veracruz, Mexico, defined a kind of Progressive imperialism concerned with many of the same reforms of Progressivism in the United States: public health, public works, education, fiscal management, and civil and military service.[21]

In addition to this technocratic agenda, the Marine occupiers pursued the goal of complete civil order in the towns, where an indignant Dominican polity resented the loss of sovereignty, and in the countryside, where nationalist guerrilla resistance persisted, especially in the eastern region. Marine tactics to ensure urban control began with Knapp's censorship decree (which applied to domestic and foreign publications, theater, and individual expression) and his order to disarm the population. In addition, Marine guards patrolled the streets of Dominican cities, and Marine intelligence officers gathered information about those opposed to the occupation. When nationalist demonstrations occurred in Santo Domingo and Santiago during the *Semana Patriótica,* or "Patriotic Week," in May 1920, the military governor jailed more than a score of writers for inciting unrest and asked for reinforcements; five hundred more Marines arrived to bolster the existing force of two thousand.[22]

The Eastern District of the Marine command included the principal sugar zone of the republic, composed of increasingly larger foreign-owned estates radiating from the cities of La Romana, San Pedro de Macorís, and Santo Domingo.[23] The U.S.-owned sugar companies prospered during the occupation, taking advantage of new property-title regulations to purchase land traditionally held in common, until they owned 80 percent of the sugar acreage in the country.[24] The expansion of cane cultivation displaced peasants from the land and increased the financial stakes of the occupation in the east, where the interests of what became known as the "American Colony" of capitalists and managers were concentrated. The tenacious native insurgency that arose there against the Marine presence threatened the estates, whose monocultural occupation of the Dominican soil fueled local resistance.[25] In response, the Marines of the Eastern District employed an aircraft squadron, based at the airfield of the American-owned Consuelo sugar estate, to locate and harass groups of "bandits," whose guerrilla tactics and knowledge of the terrain made them difficult to confront.[26] In order to isolate the guerrilla fighters in the field, the Marines gathered the rural population into "concentrations," where they used military bands to entertain the *campesinos* and speeches to convince them of the occupation's benevolent intentions. The Marines in the countryside, like their counterparts in the cities, also gathered intelligence on the membership and movements of the guerrilla forces.[27]

The Marines also recruited and trained Dominican soldiers to form the constabulary force envisioned by Woodrow Wilson, although during his administration the Guardia Nacional, as it was called, remained a relatively undisciplined force with no commissioned Dominican officers.[28] The U.S. Army had followed up on their turn-of-the-century interventions in Cuba, Puerto Rico, and the Philippines by training local forces there, but the Marines were new to the task when they established the Dominican Guardia Nacional and the Haitian Garde d'Haiti. Wilson's Republican successor, Warren G. Harding, criticized the interventions on Hispaniola during the 1920 election, and the following year a Senate committee conducted hearings in Washington and Santo Domingo on the subject of crimes committed by Marines and members of the Guardia against civilians.[29] Although they generally favored the Marines, the hearings contributed to the unfavorable publicity about the occupation that was generated in the United States, Latin America, and Europe by an articulate group of exiles and an American lobbyist, Horace Knowles. After the military government suppressed *Semana Patriótica* in 1920, the nationalist movement in the Dominican Republic grew in numbers and means. But relevant State and Navy Department officials agreed that there must be a "professionalized" Dominican military before the American forces could be extricated from the country.[30]

Brigadier General Harry Lee, who took command of the occupying Marine Second Brigade and the Guardia Nacional in August 1921, agreed that the "preliminary step" toward withdrawal was "organizing and training a native constabulary, in order to insure peace and order within the Republic after suspension of the military government."[31] Although the "National Guard" had recently been renamed the "National Police," Lee began an intensive enlistment and professionalization campaign geared to making it into a national army. He immediately opened a military academy at Haina, near Santo Domingo, and increased recruiting and training of the Policía Nacional in each of the three military districts.[32] Lee and the new military governor, Rear Admiral Samuel S. Robison, envisioned a Dominican army that would remain under U.S. Marine officers for some years after the anticipated departure of the Second Brigade.[33] But a prolonged military mission was unacceptable to Dominican nationalists, who also protested American financial control. Francisco Peynado, a moderate Dominican on good terms with the "American Colony" and the sugar companies, took up these issues with Sumner Welles, chief of the State Department's Latin American Division, in 1922.

Welles and Peynado, who shared fluency in English and Spanish and the culture of statesmanship, exchanged visits to Washington and the Dominican Republic while negotiating the terms of U.S. withdrawal. The compromise they concluded, called the Hughes-Peynado Plan after U.S. Secretary of State Charles Evans Hughes, was disliked both by the Dominican *pura y simple* nationalists (who demanded unconditional withdrawal, "pure and simple") and by General Lee and Military Governor Robison (whom Welles had excluded from his talks with Peynado). The nationalists protested against the $22 million loan contracted by Robison in March 1922, which extended American control of Dominican customs, and they resented the Dominican Republic having to recognize all the laws passed by the military government throughout its despised tenure. General Lee and Admiral Robison complained against the complete evacuation of U.S. forces agreed to by Peynado and Welles, claiming that the Dominican constabulary was not ready to take over for the Marines at the pace dictated by the Hughes-Peynado Plan. They also argued for a permanent U.S. military mission to ensure a peaceful transition of power. The final agreement prolonged the stay of the general receiver (under a treaty called the Convention of 1924) but evicted the Marines.[34]

The Second Brigade had been gradually withdrawing from their garrisons around the republic since July 1921, leaving them to the expanding Policía Nacional "as rapidly as recruits could be obtained and sufficiently trained." Under the Hughes-Peynado accord, a provisional government would take over all police activities, and the "Dominicanization" of the police would be completed by October 1922, when the provisional president would take office, less than a year after commissioning the first graduates of Haina Academy. Before the inauguration of Provisional President Juan B. Vicini Burgos, the Marines finished "concentrating" their forces in the major cities and were ready to turn over law enforcement to the Policía. They continued to train Dominican officers and enlisted men at centers in Santo Domingo and Santiago, however, with courses on "administration, topography, minor tactics, law, sanitation, signalling, military hygiene, target practice, and lectures in obedience, loyalty, patriotism and esprit de corps." A parade of "distinguished personages" visited the Dominican Republic and reviewed the troops of the Policía Nacional Dominicana during the last two years of the Marine occupation. The VIPs included the U.S. secretary of the navy, two rear admirals (one of them the commander of the Special Service Squadron based in the Caribbean), two Marines major generals (one of them the commandant of the Marines Corps), the governor of Puerto Rico, and the president of the Associated Press. The visitors were impressed with the "efficiency" of the force, which now numbered thirteen hundred, reported General Lee.[35]

The Policía supervised the national elections of March 1924 "without a single case of disorder," with Horacio Vásquez defeating Francisco Peynado at the polls. Before a crowd of Dominicans "in the greatest good humor," the American flag came down over Fortaleza Ozama, the military center of power in Santo Domingo since the sixteenth century, on inauguration day, 12 July 1924. A Cuban warship with a battalion of troops arrived to participate in the celebration, but no U.S. Marines marched in the street parade with the Dominican and Cuban troops and the floats representing the provinces of the republic. Robison, Lee, and the Cuban general reviewed the troops in private with President Vásquez three days later, and Vásquez hosted a reception in Robison's honor that was attended by the diplomatic corps. In a further expression of the transition in power, the event took place at the building that had been the headquarters of the Receivership, a massive structure with wide verandas on both floors, commanding a prime hilltop location; having been sold to the reconstituted Dominican government, this building was now the Presidential Palace. Robison reciprocated with a banquet at the Santo Domingo Country Club, founded during the occupation and already an important venue in foreign relations, for "the outgoing and incoming presidents and their cabinets, the Supreme Court, the visiting Cubans, and the Diplomatic Corps." Having relinquished power functionally and symbolically, Robison and Lee departed the next day, leaving civil order in the hands of Dominican officers who had been schooled in "the soldier's profession . . . raising them from the depths of primitive existence and ignorance to alert, keen, patriotic young soldiers and citizens."[36]

## THE EDUCATION OF RAFAEL TRUJILLO

One of those "raised from the depths" by Marine training was Rafael Trujillo, a towering figure in Dominican and Caribbean history who used the modernized Dominican military to seize power in 1930 and act as dictator for thirty-one years, maintaining one of the most durable regimes of the twentieth century.[37] Trujillo's family in San Cristóbal, eighteen miles west of Santo Domingo, was of transnational ethnic stock; his grandparents were Cuban, Dominican, and Haitian.[38] They were not counted among the *gente de primera,* although Trujillo, one of eleven children, carried himself as if he were. While still a boy, he demonstrated the fascination with personal appearance, clothing, and military decorations that suited him for a military career, earning the nickname "Chapita" for the bottle caps he collected like medals.[39] His early adulthood is somewhat obscure, but it is certain that he attained the post of *guardacampestre,* whose job "was (and is) to control Haitian cane-cutters," at the Boca Chica sugar estate in 1916, the year of the Marine invasion, when he was twenty-five years old. In 1918 he applied for a commission in the Guardia Nacional, directing his inquiry to Major James J. MacLean, a friend of his maternal uncle, Teódulo Pina Chevalier, along with a recommendation from his employer, the manager of the Boca Chica estate. Despite accusations of forgery against him that year, and perhaps a jail sentence, Trujillo received the rank of second lieutenant.[40] His subsequent rise and extended rule resulted from the education he received and the relationships he formed during the Marine occupation.

Rafael Trujillo was in the first class of native officers hastily graduated from the Haina Military Academy and commissioned in the constabulary by the end of 1921. The year before his appointment to the military academy, Second Lieutenant Trujillo had been acquitted of credible charges of rape and extortion by a commission of eight Marine officers. The court martial had no deleterious effect on his rise in the constabulary ranks.[41] He received further training in the Northern District under the tutelage of Colonel Richard M. Cutts and was judged to be a promising leader by his Marine supervisors. The young officer's apparent assimilation into the culture of the U.S. Marine Corps, reflected in the approval of his American superiors, accelerated his rise in the Dominican ranks during the occupation.

Less than a year after the departure of the final detachment of Marines (commanded by Colonel Cutts), Trujillo was promoted by President Horacio Vásquez to commander of the Policía Nacional Dominicana. He gained the rank of brigadier general in 1927, and the following year he led the effort to change the outdated name of the force from "police" to "army." The term "police" evoked the "constabulary" of the U.S. occupation, a designation one Dominican congressman called a "colonial replica." An "army" is really what the Dominican military had become under the Marine professionalization program of 1921–24 and under Trujillo's command.[42] The newly christened Ejército Nacional Dominicano, or "Dominican National Army," was Trujillo's virtually autonomous power base. He promoted the institution with a magazine, the *Revista Militar,* that praised his leadership of the force and argued for military expansion.[43]

Trujillo's control of the army made him the master of Dominican politics by 1930 and transformed the force from a surrogate for Marine occupation to an agent of Dominican nationalism. Trujillo's understanding of its use would give him greater leverage over the Dominican nation and its foreign relations than had been enjoyed by any previous Dominican leader, and he would exert his power in ways that reflected his experience during the occupation. The administrative actions of the military government, which pursued a vigorous Progressive agenda while stifling civil rights, provided a pattern for Trujillo to follow in his domestic program. His background as a Marine Corps protégé also provided the social context for his relations with the diplomatic, military, and civil representatives of the United States.

ORIGINS OF THE GOOD NEIGHBOR POLICY

The apparent failure of the military occupations on Hispaniola, and the ill will provoked throughout Latin America by "gunboat diplomacy" in the Caribbean, prompted a change in U.S. behavior. The Hoover and Roosevelt administrations adopted nonintervention, promotion of shared interests such as trade, and inter-American friendship (or "Pan-Americanism") as guidelines for their approach to Latin America, an approach that was dubbed the "Good Neighbor policy" in 1933. Though by reputation an innovation of the Roosevelt watch, the spirit of the Good Neighbor policy emerged in the early days of the republic and developed for more than a century before gaining ascendance between 1930 and 1945.

In 1820, Thomas Jefferson had advocated "a cordial fraternization among all the American nations . . . coalescing in an American system of policy."[44] Jefferson was among the first to envision a hemisphere brought together by U.S. leadership, based on republican principles of deference to one's "natural representative," which in the community of American nations would be the original American republic, the United States. His assumption of superiority over Native American and Hispanic people alike supported his claim to authority over them. Jefferson sent Lewis and Clark on their expedition among the western tribes in an early version of "good neighbor" diplomacy, eliciting cooperation through moral authority and friendly rituals rather than by force. Lewis and Clark conferred medals and certificates on the chiefs of the tribes they encountered, much as U.S. Navy vessels on "good will cruises" would come bearing gifts to Caribbean leaders in the years preceding the Second World War. In each case, the envoys' assumption was that proper relations with the people they met would be based on mutual benefit and guided from Washington.

The same assumptions underpinned the Monroe Doctrine of 1823, which extended a protective mantle to the new American republics. There was an element of republican one-for-allism in the Monroe Doctrine, if one reads that policy as a guarantee of a shared postcolonial future for the hemisphere. But there is also in the doctrine a unilateral declaration of U.S. authority over the Latin American republics (the nation's naval weakness and reliance on British support notwithstanding). This implication of U.S. domination, or at the very least the assumption of U.S. leadership, was in some ways at odds with the vision of naturally complementary interests binding the Americas together in a network of trade, conflict arbitration, defense against Europe, and shared history. The promise of a community of American republics, minus the Yankee domination, began with Simón Bolívar, who was often compared to George Washington both in terms of military deeds and a Cincinnatus-like disavowal of autocratic power.

At each juncture in the history of U.S. relations with its closest neighbors, however, the rhetoric of solidarity and protection against European aggression ran counter to the brutal logic and increasing momentum of U.S. territorial expansion and imperial ambitions. John Quincy Adams set the precedent for this dichotomy in the Transcontinental Treaty of 1819, which legitimized the strong-armed acquisition of the Floridas from Spain by Andrew Jackson, who led a military campaign against coastal territory coveted by Anglo settlers, without the benefit of prior government approval. Adams built the "no-transfer" principle into this agreement and into the Monroe Doctrine itself: land under European colonial rule could not change hands, unless the hands reached out from Washington. The same tension between expressions of good will and violent intervention marked the actions of President James K. Polk, who employed the metaphor "good neighbor" to describe relations with the American republics yet, in 1846, invaded the nearest of them, Mexico, on slim pretext in order to seize the state of Alta California, among other less coveted prizes. Fifty years later, President William McKinley's expressions of sympathy for Cuban patriots, like the depiction of Cuba in the popular press as a female waif needing to be rescued from a rapacious, decrepit Spain, also conflicted with U.S. actions.[45] After the United States intervened in the Cuban revolution in 1898, Cuba did not receive independence from Spain, but remained in a non-sovereign limbo in its relations with the United States until at least 1934, when Roosevelt agreed to abrogate the Platt Amendment of the Cuban Constitution, which sanctioned U.S. intervention there. Long before the "gunboat diplomacy" of the twentieth century, U.S. intervention among its neighbors prevented both the "cordial fraternization" and the "American system of policy" between North and South America that Jefferson had evoked. But the sentiment behind them remained and grew stronger in opposition to the increasingly overt imperialism of the United States.

The sentiment in favor of inter-American harmony and cooperation found pithy expression in the term "Pan-Americanism," cited as a major policy goal by James G. Blaine while he was secretary of state during two presidential administrations. Blaine initiated what became a long series of "Pan-American" conferences and expositions, negotiated reciprocity treaties with several of the Latin American republics, and pushed for the formation of the International Bureau of American Republics in 1889. That organization took the name Pan-American Union in 1910 and occupied a grand headquarters building in the heart of Washington, D.C. The basic aims of Pan-Americanism, like the later Good Neighbor policy, were to encourage trade, counteract European influence, keep peace, and celebrate unity. Its basic tactics, also later features of the Good Neighbor policy, were international conferences, increased diplomatic contacts, military liaison, and "good will" visits. Attempts to coordinate policy in the Americas under the banner of "Pan-Americanism" were not very successful during the early twentieth century, though, mainly because of what many Latin Americans viewed as U.S. bullying around the Caribbean as well as Latin American resistance to U.S. domination, especially on the part of Argentina, Brazil, and Chile. The Pan-American Union lost a great deal of its credibility and influence over its shrill support for U.S. entry into World War I and pressure on member states to follow suit (seven Latin American nations nevertheless remained neutral in the conflict).

President Woodrow Wilson's "Pan American visions" expanded with the completion of the Panama Canal in 1914, considered a unifying event for the Americas by the promoters of such celebrations as the Panama–Pacific International Exposition held in San Francisco in 1915 to mark the occasion. Keeping with the tradition of imagining Latin American nations as feminine, Wilson declared that "one of the chief objectives" of his administration would be to "cultivate the friendship and deserve the confidence of our sister republics."[46] He and his military representatives in the Caribbean used the ideal of progress to explain their actions in Haiti and the Dominican Republic, where occupation forces built roads, armies, and civil organizations. Another reason for intervention was friendly assistance. In Wilson's estimation, the "good neighbor" intervened to "do his neighbor service"; he considered it his "foremost duty" to bring about "the internal reform" of "unhappy neighbors." His close advisor Colonel Edward House defined a good neighbor's behavior more succinctly: he helps put out the fire in your house, but does not steal anything.[47]

Dominican intellectuals articulated their own visions of national development and neighborly behavior that did not include U.S. intervention, and they were joined by an increasing number of Latin American writers and politicians in protesting Wilson's policies. Adherents to the Latin American movement called Arielismo compared the two continents to the characters in the "brave New World" of William Shakespeare's *The Tempest,* set in newly discovered Bermuda in 1610: Latin Americans were akin to Prospero's fairy muse, Ariel; sensitive, spiritual, and wise. North Americans resembled the brutish and carnal Calaban, whom Prospero wisely kept in chains. Facing such a climate of ideas, Wilson's proposal for a Pan-American Pact during World War I had little chance for approval. The Pan-American Pact asked the other American republics to ratify the principles of the Monroe Doctrine, which Wilson interpreted to be recognition of every nation's territorial sovereignty and right to self-determination. Wilson elicited support for the pact with a vigorous campaign of naval visits to Latin American ports that one participating admiral called "festivals of enthusiasm," including a round-trip voyage to Buenos Aires by Secretary of the Treasury William McAdoo aboard the battleship *Tennessee*. Wilson also sent full ambassadors to Chile and Argentina, and dispatched naval and aviation instructors to Brazil, which already had embassy-level representation, amid calls for an "American continental type of naval science" that would integrate the air and sea forces of the hemisphere. In addition to increased diplomatic activity, trade with Latin America boomed during the war, with the volume of U.S. exports doubling and the U.S. share of the Latin American import market reaching 90 percent in the absence of European competition. Fear of U.S. domination, resentment of the presumption of U.S. leadership, and perceptions of "norteamericanos" as grasping and cold, all contributed to the Latin American rejection of the Pan-American Pact. But Wilson used the concept as the basis for his better-known League of Nations idea, which he outlined in the Fourteen Points, insisted upon at the Versailles peace conference, and pushed to the point of personal exhaustion and collapse in the United States.[48]

Wilson's Caribbean projects, and the opposition they inspired in Latin America and among U.S. anti-imperialists, shaped the regional policies of his Republican successors, Warren Harding, Calvin Coolidge, and Herbert Hoover. These three sought similar goals of progress and stability while trying, without great success, to reduce Latin American anger at "gunboat diplomacy." Although the military occupation of the Dominican Republic ended in 1924, the customs receivership continued in operation, as did the military occupation of Haiti. In addition, the Harding and Coolidge administrations deployed naval vessels, Marine landing forces, and aircraft to monitor events in all the region's republics and to quell outbreaks that disrupted the activities of the resident "American colonies" and threatened their plantations, mills, banks, utilities, and transportation systems. The small but pivotal Special Service Squadron of the U.S. Navy was formed in 1920 to perform this role and to bolster the influence of American diplomats in the regional capitals.

In the meantime, Pan-American congresses and the Pan-American Union were confined mainly to expressing the "Western Hemisphere Idea" in symbolic ways.[49] One such project was the Columbus Memorial Lighthouse to be constructed in Santo Domingo, a resolution that passed at the

Fifth Pan-American Conference at Santiago, Chile, in 1923. The Santiago conference also adopted the "Treaty to Avoid or Prevent Conflicts between the American States," better known as the Gondra Treaty, one of numerous antiwar and disarmament agreements of the 1920s, this one specific to the hemisphere. But the first meeting of "the American republics" that had a significant influence on U.S. policy was the Havana conference of 1928, when the Marine occupation of Haiti and intervention in Nicaragua drew protests, and President Coolidge traveled to Cuba to personally assure the Latin American delegates of his administration's good intentions.

The Hoover administration went even further in the direction of nonintervention. Hoover reduced the size and operations of the Special Service Squadron and narrowed the criteria for fresh intervention, although he did maintain the commitments he inherited in the Dominican Republic, Haiti, and Nicaragua. He dispatched the Dawes Commission to the Dominican Republic and the Forbes Commission to Haiti, but these blue-ribbon contingents failed to resolve the issues that perpetuated the Dominican receivership and the Haitian occupation. Also to the chagrin of Hoover and his secretary of state, Henry Stimson, the military campaign against Augusto Sandino's insurgency in Nicaragua eventually involved thousands of U.S. Marines and soldiers of the Marine-trained Nicaraguan Guardia Nacional, despite Stimson's personal attempts to end the war. This legacy of a deeply interventionist and putatively tutelary presence in the Antilles and Central America, with all the animosity it engendered within and beyond the Caribbean, also shaped the Good Neighbor policy as it developed during the administration of Franklin Roosevelt.[50]

The impulses behind the Good Neighbor policy originated, then, in the paradox between fraternity with neighboring republics and domination over them. Its positive component was its appeal for inter-American unity, based on shared interests and joint occupation of the New World. Its negative component was rejection of prior policies of intervention: "gunboat diplomacy," military occupation, and "dollar diplomacy." Its goals were consistent with overall U.S. policy toward Latin America under all its different names, a policy that has always been geared to gain national security and prosperity, by whatever means seem likeliest to work, from persuasion to invasion. By invoking Pan-American feeling, the Good Neighbor policy drew from a long tradition of ameliorative diplomacy between the United States and Latin America. By condemning intervention, the Good

Neighbor policy rejected the dominant theme in twentieth-century inter-American relations, which was U.S. imperialism, but sought just the same to take the lead in regional trade and defense.

The term "Pan-American" was in common usage by the time Hoover declared "Pan-American Day" in 1930. FDR used it synonymously with "good neighbor" to connote policy coordination, economic symbiosis, cultural appreciation, shared heritage, and intertwined destiny. Popular familiarity with the concept of Pan-Americanism resulted also from the tireless publicity efforts of the Pan-American Union, which FDR endorsed. The president of the Pan-American Union, Leo Rowe, traveled with Roosevelt when he went to the Inter-American Peace Conference in Buenos Aires, Argentina, in 1936. By then, Pan American Airways had spread southward, its Pan Am Clippers reducing the travel time between the nations of the hemisphere and inspiring romantic enthusiasm for "flying down to Rio." The 1933 movie by that name was one example of how "America" developed an appreciation for the Americas, especially after the Great Depression dashed the smug, dismissive attitude of many "Americans" for "Hispanic" people and "Latin" culture. Much of the fascination in films like *Flying Down to Rio* derived from escapist fantasy, and much of the intellectual and cultural attention paid to Latin America after 1929 was utopian in orientation, but they contributed to the attraction.[51]

Cultural affinity for Latin America arose in the United States independently from the efforts of presidential administrations to establish a policy of nonintervention and friendship in the hemisphere. Fads included the *vogue noir* for Haiti, especially its African religion; "the enormous vogue for things Mexican," like the work of its famous mural painters; the tourist droves taking Cole Porter's advice to "See You in C-U-B-A" during Prohibition; the proliferation of travel books written about Latin American destinations by authors increasingly attentive to local cultures; the rumba and tango dance crazes; and movies with Latin American subjects from *The Emperor Jones* (1933) to *Blondie Goes Latin* (1942).[52] The new interest in and acceptance of the societies to the south among segments of the general population prepared the way for the Good Neighbor policy's enthusiastic acceptance in the United States and was in turn stimulated by Roosevelt's initiatives.

FDR picked up on the prevailing trends in U.S.-Latin American relations and animated them with his "Good Neighbor" rhetoric and 1936 pledge of nonintervention, issued by him personally at the peace conference he had called in Buenos Aires. The campaign to improve relations intensified during Roosevelt's second and third terms, when the onset of the Second World War hastened his efforts to unite with his neighbors. During those years, the Roosevelt administration forged a military alliance with Latin America at the Lima (1938), Panama (1939), and Havana (1940) conferences; loaned money and supplied arms to the nations that cooperated; and created an Office of Inter-American Affairs in the State Department. That organization delivered a barrage of pamphlets, posters, movies, and radio programs "south of the border" to stimulate good will among the Latin American public. The U.S. public continued to divert attention to Latin America during the war years, as well, with the Roosevelt administration pointing the way. Contemplation of (and fantasies about) Latin America, the only region in the world that was not a theater of combat, offered the same kind of escapist break from the war that it had offered during the depression. In the early 1940s, the Good Neighbor policy flowed together with the war effort, but it also combined with such powerful cultural forces as Walt Disney—who produced the government-inspired cartoon _The Three Caballeros_ (1945), starring Donald Duck, a Brazilian parrot, and a Mexican fighting cock—and Carmen Miranda, the Brazilian actress who became the symbol for the United Fruit Company in marketing Caribbean and Central American bananas.[53]

Other Latin American actresses popular during the period of the Good Neighbor policy were Dolores del Rio, from Brazil, and María Montez, from the Dominican Republic. These women, whether playing in a Latin American role like del Rio in _Flying Down to Rio,_ or in an entirely unrelated one like Montez as Sheherazade in _Arabian Nights_ (1942), presented a more attractive side of their home nations to theatergoers on the home front than did the authoritarian leaders of those states, Getulio Vargas and Rafael Trujillo. The wartime cooperation of Brazil, just a bomber's flight from North Africa, and the Dominican Republic, astride the approaches to the Panama Canal, was necessary for the defense of the hemisphere, their undemocratic political systems notwithstanding. The Good Neighbor policy facilitated the requisite bonding with these and other nations by promising all Latin American leaders, dictators included, that the United States would not intervene in their affairs. Simultaneously it directed public attention at home away from those neighbors ruling with the iron fists and toward those dancing with the fruit hats.

The Good Neighbor policy was a qualified success, but it had the unfortunate effect of strengthening military regimes, which were justly criticized for mistreating their citizens and menacing their neighbors. Some of the opprobrium incurred by Latin American dictators rubbed off on the U.S. government for its self-serving complicity with them—or, at best, its principled adherence to nonintervention—and its resulting refusal to oppose them. The most disruptive of these authoritarians was Trujillo, who was no short-lived Emperor Jones, although to a point his career paralleled that of the character performed by Paul Robeson in both the stage and movie versions of the Eugene O'Neill play *The Emperor Jones;* indeed, the first production of the play (1924) and the release of the movie (1933) bracketed Trujillo's rise to power. Both Rafael Trujillo and Brutus Jones were charismatic men of color who ascended from common origins on the strength of personality, who made the most of an opportunity presented by white foreigners, seized power for themselves, exploited the relationship with their erstwhile mentors, and ruled on the dictates of their personal wealth and vanity. But Emperor Jones overstepped himself and fell in short order, his enemies hunting him down in the wilds of the island he briefly ruled. Conversely, Trujillo survived to defend and augment his absolute power for thirty-one years before being assassinated, hunting down his own enemies with tremendous energy both on and off the island he dominated throughout that long period. The consolidation of the Trujillo regime and the evolution of the Good Neighbor policy were intertwined in ways that reveal a great deal about both. That history begins with the coup that brought Trujillo to power, known as the Dominican Revolution of 1930.

CHAPTER TWO

✦

# The Dominican Revolution of 1930 and the Policy of Nonintervention

U.S. Minister Charles B. Curtis spent a busy Sunday working at the cramped legation offices in Santo Domingo. It was the middle of February 1930, and he had been kept "on the jump every minute for several days" as the deadline for nominations to the May elections approached. The new minister had been "having a wonderfully interesting time" since his arrival in the Dominican Republic five weeks before, and although he anticipated another busy week ahead, he was confident there would be ample time for "some golf and swimming until the elections themselves draw near."[1] He was to be disappointed. The next morning Curtis would be astonished by the appearance of the Dominican "President, his wife, the Vice President, more than half the members of his cabinet, the Presidents of the Senate and Chamber, and a score of others" at the door of the U.S. legation, requesting political asylum.[2] The Dominican Revolution of February 1930 took him by surprise. Although he tried frantically to shape the events that followed, Curtis was unable to prevent General Rafael Trujillo from riding to power on a wave of military violence during the ensuing spring and summer.

## NONINTERVENTION AND MILITARY RULE

The Dominican Revolution of 1930 began in the northern Cibao Valley, as many previous political uprisings in the Dominican Republic had, with the frustration of rival political leaders currently out of power.[3] In this case, the fear of the continuation in office of Horacio Vásquez, president since the end of the U.S. occupation in 1924, prompted Rafael Estrella Ureña and his followers in Santiago to take up arms against the incumbent. The arms were supplied by General Trujillo, who ordered his army not to hinder the rebel force, which then took Santo Domingo and prompted the unexpected appearance of Vásquez and his entourage at the door of the U.S. legation. Minister Curtis asked for a warship from the Navy's Special Service Squadron, based in the Caribbean, to support the Vásquez government, but the developing U.S. policy of nonintervention would not allow this step. Curtis then tried to prevent Trujillo from becoming a candidate in the subsequent election of May 1930, but without the threat of intervention Curtis's influence waned. Trujillo commandeered both the campaign and the election through intimidation and established what amounted to martial law over the republic, remaining its effective leader for thirty-one years.

That Trujillo was able to come to power despite the strenuous efforts of the U.S. minister was owing to two recent changes in the Dominican political equation. One was the presence of a standing army of more than two thousand trained men armed with modern rifles, the Marine-established Ejército Nacional Dominicano, over which Trujillo had complete control.[4] There would be no return to internecine disorder in the Dominican Republic so long as the military cohered. The other change in circumstances was the inability of the U.S. minister to summon U.S. Navy warships to enforce the terms of his mediation of the conflict. The Hoover administration's rejection of intervention as a tool of regional policy precluded the use of force, although Curtis was slow to accept this curtailment of his power. This new combination of Latin American military strength and U.S. nonintervention, which also affected several other republics in the Greater Antilles and Central America, came together in the Dominican Revolution of 1930 to set the pattern of international relations in the Caribbean area under the Good Neighbor policy. Given the development of the region's armed forces and the disavowal of military threats by the United States, one of the central features of the policy was acquiescence in the rise of authoritarian regimes. Caribbean "strongmen" like Trujillo fulfilled what Secretary of State Henry Stimson called "the main thing in Latin American countries": they were "popular with the Army."[5]

A series of political transitions in the Caribbean republics in the 1930s tested and underscored the policy of nonintervention. In addition to the Dominican Republic, dictators came to power in Guatemala, Honduras, El Salvador, Cuba, and Nicaragua as a result of coups and revolutions. These events demonstrated changes in the forms of U.S. hegemony, which after 1930 rarely included the hostile presence of warships. They also brought new forms of nationalism in many of the Caribbean republics, where modern military organizations now dominated the political landscape. U.S. diplomats "in the field" continued to work on behalf of the elite class, or "better sort," who lost power to the military, but they did so from a diminishing diplomatic power base. On the other hand, the establishment in several republics of military rulers, especially those like Trujillo who felt a personal affinity for the U.S. Marines, advanced U.S. strategic aims later in the decade and increased the diplomatic role of American military officers.

This examination of the Dominican watershed of 1930 will examine the dynamic between rising militarism and the policy of nonintervention, an interplay influenced by personal, class, and bureaucratic antagonism and rivalry between actors with conflicting allegiances. It will follow the shift in effective control of the Dominican Republic and its foreign affairs from the U.S. citizens who had supervised the nation's military, diplomatic, and financial domains for much of the time since 1904 to the aggressive, consolidated, and nationalist regime of Rafael Trujillo, who, despite his talent for maintaining stability, was never a "client" ruler following instructions from Washington. And it will demonstrate a typical case of how the U.S. policy of nonintervention adopted in Washington was slow to register in the State Department's foreign missions, where individual diplomats frequently had to be restrained from their traditional role of dictating solutions to internal problems.

THE VÁSQUEZ ADMINISTRATION

When the Marine occupation of the Dominican Republic ended in 1924, Horacio Vásquez and his *horacista* followers, winners of that year's election, were left in control of the government. Vásquez remained on good terms with the United States during the next six years, fostering ties with U.S. diplomats and businessmen and maintaining order through the armed forces, commanded by Rafael Trujillo after 1925. In 1928, Vásquez prepared to extend his term from four to six years, requiring a manipulation of the Dominican Constitution. The State Department authorized Minister Evan Young to register "strong disfavor" of the move, but Young was not opposed to the Vásquez regime's continuation in office. He summarized his reasons to Secretary of State Frank Kellogg in October 1928: "These countries have need of a man of his type at the head of their affairs. They are democracies more in name than in fact. . . . Above everything else, these countries need peace, but . . . it requires a strong hand to maintain stable conditions."[6] Young counseled his superiors in the Coolidge administration that "friendly advice" should be the extent of U.S. action. Kellogg agreed.[7] Kellogg, a former senator, also agreed with William Borah, Republican of Idaho and chair of the Senate Foreign Relations Committee, that intervention was ill-advised and interfered with, rather than promoted, the expansion of U.S. business interests. Such was the position as well of Minister Young, who left his post in Santo Domingo to become the vice-president for public relations of Pan American Airways, an organization that required its own brand of good neighbor diplomacy to conclude operating agreements with Latin American governments. Secretary of Commerce Herbert Hoover, who promoted the international efforts of his department under Harding and Coolidge, was also interested in Latin American business opportunities, and he agreed that government intervention was less effective than private enterprise in boosting trade.

Hoover took office as president in 1929 with "the desire to maintain . . . the relations of the good neighbor" with Latin America, ten countries of which he visited on a seven-week "good will" tour between his election and inauguration.[8] He contended that "no policy of intervention" had existed under Coolidge, and he sought to refrain from meddling himself, although he continued the military commitments in Haiti and Nicaragua to fulfill prior agreements.[9] Noninterference was also the stated Dominican policy of Hoover's administration, although the U.S. General Receivership quietly continued to collect Dominican customs under the terms of the Convention of 1924. While Vásquez remained in power, the U.S. legation in Santo Domingo applauded the low-profile stance. First Secretary John Moors Cabot reported that the Marine occupation had left a tender wound, making the Dominicans extremely sensitive to any hint of U.S. interference in Dominican affairs and quick "to resent any slight, any tactlessness" on the part of U.S. representatives.[10] Cabot reported that the Dawes Mission, sent in March 1929 to set up a plan for payment of the Dominican debt, was the object of such resentment; President Vásquez's "prestige suffered perceptibly" as a result of its presence.[11] Cabot argued that the "policy of non-interference, of sincere friendliness, and of quiet unofficial helpfulness" had much happier results. It brought greater prestige to the U.S. government and made the Dominican government more willing to accept the legation's advice. Cabot reported that "even the immediate and selfish interests of the U.S. are better served by the present policy."[12] The State

Department under Hoover and Secretary of State Henry Stimson sought to implement this policy throughout the hemisphere, hoping for the same results it seemed to be having in the Dominican Republic.

Vásquez laid the groundwork to succeed himself for another six-year term in 1930, again in violation of the Dominican Constitution, and exhibited an "imperial tendency" and "trend toward one man government" noticed at the U.S. legation. Careful to "pamper" the Dominican Army, Vásquez "favored General Trujillo in every serious controversy" stemming from the army's increasing pushiness, measures that were essential to his continuation in office.[13] Legation observers noted that Trujillo had converted his soldiers "into a group of personal followers," and although they considered him "too clever to be disloyal" to Vásquez they "expected [Trujillo] to produce some fireworks after the retirement" of the president.[14] But with Vásquez showing no sign of vacating the presidency, Minister Young reported that "uncertainty . . . characterized the political situation" in Santo Domingo, especially after Vásquez went to the United States for an operation at Johns Hopkins Hospital in October 1929. As Young prepared to leave his post in December 1929, he reported that "the attitude of General Trujillo looms as a gigantic question mark upon the backdrop of the Dominican political stage."[15]

First Secretary John Moors Cabot remained as chargé d'affaires after Young's departure. Cabot, twenty-eight years old, was born in Cambridge, Massachusetts, and went to Harvard, like most of his Boston Brahmin clan. He had a degree in modern history from Oxford and was the author of a book on racial conflict in Transylvania, but he was new to the Foreign Service. He was humorous and affable in public, put derisive and condescending in private, revealing attitudes that inclined him to underestimate the intelligence and determination of the contenders for Dominican political power. The events about to occur in the Dominican Republic, only Cabot's second post, would teach him a great deal in a few hectic months.

Cabot recognized that Vásquez was "definitely disinclined to court the dangers inherent to dismissing" Trujillo, but he believed that the president, who returned to Santo Domingo in early January 1930, had a "hold upon" Trujillo that was almost "comical." Trujillo and two others behaved "like three timid school boys caught by the master in some prank," said Cabot, when Vásquez accused them of plotting against him during his absence.[16] Cabot's misjudgment of the distribution of power between the civilian chief of state and the military commander, a mistake repeated frequently by U.S. diplomats as militarist nationalism swept the region in the early 1930s, was the main reason why the United States was so unprepared for the events of February 1930. Cabot's perception of the president's power over the general was adopted by the new minister, Charles B. Curtis, upon his arrival in Santo Domingo in January.

## THE REVOLUTIONARY CONSPIRACY

Rumors that a revolution had broken out in the north prompted the U.S. and British legations and the three foreign banks in Santo Domingo to "hoist their flags" on Sunday morning, 23 February, as a symbolic guard against whatever violence might ensue. The Cuban minister called a meeting of the Diplomatic Corps that day to "ask the American Minister whether the United States Government was prepared to protect all foreign interests," but Curtis did not attend.[17] Not until the arrival of President Vásquez and his panicky government at the door of the legation the next morning did Curtis act, and then he did so without consulting the other diplomats. Knowing that the Dominican Army could easily repel the "twenty-five automobiles full of armed men" that constituted the revolution, Curtis was not convinced that Vásquez and his party were in jeopardy. He telephoned General Trujillo at his headquarters in Fortaleza Ozama on the other side of the city and, having received the commander's reassurances, comforted Vásquez with the news that Trujillo, and hence the army, "was entirely loyal to the President." Curtis was unaware, however, that the weapons bristling from those cars full of rebels on the highway had been transferred by Trujillo from the fort in Santo Domingo to the one in Santiago, where they were surrendered to the rebels following a mock battle.[18] Trujillo was in on the plot to oust Vásquez.

Curtis apparently did not stop to consider that a shrewd politician like Rafael Estrella Ureña, the reputed leader of the revolt, would not undertake a cross-country revolutionary motorcade unless he was confident of the acquiescence, if not the support, of the strong Dominican Army. Convinced of Trujillo's loyalty and recognizing the legitimacy of the rebels' opposition to the illegal candidacy of Vásquez in the May elections, the minister convinced Vásquez to leave the legation and advised him to compromise as much as possible with Estrella Ureña's demands.[19] This meant securing the resignation of Vásquez's vice-president, José Alfonseca, which Curtis did on his own volition, and persuading Vásquez to withdraw from the May ballot, which Curtis tried to do. Vásquez said he would take the demand "under consideration," and departed the legation.[20] Curtis took two other actions at this early juncture. First, he sent a telegram to Washington with news of the revolt and, in response to a query from Joseph Cotton, acting secretary of state, confirmed that "the National Army and its Commander in Chief are true to the President."[21] Second, he dispatched First Secretary Cabot to Santiago to intercede with the rebel leader in order to arrange a truce. Cabot hurried north and sought out Estrella Ureña in an attempt "to stop the revolution by sweet reason, when the leaders there knew that it would succeed, due to the army's treachery." After a night of shuttling between the rebel leaders in Santiago and the lines that had been formed by the government and rebel troops north of Santo Domingo, Cabot was able to halt the rebels' advance pending a meeting between Vásquez and Estrella Ureña.[22]

No one told Trujillo, however, and he continued to play his part according to the original script of the rebel conspiracy. He informed Curtis "that the government troops had been outflanked and partly surrounded by the much more numerous revolutionary forces," who he said would soon take the capital. When a peaceful night in Santo Domingo ensued, Curtis decided to drive out of the city himself to find out what was happening. He encountered the government lines intact, neither "outflanked" nor "surrounded," and its leader in possession of the cease-fire agreement that Cabot had arranged and about which Trujillo knew nothing. Trujillo was also unaware that Vásquez had relieved his fellow conspirator, Colonel Simón Díaz, as field commander and placed an officer who knew nothing of the conspiracy in command of the government troops, which is why the choreographed rout had not taken place. Thus Trujillo had prematurely announced the army's staged defeat to Curtis, revealing his integral role in the revolution, although he did not shy from following through with the plan after realizing he had blown his cover. He recalled the loyal officer and put Díaz back in charge of the troops in the field, a move that "at least relieved the legation of any anxiety concerning the possibility of bloodshed between the government and revolutionary forces."[23] British Minister W. H. Galienne reported that Estrella Ureña and Díaz had in fact combined their men to advance on Santo Domingo, crediting reports that the government "troops have deserted and joined the revolutionaries."[24]

## "WITHOUT SHOW OF FORCE"

With the fall of the Vásquez government imminent, Curtis asked the State Department to send a warship to Santo Domingo. Curtis was a lawyer and a career diplomat, having joined the State Department in 1907 at age twenty-eight, but Santo Domingo was his first appointment with the rank of minister. Like Franklin Roosevelt, Curtis attended prep school at Groton and graduated from Harvard, but unlike his fellow New Yorker, he was brittle and sensitive to slights. Born in New York City and trained in law at Columbia University, he had served in several European and Latin American posts, including a brief stint in Santo Domingo eighteen years earlier. He spent most of his career in cosmopolitan cities like Saint Petersburg, Constantinople, Rio de Janeiro, and most recently Havana. Santo Domingo was something of a backwater in his estimation; the U.S. minister in such a place, Curtis assumed, was the ultimate authority in any unruly dispute among the locals, who should accord him profound respect and follow his advice. He knew that U.S. diplomats had frequently enjoyed the power to conjure up naval vessels for "moral effect" in cases of unrest in the Caribbean republics, a practice that increased the gravity of their counsel in mediating disputes. The U.S. Navy Special Service Squadron stood ready in the Canal Zone to be on hand for such occasions. Curtis and Cabot had been able to dissuade Vásquez from resigning on two successive mornings and had prevented the revolutionary forces from taking Santo Domingo simply by invoking the prestige of the U.S. legation, but they knew that the silhouette of a naval cruiser on the horizon would make them the unquestioned arbiters of the situation.

Curtis first asked for naval muscle on the evening of 24 February, when he thought the rebels would be driving into town at any minute, and repeated his request the next morning.[25] Several Navy ships were moved to "within a relatively few hours" of Santo Domingo, but Acting Secretary of State Joseph P. Cotton informed Curtis that his priority was "to handle this situation without show of force." Cotton was "virtually in charge of the State Department" during Secretary of State Henry L. Stimson's long absence at the London Naval Conference at the time of the Dominican revolution. One of the leading lights of Harvard Law School's memorable Class of 1900, Cotton had been meat director in Hoover's World War I Food Administration, and he traveled with President Wilson to Europe in 1918.

He was also an old friend of Stimson, who was himself a legal prodigy and graduate of Harvard Law, although the two men differed in temperament. Stimson was austere and obstinate, while Cotton operated within a "cloak of irony" and wit.[26] Cotton summarized the basic argument of the policy of nonintervention to Curtis in urging him to conduct diplomacy without the gunboat. "If you can do it," he wrote, "it will materially strengthen our position in the Dominican Republic and in the rest of Latin America."[27]

Cotton also advised Curtis to reduce the likelihood of endangerment to American lives through "the establishment of a new zone where Americans . . . would be safe."[28] Cotton was previewing a strategy that Stimson would make official policy a year later. The "Stimson Doctrine," announced in April 1931, placed new restrictions on the familiar "American lives and property" justification for intervention: "The State Department does not propose to abandon protection of American lives; it merely asks Americans desiring such protection to come to places where protection can be really extended and with a minimum of interference in the internal affairs of the country where it is applied."[29] The right to intervene to protect "lives and property" would not be renounced by the United States until the Buenos Aires Peace Conference in 1936, but in the meantime the Hoover administration sought to narrow the grounds under which such protection might be invoked. In response, Curtis warned that "unorganized street fighting and rioting" might start at any minute, an eventuality he said that would require the presence of a warship immediately, not "within a relatively few hours."[30] But Hoover himself ended the discussion with a statement to the press that there was no thought of sending American troops to the Dominican Republic since the revolution posed no danger to American citizens.[31]

Unable to summon a U.S. warship, Curtis supported British Minister Galienne's decision to call for help from a Royal Navy vessel, HMS *Wistaria,* which the Foreign Office had authorized him to do. By Wednesday morning, 26 February, the capital's "streets [were] full of armed rebels . . . mostly a wild and poverty stricken lot without shoes or proper clothing," and Curtis concurred that "the presence of a British ship would be helpful." Galienne observed that "the American Government is obviously more afraid of the obloquy they would incur by landing troops than they are of danger to American property," hence Hoover's refusal to dispatch a gunboat. The *Wistaria* was at the British minister's disposal, however, because "no one suspects [the British] of a desire to annex the country or govern it." But by the time Galienne's cable to *Wistaria* reached the British colony of Dominica, the ship's last port, she had departed and could not be contacted to come to the rescue.[32]

Although denied the support of naval forces, Curtis and Cabot were authorized to continue offering "assistance" to both sides of the conflict in reaching a "peaceful and orderly arrangement."[33] Cabot's truce held the rebels in their position for two days while he and Curtis compiled a list of their demands for Vásquez, but when Cabot drove back to the rebel lines after midnight on the third day to report the cooperative attitude of the government, they were gone. Estrella Ureña led the revolutionary forces into Santo Domingo at dawn on Dominican Independence Day, 27 February, entering without opposition from Trujillo, who remained ensconced with his troops at Dominican Army headquarters in Fortaleza Ozama.[34]

Curtis and Cabot were angered by Estrella Ureña's breach of the truce; as American diplomats with Latin American experience, they were unaccustomed to having their "quiet unofficial helpfulness" ignored. Despite Cotton's clear instructions to the contrary, they could not restrain themselves from threatening Estrella Ureña with military intervention in their attempts to reassert their "unofficial influence" in the situation. When Estrella Ureña said he would attack the presidential mansion to speed Vásquez's cooperation, Cabot warned him, with Curtis's permission but without the knowledge of anyone at the State Department, "that if he did, we'd have a warship here pronto." Estrella Ureña then "climbed down" and cooperated with the legation's efforts to mediate a transfer of power.[35] Curtis and Cabot knew that the only warship to arrive on the scene would be the one sent by Britain, and Cotton had already advised the British government that its presence was unnecessary.[36] For the moment, though, Cabot's bluff went unchallenged, and the legation's efforts to shape the outcome of the revolution continued with the threat of force hanging in the air.

MEDIATION

After a few scattered volleys of gunfire on the morning of 27 February, most of them apparently into the air, the rebels were in control of Santo Domingo and talks between Vásquez and Estrella Ureña, orchestrated by the U.S. diplomats, began. Curtis first had to convince Vásquez for the third time in four days not to resign, but then he was able to bring him together with Estrella Ureña at the U.S. legation.[37] The small size of the offices, where one could not have a visitor "without hunting up the shoe horn," made them an uncomfortable venue for negotiations.[38] So the talks were moved to the more commodious presidential mansion, where they continued for two more days despite "an enormous mob of bootblacks, greengrocers and scrubwomen moiling through the entire mansion." Cabot reported to a friend that the Dominican cabinet had to meet in the hall, "each minister whispering loudly to the next one 'We have no arms . . . We are betrayed' . . . and all Santo Domingo listening in."[39] Curtis and Cabot mediated a peaceful and technically constitutional transition of power that had Vásquez appoint Estrella Ureña as his secretary of state for the interior. Estrella Ureña would then become interim president upon the resignation of both Vásquez and his vice-president, Alfonseca. The electoral laws that Vásquez had altered in preparation for his self-succession were restored, the rebels' arms were surrendered to the new government (essentially given back to Trujillo), and both sides agreed to keep the peace in order to facilitate the May elections.

Curtis himself injected one final important item into the agreement between Vásquez and Estrella Ureña. Curtis suggested that Trujillo, "having repeatedly betrayed the government," be disqualified as a candidate in May. Vásquez, who had been the one betrayed, and Estrella Ureña, who felt threatened by the general, were both eager to include such a provision. Acting Secretary of State Joseph Cotton was not so enthused, and when Curtis noted that Trujillo's exclusion from politics (and, if possible, from the army) could "hardly be accomplished without the assistance of the legation," he refused to support the idea.[40] Once again, the diplomats "in the field" decided to proceed alone. Curtis informed Estrella Ureña "that the legation would under no circumstances recommend the recognition of a government headed by" Trujillo. This made it seem as if the legation held the key in the matter of recognition, when actually the State Department was moving toward a policy of recognizing de facto governments of any stripe in Latin America. As a result of Curtis's involvement, Trujillo's disqualification as a candidate was written into the agreement purporting to end the revolution. But the agreement would fail to prevent the coup that Trujillo had set in motion when he allowed Vásquez to fall.

After a week of energetic interference in Dominican politics, Curtis and Cabot would "view with satisfaction" what they had accomplished. There had been "virtually no bloodshed or property loss," and resident Americans had escaped all injury. The "ultimate solution" had been peacefully negotiated and had complied with "all legal and constitutional forms." The legation staff had "indulge[d] in no action distasteful" to the Dominican Republic but had instead earned the "deep appreciation" of both sides by mediating. Curtis concluded that "friendship for the United States . . . increased rather than decreased as a result of the revolution." Curtis was equally proud that "Trujillo was blocked in his plan to become Acting President," although that provision of the legation's "ultimate solution" was by far the most fragile.[41]

John Moors Cabot, who had slept very little for several days, reported exuberantly to his friend that the legation looked like "a house after an all night whoopee party . . . except that correspondence took the place of empty bottles and glasses."[42] He and Curtis were praised in the press and at the State Department for their mediation of the revolution. The *New York Times* credited Minister Curtis with bringing "the conflicting parties together" to end the revolution. This was particularly significant, the story continued, because "it is the first time that such a political dispute has been handled without bloodshed and violent clashes."[43] The *Boston Herald* preferred to credit First Secretary Cabot in an imaginative account of his mission to Santiago under the headline "Boston Boy Halts Near Revolution: Young Cabot in Risky Ride Brings About Truce." The story reported that Cabot had driven his "red roadster" through "whistling bullets" to locate the rebel force, concluding that "his exploit is undoubtedly among the most brilliant in American diplomatic records."[44] The State Department commended Curtis for his part in the negotiations and promoted Cabot two ranks for "exceptionally meritorious service." The U.S. consul in Puerto Plata, William Bickers, was also recommended for promotion for his peacemaking intervention there.[45]

"A MOST FRIENDLY SPIRIT"

The diplomats had little time to savor these plaudits. It was soon evident that the keystone of the negotiated settlement—the removal of Trujillo from the Dominican hustings—would not hold.[46] The general had not facilitated the revolution only to be eliminated by an agreement between his political rivals, who were militarily weak, and the U.S. minister, who was unable to provide naval support for his demands. The Dominican Army was still under Trujillo's personal control and could easily be made to play the role of Praetorian Guard for its commander. Curtis realized that Trujillo's candidacy was a distinct possibility "in spite of the terms of the agreement," and he foresaw the use of the army to ensure Trujillo's victory in the election.[47] Barring the appearance of a gunboat, Curtis's ability to prevent or alter this scenario depended on the refusal of the U.S. government to recognize a government headed by Trujillo, should he come to power. Curtis tried to influence this decision through his reports to Washington, reports that now became a virtual torrent of calumny at Rafael Trujillo.

The lines of reasoning along which Curtis and Cabot developed their argument against recognizing Trujillo, and the corresponding sources of the deep personal antipathy they developed toward him, are encapsulated in their dispatches during early March 1930. First was the expectation that Trujillo would prove to be a despot: "He expects the army to terrorize the voters. If General Trujillo succeeds in his desire to be President, it seems likely that the Dominican Republic will have to endure a prolonged military dictatorship."[48] Curtis was generally opposed to the development of authoritarian rule (he had been candid, and quick, in describing the Gerardo Machado regime as a dictatorship in his reports as chargé d'affaires in Cuba in 1929), but he particularly objected to Trujillo's rise because of the general's betrayal of the apolitical mission of the Dominican armed forces. Trujillo's subversion of the political process (or, rather, his failure to support Vásquez's subversion of the political process) was compounded in the minister's eyes by the worthlessness of his personal guarantee of loyalty to the Dominican government and, by extension, to the government of the United States, which meant Curtis himself. "The government of the United States . . . organized here a well-drilled standing army with the idea that it should be a firm support for the President and prevent uprising against him. . . . The small army . . . was undoubtedly capable of rendering the services for which it was created; its chief, however, fully appreciated the power which laid in his hands and . . . is determined to use it for the purpose of putting himself in the Presidency."[49]

Finally, Curtis and Cabot were disdainful of Trujillo's lower-class social status and that of his followers. Both diplomats were upper-class, white Easterners who favored the politics and companionship of the traditionally dominant political and economic class in the Dominican Republic, an oligarchy of light-skinned, well-educated elite families in the cities of Santiago, Puerto Plata, and Santo Domingo. They were especially close to those members of Dominican "high society" in the capital who socialized with the "American Colony" of businessmen, diplomats, and their families. Trujillo's hardscrabble San Cristóbal upbringing and military vocation placed him outside this privileged circle. Curtis claimed that his social and moral aversions to Trujillo were shared by all classes of the Dominican population, high and low: "Among all of the more prominent men in the Republic it is to be doubted whether anyone . . . was hated by such a large number of persons as Trujillo. His birth caused the upper classes to turn up their noses; his cattle thieving and similar offenses alienated many peasants; and his 'love affairs' caused many to thirst for vengeance."[50] The skin color and lack of education of some of Trujillo's collaborators were also unacceptable to the U.S. diplomats. Cabot disdained the social rank and racial composition of the interim cabinet members, reporting that "three are negroes and two can't read and write," and Curtis attacked Trujillo's first cabinet for including "a mulatto murderer," "an illiterate Syrian," and "an estimable nonentity of limited intelligence."[51] The minister's enmity for the general was in contrast to his growing regard for the acting president, Estrella Ureña, a light-skinned member of the Santiago elite. He had "made an excellent first impression" on the diplomats.[52]

Trujillo formally declared his candidacy on 17 March 1930, with the cowed Estrella Ureña in the vice-presidential spot on the ticket. Estrella Ureña, acting president since the revolution, confessed to Curtis the next day that Trujillo "was dominating him and preventing him from promising real results from the army during the election [i.e., that they would not intervene] with the result that these could not possibly be fair." Estrella Ureña asked Curtis "to make it publicly known that the American Government would not recognize Trujillo as president in view of the agreement reached through the legation's mediation which ended the revolution." Curtis requested authorization from the State Department to announce as much, arguing that "a revolution by or against Trujillo is certain unless we can eliminate [him]."[53] Joseph Cotton rejected the idea in Washington, repeating the conclusion that "scrupulously avoiding even the appearance of interfering" had put U.S. relations with the Dominican Republic "on a very sound basis" in the years since the end of the occupation, the recent deep involvement of Curtis and Cabot notwithstanding. He agreed with Curtis that Trujillo's role should be as guarantor of a fair election rather than as candidate, but he would allow Curtis to make only "a personal appeal" to the general to stand down. Cotton's message left the minister little leeway: "The Department cannot emphasize too strongly the necessity of making your appeal in a most friendly spirit. For your strictly confidential information the Department desires you to know that it expects to recognize Trujillo or any other person coming into office as a result of the coming elections and will maintain the most friendly relations with him and his government and will desire to cooperate with him in every proper way."[54]

Cotton pointedly suggested that Curtis invite Colonel Richard M. Cutts, one of Trujillo's former Marine superiors, to come from his station with the Marine occupation force in Haiti to exert his "great personal influence" on Trujillo to do his duty. Given Trujillo's personal identification with his Marine mentors and comrades, a "personal appeal" from Cutts would carry far more weight than one from the openly antagonistic Curtis.[55] The subsequent five-hour meeting between Trujillo and Cutts set the tone for future relations between the general and U.S. military officers, characterized by apparent mutual approval based on a shared military culture and a set of priorities oriented toward strict civil order. Cutts reported and seemed to accept Trujillo's assurance that the overthrow of Vásquez was "not a real revolution, the whole thing being merely a demonstration," and that he was not "a candidate of force." He also conveyed Trujillo's impression "that the local State Department Representatives are against him" (which in fact they were), giving his opponents "a great and undue advantage."[56] Far from discouraging Trujillo's candidacy, Cutts lent a sympathetic ear to his fellow officer, who he thought was misunderstood by the diplomats. Other Marine Corps representatives in the future would also commiserate and cooperate with Trujillo.

Without the diplomatic ammunition necessary to force Trujillo to abide by the peace agreement, Curtis and Cabot met with great frustration "trying to make people live up to their promises. Trying to keep the country on an even keel. And all without any means of making anyone behave."[57] Cabot complained to Winthrop Scott, the State Department official most sympathetic to the legation's plight, that Trujillo had "broken three major promises to the legation" and had treated the peace agreement "as a scrap of paper." Cabot pleaded for greater powers of enforcement: "I frankly do not see how diplomatic relations can be carried on with the Dominican Republic if Dominican leaders are going to be permitted to break promises with impunity."[58] Claiming that the legation "could have retained neither its self-respect nor the respect of either the country or of General Trujillo" without opposing the latter's candidacy, Curtis continued to predict that "unless the United States takes a stand versus the government strong enough to make Trujillo withdraw," a much more violent revolution was certain to result and "within a couple of years military intervention will become inevitable."[59] British Minister Galienne reported the general impression that the U.S. legation had lost control of Dominican affairs: "The better-informed Dominican seems to feel that the position has been handled in too diplomatic a fashion by the United States Government, and that there is no longer the great fear that American marines would enter at the first disturbance or unconstitutional action."[60]

The Dominican Revolution of 1930 and Trujillo's subsequent rise had tested the resolve of U.S. policy makers to maintain the policy of non-intervention, even as diplomats "in the field" recommended abandoning the policy and acted at times as if it had already been abandoned. Cabot had foreshadowed his mixed feelings in an assessment of U.S. policy in the Dominican Republic written six months earlier, in which he condemned the Marine occupation for doing "immeasurable harm" to Latin American relations and encouraging "Anti-Americanism." He noted in contrast that during 1924–29, "the preservation of domestic political tranquillity . . . together with the protection and promotion of American interests" had been achieved "without the remotest threat of using the 'big stick.'" Cabot nevertheless argued for the possibility of vigorous U.S. interposition should the Dominican government again become unstable. "The policy of non-interference and quiet helpfulness cannot in themselves indefinitely prevent the outbreak of armed disturbances. If and when that contingency arises, it will again raise the question whether another policy is required; whether the U.S. must not again resort to armed intervention."[61]

But after the outbreak of hostilities in February 1930, the State Department held firm in its refusal to make a demonstration of force or to authorize its diplomats to make official protests about the major issues: the means by which Trujillo seized power and his personal duplicity toward the U.S. legation. Curtis and Cabot were empowered to offer their assistance in a personal capacity only, without the authority of the State Department to endorse their words and actions.[62] Although they acted independently in attempting to shape the outcome of the revolution, interjecting themselves onto the lines of battle and into conferences between the rival groups, they were powerless to prevent Trujillo from emerging as the ultimate victor. The ironic result was that their efforts to corral the Dominican political stampede were commended by the State Department, inasmuch as an agreement ending the "revolution" was concluded without the aid of a warship, but the policy of nonintervention ruled out their political ban on Trujillo and greatly reduced their influence over subsequent events. The weakness of the diplomats later became clear with the election and recognition of Trujillo.

## THE ELECTION OF 1930

The legation's protests notwithstanding, Trujillo began his push for the presidency surrounded by a group of social outsiders whose "combined net political tonnage," estimated Cabot, was "approximately equal to that of one Persian kitten (drowned)."[63] But for all their lack of political experience, Trujillo's followers were thorough in their intimidation of his opponents in the National and Progressive parties, who combined to form the Alianza Party. Army personnel "going about in civilian clothes heavily armed" ran his election campaign, in which Curtis reported that "murders, plunders, assaults and outrages" took the place of rallies and speeches.[64] On the night of 4 April 1930, soldiers fired on the Alianza leaders, including the candidates Federico Velásquez and Angel Morales, as their car caravan proceeded through the Cibao Valley.[65] The "intimidation and terrorism by the Army" included "overthrowing" those municipal councils and town mayors who would not cooperate in rigging the election and "disarming the people" (as well as the bodyguards of Trujillo's opponents).[66]

The Dominican press recorded assaults and jailings of opposition party leaders and attacks on rival political gatherings. A rally near Fortaleza Ozama, for example, was broken up by a crowd throwing rocks from "Parque Trujillo" across the street.[67] Tulio Cestero, the Dominican minister to Spain, was among a network of Dominican elites in Europe who circulated newspaper clippings on these events among themselves. Their personal commentary on what they read had an air of resignation; the coverage had a familiar ring to it. Cestero's correspondent Enrique Deschamps, at the Institute of American Economy in Barcelona, was more alarmed than most at the rise of Trujillo. "¡Que horror!" he wrote, "if we have to go back to military presidents, I think we will suffer gravely." But in "las danzas políticas dominicanas," he added, one could expect violence to cut in.[68]

On 7 May 1930 the entire Junta Central Electoral, or electoral commission, resigned over the refusal of the Dominican armed forces to retire to their barracks, and the week after that (just two days before the election) the Alianza Party announced a boycott of the election.[69] Curtis reported that "law has ceased to exist," there being fewer political freedoms than during the infamous dictatorship of Ulises Heureaux. He concluded that Trujillo, already in de facto control, proceeded with the elections simply to give "the semblance of constitutionality" to his seizure of power. This would strengthen his case for U.S. recognition of his government.[70]

The "shot-gun elections" went ahead on schedule. "Almost nobody voted," yet the returns showed more votes than there were registered voters, almost all of them cast for Trujillo.[71] U.S. Consul Bickers in Puerto Plata reported that "the election was regarded as a joke even to those in control of the voting booths."[72] Trujillo moved quickly to seal his absolute victory, jailing his defeated opponent, Federico Velázquez, and prompting "all the other opposition leaders to scurry for shelter" or into exile, most notably the defeated vice-presidential candidate Angel Morales, who would become the most prominent and respected of Trujillo's enemies abroad.[73] Two days after the poll, "a gang of toughs" (called *La 42,* supposedly after one of the units of the Marine occupation) broke up a session of the appellate court and sacked its chambers as it was "about to declare the elections illegal." Three judges hurried to the legation for asylum, and "The 42" continued "tearing around Santo Domingo in an unlicensed car," terrorizing the inhabitants.[74]

The litany of campaign violence recounted by Curtis had momentarily confused Acting Secretary Cotton, who asked the Latin American expert Dana Munro, "Does [Curtis] mean that Trujillo controls or nobody controls?" Munro, who had been in the State Department's Division of Latin American Affairs since the Wilson administration, replied: "I think he means that Trujillo controls the army and is using it to oppress his opponents," adding wearily that "events like these are not unusual in Caribbean elections."[75] What was unusual was the inability of the U.S. diplomat on the scene to do anything about it.

RECOGNITION POLICY

Cotton's distinction between anarchy ("nobody controls") and bullying ("Trujillo controls") was an important one in the State Department's policy on recognition, which was the prevailing issue in the wake of Trujillo's election and one of the contested features of the early Good Neighbor policy. The practice was to recognize de facto regimes, so long as they met certain conditions. Most important, they had to be in firm control. Assistant Secretary of State Francis White advocated in 1924 that "if a strong man is in office . . . we should by all means be friendly to him and if he continues in office more than the constitutional period . . . I feel that we should by all means be on friendly terms with him so long as he protects our interests."[76] Vásquez, for all his manipulations of the Dominican Constitution and electoral laws, enjoyed such support while he seemed to control Trujillo and the army. With Trujillo having cut out the middleman, the criteria for success remained the same for what Secretary of State Henry Stimson considered to be "one of our most important experiments": "the Dominican experiment." Stimson wanted Dominican affairs to continue "running pretty well" during the Trujillo administration, as they had under Vásquez.[77] The smooth operation of the U.S. General Receivership of Dominican Customs and the redemption of the Dominican foreign debt depended on civil order, which had been imposed in the republic for the previous fourteen years, first by the Marines and then by the Dominican Army. "Colonel" Stimson, a former secretary of war and governor-general of the occupied Philippines, emphasized the importance of military support for the government. Speaking to Senator William Borah in November 1930, Stimson explained why the United States did not intervene in a similar situation in Cuba, where Gerardo Machado had extended his rule and intensified his repression: "[The Machado regime] was not the government that we should care for in America, but that it seemed to be in full control in Cuba; that it was popular with the Army, and that that was the main thing in Latin American countries."[78] But Stimson's criteria for recognition were not enumerated publicly until the following spring, when he issued an explanatory press release. His three prerequisites were, first, that the government to be recognized have "control of the administrative machinery"; second, that there exist "no active resistance to their rule"; and, third, as a function of such stability, that it was "willing and apparently able to fulfill [its] international obligations," especially the repayment of foreign debts.[79]

But State Department policy on recognition of Caribbean governments was still clouded by Hoover's adherence to the Washington Treaty of 1923. This agreement between the five Central American republics, which the U.S. government had approvingly mediated, stated that regimes coming to power illegally in any of those countries were categorically ineligible for recognition by foreign governments. Hoover had not renounced this formula in his policy toward Central American affairs, and the State Department continued to use the Washington Treaty to reduce revolutionary disquiet, leaving some doubt as to the extent of its geographical application.

On the day of the rigged Dominican election, the *New York Times* printed a statement from Assistant Secretary of State Francis White, who had supervised Latin American relations since 1922. White's press release extolled the nonrecognition policy in terms not specific to Central America: "In recent years the United States has made a great departure and, I believe, a step forward in refusing to recognize the governments of States that have secured control through criminal or unconstitutional methods. . . . All Americans should be proud of our record in this respect."[80] The principles of the Washington Treaty were also applied by Acting Secretary of State Joseph Cotton in Haiti the following month, when the "Hoover plan" for Haitian elections was instituted by the Forbes Commission.[81]

Despite the Washington Treaty, the tests of constitutionality and criminality would not be applied in the case of the Dominican Republic. Instead, the State Department's intention in 1930 "would be to recognize Trujillo even were the elections palpably fraudulent or the result due to intimidation by the military forces," as "the Department desires to avoid as much as possible the possibility of any intervention or interference in Dominican affairs."[82] Not only was Trujillo in complete control of the Dominican armed forces, he was judged by Colonel Cutts to be "probably more Americanized than any other Dominican" as a result of his Marine training.[83] The qualities that Cutts admired as "American," efficiency and authority, would empower him to maintain stability in the Dominican Republic, as observers less partial than Cutts also believed. Trujillo had the best chance to prove the Dominicans' "ability to govern themselves," as a *New York Times* report on the May election phrased it. If successful, the "policy of nonintervention will have proved more than ever justified."[84] But the State Department did not communicate its intention to recognize Trujillo, either publicly or through diplomatic channels. Washington's silence kept alive the threat that Trujillo would not be recognized, and perpetuated political uncertainty in the Dominican Republic even after his landslide election.

### THE "GUNMAN GOVERNMENT"

Recognition was one plum that Trujillo could not obtain by force, and so he attempted a reconciliation with Curtis.[85] The president-elect sponsored a dinner for the minister and indicated he "would soon turn toward the legation and the government of the United States for assistance." He displayed "effusive cordiality" toward his American nemesis but failed to assuage the latter's bitterness.[86] If anything, Curtis became even more deeply indignant as he watched Trujillo and the "traitors and demagogues" surrounding him "violating the liberties of the Dominican people with a weapon forged by the Military Occupation." The policy of nonintervention had undermined his authority and increased his resentment of a Dominican president immune to his "personal appeals" and "friendly advice." "Although the policy of non-intervention has avoided for the moment the danger of stirring up Dominican and Latin American resentment against the United States, the failure of the present government to fulfill its promises and to observe the Agreement which had been reached through the legation's mediation, has so shaken confidence in the ability of the legation to carry out its policies that it would be impossible for it to play again the role which it played in the revolution of February."[87]

British Minister Galienne also discerned that "recognition of General Trujillo's government would be a further severe blow to the prestige of American diplomacy here and the power and influence which the American Legation used until the February revolution would probably disappear." In his view, "'big business' in this country, represented by the Cuban-Dominican Sugar Co., the National City Bank of New York, the petroleum companies and others, is undoubtedly supporting General Trujillo" and "using influence at Washington" to gain recognition for him. "The situation, as I envisage it," reported Galienne, "becomes a duel between American business on the one hand and American diplomacy on the other."[88]

Dominican politics had not passed entirely out of the orbit of the U.S. legation, though, so long as uncertainty over the U.S. government's recognition of Trujillo encouraged resistance to his regime. Cabot wrote that "rumors of revolution and assassination fill the streets and drawing rooms" while this question remained unanswered.[89] The legation staff did nothing to quell the "rumors" in the "drawing rooms" of Trujillo's elite opponents, but enjoyed watching Trujillo twist in the wind while the Hoover administration said nothing on the subject of recognition. The brunt of the pressure fell on the new Dominican minister to the United States, Rafael Brache, who took the position Angel Morales had occupied before the coup. "We are quietly snickering over the painful predicament of the Dominican Minister in Washington, who went to Washington with Just One Object in mind. Poor dear, he didn't know that before he went Washington had already decided to do the very thing he wanted. . . . Later on we were vastly amused to hear that he had sent telegrams which fairly sweated blood because he hadn't been able to accomplish a thing (not knowing that it wasn't necessary). . . . [E]verything had been decided in March, before he'd arrived."[90]

In the first week of June 1930, the first spark of revolution against Trujillo was kindled by the defeated opposition.[91] He extinguished it rapidly:

> The Genial Grafters (that's the crowd that got kicked out in February) have been getting sorer and Sorer and SORER at the Gunman government (that's the present administration), until they finally bust right through their waistcoat buttons (that excluded automatically 99 44/100% of the population). So they started a revolution, which consisted of the leaders playing hide-and-seek in the town with the government, while their followers laid it in the bush. Well, the government retaliated by pinching everyone who still retained a waistcoat and wasn't in hiding (which meant that they were all innocent). After about twenty-four hours all the outs who were playing hide-and-seek in the bush got bored and returned to town, which leaves those in town rather on the end of a limb.[92]

Although in personal letters Cabot described Dominican politics with comic derision, the intensification of violence and intimidation against Trujillo's opposition was very real. A "gang of assassins" murdered Virgilio Martínez Reyna, the prestigious leader of the Partido Nacional and candidate for senator from Santiago in the boycotted election, along with his pregnant wife. A group of armed men detained and threatened Arturo J. Pellerano Alfau, director of the anti-Trujillo newspaper *Listín Diario,* and his family.[93] The newspaper offices themselves had been attacked ten days earlier.[94]

In the midst of this time "when wild excitement seem[ed] to be breaking out at every point," Minister Curtis "developed a case of colly-wobbles," as Cabot put it, and had to go on leave.[95] As a result, he was not there when the warship he requested back in February finally arrived in June, although it came for a very different purpose than the one he intended. The cruiser *Sacramento* of the Special Service Squadron paid a "good will visit" to Santo Domingo for five days, during which an exchange of courtesy calls, receptions, and meals took place at the presidential mansion, the U.S. consulate, and aboard the ship. These meetings left no doubt that, although Rafael Estrella Ureña continued as interim president, it was General Trujillo who controlled the country.

Trujillo made this clear in a meeting with Commander W. W. Smith and the officers of the *Sacramento* when he "somewhat theatrically" solicited their opinion of Samaná Bay, "suggesting that perhaps arrangements could be made for its survey by American naval vessels, some of which could then be stationed there permanently." Chargé Cabot reported that "the conversation regarding Samaná Bay was short and indefinite, but the meaning General Trujillo desired to convey was absolutely clear; he wished to lease or sell it to the United States as a naval base."[96] The Commission on Navy Yards and Navy Stations had already completed a secret survey of the bay and concluded that it "possessed superior advantages over any other position as a main base for the defense of the Caribbean," although in response to Trujillo's overture Stimson and Navy Secretary Charles Francis Adams agreed that the United States "entertains no desire" to acquire the bay.[97] Naval planners may have had professional interest in the strategic qualities of Samaná, but the new orientation of Caribbean policy would not permit further strengthening of the naval presence in the region; in fact, the number and size of the vessels attached to the Special Service Squadron were reduced during the balance of Hoover's term, and their "good will" cruising was curtailed. The intention of the policy of reduced naval forces in the region was to reduce the level of indignation they inspired on the part of Latin Americans who viewed battleships as symbols of imperialism. *Listín Diario* made the point in an editorial on "the presence of the cruiser *Sacramento* in Dominican waters," which presence was "contrary to nationalist feelings." The *Sacramento* was particularly "connected to the nexus of hatred and pain" caused by the Marine invasion and occupation, having taken part in the bombardment of the Dominican coast in 1916.[98]

By the time Trujillo's offer, with its implicit message of control and cooperation, crossed the desks of the highest ranking officials at the State and Navy departments, his domestic opponents' resistance had been broken. Cabot understood that "no good purpose would be served by concealing longer" the intention to recognize Trujillo. Further delay would result only in further intimidation of elite Dominicans (Cabot's waistcoated and "genial" associates) by the "gunmen" of the new regime (equated by Cabot's term with the peasant "bandits" formerly pursued by the Marine government).[99] Cabot ended his personal policy of being "discreet to the point of secretiveness" on the question of recognition.[100] He asked for and was granted permission to reveal to Trujillo, who was due to be inaugurated in three weeks, that he would be recognized by the United States, thereby ending the "absurd rumors" to the contrary that had been "prejudicing political and economic conditions."[101]


## TRUJILLO'S "CORONATION"

As standard procedure dictated, Charles Curtis (still on leave) was designated "special ambassador" to Trujillo's August inauguration, an announcement that neither party greeted with enthusiasm. Trujillo now first displayed his strategy of courting well-connected political allies and lobbyists in the United States in order to circumvent the opposition of the legation to his goals. Wanting someone to be accredited who had greater political clout (and more personal respect for him) than Curtis, Trujillo had in mind the attorney and "well known socialite" Edward E. Gann, the brother-in-law of Hoover's vice-president, Charles Curtis (no relation to the minister).[102] Trujillo had hired Gann as a lobbyist when he "apparently feared that he might not be recognized." Vice-President Curtis approached Secretary of State Stimson at a cabinet meeting to relate Trujillo's desire to have Gann appointed special representative. Stimson told the vice-president that the State Department rarely dispatched special representatives, adding that Trujillo "is coming into office as a result of revolutionary disorders in the Dominican Republic and this inauguration would seem to be a particularly inappropriate occasion to make any exception."[103] Trujillo also cultivated a relationship with Governor Theodore Roosevelt Jr. of Puerto Rico, whose help he believed "would be much more useful" than that of the U.S. legation in trying "to obtain for him the firm support" of the U.S. government.[104] Favorable relations with the governor of Puerto Rico also helped Trujillo to keep a close eye on the activities of the many opposition leaders who took part in the "exodus" to that island after the May elections.[105] Both Governor Roosevelt and his predecessor, James Beverly, coordinated with the Detective Bureau of the Bureau of Insular Affairs, the Dominican legation in Washington, the Federal Bureau of Investigation, and the secretary of war to "carefully watch" the many exiled Dominican politicians in Puerto Rico (including Horacio Vásquez).[106]

Trujillo's "coronation," as he himself "facetiously" called it, took place on Dominican Restoration Day, 16 August 1930. Cabot reported that it was "the most grandiose and gorgeous inauguration which the country has ever seen . . . such as few incoming presidents would deem in conformity with republican simplicity." Far from humble republicanism, the grand style of nationalism characteristic of what would become the Era of Trujillo was reflected in its ritual commencement. Wearing a gold-braid uniform made in Paris and the cockade hat of the dictator Ulises Heureaux, the new president paraded through five triumphal arches on Avenida 27 de Febrero (four erected by foreign "colonies" of entrepreneurs and immigrants, one by the U.S.-dominated sugar industry) accompanied by "virtually the entire army in their dress uniforms."[107] The capital was decorated with twenty thousand Dominican flags (some paired with the flags of the other American states), and packets of confetti and streamers were distributed in the "poor neighborhoods" (although Cabot suspected that the "alms . . . distributed to the poor [were] from the public moneys which Trujillo has diverted to his personal bank account"). Government buildings, clubs, and businesses were "illuminated," and there were fireworks in central Parque Colón. The general was now also the president.[108]

## THE SAN ZENÓN HURRICANE

As Trujillo consolidated his dictatorship of the Dominican Republic, the State Department did what it could to conduct uneffusive relations with Trujillo. The bilateral relationship might be characterized as "correct," a term that can mean a great many different things in the performance of foreign relations in two countries by several different organizations. During Trujillo's first year in power, while Charles Curtis remained as minister, "correct" relations in Santo Domingo meant icily hostile, while those in Washington meant politely standoffish. Even when, less than three weeks after Trujillo's inauguration, the San Zenón hurricane demolished Santo Domingo (on 3 September 1930), the political and personal repercussions of sending relief to the stricken capital were foremost in the minds of U.S. diplomats there and in Washington. The State Department would not authorize Trujillo's request for fifty U.S. Marines to be sent ashore to help maintain order, fearing the symbolic use he might make of them, and Curtis obstructed other aid efforts in an effort to "swat" the new Dominican leader. This revealing episode merits a closer examination.

The San Zenón hurricane flattened all but the ancient capital's stoutest colonial structures and wrecked the only bridge across the Ozama River, reducing the city to a field of rubble. Although estimates vary, perhaps as many as six thousand Dominicans were killed, and the survivors faced a nightmare of bad water, decaying bodies, and shortages of food and medicine.[109] The U.S. legation offices and the minister's residence, across the street from each other, were "unroofed" by the storm as well.[110] The aftermath of the disaster encapsulates the political dynamic in the Dominican Republic at the outset of the Trujillo regime, with its lines of personal antagonism between Trujillo and Curtis, and of bureaucratic rivalry between the diplomats and naval officers of four nations over what forms of relief would be carried out and by whom. These politics of relief were shaped by the aggressive style of foreign relations adopted by the newly inaugurated and internationally recognized President Trujillo, and they are revealed in reports from the USS *Grebe,* the first vessel to arrive after the storm, and from Marine Major William B. Sullivan, sent as a Navy Department liaison officer and translator for the Navy relief effort.

The *Grebe* encountered a swollen, surging Ozama River with a wreck blocking its entrance when it reached Santo Domingo from San Juan early on 6 September 1930. For three days afterward, the ship's company worked unloading relief cargoes brought by other ships and navigating the dangerous approach past the wreck against the river current to the city. Only eight sailors went ashore, those to guard trucks carrying supplies from the dock against "thieving by the native soldiers and others."[111] When Major Sullivan came on the scene on 9 September, he found that Colonel Richard Cutts in Haiti had done "quick work" in sending medical supplies after the hurricane, and the Marine Air Corps planes stationed in the Virgin Islands had established relief flights. An officer of the Navy Medical Corps was also supervising five "hospital units," but that was the extent of the U.S. commitment.[112] The reason more had not been done, said Sullivan, was the "apparent" fact "that relations between the Minister and the president are so strained as to make work here difficult." Trujillo had already asked the State Department, Navy Department, and Governor Roosevelt of Puerto Rico for a contingent of fifty Marines to provide assistance, but the State Department referred him to Curtis, saying that "requests for Marines" had to be made "by the President" directly to the U.S. minister. The personal deadlock between Trujillo and Curtis precluded that, despite Sullivan's "opinion that the Marines should be here for the good effect they would have on the Guardia."

> Mr. Curtis the Minister was outspoken in his criticism of the President. He says that the President tries to humiliate him and he (the Minister) is ever on his guard to thwart the efforts of the President.

Mr. Curtis stated to me "Colonel Cutts is an admirer of the President but *I* am not." He is ever on the look out for a chance to "swat" the President, to use his own words. Mr. Curtis stated to me that "I must watch my prestige, for I have to live here when this is over." This was brought out when Mr. Curtis told me the President had endeavored to "by pass" him on several occasions in communicating with various departments in Washington.[113]

With the city in ruins, Curtis sought to channel the Navy and Marine relief efforts through his office for the sake of, he reiterated to Sullivan, his "prestige." This was evident when Trujillo requested that one of his Marine comrades from the occupation, Major Thomas E. Watson, be appointed as food administrator. The State Department asked Curtis whether Major Watson's appointment should be as "attaché" or "relief worker." "The Minister stated to [Sullivan] very gleefully that he would certainly ask for Watson as Attaché, because the Department had informed him that Watson is a friend of the President. 'Now' said Mr. Curtis 'if Mr. Trujillo wants Watson for food administrator or anything else he will have to ask *me*.' (The word me being accented)."[114] To Sullivan, "the mission" of relieving the "emergency" was "to accomplish the most in the shortest time and in the most direct manner," to which Curtis agreed with one important caveat: "There were a great many things that could be accomplished," he said, " 'If Trujillo would only ask me.' "[115]

On 9 September, the same day Major Sullivan arrived to act as liaison, the appearance of first a Dutch and then a British warship brought an international dimension to the dispute over hurricane relief. The Dutch ship, the cruiser *Arend,* immediately did what the United States had shied away from since the storm; it sent a party of twenty "bluejackets" ashore to clean the streets and Fortaleza Ozama. The British chargé then offered to disembark a shore party from the cruiser *Danae,* which arrived in the afternoon; Trujillo "accepted the offer and asked for 60 or 70 armed men to come ashore to relieve the Guardia."[116] The captain of the *Danae* informed his counterpart, Captain Petri of the *Grebe,* that the "armed guard" would be "for the purpose of maintaining order" in the city, news that alarmed the U.S. Navy and Marine officers on the scene, including Major Sullivan, who informed Curtis.[117] Curtis, however, "thought the President was making a foolish move. . . . He said it will be good propaganda for the outs who will say the President could not handle the situation without calling for foreign troops." Sullivan then left a message for Trujillo that "to bring an armed force ashore from the British Cruiser would lay him open to adverse criticism," so Trujillo asked that the British come unarmed to clean the streets, as the Dutch had.[118] The British captain would not send sailors to do manual labor "since there were sufficient able bodied natives in Santo Domingo to do such work," but he agreed to send them as supervisors. Captain Petri advised him to the contrary, pointing out "that sending parties ashore in a supervisory capacity would have a tendency to irritate the natives." From Petri's perspective, Trujillo's request for British assistance "was a gesture on the part of the President to flout the authority of the United States since it was apparent that Americans are none too well liked."[119] It was Sullivan's "candid opinion that [the] President was asking for the British Bluejackets as a slap at the American Minister for balking him in getting our Marines."[120]

Trujillo's foreign policy in San Zenón's aftermath demonstrates the sophistication with which he would play on the bureaucratic rivalries between his Marine sympathizers and his Department of State enemies, and on the sensitivities of both concerning U.S. hegemony in the Caribbean. In this case, he had "bypassed" the uncooperative U.S. minister, established ties of gratitude and shared accomplishment with the providers of relief in the Marine Corps and Navy (who sided against Curtis), and involved the Dutch and, very nearly, British forces in the relief effort in a dextrous manipulation of three nations' representatives. Although Curtis thought the use of foreign shore parties would detract from Trujillo's projection of power, the appearance of Dutch sailors in the streets with shovels and the acceptance of the British offer of assistance were symbolic of Trujillo's ability to choose options other than those laid out for him by the United States, thus constituting an assertion of national sovereignty. Curtis, with State Department support, had prevented Trujillo from involving more than a handful of Marines in the relief effort despite the Marines' willingness to help. Barring American involvement, British participation in the San Zenón cleanup was narrowly averted by advice from the ranking American military officers on the scene, Sullivan and Petri, who acted to protect Trujillo's political interests from damage by Curtis, and to defend the Navy's control of relief operations from its imperial competitors. The officers and minister alike based their actions on the political dynamics, rather than the manpower requirements, of storm relief.

In a sense, the San Zenón hurricane was the culmination of the drawn-out coup that was initiated by Trujillo in the February "revolution" and confirmed in his coerced election and gaudy inauguration. Trujillo's quick response to the catastrophe gained him the grudging respect of some important people in Washington, like Henry Stimson, who privately judged that he was "panning out to be a very good man." Impressed by Trujillo's ability, Stimson sought to help him by relieving the Dominican debt crisis, as the following chapter will detail.[121] Also in the wake of the storm, Trujillo asserted complete authority over the rebuilding of the city, which he would rechristen "Ciudad Trujillo" in 1936, giving him the ability to reorient the social organization of its population to reflect his control.[122] Trujillo's reconstruction of Santo Domingo, including a new bridge over the Ozama and greatly improved port facilities, deepened the respect that many Marines and Navy officers already had for him, while his reconfiguration of Dominican society through grandiose personalism (symbolized by naming the new bridge, the new port, and the city itself for himself) heightened the diplomats' distaste for him.

## THE "NECESSITY OF CORDIAL RELATIONS"

U.S. acceptance of the accession to power of a military tyrant would not go without examination and criticism, however. During the autumn of 1930, Curtis and Cabot reported that "fifty or sixty members of opposed or loosely connected factions have met death by violence since the election." They gave details of rape and torture perpetrated by members of the army.[123] Cabot discarded the various euphemisms he had employed and labeled the government a "virtual dictatorship" under which political freedom and private rights were things of the past.[124] But Curtis had to admit in January 1931 that it was equally certain that "the strictest order [was] being maintained throughout the length and breadth of the country and that the credit for this is due to President Trujillo alone."[125] One of Tulio Cestero's correspondents in Santo Domingo agreed with this assessment, reporting to him in February 1931, that "everyone fears [Trujillo] and obeys him. . . . The country needs a man, and it found one. Peace is a fact."[126] Henry Stimson was accepting of the Trujillo regime for the sake of the stability it engendered, although he stopped short of embracing it. When Governor Roosevelt of Puerto Rico lobbied to fulfill Trujillo's desire for a U.S. military commission "to train his army," Stimson understood that this would help Trujillo "stay indefinitely in power," and he opposed the idea.[127]

A series of articles by Drew Pearson on the scale of repression practiced during Trujillo's first six months in office appeared in American newspapers in February 1931, taking the State Department by surprise. Pearson's motivation to write the articles, and the information he disclosed in them, came from Sumner Welles, a strong ally of the Dominican exiles and future undersecretary of state under Franklin Roosevelt.[128] The tone of the reports was sensationalist, but after an internal inquiry into the facts of the matter (including the wider circulation around Foggy Bottom of many of the legation's earlier cables, which had not been read by many officials when they came in) State Department officials were "shocked to find that the picture is even more lurid than Mr. Pearson paints it."[129] The publicity was unwelcome, and the reasons why were outlined by First Secretary Cabot, who was witness to the entire tableau of Trujillo's drawn-out coup and who directed a lengthy "Memo Regarding Policies toward the Trujillo Government" to his superiors at the State Department. His encapsulation of the quandaries presented by the policy of nonintervention toward a dictatorship merits an extended quotation:

> The Department has at various times emphasized to the legation in Santo Domingo the necessity of cordial relations with the Trujillo regime and with Trujillo himself. . . . I submit that a desire to maintain an attitude of cordiality and sympathy should not preclude an adequate taking into account of the following points:
>
> 1. Trujillo came into power by gross treachery to the man who made him commander of the army and in spite of promises made to the legation.
> 2. He won the elections purely and simply by force.
> 3. He has (in my opinion) almost no support in the country outside of the army; he appears to be intensely hated by the great majority of the Dominican people. . . .
>
> It must be pointed out that it is generally thought in Santo Domingo that the American government is positively favoring Trujillo. Color is lent to this belief by the following:
>
> 1. Trujillo was raised from the gutter by the Marine Corps and started toward this present position.
> 2. He is known to have been in close contact with Colonel Cutts from the Evacuation to the present moment. . . .

4. The American government promptly recognized the Estrella Ureña and Trujillo governments. . . .

Is it advisable for the American government to show what appears to be marked favor to a thoroughly unpopular, unscrupulous, and perhaps unstable government, or even to bolster it?[130]

Cabot had summed up the basic challenge for U.S. policy toward Trujillo and other rulers like him: how to walk the line between interference and advocacy. This policy debate has continued to shadow U.S. relations with military regimes everywhere since the 1930s, although the question has been especially pressing as it concerns the Caribbean area, where U.S. influence has been deep and is often thought to be decisive.

Henry Stimson was a great believer in wielding what he called "the club of public opinion," which was "a live factor which can be promptly mobilized and which has become a factor of prime importance in the solution of the problems and controversies which may arise between nations."[131] Why, then, did Stimson not apply this form of pressure to the Dominican Republic in an attempt to persuade Trujillo to curb the brutality of his rule? Stimson preferred to divert critical public attention from authoritarianism in the Caribbean and the discernible links between militarist repression and the policy of nonintervention. One respect in which the Hoover administration's Latin American policy set the precedent for Roosevelt's loudly proclaimed "Good Neighbor policy" was its selective use of the "club of public opinion." Rather than criticize authoritarian regimes in the Caribbean, Hoover and Stimson pledged nonintervention in neighbors' affairs. The policy aimed to reconfigure the entire hemisphere's perceptions of the United States and to elicit the kind of comment made by the Cuban newsman Carlos Silva Vildosola, who said Hoover's Latin American policy constituted "a new form of legitimate imperialism: that of cooperation."[132] The tactic of censuring the Trujillos of the hemisphere threatened to bring further charges of arrogance and interference against the United States and offered no guarantee that conditions would improve for people living under dictatorships. Hoover and Stimson would have preferred to carry on relations with nations that combined stability and representative government, but they were not willing to achieve that ideal at the cost of playing the policeman again in Latin America.

When possible, the State Department tried to prevent unfavorable publicity about Trujillo from soiling its record, as it did when Drew Pearson prepared another gory article concerning the Dominican Republic. Learning of this "unpleasant" coverage, Winthrop Scott of the State Department took immediate action. Scott, soon to become undersecretary of state, held a low personal opinion of the Trujillo regime, and he knew Pearson's information in the first series of exposés was accurate, but he "hastened to prepare a Press Release so as to forestall any wrong slant."[133] The journalistic "slant" that State most wanted to avoid was that Trujillo was a protégé of the United States. The image it hoped to project was that the U.S. government was completely impartial, abstaining from both interference and judgment, neither disapproving nor advocating. This turned out to be an awkward posture to maintain as Trujillo cultivated friends and allies in the United States (Marine officers, lobbyists, publicists, and businessmen) and developed his aggressive international policy during the 1930s. But before examining further the role of public relations between the two countries, the problems posed by the Great Depression should be considered.

Coppin State
Alfred Anna Voglibain
410-747-
Thursday 7971

Environment moses
University Liberia

Thursday University
Jim Turley

Bola George
Nigeria

April 8 Inaugration

Electronic registration

Urban League

11/3/09 - staff meeting

Bill Bentley: ProCAP
- _Erasures_          SenCAP

D'Ambra    eastern house

Achebe

◆

# CHAPTER THREE

# The Bankrupt Neighbor Policy:
# Depression Diplomacy and the Foreign
# Bondholders Protective Council

The global economy of the twentieth century is interdependent; it is a familiar economic metaphor that when the United States sneezes, the whole world catches a cold. But on 29 October 1929, when the United States caught a cold, Latin America contracted pneumonia. The stock market crash began the Great Depression, which spread quickly through the hemisphere and began an extended period of economic hardship and political uncertainty in Latin America. Many nations there were already deeply indebted to banking houses in New York, and the economic dislocations that radiated from stricken Wall Street were sufficient to bring those dependent economies to the brink of collapse. As the value of agricultural commodities plummeted, government revenues declined and it became increasingly difficult for those countries to continue paying their foreign debts. Their customary sources of credit in New York dried up completely within a year of the crash, even as the clamor for repayment being sounded by the U.S. holders of Latin American bonds grew more strident.[1]

## THE GREAT DEPRESSION

Latin American nations, provinces, and municipalities began to default, a situation that put the State Department in a difficult position. Since 1922, its policy had been to review all foreign loan proposals from U.S. banking establishments and bond houses. The department passed judgment on the compatibility of the loans with U.S. foreign policy but did not reflect on the risk of default that such loans might encounter. Many who had purchased Latin American bonds nevertheless viewed this system of review as a State Department guarantee of their investments. As the global crisis deepened, the epidemic of defaults led the bondholders to demand a cure from the State Department. Most of the defaulted loans were relics from dollar diplomacy and from the stock market frenzy of the 1920s; many had been arranged with unscrupulous Latin American regimes, and often the terms of the loans were akin to extortion. Even so, the onus of having "approved" these threatened issues fell squarely on State.[2]

Along with the protectionist Smoot-Hawley tariff, the Latin American debt problem was one of the major reasons why Hoover's brand of Good Neighbor diplomacy was not more successful or widely recognized.[3] The Hoover administration's depression diplomacy attempted to reconcile the competing interests of the Latin American debtors and their American creditors, but caught criticism from both sides. Hoover and Stimson did not subscribe to the use of government muscle for the collection of private debts, and they sought to keep the U.S. government above the financial fray.[4] But the banking houses and their bond investors cited the State Department system of "approval," claiming that certain foreign bonds were salable only because they had the apparent blessing of the U.S. government. The government, they reasoned, was responsible to its bondholding constituents and should pressure the Latin American nations into honoring their obligations, depression or not. The defaulting nations looked to the State Department for understanding of their desperate financial plight, and they looked to Hoover to be a "good neighbor." The debtors wanted new loans or moratoriums on their existing obligations to prevent economic collapse. In response to these competing expectations, Hoover's diplomacy avoided both the appearance of coercion and the appearance of favoritism. The Hoover administration tried to show that the government would not serve the powers of Wall Street, nor would it bail out bankrupt borrowers.[5] The State Department exerted no public pressure on foreign governments, but it did not come to their aid either. This approach made enemies on both sides of the foreign debt issue.

## THE DOMINICAN DEBT

The holders of Dominican bonds had especially high expectations that the U.S. government would have to act on their behalf, because the Convention of 1924 explicitly authorized U.S. intervention in the case of a default. Besides, the General Receivership gave the United States control of Dominican external revenues and supervision of the Dominican government's budget. The Receivership had been the most important part of Theodore Roosevelt's effort to overhaul Dominican finances and prevent interference from European creditors; as such, it was the very ideal of the Roosevelt Corollary. Its life was extended by the Convention of 1924, negotiated by Sumner Welles and Francisco Peynado as part of the procedure to end the military occupation of the Dominican Republic. By 1930 it had become one of the most stable institutions in Dominican history, lasting longer than the Haitian occupation, the dictatorship of Ulises Heureaux, or the U.S. military government. But it had also become the appendix of U.S. Caribbean policy, a remnant of anachronistic methods remaining from an earlier way of conducting foreign affairs. Another vestige of intervention was that the U.S. dollar circulated as the republic's legal tender, as it would until Trujillo established the Dominican peso in 1947. In accordance with the Convention of 1924, the priority of the customs receivership was to pay off the Dominican bond issues of 1922 and 1926. The 1922 loan of $22 million had been arranged by the U.S. military government itself in order to refinance the existing Dominican debt, fund road construction, and establish a constabulary force. The $25 million loan of 1926 had been authorized in the Convention of 1924 as a way to boost the Dominican government out of the financial straits bequeathed to it by the U.S. occupation. Whatever was left constituted the external revenues for use by the Dominican government.[6] The big problem facing Rafael Trujillo when he came to power in 1930 was that the amount of money coming into the customs houses had dwindled disastrously, and there was none left to run the government. Trujillo hoped the U.S. government would help him through the crisis, since the customs receivership controlled Dominican revenues.[7]

In the spring of 1931, Hoover and Stimson announced that the U.S. government was unable to assist bondholders whose securities were in default.[8] This was tacit acceptance of the Drago Doctrine, long a pillar of the Latin American case against intervention, condemning government action to collect private debts. In this way, the Hoover administration laid the groundwork for a more congenial stance toward its depressed neighbors. But the Drago Doctrine was no longer sufficient to rescue the bankrupt nations, which asked Hoover to defer their interest and amortization payments until a general financial recovery occurred. Hoover had set a precedent for this action in June 1931, when he proposed a moratorium on intergovernmental debts, like those remaining in Europe from World War I.[9] But intergovernmental debts were clearly subject to government action, whereas the private loans contracted in Latin America were not, said Hoover. The separation between public and private jurisdictions lay at the heart of Hoover's conception of liberal government; although Hoover felt fully justified to wade into the melee of reparations and government loans, he could accept nothing beyond the role of interested spectator where private lenders did business. Even so, the Latin American borrowers were encouraged by Hoover's proposal to suspend payments in Europe, and they rallied around the panacea of a general moratorium on all debts, public and private.[10]

But Hoover denied that any steps could be taken "concerning South American debts," since private debts were not subject to an executive moratorium, and he took no public action.[11] He saw fit, however, to exert unofficial governmental influence to lessen the financial crises in individual countries. Although the defaulting nations received no sweeping pardon of their contractual obligations from Hoover, he acted behind the scenes to aid them. Hoover and his Latin American policy makers recognized that a financial collapse in the Dominican Republic would serve no one's interests; the nation would risk anarchy, the bondholders might lose their investments, and the customs receivership would be caught in the middle. To avoid this, the State Department quietly pressured Trujillo into declaring a temporary, provisional moratorium on foreign debt payments: the Dominican Emergency Law of 1931.

In the case of the Dominican debt moratorium, Hoover's public posture and his official actions were in conflict. His belief in the separation of public and private affairs was mediated, first, by his pragmatic insistence on stability and, second, by his desire to improve relations with a strengthened and more orderly Caribbean region. In public, Hoover and Stimson continued to stress their inability either to aid the lenders with the collection of the debt or to cooperate with the borrowers in emergency measures to cease payment. Yet in backstage negotiations with the government of Rafael Trujillo, Hoover's State Department aggressively advocated a moratorium on the Dominican debt. Although it meant infringing on private contractual obligations, the United States sought to strengthen General Trujillo's fledgling regime and to establish solid and neighborly relations with it.

The Dominican Emergency Law of 1931 also achieved two other goals of the Hoover administration's Latin American policy. First, it avoided the appearance that the U.S. government was acting against the bondholders' interests. With Senator Hiram Johnson already convening embarrassing hearings in the Senate on the subject of bond sales, the State Department could not openly advocate a moratorium on debt payments.[12] Instead, the bondholders had to be finessed into accepting the cessation of payments while U.S. diplomats stood by clicking their tongues at the prodigal Dominicans. Second, and more important, it adhered to the Hoover administration's strict prohibition against further entanglements in Latin America. Hoover and Stimson were committed to extricating the government from its expensive military involvement in Nicaragua and Haiti, and they were opposed to deepening or extending its responsibilities in the Dominican Republic. So the debt moratorium had to be arranged without any new methods of control, like a U.S.-appointed supervisor of Dominican finances or an extended term for the customs receivership.

Throughout Latin America, the chain reaction of financial crises began with falling commodity prices. In the Dominican Republic, these all-important cash crops were coffee, cacao, and especially sugar. Low agricultural prices in the United States resulted first in greatly diminished earnings for the plantation owners themselves, which in turn meant less business for factors and merchants and sinking wages for Dominican labor. Sales and imports of all kinds of goods slowed to a fraction of their normal pace as the income of most Dominicans neared the subsistence level. For the Dominican government, which relied on sales and excise taxes and customs receipts for most of its income, these trends meant disaster.[13] To add to the problem, the service on the foreign debt more than doubled in 1930, as interest on a large portion of the principal became payable under the terms of the loan.[14] Soon after this new obligation went into effect, two representatives of the Brookings Institution traveled to Santo Domingo to assess the damage wrought by the depression. Their report described a desperate state of decline in the republic. With Trujillo not yet steady in the saddle, the shaky political situation made a speedy financial recovery unlikely, while the economic crisis in turn threatened civil disorder.[15]

In the midst of this economic collapse, the San Zenón hurricane hit Santo Domingo. With hurricane relief now paramount, the Dominican government was unable to service the debt even at the cost of denying itself any income for normal administrative expenses.[16] Trujillo's strategy to cope with the disaster was to push for a new loan. He declared to the State Department his intention to honor every cent of his debt service despite the storm damage, concluding that this adherence to principle was his best hope for a "prompt and real reconstruction" through outside funding.

Dominican Secretary of the Interior Elías Brache, an experienced politician who had been one of the signatories of the Hughes-Peynado agreement, instructed his brother Rafael, minister in Washington, to make Trujillo's pledge "known to the American Press."[17]

## THE MORATORIUM

In response, longtime General Receiver of Dominican Customs William Pulliam recommended arranging a moratorium on the Dominican debt.[18] Pulliam had entered the U.S. Customs Service in the Philippines in 1898, serving there for six years under Governor-General William Howard Taft, who then became secretary of war in the Roosevelt administration. Taft appointed Pulliam to head the Receivership in 1907, and he had been the steward of the Dominican debt for most of the time since then. As such, he was the "only individual . . . who must say no [to] the supreme authority," meaning Trujillo, whom he disliked.[19] He was accustomed to wielding considerable influence in the Dominican capital but was often at odds with the new government, which sought to replace him. Pulliam's opinion of what to do about the Dominican depression, based as it was on his intimate knowledge of the nation's finances, carried considerable weight at the State Department. Minister Charles B. Curtis shared Pulliam's distaste for Trujillo but argued against a moratorium. He stressed the need to maintain the Dominican credit rating, which would be irreparably damaged by a suspension of payments.[20]

In an effort to clarify this conflicting advice, the State Department dispatched an investigative mission to Santo Domingo. The mission, headed by U.S. Representative and former Assistant Secretary of the Treasury Eliot Wadsworth, sailed for the Dominican Republic on 25 September. After spending a week picking through the rubble of the capital and navigating the maze of the Dominican government's budget, Wadsworth made his report. He agreed with Pulliam on the need for the suspension of amortization payments, recommending a two-year moratorium, but he also agreed with Curtis, recommending that the Dominican government be stabilized with a significant cash advance.[21] Trujillo himself resisted plans for a moratorium, because that would jeopardize his grandiose plans for a $50 million loan to restructure the entire Dominican debt.[22]

Stimson believed that Trujillo could prevent the revenues made available by a moratorium from being intercepted by what he termed Dominican "vultures" and "politicos," but he still opposed a new loan.[23] Stimson had visited the Dominican Republic in 1917 and had befriended General Receiver Pulliam, with whom he still corresponded. He felt he had a clear view of the Dominican character, had concluded that "improvident borrowing" had been the source of the Dominican Republic's woes, and accordingly opposed any increase in the foreign debt.[24] Trujillo still sought a loan instead of a moratorium, sending an "economic mission" consisting of the Dominican secretaries of finance, the interior, and the presidency to New York to secure one. Stimson decided to allow Trujillo to find out the hard way that, if the State Department could prevent it, no loan would be forthcoming.[25] As a result, several Dominican loan proposals were shot down by the State Department during late 1930 and early 1931. The loans were secretly promoted by Trujillo's Marine Corps friends and backed by reputable New York lenders and construction firms, but no matter what their terms they were all rejected in Washington.[26] State Department officials rejected small loans as being insufficient to alleviate the problem, large loans as too great a commitment for the bankrupt nation. The publication of the harshly critical Drew Pearson articles in February 1931, especially the one detailing the loan proposals, ended for the moment the possibility of fresh funding for the Trujillo regime.

By repeatedly turning back Trujillo's attempts to secure a loan, the Hoover administration quietly orchestrated a default on the Dominican debt. The Dominican government was forced to implement the moratorium that the State Department had privately prescribed for it, which was codified in the Emergency Law of 1931. The crux of the resulting law was that the Dominican government would suspend amortization payments and establish its own kind of receivership. The U.S. General Receivership would continue to collect a portion of the customs receipts to pay the interest on the 1922 bonds, but the rest of the revenues would be gathered by a "Special Agent" (also a U.S. citizen) employed by the Dominican government. The money in this "Emergency Fund" was to pay the interest on the 1926 bonds, the special agent's expenses, and a monthly disbursement of $125,000 to the Dominican government. The remainder of the emergency fund, if there was any, was earmarked for amortization. The moratorium had a life of two years.[27]

In keeping with the depression diplomacy of the Hoover administration, Henry Stimson's response to the Emergency Law played to both sides of the issue. For Latin American consumption, he evinced sympathy for the economic straits of the Dominican Republic and encouragement for Trujillo's efforts to pay his bills.[28] For the benefit of the bankers and bondholders, he adopted a tone of grudging acquiescence in a regrettable turn of events, assuring them of his continued vigilance. Significantly, he also reminded them that the preservation of law and order in the Dominican Republic was prerequisite to the payment of its external accounts.[29] An orderly bankruptcy procedure was preferable to financial collapse and possible chaos.

Hoover and Stimson had acted in what they considered the best interests of the beleaguered republic. Herbert Hoover was a bootstrap-tugging product of early Progressivism, an Iowa orphan and frugal Quaker who became a millionaire by dint of education (Stanford University's first graduating class) and hard work (years of mine engineering in forbidding terrain in places like China and western Australia). Henry Stimson was wellborn, the occupant of a Long Island estate, but he agreed with the president that granting loans or giving handouts was not the solution to poverty. Rather, the wise and good creditor would postpone collecting debts from his hard-hit neighbor, thereby allowing him time to get back on his feet. Then that neighbor would be a grateful ally, not a sniping recipient of charity. They felt unable to express these views publicly for fear of revealing that the Convention of 1924, with its contractual guarantees to the bondholders, was a dead letter. So they stymied the Dominican government's projects with bureaucratic stipulations and incomplete information, repeatedly frustrating Trujillo's initiatives with Kafkaesque maneuvering. Trujillo and the members of his economic mission must have felt like so many Josef K's, unaware of sanctions from Stimson's high court, as they felt their way through a maze of conditions toward the final solution of a moratorium.

Trujillo himself saw the Emergency Law of 1931 in its true light. He regarded the program as a diplomatic smoke screen thrown up by the State Department to conceal its real agenda from the bondholders, who under the Convention of 1924 had the right to expect more strenuous action on their behalf from their representatives in Washington.[30] Trujillo cooperated by finally declaring bankruptcy and accepting the moratorium, but soon afterward he began acting on his own. He withheld money from the "special agent's" collection of customs to establish a reserve fund. Another $250,000 went into a fund for Trujillo's personal benefit. He also printed valueless bonds to finance a portion of the government's operating expenses and diverted $7 million from the bondholders to reduce his domestic "floating debt." Among the republic's many creditors, the Red Cross was supposedly the top priority for repayment, but the bill owed to them from the San Zenón hurricane relief effort went unpaid. More politically expedient payments went through, like those to cover unpaid government salaries. Since Trujillo's wife ran a lucrative business in discounting government paychecks, which were perpetually in arrears, payment of overdue salaries was also a transfer of money to Trujillo's personal coffers.[31]

Another of Trujillo's significant violations of the moratorium arrangement was his attempt to establish an air force with money from the debt suspension. When Stimson learned that a Trujillo agent had been seeking a $100,000 credit to purchase aircraft in the United States, he demanded an explanation.[32] Trujillo reported that no military planes would be acquired until the necessary money had been saved from the military budget and that only aircraft for a commercial service would be bought in the meantime.[33] Two planes were accordingly purchased by the National Aviation School for that purpose, but it turned out that these "commercial" carriers came equipped with bombs and machine guns.[34] The National Aviation School became the official title of the Dominican Air Force, which later became the most powerful in the Caribbean region. The moratorium may have calmed the waters of U.S.-Dominican relations, but Trujillo continued to rock the diplomatic boat with subterfuges like these in violation of both the Convention of 1924 and the Emergency Law of 1931.

Why did the State Department remain quiescent as these provocations mounted? With the Hoover administration trying to carve out a reputation for noninterference in its neighbors' affairs, no advantage could be gained by making Trujillo toe the line of the Emergency Law, which was essentially a legal fiction. The Dominican debt moratorium was among the first timid steps taken by the administration to improve hemispheric economic relations and establish a correspondingly flexible foreign policy toward Latin America.

The Dominican situation also shows how hesitant Hoover and Stimson were to accept the consequences of their depression diplomacy, and it demonstrates their reluctance to offend any of the interested parties. As a result, they managed to offend them all. Unable to declare the Convention of 1924 an unworkable anachronism, they nibbled at its edges until bankers, bondholders, and Dominicans all found common ground in their frustration. The bottom line was the desire of Hoover and Stimson to step away from commitments like those represented by the convention, but to do that they needed reasonably dependable sources of authority to assume responsibility. Authority in the Dominican Republic meant Rafael Trujillo, a dictator who nevertheless had established order and continued interest payments. The Hoover administration arranged the Dominican moratorium to give Trujillo time to get his financial house in order after the devastation of the hurricane. But the moratorium was only a stopgap measure that left intact the Convention of 1924 as the prime obstacle to a truly noninterventionist, "good neighbor" relationship between the United States and the Dominican Republic.

## THE FOREIGN BONDHOLDERS PROTECTIVE COUNCIL

Hoover's efforts notwithstanding, the Latin American debt crisis continued to be a mess. The more U.S. policy makers attempted to influence events, the deeper they involved themselves in the internal politics of the defaulted nations. The convoluted diplomacy that led to the Dominican debt moratorium is evidence of the Hoover administration's reluctance to elaborate its responsibilities in Latin America and of the difficulty it encountered in trying to shape a hemispheric policy while maintaining a hands-off attitude. In the subsequent negotiations to resolve the Dominican default, both the Hoover and Roosevelt administrations searched for a diplomatic surrogate that could assume responsibility for the sensitive issues posed by the debt crisis. That search led to the device of bondholders' protective committees, representative organizations that could negotiate directly with bankrupt governments for the continued payment of their debts.

Forty separate protective organizations appeared during the Hoover administration to deal with the epidemic of default.[35] The proliferation of protective organizations, none of them receiving direction from the State Department, led to a good deal of confusion and rivalry.[36] The Hoover administration attempted to resolve these squabbles by creating a central bondholders' organization, using England's Foreign Bondholders Protective Association as its prototype, but this plan was still being developed when Hoover left office and Franklin Roosevelt took over.[37]

One of the few substantive resolutions to come of the failed London Economic and Monetary Conference of April 1933 was a unanimous call for the formation of government-sanctioned protective organizations to represent the private creditors of bankrupt nations. A provision for such a body in the United States was written into Title II of the Securities Act of 1933, also known as the Johnson Amendment. Under this plan, the Federal

Trade Commission would appoint the members of the organization and the Reconstruction Finance Corporation would fund it. But Congress left the president a great deal of latitude in this regard: the Johnson Amendment would be put into effect only by a proclamation from Roosevelt, who could opt instead to create a committee of a different nature. Interested constituencies both in the United States and abroad watched closely to see who would serve on, and whose interests would be served by, such an organization.

The question of whether the organization would be a public or a private agency was central to the international debt issue. Roosevelt wanted to separate the government from the touchy negotiations that would be the daily fare of the new bondholders' committee. To entrust such negotiations to an organization closely identified with the government would invite from Latin America charges of interference and disregard for Latin American sovereignty. But a private committee without government clout would have a weak bargaining position vis-à-vis the debtor states and would run the risk either of being bullied by foreign governments or fading away like many of its predecessor organizations. That would be viewed domestically as an abdication of the State Department's perceived responsibility toward the bondholders.

The resulting compromise was a national bondholders committee, the Foreign Bondholders Protective Council (FBPC). The FBPC allowed the U.S. government to assume the role of interested spectator to debt negotiations without being accountable for their outcome. The council was integral to the Good Neighbor policy, but it has not received attention in proportion to its importance. Without the FBPC to handle the volatile issue of bond defaults, Roosevelt's diplomatic initiatives toward Latin America might well have bogged down in the controversy over foreign debts.[38]

The FBPC followed the same basic plan, designed by Herbert Feis, that Hoover had been ready to implement. It was a nonprofit organization with prominent private citizens as trustees, initiated by the government but not part of it. Feis, a Ph.D. in economics from Harvard with a decade of college teaching experience, joined the State Department at Henry Stimson's request in 1931. He made a strong case for this proposed arrangement in a memo written soon after Roosevelt's inauguration: "*This has been visualized by the State Department as a step away from dollar diplomacy, and not toward it.* In the absence of such an organization it is almost inevitable that the government will be dragged into various situations in an effort to protect the American investors against unfair or discriminatory treatment. If an adequate and disinterested body were formed, the Department could keep aloof."[39]

In September 1933, Roosevelt invited a group of aging power brokers recruited by Feis to a meeting in Washington.[40] Appealing to the expertise and patriotism of such men as former Secretary of War Newton Baker and former Secretary of the Navy Charles Francis Adams, Roosevelt and Secretary of State Cordell Hull "requested" that they create a committee of "disinterested individuals" to represent the collective interests of U.S. bondholders.[41]

The FBPC, being neither public nor fully private, offered a number of advantages for the Roosevelt administration. The State Department could suggest that the council was its designated surrogate in financial diplomacy while disclaiming responsibility for resolving defaults. Still in blueprint form when Hull left for the Montevideo Conference in November, the FBPC provided him with an official stance regarding Latin American debts. He told the Latin American expert Samuel Guy Inman on the steamer to Uruguay that "the bondholders were not going to be able to use State as a collection agency any more," and during the conference he "made a fine impression by declaring that the Roosevelt Administration is not backing nor helping in any way the bankers who over-sold the recent enormous loans."[42] Armed with this disavowal, Hull was able to propose the FBPC as an avenue for future negotiations on the growing number of defaults. In response to a resolution by the Mexican foreign minister for a seven- to ten-year moratorium on all amortization payments and a reduction of interest payments to 3 percent, Hull emphasized that the debts in question were those of "private American investors" whose interests were now in the hands of the new protective council. With the support of Argentina's influential foreign minister, Carlos Saavedra Lamas, Hull persuaded the conference to table the resolution and to subscribe instead to the FBPC alternative.[43] One of the major stumbling blocks to economic diplomacy was thus removed even before the council's incorporation.

The two most important figures in the FBPC during the 1930s had been the two most important architects of Hoover's Latin American policy at the State Department: J. Reuben Clark and Francis White. Clark, whom Herbert Feis described as "a really hard-fisted Mormon," was undersecretary of state for his good friend Hoover and author of the *Memorandum on the Monroe Doctrine* (1928), the administration's published repudiation of the Roosevelt Corollary and its justification for "police" intervention.[44] He left Washington in 1929 to serve in Mexico as counsel to another friend, Ambassador Dwight Morrow, subsequently becoming ambassador there himself. Francis White was the institutional memory of the Latin American Division going back to 1922, when at the age of thirty he became its chief, and he served as assistant secretary in charge of Latin American affairs for six years. A member of the Baltimore elite and a Yale graduate, he felt betrayed in April 1933 by his old friend Sumner Welles, who got the ambassadorship to Cuba that White badly wanted, and he left government service soon after.[45]

Roosevelt made use of Hoover's best officials by creating a sanctuary for them in the FBPC. Clark and White shared a firm personal conviction about the sanctity of the contractual arrangements they were to represent, and they were certain to drive as hard a bargain with the nations in question as they possibly could. The State Department of Roosevelt and Hull would benefit from the FBPC's hard-line approach, yet would avoid being directly associated with it. As for the council's power to negotiate, the State Department sent diplomatic signals that, while technically a private concern, the council was of singular interest to the government. The inclusion of such luminaries as Clark and White gave the council clout, as did the continued interaction of these men with the State Department. This close connection was highlighted by Clark's participation in Hull's delegation to the Montevideo Conference in 1933. Hull informed journalists that the "high-class, clean-cut" commission would prevent the "name" of the government from being "hawked and peddled" in default situations.[46]

The many different constituencies interested in foreign defaults had a stake in the FBPC. The chairman of the New York Federal Reserve Bank, J. Herbert Case, elicited the support of the chairmen or presidents of General Electric, General Motors, IBM, J. P. Morgan, U.S. Steel, and Standard Oil for the FBPC.[47] The council's declaration of purpose was carefully written to address the needs of small creditors. The nation's traders were cheered by the news that increased "buying power" was another declared goal of the FBPC.[48] But the schizophrenic nature of the FBPC also reflected struggles within the Roosevelt administration over economic policy, especially toward Latin America. Roosevelt had little regard for Wall Street's problems in the world and was primarily concerned with clearing the debt problem from the path of the Good Neighbor policy.[49] Hull wanted to resolve the debt problem without "jeopardizing larger trade" with other countries.[50] Sumner Welles preferred a tough stand on Latin American debts, which he believed should be repaid. The FBPC was given the task of pursuing these competing agendas.

## JOSEPH E. DAVIES

In preparing for further negotiations on the Dominican debt, Rafael Trujillo added a powerful weapon to his own diplomatic arsenal in 1933. He enlisted the services of Joseph E. Davies, a wealthy lawyer and close friend of both Roosevelt and Hull, to be the advocate of Dominican interests in Washington and "financial mentor to President Trujillo."[51] U.S.-Dominican relations changed significantly when Davies began to represent Trujillo in Washington and New York. Davies, who became a millionaire handling litigation for foreign governments through his Washington, D.C., law practice, told his new client that no troublesome "underlings" like the new U.S. minister, H. F. Arthur Schoenfeld, who replaced Charles Curtis in August 1931, would prevent him from taking the Dominican case to the "highest circles" of the U.S. government. Davies had been a stalwart of the Democratic Party since the Wilson administration, which he served as federal trade commissioner, and he knew the corridors of power in the capital intimately. He began his lobbying for Trujillo by meeting with Assistant Secretary Jefferson Caffery at the State Department in June 1933. Davies "argued strongly" at this session for a four-year extension on the moratorium on Dominican debt payments and intimated that the State Department was really powerless to prevent it. Trujillo could extend the moratorium unilaterally, said Davies; he could even suspend interest payments if he wanted to, and "there was no likelihood of serious objection being made by the American government." Jefferson Caffery closed the conference by referring Davies to the national bondholders' organization that would soon be created.[52]

Undersecretary of State William Phillips sent Roosevelt a memo entitled "The Dominican Situation" about a month after Davies's presentation at Foggy Bottom. Phillips, a friend and supporter of Roosevelt despite being a Republican, returned to the State Department in 1933 to fill the same second-ranking office there for FDR that he had for Warren Harding. Phillips reminded the president of "the responsibility of the United States government toward the bondholders," an obligation that would put the administration "in an embarrassing position" if the Dominican government acted on its own. He contended that the bondholders' group envisioned in the Johnson Amendment was the solution since it would "be able to act as an intermediary between the Dominican government and the American bondholders." He stressed the need for Roosevelt to invoke the Johnson Amendment before Trujillo acted on Davies's threat of unilateral action.[53] Edwin Wilson, the chief of the Latin American Division, agreed that State should continue to play "wait-and-see" until the creation of a bondholders' group, which could take over the portfolio of Dominican finances. Wilson also felt that State Department policy should forestall Trujillo and Davies from moving on their own. "This was essential," he said, "if the American Minister is to enjoy any authority."

Minister H. F. Arthur Schoenfeld [pronounced "shernfeld"] himself already suspected that he had little authority in his new position. Schoenfeld came from an academic, diplomatic family; he was the son of a professor, and the brother of a career Foreign Service officer like himself. A graduate of George Washington University in Washington, D.C., Schoenfeld studied law there before he joined the Foreign Service. He had nearly two decades of experience as a diplomat despite being only forty-two years old, including service in Mexico with Ambassadors James Sheffield and Dwight Morrow, who helped him advance to the rank of minister in 1928, first to Bulgaria and then to Costa Rica. He left the State Department to take a job with International General Electric in 1930, but after a year plagued with health problems he decided to return to diplomatic service as minister in Santo Domingo. After two years at his post, Schoenfeld noted on Trujillo's part "a polite but unmistakable skepticism as to what, if anything besides himself, the American Minister represented." The transition period between the Hoover and Roosevelt administrations demonstrated to him, however, that "the Dominican government is just about as sensitive to political changes [in the United States] as the mimosa is to the touch of a hand," resulting in the intensified lobbying campaign after Roosevelt's inauguration in March 1933. Joseph Davies had visited the State Department and the Oval Office, conducting talks about which Schoenfeld was told nothing.

Schoenfeld also considered Trujillo's outspoken desire to retain him as minister in Santo Domingo somewhat humiliating. He asked Phillips to give him "a clear perception of our considered policy . . . particularly with precautions taken against any crossing of wires in representing that policy to the Dominican government."[54] There was little chance of crossed wires while no wires were being sent to the legation, however. The chargé d'affaires in Santo Domingo, James E. Brown, confirmed that "the most basic matters between the Dominican government and the State Department have recently been carried on through Mr. Davies. . . . [N]othing, not even memoranda of conversations, of any importance has come to the Legation from the Department."[55]

In the meantime, Trujillo's backdoor links to the new administration were strengthened by the arrival of a new U.S. special agent to the Dominican Emergency Fund, Major Oliver Newman. Newman was well connected, having been an aide to Wilson at Versailles, and received his nomination for the post from an old friend and fellow Democratic Party stalwart, Secretary of State Cordell Hull.[56] His background in the military (he was a West Point graduate), journalism (he had experience at both the *Washington Post* and the *Washington Times*), and advertising (his most recent career path) made him attractive to the Trujillo regime, which received favorable treatment in Newman's subsequent work as the Santo Domingo correspondent to the Associated Press. The incumbent special agent, William E. Dunn, had run afoul of Trujillo, who waved a pistol at him during his last audience with him.[57] Dunn was in the United States unaware that he had lost his job when Trujillo had Major Newman move into Dunn's own house. Dunn's possessions and papers were unceremoniously boxed and removed, and his servants were told that Major and Mrs. Newman were the house guests of the family.[58] The most important part of Newman's job dealt with the surplus that had accumulated in the Emergency Fund, money that was earmarked for amortization but that had been retained in defiance of the Emergency Law. Joseph Davies soon claimed jurisdiction over the surplus, which totaled more than half a million dollars.[59] With Newman's arrival in Santo Domingo, Davies now had an ally to guard the Emergency Fund from the FBPC, a bargaining chip that gained value with each month's customs receipts.

Sumner Welles was the new assistant secretary of state in charge of Latin American affairs (a position he first held in 1921, when he was only twenty-eight). This fact posed tremendous problems for Trujillo and Davies, because the Dominican Republic was of particular interest to Welles. He had spent a great deal of time there between 1922 and 1924 to negotiate the treaty that ended the U.S. Marine occupation, and he had written a two-volume history of the country, *Naboth's Vineyard* (1928), named for the biblical allusion employed in the famous speech delivered by his great-uncle, Senator Charles Sumner. Welles was also a member of the commission led by former

Vice-President Charles Dawes to investigate the Dominican debt in 1929, when Welles first took notice of corruption and abuse of power by the commander of the army, Trujillo. Welles had subsequently opposed Trujillo's rise, warning Horacio Vásquez not to allow the army chief to change the Dominican armed forces from a police organization into a national army. After Trujillo came to power, Welles urged the leaders of the Dominican exile opposition, who were friends of his from the 1920s, to send him regular reports, and he gave the information to journalists he knew in order to publicize the "fraud and violence" of the dictatorship.[60] Welles of New York was another suave product of Groton and Harvard, like his personal acquaintance Franklin Roosevelt, whose wedding to Eleanor he attended. He and his wife, the heiress Mathilde Townsend, occupied both a grand mansion on "Embassy Row," in Washington, and sweeping Oxon Hill Manor overlooking the Potomac nearby in Maryland.[61] After a brief assignment to Havana as ambassador in the midst of the Cuban Revolution of 1933, he returned to Washington to compete with Cordell Hull for direction of Roosevelt's Latin American policy.

Although he was charming to his friends, Welles was humorless and rigid in public life, prompting one diplomat to comment that he looked as if he had "swallowed a ramrod in his youth."[62] He immediately set himself against Trujillo's plans. He took an aggressive stand with regard to the Dominican debt in August 1933, proposing a plan for extending the moratorium that stipulated the unconditional remittance of the Emergency Fund surplus as a prerequisite. More provocatively, he also pushed for political reform in Trujillo's authoritarian regime: "We should make known to Trujillo our opinion as to the necessity of free political organization and free elections. . . . [T]here is a matter of major policy involved here and it is essential that there be ample liberty for the opposition groups to organize and take part in the coming elections, since if this is not done the Department will come in for criticism for having kept Trujillo in power."[63] After more than three years of State Department reticence on the subject of Trujillo's authoritarianism, an influential policy maker was at last suggesting that the U.S. government use its leverage against the dictator. Welles demanded the restoration of fiscal integrity in the Dominican Republic under the guidelines he himself had drafted in the Hughes-Peynado Plan and the Convention of 1924. Minister Schoenfeld, who was increasingly isolated at his post in Santo Domingo, was cheered by Welles's return: "At times the Department has come within an ace of being jockeyed out of position but the frequent changes in personnel up there were doubtless responsible for this and I fancy Sumner Welles, now that he is on the job, will not be easy to wheedle out of standing up for his pet Convention."[64]

Even so, Schoenfeld was taken aback by Welles's agitation for political reform. He, Caffery, and Wilson seem to have taken it upon themselves to prevent Welles's position from being communicated to the Dominican government.[65] They apparently understood better than Welles that his demands could discredit the Good Neighbor policy. Although Schoenfeld was empowered to bring up the question of political freedom, he adopted a mild stance. Trujillo was already inclined to believe, with good reason, that Welles was determined to "overthrow" him.[66] Welles's letters to the Dominican Republic (and sometimes to New York!) were routinely "rifled in the mails" by Trujillo's agents, so his animosity toward Trujillo was well known.[67] Any mention by Schoenfeld of Welles's demands would have set off loud protests in Trujillo's controlled press and might well have wrecked Cordell Hull's agenda at the upcoming Montevideo Conference.[68]

Even Schoenfeld's informal request for remittance of the surplus fund brought a swift response from the Dominicans' lobbyist. Joseph Davies sent an "Informal Memo" to his friend Hull asking that Schoenfeld's request be withdrawn. Familiar with how to get attention at State, Davies asserted that the surplus fund was important "in connection with the preservation of an orderly government" in the Dominican Republic. Insistence on payment by the U.S. government "might be construed as . . . useless and needless offense to a friend of the United States." Demanding payment was not the neighborly attitude, said Davies, especially since "no bondholders are complaining," and "a strong, stable government has been maintained and property has been protected."[69]

Davies then extended his efforts to the Senate Foreign Relations Committee, informing Chairman Key Pittman that the Dominican Revolution of 1930 "was led by a group of younger men, graduates of great universities of the world, who were desirous of improving their government, and the condition of the Dominican people." He told Pittman that their leader now needed U.S. approval of a moratorium in the name of "common humanity." Pittman wrote to Hull about the matter, and the secretary replied that no legislative action was needed.[70] Davies and Special Agent Newman met with Hull personally on 7 November 1933 to ask for an extension of the moratorium, due to expire at the end of the year. Replying to Davies's request for a four-year moratorium, the secretary referred him to the nascent Foreign Bondholders Protective Council, which he said would be "the proper channel" for further action.[71]

## THE DOMINICAN BOND NEGOTIATIONS

Less than a week later, Hull announced the formation of the FBPC to deal with the problem of defaulted foreign bonds. He said, "It is this organization of disinterested citizens charged solely with safeguarding the rights and interests of American bondholders that foreign debtors must satisfy if they are to conserve *vis a vis* the American public the standing of honest debtors. *The problem is not inter-governmental.*"[72] Roosevelt pointed out at a subsequent press conference that "the United States is not owed any money by any of the South American republics and it is therefore a matter between those republics and any of the bondholders."[73] A circular sent to all diplomatic and consular officers in January 1934 reported the incorporation of the FBPC, which it said was "to be independent of the government in the conduct of its affairs and to act solely on its own responsibility."[74] Minister Schoenfeld was alarmed that the arrangement to bring in the FBPC would be a "waiver" of government responsibility, but that was precisely the intention of the State Department.[75]

The president of the FBPC was J. Reuben Clark, who "knew absolutely nothing about Dominican affairs" when he accepted the council presidency.[76] State Department officials led by Sumner Welles influenced his view of Trujillo by giving him access to confidential State Department files. This tactic was intended especially to counteract the information provided to Clark by Joseph Davies.[77] Davies objected to the cooperation between the "independent" FBPC and the Department of State, protesting to Hull that "conspirators" and "enemies" of the Dominican Republic were plotting to turn the FBPC talks against Trujillo (Davies probably had Sumner Welles in mind). He reminded Hull that Trujillo was a "Good Neighbor" who would "undoubtedly" be reelected by a large margin.[78] State Department leaks to Reuben Clark became more discreet as Davies's suspicions grew. Although no longer offered copying service on his visits to State, "Mr. Clark, however, might find something . . . on a desk in the Department and might inadvertently take it off with him for a day or two and have a copy made."[79] Davies was not to be shown any documents, as in "this case . . . he was not an American, but a Dominican."[80]

Some of the most revealing information made available to Clark originated at the U.S. legation in Santo Domingo. Schoenfeld had received a copy of the 193-page book that Davies published to make Trujillo's case; the book had been sent by Davies to the FBPC, the State Department, and fifty leading banks and public leaders in the United States.[81] Schoenfeld's second secretary, James Gantenbein, was assigned to prepare a rebuttal. Gantenbein had a knack for these issues (he was about to be sent to Harvard University by the State Department to study foreign bond defaults), and he shared Schoenfeld's conviction that the Convention of 1924 should be restored and that the U.S. government, not the FBPC, should see to it. Gantenbein's 60-page memo refuted Davies's book point by point, concluding that the financial crisis of 1931 had "ceased to exist." He contradicted Davies's assertion that the Dominican government had "cut its expenditures to the bone," calling attention to Trujillo's ambitious military buildup and public works. He recommended abolishing the Dominican Navy, reducing the army and public works budgets, and cutting government salaries.[82] Officials at State arranged for Gantenbein's memo to slip "inadvertently" into Reuben Clark's briefcase.[83]

Sumner Welles thought that the Dominican Republic presented "more cause for worry than any other country of Latin America." He read Schoenfeld's official dispatches and carried on a personal correspondence with the minister as well, sharing with him an increasingly pessimistic view of the Dominican government.[84] Welles and Schoenfeld both considered the customs receivership to be an important "restraint" on Trujillo, and they wanted to reinstate it as part of a default settlement. The difference between their positions was that Welles wanted the FBPC to take the blame for reinstating the Convention of 1924, which one Dominican newspaper called an "arduous yoke."[85]

Secretary of State Cordell Hull, on the other hand, expressed apprehensions about restoring the convention. Hull of Tennessee had been a U.S. senator, and although his great interest was international trade, he had no diplomatic experience, nor much inclination; Roosevelt had nominated him to the top foreign policy post in order to gain southern and conservative support. With his southern twang and distaste for parties, Hull was in some ways the opposite of the cultured Sumner Welles, who was "something of a hedonist" in Bond Street suits.[86] The two came into increasing conflict on a variety of issues, especially after Welles became undersecretary of state in 1937; one of these issues was policy toward the Trujillo regime.

Hull had no attachment to the convention Welles had put in place in

1924, and he was influenced by a note from the new Dominican minister in Washington, Roberto Despradel, in which the Dominican government threatened to spend the surplus fund unilaterally "without formality of final accord with the United States." Despradel, a lawyer and journalist, had been one of the "two main conspirators" backing Trujillo in the Revolution of 1930, planning the coup with Rafael Vidal from Fortaleza Ozama itself. He and Vidal were the writers who produced Trujillo's military magazine in the late 1920s, and he expressed the Dominican position forcefully to Hull.[87] Despradel complained that "my people cannot understand why we have spent a year on this case without settling it," since the Good Neighbor policy "should have made technicalities harmonize with policy."[88] Hull told Clark that he feared the Dominican government "would decline" the FBPC demand for the reinstitution of the Convention of 1924 "and thus snub this government." He pointed out that "of course no measures of coercion would be used by this administration, and he indicated that President Trujillo was probably aware of this fact."[89] Hull opposed U.S. intervention of any kind, so long as civil order prevailed. His great fear, as he put it with his distinctive lisp, was "when chaos breaks out in one of those countries, and armed bands go woamin' awound, pillagin' and murderwin' Amewicans," in which case Roosevelt would have to do something in order to be "we-elected."[90] There was little danger of such an outbreak under the Trujillo regime.

Clark's subsequent negotiations with Davies show that Welles's coaching prevailed over Hull's caution in convincing Clark to push to bring back the Convention of 1924. The information provided to him at the State Department gave Clark a very strong bargaining position. Davies became "very much wrought up" about Clark's access to State Department files, and their first day of discussions together ended with Davies threatening to complain to his friend Franklin Roosevelt about the "poisoned reports" that Clark had read.[91] Two days later, Davies made a more personal appeal to Clark. The high amortization payments demanded by the FBPC were unacceptable, Davies said, and he would be fired if he reported Clark's position to Trujillo, thereby losing "one of his best clients." Clark responded that the FBPC "was more or less inclined to laugh" at Davies's counterproposal of ½ percent amortization payments.[92] Negotiations for a settlement without the reestablishment of a full-fledged receivership were "idle motions," said Clark, since the Dominican government had a "history" of breaking promises.[93] Davies said "his man" Trujillo "was an exception." Davies also revealed to Clark that he held some Dominican bonds himself, which guaranteed his objectivity. Clark replied that if this were true he "would try to protect his [Davies's] interests also."[94]

During July 1934, the Dominican position moved closer to Clark's State-inspired demands, which included the reestablishment of the Convention of 1924 and the resumption of interest payments.[95] Hull continued to disassociate his department from the negotiations, telegraphing Schoenfeld that they were "solely the concern of the Dominican government and the holders of Dominican bonds" and instructing him to "scrupulously avoid the creation of the impression that the Department is intervening in any way at this time."[96] Schoenfeld knew better, having learned about the information leaks to Clark. He was anxious to see a settlement concluded in order to normalize diplomatic relations, which "had been for several weeks approaching a state of tension" in Santo Domingo.[97] The FBPC Board of Directors also wanted "some substantial settlement, such as that which might be arrived at in the Dominican situation," to publicize with a series of radio broadcasts and a circular statement to American banks.[98] The FBPC Executive Committee empowered Clark to "go forward without any further consideration and try to wind the negotiations up."[99]

### THE DOMINICAN DEBT AGREEMENT

The FBPC reached an agreement with the Dominican government in August 1934, mainly on Clark's terms. The accord was a public relations victory for the Roosevelt administration. It placed the FBPC squarely on the diplomatic map as the Department of State–approved arbiter of foreign bond defaults, and it inspired favorable press reactions which further solidified the position of the council. The London Times reported that the Dominican agreement "may prove to be the first step out of the morass of Central and South American Loans in which the public of the United States finds itself."[100] The Wall Street Journal dismissed criticism that the FBPC was banker-controlled, and the New York Herald Tribune called the FBPC "an admirable body, intent on quiet missionary work in favor of American investors and not greatly concerned with the praise that it merits."[101] The State Department called the agreement "a signal demonstration of the practical effect of the Rooseveltian policy in Latin America. Settlement was made through the instrumentality of a Rooseveltian Agency, to wit, the FBPC, Inc."[102] The Dominican debt agreement was the first tangible evidence of the policies articulated by Hull at the Montevideo Conference. It confirmed the U.S. policy of nonintervention in the hemisphere and its resolve not to act as bill collector for private debts. This was an important step toward more cooperative relations between North and South America.

The Dominican government issued its own press release, drafted by Joseph Davies, which added to the chorus of approbation: "The Dominican Republic is appreciative of the fact that there should have been created so distinguished and disinterested a group of American citizens, such as the FBPC. . . . The Dominican Republic is appreciative of the Good Neighbor policy of President Roosevelt and Secretary Hull which made this adjustment possible."[103]

The second issue of Trujillo's *Boletín de Relaciones Exteriores* [Bulletin of Foreign Relations] trumpeted the agreement as a "transcendent step" toward reestablishing Dominican credit and was careful to point out the privileged status of the FBPC in the eyes of the Roosevelt administration, thereby implying that the agreement had an intergovernmental nature.[104] There was an immediate warming in the chilly diplomatic atmosphere of Santo Domingo, as well.[105] Dominican officials, who promised "to resume . . . cordial and close cooperation" with the United States in appreciation of the "friendly and generous" spirit of the Good Neighbor policy, told Schoenfeld to expect "practical proof" of their good will through "early action" on cases of abuse of American business interests.[106]

The personal and bureaucratic machinations that led to the final terms of the Dominican debt readjustment, however, indicate that the Good Neighbor policy was not yet the gospel of the State Department. The Roosevelt and Hoover administrations shared a desire to shift the responsibility for the Dominican debt situation away from the U.S. government, and both came to view the instrument of an independent bondholders' committee as the answer. After a period of confusion occasioned by the change in administrations, Roosevelt opted for a national version of the committee idea to address all foreign bond defaults and clear the way for the Good Neighbor policy. Officials at the State Department, however, were divided as to the proper stance that the FBPC should assume in its negotiations with foreign governments and the proper amount of influence that the State Department should wield over the organization. Sumner Welles initially pushed for an interventionist political agenda for the negotiations in hopes of forcing reforms on Trujillo, but his subordinates decided on their own not to press the hard line he advocated. The undersecretary's view was also not acceptable to Hull, who had been embarrassed by Welles's intrusion into Cuban affairs during his mission there. Hull was also apprehensive about Welles's other argument, which was that the FBPC should demand the reestablishment of the Convention of 1924 and the customs receivership.

The final draft of the Dominican agreement with the FBPC revived the Convention of 1924, as Welles wanted, but was silent on the issue of dictatorship, as Hull insisted. This compromise was largely the result of actions taken by subordinate State Department officials in Washington and Santo Domingo, rather than by Hull and Welles themselves. Those in Washington, Assistant Secretary Jefferson Caffery, the Latin American Division chief Edwin Wilson, and the Dominican "desk officer" Joseph F. McGurk (who became ambassador to the Dominican Republic in 1945), downplayed Welles's political agenda, always making it clear in their reports to Hull that Welles's views were his alone. In Santo Domingo, U.S. Minister Arthur Schoenfeld chose not to convey to Trujillo Welles's suggestion that internal political processes had to change before relations could be considered "normal."[107] But this group did support Welles's case for restoring the Convention of 1924. Using information provided by Schoenfeld and James Gantenbein, Wilson and McGurk made certain that Reuben Clark had the evidence he needed to take a hard line in his negotiations with Joseph Davies. The close friendship between Welles and his wife Mathilde, Schoenfeld and his wife Aïda, and General Receiver William Pulliam and his wife Muriel might also account in part for their insistence on preserving the post held by Pulliam, the "dean" of the American Colony in Santo Domingo.

Trujillo accrued benefits from the agreement that offset the unwelcome reappearance of a fully empowered customs receivership in the Dominican Republic. Some of the benefits were financial, amounting to an extra $2.4 million in revenues for Trujillo to spend.[108] Other benefits were political: Trujillo gained prestige in the hemisphere and in his country by demonstrating his own brand of Good Neighbor diplomacy and weathering the Dominican financial crisis without suspending interest payments on the foreign debt. Trujillo also learned that U.S. officials responded with alacrity when he mixed his threats of unilateral action with testimonials of cooperation. He remembered this lesson in his subsequent relations with the United States, combining Good Neighbor rhetoric with anti-imperialist denunciations in order to keep U.S. diplomats off balance. The participation of Joseph E. Davies in resolving the issue had proved the benefits of employing well-connected lobbyists to press his interests abroad, although their services were expensive. Davies submitted a bill to Trujillo for $1,180,000 but eventually settled for $480,000.[109] Finally, Trujillo treated the FBPC agreement of 1934 as a scrap of paper, just as he had the Emergency Law of 1931. He correctly understood that Roosevelt and Hull were not concerned with the actual operations of the agreement, but rather with the benefits of having agreed.

Most State Department officials in the Roosevelt administration wanted to remove the interventionist customs receivership from the Dominican Republic but as yet "did not feel sure enough" of Trujillo to take that step.[110] The Good Neighbor policy had been declared, but they could not follow through to the policy's logical conclusion: unilateral abrogation of the Convention of 1924 and the return of Dominican customs houses. As Trujillo consolidated his power, the danger of financial collapse diminished, and the Roosevelt administration accelerated its search for a way out of Dominican affairs in order to keep the Good Neighbor policy's promise of an end to intervention in all its forms. Before the receivership could be removed, domestic political considerations demanded that the bondholders get a return on their investment in the Dominican Republic. Dominican financial recovery and payment of the Dominican debt in turn required the stability that seemed to be offered by the Trujillo regime, however repugnant it was to observers at the State Department and in the press. Even so, the United States continued to collect Dominican customs until the Hull-Trujillo Treaty of 1940, which will be examined in Chapter 7. In the meantime, with his total authority established in the republic, Trujillo himself emerged as the greatest source of instability in U.S.-Dominican relations. His violent and unpredictable personality was the major stumbling block to a settlement in the debt issue, even though he had brought order to a country where order had been rare. As U.S. officials found out, the benefits of a "stabilizing" dictatorship could be canceled out by an unreliable dictator.

◆

# CHAPTER FOUR

# What Will the Neighbors Think?
# Dictatorship and Diplomacy
# in the Public Eye

Franklin Roosevelt had been in office less than a month when Sumner Welles advised him to proclaim a new Latin American policy that would go beyond the "good will and pious wishes" of his predecessors.[1] In his draft of Roosevelt's Pan-American Day speech, 14 April 1933, Welles repudiated the "erroneous interpretations" of the Monroe Doctrine that justified U.S. intervention, and extolled "the principle of consultation" and the "promotion of commerce" as the bases for improved hemispheric relations.[2] The most enduring effect of the address was that the term "good neighbor," which Roosevelt had used in his inaugural address to characterize his overall foreign policy, became identified specifically with the Latin American policy of the new administration.

## "PREACHING AND PREACHING AGAIN"

The adoption and repetition of the "good neighbor" metaphor was mainly what set Roosevelt's early Latin American policy apart from Hoover's, since both administrations accepted the principles of nonintervention, consultation, and commerce, and neither was consistent in acting on them. Although Hoover traveled to ten Latin American nations after his election, created Pan-American Day, and also occasionally employed the term "good neighbor," he was outdone by his successor both in logging "good will" miles and in packaging policy for consumption farther south. FDR was also a better speaker than Hoover, seeming to give substance to rhetoric simply by stating it with confidence and expansiveness. Along the way, Roosevelt transformed "good neighbor" from a useful phrase, one that had hovered in American political parlance for a century, into a distinctive slogan for his version of the "Western Hemisphere idea." "Good neighbor" was supposed to invoke cooperation, friendship, and reciprocity, and it included everything the Roosevelt administration wanted from Latin America (a list that changed with conditions). The nebulous quality of the Good Neighbor policy (one is tempted to use the plural form of the noun) and the divergence of opinion about what it meant suited the new president, who was a master of innuendo, ambiguity, paradox, and the manipulation of disparate personalities.[3] "La política del Buen Vecino" became the subject of widely diverging individual interpretations by the Latin American leaders toward whom it was directed (who had lists of their own about what they wanted from the Roosevelt administration). One of Trujillo's sycophantic biographers, Abelardo Nanita, offered this Dominican view of the Good Neighbor policy: it had replaced the "task force" policy with "friendly pleading" for "defense and commercial expansion."[4] As Roosevelt himself allowed, the Good Neighbor policy in its early stages was all talk; the president described "the method . . . used in our Latin American relationships" as "preaching and preaching again" and "the iteration of moralities."[5]

"Preaching" brought few tangible benefits to the Dominican Republic during Roosevelt's first term and a half in office. His administration put the portfolio of Dominican financial problems in the hands of the unsympathetic Foreign Bondholders Protective Council, which argued successfully for the continuation of the interventionist General Receivership of Dominican Customs. Cordell Hull's campaign to conclude bilateral commercial-reciprocity treaties in Latin America did not extend to the Dominican Republic, which was prevented from concluding them with other nations under the terms of the Convention of 1924. Nor did Hull improve tariff treatment or increase the "paltry" quota for sugar, the principal Dominican export, in the U.S. market. The Sugar Act of 1934, part of the New Deal's Agricultural Adjustment Act, reserved only 4 percent of the domestic market for foreign sources other than the Philippines (still under the rule of the War Department) and Cuba. Not until 1937 was the Dominican share enlarged somewhat, and even then less than thirty-two thousand tons of Dominican sugar entered the United States.[6] Furthermore, the State Department denied Trujillo's requests to be invited to visit the United States and form an even closer relationship with the American military. From the perspective of Dominican interests, the Good Neighbor policy was mainly rhetoric and symbolism.

Trujillo's foreign policy was even more oriented to the manipulation of public impressions than Roosevelt's. Trujillo tried to control the depiction of his regime in every medium he could possibly influence, both domestic and foreign. He publicized Dominican progress and his personal leadership wherever he could, and he applauded the Good Neighbor policy's blanket pledge of mutual respect, which conferred approval on his regime. The Good Neighbor policy had done away not only with "the old school of the 'big stick,'" contended an editorial in *La Opinión* in 1934, but had also abandoned "the sinister policy of 'prestige,'" meaning deference to U.S. leadership.[7] Trujillo embraced this interpretation of the Good Neighbor policy to enhance the international position of the Dominican Republic and his role as a Latin American leader. With his activist and image-oriented foreign policy, Trujillo seized and held the initiative in the bilateral relationship with the United States, eliciting a mix of responses from American officials that revealed one of the basic dilemmas of the Good Neighbor policy: How does one treat the dictator next door? This chapter will review Trujillo's consolidation of power, survey the tactics of his campaign to make himself "the preferred object of the world's attention," and gauge the effect that such publicity had on the Good Neighbor policy.[8]

### "THE UNDISPUTED MASTER"

Trujillo's rise to power was owing to his personal domination of the military, and military intimidation was the foundation of his social and political domination of the country, which "became complete" by 1932.[9] During his first two terms as president, Trujillo carried out virtually a reign of terror against actual and potential opposition to his authority. When a series of bombings took place in 1934 in Santiago, capital of the "historically turbulent" Cibao Valley, Trujillo traveled to the scene with the bulk of his army and appointed a "Special Commissioner" for the region, General José Estrella, who was under apparent instructions to "suppress . . . with great ruthlessness, any opposition" to the regime.[10] Estrella's death squads, led by an agent known as *El Cubano,* murdered young men belonging to Santiago's elite families in "a systematic elimination of the more outstanding elements known as antagonistic to the Trujillo regime . . . removing them by assassination." The victimization of these "better elements" brought home to the staff of the U.S. legation the extent of the violence of Trujillo's methods of control. The abuse of workers, such as the shooting of "a number" of *campesino* leaders who were resisting the extraction of free labor for public works in 1937, reached diplomats' ears as rumors, because their contact with the lower social classes in the republic was very limited.[11] But the abuse of upper-class Dominicans, especially *capitaleños* belonging to the social circle of Santo Domingo's elite clubs, was much more evident and personally appalling to those reporting on Dominican affairs for the State Department.

The diplomats' personal knowledge of the regime's forms of political intimidation (assassination, torture, imprisonment, the denial of due process) was most graphic when the victims were their acquaintances; these events accelerated the process of learning about, and coming to despise, the regime. Charles B. Curtis had gone through that process during the violent year of 1930, but his successor, H. F. Arthur Schoenfeld, was slower to grasp the scale of Trujillo's oppression and to identify it as a problem for U.S. policy. Prominent Dominicans continued to go into exile, most notably Rafael Estrella Ureña, suggesting something was amiss. Estrella Ureña, the Cibao politician who led the public phase of the Revolution of 1930, had been serving as both vice-president and foreign minister since the inauguration of the Trujillo government in 1930. He departed in August 1931 as if going on vacation, and was given a fond farewell at the dock by the Diplomatic Corps, a sight that prompted Trujillo to remove him from the office of *canciller*. Estrella Ureña remained the constitutional vice-president while in exile until he was impeached in absentia in December 1931.[12] Despite such unusual internal politics, Minister Schoenfeld praised Trujillo's "vigor" and "determination to enforce honesty" in the government, and cited his "moral authority in the country."[13]

Schoenfeld reported "rumors" of "alleged political murders" but judged them to be "exaggerated."[14] The legation's outline of Trujillo's first term provided details of just two killings, both taking place during spring 1933, only because the dead were Puerto Rican citizens: one had been arrested at a baseball game for making "remarks" about the president, then was "shot while trying to escape"; the other had been taken to "a lonely spot" and executed after several days in prison.[15] Restrictions on the press and the danger of speaking openly about such matters prevented the details of other cases from reaching the legation. This changed in March 1935 when Oscar Michelena, a prominent member of Santo Domingo society, was arrested for conspiracy. The Michelena family was from Puerto Rico and had extensive sugar lands near Santo Domingo. Santiago Michelena, Oscar's father, was one of the founders of "El Country Club," the social hub of the

American Colony in the capital, to which his son also belonged. Michelena was a personal friend of both Schoenfeld and Welles, and his sufferings at the hands of the regime brought startling evidence to them of Trujillo's cruel methods, causing Schoenfeld to refocus his attention on the nature of the dictatorship.

After his arrest, Oscar Michelena and twenty others accused of conspiracy were taken to Fortaleza Ozama, where Trujillo himself struck them in the face with a riding whip.[16] Later Michelena was taken to "El Aguacate," a large avocado tree on the Ozama River bluff, and beaten again, this time with knotted electrical wire. He spent the first forty-three days in the clammy, ancient dungeons of the fort without any opportunity to wash or change his clothes, and was refused quinine for the malarial fever he contracted.[17] But Michelena had the advantage of influential acquaintances, who sought a way to free him. Schoenfeld sent a dispatch describing Trujillo's assault on Michelena and the others at the time of their arrest (treatment, the minister had discovered, that was common "procedure" in "the President's method of dealing with political prisoners"), and Welles forwarded the report to Hull as "a graphic presentation of present conditions in Santo Domingo."[18] Assuming Michelena to be a Dominican citizen by birth, Schoenfeld felt unable to intervene on his behalf until Welles provided the justification; Michelena, having Puerto Rican parents, had been registered as an American citizen in the early 1920s.[19] With Hull's approval, Welles authorized Schoenfeld to demand an immediate hearing for Michelena, who had not been charged with a crime, and access to him after ten weeks of his being held incommunicado, "to ascertain whether he has been subjected to inhuman treatment."[20] Trujillo then released Michelena "as an act of courtesy" to Schoenfeld, who had refrained from making any formal "demands" but had hinted at his authority to do so.[21]

Schoenfeld learned firsthand of life inside Trujillo's prisons from Michelena, who also lost his sugar estate in a foreclosure suit during his incarceration.[22] Michelena's experience of physical and psychological abuse opened Schoenfeld's eyes to the regime, as reports from Dominicans in exile had done for Sumner Welles. When Alfredo Ricart, another elite Dominican on good terms with the American Colony, informed Schoenfeld "that perhaps thousands, and certainly hundreds, were generally thought to have been executed by summary procedure or without legal procedure of any kind," he did not dismiss the report as "exaggeration" or "rumor," as he previously had been inclined to do.[23] The repeated incidents of "prominent" captives dying in prison even prompted "an explanation" from Secretary of Justice Juan Tomás Mejía (whose brother Luis, an exile in Caracas, published accounts of the regime's repression). The statement appeared in *La Opinión* and was forwarded by Schoenfeld to Washington: "It is a misfortune when a political prisoner commits suicide, because the enemies of the government find it convenient to alter the facts and to assert that it involved summary execution."[24] "Owing to the efficient and ruthless methods" of the regime, reported the legation in reviewing the seventh year of Trujillo's rule, not "a stir of activity" threatening to the government took place.[25]

Trujillo also used the Partido Dominicano, founded in 1932, to make himself "the undisputed master of every phase of Dominican life," as Schoenfeld judged him to be in 1936.[26] By 1934 the Dominican Party was the only "organized political party" in the country, as Trujillo prepared for his landslide reelection in May.[27] By that time, membership in the Partido Dominicano was virtually mandatory to avoid harassment by the authorities; during Trujillo's second term, though, membership alone became inadequate. The party's Council of Honor, established in September 1934, purged "indifferent or unenthusiastic members" from the party ranks, with the usual result that the individuals would also be fired from their jobs.[28] A notice from Secretary of State for the Presidency Bonetti Burgos "to the Merchants, Industrialists, Managers, etc." of the republic, published in *La Opinión* in March 1935, called upon them to "control and exercise the most active vigilance over all the employees whom you have enrolled." It was "not sufficient," the notice read, for prospective employees to "show a card of enrollment in the Partido Dominicano"; their behavior was to be subject to continual scrutiny and judgment.[29] An inquisition in the form of permanent "courts of honor" tried Partido Dominicano members suspected of being "doubtful, indifferent, or who do not react with enthusiasm to all decisions of the Party." "Suspension or expulsion" as a result of these trials, which took place on forty-eight hours notice to the accused, was "tantamount to banishment from all fields of profitable endeavor in the country," judged one legation observer.[30] More of those "fields of profitable endeavor" came under Trujillo's personal control every year; by the end of his second term, his family held monopolies over salt, meat, dairy products, tobacco, shoes, lumber milling, truck and mule transportation, edible oil production, insurance, plantains, peanuts, charcoal, bordellos, and military contracts for supplies and laundry.[31] His youngest brother, Héctor, whom Trujillo had brought into the military in 1926, had the greatest success of the dictator's ten siblings, rising to command the Dominican armed forces and later to be president.

The centralization of the party and its merger with the Dominican government continued with an "extraordinary session" of its leadership in October 1936, which passed statutes to eliminate the "romantic and not constructive" notion of opposition. Authority over government employment shifted to the Supreme Directive Board of the Partido Dominicano, furthering what a legation report called the "trend toward totalitarianism under the control of President Trujillo."[32] A circular to all members of the Partido Dominicano in 1937 indicated that the real key to "patriotic zeal" was "to be also faithful and vigilant in informing with exactness the President of the Republic . . . of anything that may be contrary to his work of government or his political interests." The message warned "those who may be indifferent" that informers "who offer the Chief of the Party and of the State . . . news that may be of political interest" were bound to replace them in their positions.[33] Trujillo constantly shuffled the incumbents in government positions to prevent the rise of rivals, purging and reinstating officials at his whim. Individuals forced out of their executive jobs or legislative seats faced social ostracization, as well, and sometimes imprisonment. A large shake-up, accompanied by headlines in the newspaper and humiliation for the victims, had the flavor of a "truly Florentine imbroglio," with the effect always being the "strengthening of the President's control."[34] The importance of informing on enemies of the state had already been stressed to Dominican children in the text of the "Civic Primer" distributed in the schools beginning in 1933.[35] The Carta cívica was Orwellian in tone and content: "Love your country above all things and obey your government, as the best way of attaining the nation's happiness, which is your happiness. . . . If a man passes by your house who wants to change the present order, have him arrested. He is the worst of bad men. . . . He is your worst enemy."[36] The Partido Dominicano was superceded by the Partido Trujillista in 1942, retaining the same basic form under a more accurate title.[37]

The regime also elaborated a personalist political ideology based on the all-encompassing figure of the dictator, who was identified with material progress, civil order, and public spectacle. This ideology extolled the one-party system, which had all the governmental branches of a constitutional democracy but was said to be more efficient and conducive to national solidarity because it had Trujillo as its unquestioned central leader. Trujillo's establishment of a one-party state was supported by the dissemination of this way of thinking in the Dominican press, which was under Trujillo's complete control by early 1934. Juan Bosch, soon to become an exile and later, after Trujillo's death, to lead the political battle against his legacy, summarized the logic of the president's expanding power in January 1936. His article in *Listín Diario* was based on a series of public speeches by Trujillo, who had become, wrote Bosch, "at one and the same time Chief of the Government and Chief of the Opposition." Sedition was not only illegal (as it had been under the Marine occupation and, since November 1932, under the Trujillo regime), it was unnecessary: "Before the people grumble, he anticipates denunciation: he sees the blot and shows the nation."[38] Trujillo was *El Jefe,* "The Chief," because of his relationship with "the will of the people," explained *La Opinión* in an analysis of democracy in December 1936. A "normal democracy" was where a leader was elected for "a definitive period," said the editorial. When a leader "maintains himself in power" even though "the people do not support him," it continued, "that is not democracy." Neither case applied to Trujillo: "If the people consider the one who governs so necessary that they give him permanent power, that is super-democracy."[39] Even as Trujillo stepped down from the presidency in 1938, it was clear that he still wielded "permanent power" in the Dominican Republic, where his name and image had become ubiquitous.

## "DOMINICAN GOD"

The *trujillista* ideology dictated that one of the main functions of public life was the perpetual deification of *El Jefe* through rhetorical homages, nationalizing rituals, and the proliferation of images and place-names associated with him. The process by which Trujillo's name and image were conflated with the Dominican nation itself began in earnest on Dominican Independence Day, 27 February 1933, when the title "Benefactor of the Republic" was bestowed on him.[40] The title was changed to "Benefactor of the Fatherland [*la Patria*]" later that year at a ceremony in the capital of the Cibao region, Santiago, on the most important regional holiday, Restoration Day, 16 August.[41] The composition of rhetorical homages to Trujillo developed into an art form in the Dominican press and in public speaking during his tenure, exemplified by a newspaper contest held in November 1934 to find a new "apotheosis," or honorary title, for *El Benefactor.* Contest entries, printed in the form of signed letters from citizens, appeared on the front pages of the capital's press for weeks afterward. Some of the suggestions, translated by the legation staff, were the following: "President-for-Life," "Admiralísimo," "Emperor," "Super-Man," "Super-Great Citizen," "Greatest Illustrious Creator of Generations," and "Dominican God."[42] Speeches and toasts extolling the president in similar terms became standard fare at all public functions, and their texts frequently appeared in newspaper accounts of the events. Those omitting the requisite praise for the president at meetings and social occasions faced harassment.[43] The press and the U.S. legation both followed the travails of Ramón de Lara, a Santiago doctor who neglected to praise Trujillo in a speech he gave at a party and who was subsequently harassed and imprisoned by the regime. Vice-President Jacinto Peynado's words at a ceremony in November 1935 are characteristic of this discourse of adulation: "He knows everything. He realizes everything. He has a super-vision for the inscrutable. . . . His brain is a fountain of vivifying purposes."[44] The implication of Trujillo's omniscience was repeated in the phrase "Dios y Trujillo," which appeared on Dominican documents beginning in October 1935 and glowed in neon over Peynado's house.[45] One pamphleteer compared Trujillo to Buddha, Confucius, Christ, and Mohammed in concluding that, since he was the "immutable and super-powerful creator of a new life . . . Trujillo is God."[46]

The elaborate nationalizing rituals characteristic of the Trujillo regime had the combined effect of promoting the sovereignty of the Dominican Republic and attributing its benefits to Trujillo. Extensive celebrations were staged on Independence Day, Restoration Day, Trujillo's birthday, and an increasing number of occasions commemorating diplomatic achievements, visits by dignitaries, and new honors for the "Benefactor." Sometimes an event combined several of these categories into a single moment, as when "a school-children's medal" was "presented to the President and to his infant natural son" during the visit of Haitian President Stenio Vincent in February 1935. "A distinguished gathering" including Vincent, the Diplomatic Corps, and "high officials" of the Dominican government attended the ceremony, which transformed the occasion of Vincent's visit (an important step toward a treaty settling the tense border dispute with Haiti) into a spectacle that was simultaneously patriotic and personalistic.[47] In rituals such as these, Trujillo incorporated foreign representatives into the effort to publicly define Dominican nationhood.

The largest gatherings, the "Civic Reviews" first held in 1933, were convened to impress *campesinos* with Trujillo's power. Drawing crowds of ten to twenty-five thousand people, the mass rallies were "considered practically

a public holiday," including transportation courtesy of the Partido Dominicano, distribution of free food and clothing, and speeches by Trujillo and
his supporters. The theme of "Civic Review" rhetoric was Trujillo's protection of "the lives and interests of those who water the land with the
sweat of their work" but who always got "the worst part" of any revolution. Trujillo, however, had "saved" the republic from revolution and, as "a
man of the pastures" himself, identified with the farmers.[48] At an address to
a rural audience in Esperanza in January 1936, Trujillo linked this appeal to
the working people with an excoriation of the elites he had displaced from
power, saying: "There is a class of persons who inspire me with scorn: those
who consume in leisure the hours of work for which the nation pays."[49]
The mottoes inscribed on the base of the first statue of Trujillo, erected in
his birthplace of San Cristóbal in 1935, amplified these themes of working-
class protection and identification. The mottoes were these: "There is no
danger in following me," which was also the motto of the Partido Dominicano, and "My best friends are workingmen."[50]

The proliferation of statues, busts, and portraits of Trujillo mirrored the
growth of his power and was visual evidence of what Arthur Schoenfeld
called his "all-absorbing personal domination" of the Dominican Republic.[51] The "intensive campaign" to finance a statue in Santo Domingo, following the well-publicized efforts to do so in San Cristóbal, elicited a 10
percent payroll deduction from government officials and public donations
from other "contributors."[52] Cities around the country followed suit with
civic campaigns of their own, beginning with the unveiling of a bronze
bust of Trujillo in La Vega on his birthday, 24 October 1935.[53] At the time
of his assassination, an estimated eighteen hundred sculptures of the Generalísimo sat in public squares and buildings throughout the Dominican
Republic, one for every ten square miles.[54]

The transfer of names associated with Trujillo to the landscape of the
country was a related development that further dissolved the boundary between the man and his dominion. The dictator's personal names and those
of his family replaced some of the oldest European place-names in the
hemisphere in a flurry of rechristening beginning in 1934, when the western portion of the Province of Santo Domingo became the Province of
Trujillo, with its capital in the town of Trujillo's birth, San Cristóbal.[55] The
center of Santo Domingo's colonial district, a square named for Columbus
outside the oldest cathedral in the New World, was renamed Parque Ramfis
for Trujillo's infant son early the following year.[56] Later in 1935, a proposal

to change the name of Santo Domingo itself to Ciudad Trujillo gained support, although Schoenfeld told Foreign Minister Arturo Logroño that "to
change the name of the oldest permanent European settlement in America
by giving it the patronymic of a living public official . . . would be deemed
absurd" by the rest of the world.[57] Nevertheless, the Dominican legislature passed the measure and the city became Ciudad Trujillo in January
1936, with front-page coverage by the *New York Times*.[58] Legislative bills to
assign the names of various Trujillos to streets and parks in towns throughout the country subsequently filled the agenda of the Dominican Chamber
of Deputies; thirteen of them were introduced on one day in September
1936.[59] The U.S. legation reported soon after that "even the smallest village
has changed the name of at least one street, usually the principal one, naming it after the President or one of his family."[60] A law passed at the same
time designated the highest mountain in the Antilles, formerly named for
the Dominican founding father Juan Pablo Duarte, as Pico Trujillo.[61]

Trujillo's eponymous "re-construction of the Fatherland" extended to
each new structure of his ambitious public works program.[62] Four of the
first six bridges constructed by his government were named for his mother,
his father, his grandmother, and his son. Three of the most important spans
he reserved for himself: "San Rafael Bridge," a suspension bridge across the
Río Yaque del Norte constructed by John A. Roebling's Sons of Brooklyn
Bridge fame; the "Generalísimo Trujillo Bridge," which carried the new
highway across the Yuna River; and the "Trujillo Bridge," built over the
Ozama River at Santo Domingo to replace the one wrecked by the 1930
hurricane.[63] Public facilities from schools to watering troughs bore Trujillo monikers of one sort or another.[64] The system of associating Trujillo
with the republic's material progress was institutionalized by the declaration of the "Era of Trujillo, Benefactor of the Fatherland," in January 1939.
Henceforth, all municipal and national public works were required to have
a bronze plaque bearing that inscription and giving the date of their construction.[65] The "Era of Trujillo" continued along these lines for the next
two decades, with the development of Dominican infrastructure serving as
a perpetual paean, a tribute in concrete and steel, to the dictator.

The elevation of Trujillo from president to a kind of demigod took place,
then, in very public modes: hyperbolic tributes, civic ritual, geographical
reorientation, and public works. The creation of a cult of personality focusing on the dictator, participation in which was virtually mandatory for
Dominican citizens, was evident to the most casual observer of Domini-

can affairs. Supporting and enforcing this system were the less ostentatious but more keenly experienced authoritarian practices of party discipline, physical intimidation, and psychological terror. Though less noticeable to visitors, the repressive methods of the regime were publicized by Dominican exiles abroad, and particularly brutal incidents found their way into print in the foreign press. The personalism and authoritarianism of life in the Dominican Republic, occurring as they did on a grand scale, tended to elicit strong reactions, both positive and negative. Trujillo sought to control the nature of public commentary about himself and his government, both in his own country and in the United States, in a variety of ways. These efforts included generating favorable publicity, cultivating influential allies, evoking and promoting shared symbols, and mimicking Roosevelt and his policies. First and most basic of these strategies, however, was the one that worked with complete success within the boundaries of the Dominican Republic: censorship.

## CENSORSHIP

Trujillo's domestic control over political discourse was based on a sweeping sedition law passed in November 1932, which forbade "the dissemination" of opposition views "by means of writings, speeches, printed matter, drawings, engravings, pictures, emblems, or false rumors."[66] Violators could be imprisoned for a year and, as of 1935, could have their property confiscated (as Oscar Michelena found out).[67] This blanket proscription of criticism ended the political independence of the Santo Domingo daily newspaper, *Listín Diario,* competitor of the Partido Dominicano mouthpiece, *La Opinión.* The editor, Arturo Pellerano Sardá, was jailed after publishing a dissident's letter referring to places "where democracy is not a myth," in March 1933.[68] His incarceration was brief, but its effect on him was profound. Pellerano Sardá joined the Partido Dominicano the week after his release, and was elected to the Chamber of Deputies before the end of April.[69] His "return from the political wilderness" was so complete that *Listín Diario* replaced *La Opinión* as the recognized government organ in early 1934.[70] The Dominican Republic had seven daily newspapers and four magazines in 1936, all controlled by the regime.[71] The close coordination of the press with the regime, said a *La Opinión* editorial that may have originated in the National Palace, gave the medium "influence" and "effectiveness." Like the "super-democracy" construction of authoritarianism, this reading of the controlled press compared it favorably to the free press, which "believed itself very free, because it was allowed to speak without attention being paid to it." Since newspapers under Trujillo were the principal source of information about what the regime expected from its citizens (like contributions for a statue of Trujillo or suggestions for a grander "apotheosis" for him), Dominicans hoping for advancement took their cues from the press in order to render the "enthusiasm" required by the Partido Dominicano. The intentions of the regime could be fulfilled simply by printing them in "the serious press, the modern press, the press served by citizens desirous of the progress of their country," while "foolish pamphleteers and publicity seekers" faced prison for sedition.[72]

Criticism from abroad, whether in the form of pamphlets, publicity, or private correspondence, elicited sometimes "frantic efforts" to prevent its distribution.[73] Following *Cosmopolitan* magazine's publication of a scathing report on Latin American dictators, including Trujillo, in 1936, the Dominican legislature prohibited the importation of bad press.[74] Censorship also extended to the mails, which the Dominican authorities carefully screened. Fabio Fiallo, a poet who ran afoul of sedition laws under the Marines and Trujillo both, complained that "the most interesting" of his letters became "hostages of hate" and never reached him.[75] Oscar Michelena sent his letters from exile and editions of foreign newspapers back to Santo Domingo via the General Receivership to avoid this fate, further widening the gulf between the customs chief William Pulliam and the regime.[76] Even the U.S. legation staff was subject to the intrusive scrutiny of Trujillo's security apparatus, receiving letters that often "bore indications that they had been opened by the postal authorities."[77] Diplomats exchanged correspondence via the diplomatic pouch, which was immune to search, whenever possible.[78] Some contraband commentary did find its way into circulation, but the regime was mostly successful in both sanitizing the domestic press and preventing the introduction of outside criticism.

Paradoxically, Trujillo constructed new transportation facilities linking the Dominican Republic to the United States and Europe, allowing more visitors to come view his accomplishments, but increasing the likelihood of adverse publicity coming in or going out. New port facilities in Ciudad Trujillo encouraged the vessels of the New York and Port Rico Steamship Company to provide more regular sailings to the Dominican Republic, stimulating competition from other lines like the Bull Insular Line and the German Horn Line. Airport facilities, first at San Pedro de Macorís in 1934 and then in the capital, allowed Pan American Airways to schedule stops in those cities. Despite the proliferating means of travel available to him, Trujillo "had never been outside the Island of Hispaniola" until 1939, and he remained, as the British minister phrased it, "wholly ignorant of the world beyond it, whilst the never ceasing flattery with which he is plied by those who admire or fear him blind him to his own relative insignificance."[79] Once he began to travel, Trujillo's ambitions and his efforts to generate praise for his leadership (examined below) expanded with his worldliness. Throughout the period, the dictator's ability to prevent unfavorable depictions of his regime from circulating in the Dominican Republic contributed to his cult of personality there, which in turn drew the attention of a world increasingly concerned with the practice of dictatorship.

It was a more difficult and sensitive task to prevent criticism from being composed and printed in the foreign press in the first place. "Local people could not dare to send abroad the whole truth" of the harsh political realities in the Dominican Republic, but foreign journalists posed a problem for Trujillo. When the Associated Press reporter Lester Posvar attempted to transmit an unfavorable report by telegraph in February 1931, the authorities interfered. Posvar was detained and taken to court, and the office of All America Cable Company was "searched for evidence against the opponents of the Government," presumably Posvar's sources for the story.[80] Trujillo's intimidation of the reporter and of the U.S.-owned telegraph company immediately backfired. A four-part exposé on the regime by the columnist Drew Pearson ran on the front page of the *Baltimore Sun* and other papers soon afterward (the first headline read "San Domingo Is under the Sway of Terrorists"), with most of the second installment devoted to the treatment of Posvar and All America Cable ("San Domingo Suppression of News Revealed by Writer").[81] Minister Charles Curtis also protested the harassment of the cable company.[82]

Sumner Welles provided the impetus for both Posvar and Pearson to investigate and file critical reports on Trujillo. Welles wrote to Angel Morales before Trujillo's election in 1930 that any "official action" the Hoover administration might take before the upcoming Dominican election would be "legitimately criticized as intervention," but if "public opinion" in the United States were "roused" by news coverage of assaults and electoral fraud, it would "come out strongly for action on the part of this Government." Welles asked the general manager of the Associated Press, whom he had "known for many years," to dispatch a reporter to cover the election, and Posvar was put on the assignment.[83] Welles met with Drew Pearson twice just before the columnist published his scathing series, each time following up with memos answering Pearson's questions and summarizing the information provided by Angel Morales, Federico Velásquez, and William Pulliam.[84] The articles, which contained many of the "true facts" provided by Welles, proved to be of "even greater usefulness" than Welles had hoped, calling "the history of the last year in the Dominican Republic . . . forcibly to the attention of the most important members of the Government of the United States." Welles was sure that the Hoover administration's rejection of Trujillo's loan proposals was, to "a very considerable extent," owing to the "very graphic" negative publicity he himself had generated. He encouraged Velásquez to write an article about the Pearson series for publication in the Puerto Rican press, since the series itself was copyrighted and could not be directly translated into Spanish.[85] Welles himself was censored in the Dominican Republic, where *Naboth's Vineyard* was unavailable until 1939; one particular passage, dealing with the low quality and social standing of Guardia Nacional officers recruited by the Marines, may have been particularly galling to Trujillo.[86]

Trujillo's attempt to suppress bad publicity by harassing a foreign reporter had produced more unfavorable judgments about his regime than it had prevented. Thereafter, Trujillo found more subtle means to control the channels of information. Dominicans learned the risks of speaking their minds to journalists, who now received very solicitous attention from the government. Those whose employment in the service sector brought them into frequent contact with foreigners (hotel staff, taxi drivers) were said to heed an idiomatic warning: "Flies don't fly into closed mouths."[87] Still, an article in the March 1936 *Foreign Policy Reports* excoriated "Dictatorship in the Dominican Republic" in great detail.[88] The Dominican minister in Washington, Rafael Brache, protested the piece to the Foreign Policy Association, whose president defended its accuracy. The report, he said, was "based on data supplied by prominent members of the American colony."[89]

EXPATRIATES AND EXILES

Control of the members of the American Colony resident in the Dominican Republic was a more complicated proposition for the regime than control of Dominican citizens. On one hand, Trujillo encouraged the growth of the U.S. presence in his country, announcing in the pages of his New

York publication that he had "opened the gates to foreign capital."[90] More than ten thousand U.S. citizens were Dominican residents in late 1934, claimed *Dominican Republic* magazine in a wild overestimate, with "still room for many more."[91] In 1935, a year before the article in *Foreign Policy Reports,* Trujillo had acted to assuage the feelings of the American Colony, traumatized by the overthrow of their cultivated friends in the 1930 revolution, by enrolling two former Vásquez stalwarts in the Partido Dominicano and placing them in the cabinet posts most closely associated with foreign nationals: Andrés Pastoriza for Agriculture and Labor, and Alfredo Ricart for Commerce and Industry.[92] The British legation reported that Pastoriza and his wife and the numerous well-connected Ricarts "mixe[d] freely with the English and American colonies."[93] On the other hand, Trujillo exerted greater control and taxation over the business interests of the American Colony, principally sugar cultivation and utilities, than its members were accustomed to. The government instituted a sugar export tax on foreign-owned estates in 1934 to exert pressure on the Foreign Bondholders Protective Council for a debt settlement, and although the tactic failed to sway Reuben Clark, it demonstrated Trujillo's willingness "to sacrifice American interests" for his purposes.[94] The list of "controversial matters with the Dominican government affecting American interests" that Sumner Welles requested in August 1934 included complaints from several U.S.-owned companies: the Santo Domingo electric company (owned by Chase National Bank), the Dominican telephone company (owned by Associated Telephone and Telegraph), Pan American Airways, and American Bridge Company.[95] Several firms doing business in the Dominican Republic lost their tax-exempt status as the result of an amendment to the Dominican Constitution and the formation of a Public Utilities Commission.[96] Next, a stiff punitive tax against the eviction of squatters from private land, capable of being "evoked capriciously and without appeal," was placed like a "sword of Damocles hanging over the heads" of the foreign sugar estates.[97] The dictatorship may have imposed civil order in the country, but there was little stability in the Dominican business climate after Trujillo came to power.

Trujillo also expected the members of the American Colony to participate in the rituals of his self-glorification and to help finance public celebrations and public works. The same year the sugar tax went into effect, for instance, Edwin I. Kilbourne, manager of the vast Consuelo estate near San Pedro de Macorís, paid for the construction of "Ramfís Bridge" across the Higuamo River and hosted lengthy festivities honoring its four-year-old namesake.[98] After the publication of the critical *Foreign Policy Reports* article, the regime increased its pressure on the American Colony. Resident Americans received letters from the government soliciting their opinions of Trujillo, partly to generate quotations from them to counter the charges made in the article and partly to remind them that their fortunes hinged on Trujillo's good will. The legation did not protest the impropriety of the opinion poll because of concern for Dominican cooperation at the upcoming Buenos Aires Inter-American Peace Conference.[99] Thereafter, the integration of the American Colony into the public life of the Trujillo regime increased, reflecting the pacification of the expatriate community in the Dominican Republic.[100] The American-owned brewery in the Dominican Republic also took part in Trujillo's titular aggrandizement, changing the name of its beer from "Reina" to "Presidente" in 1936.

The Dominican exiles were the principal source of agitation against Trujillo throughout his period in power. Beginning with the exodus of his political opponents immediately after the tense election of 1930, the community of Dominican exiles in New York, San Juan, Port-au-Prince, Havana, and Caracas grew throughout the decade. The three most visible of them were Rafael Estrella Ureña (the ousted leader of the 1930 revolution) and Federico Velásquez and Angel Morales (the candidates of the opposing presidential ticket in the boycotted election of that year). They were joined by an intermittent stream of refugees from Trujillo's political violence, among them Oscar Michelena. Even the Dominican minister to Washington, Rafael Brache, elected to remain in exile in the United States rather than return to face accusations from the Partido Dominicano in 1936.[101] The exiles hatched plans for an invasion of the Dominican Republic and organized to condemn the Trujillo regime.

The prominence of Sumner Welles in the Roosevelt administration increased Trujillo's "nervousness and anxiety" concerning the exiles' projects, which Welles was accused of abetting.[102] After Welles went to Cuba in spring 1933, the Dominican minister in Havana, Osvaldo Bazil, approached him on the matter. Bazil said Trujillo had "intercepted correspondence" proving that Welles was "prejudiced against Trujillo [and] actively encouraging the activities of the Dominican revolutionaries in the United States." Welles defended his relationship with Morales and Velásquez, whom he "would always be glad to see as personal friends," and denied any further interest in their affairs. Bazil then made a series of requests that demonstrated the importance Trujillo placed on Welles's amity. Would Welles go to Santo Domingo as a "guest at the presidential mansion for two or three days" to show "the Dominican people" that he "was a personal friend"? Would he make "a public statement" to that effect? Welles declined to cooperate in these public demonstrations, and he also demurred on the idea of Trujillo coming "incognito" to Havana to confer with him.[103] Although Welles refused to play the part of good neighbor to Trujillo, neither did he conspire with the exiles against the regime. Once he returned to government service with the Roosevelt administration, Welles curtailed his efforts to ignite public opinion against Trujillo and avoided any implication that he might be assisting their plans. The Federal Bureau of Investigation and State Department special agents began investigating the activities of the exiles during the Hoover administration, in early 1932, and continued their surveillance after the change in administration, subsequently reporting to Welles.[104] On the eve of Roosevelt's inauguration, Estrella Ureña had cultivated "several wealthy American backers" and ordered enough weapons to arm "about one hundred ex-servicemen and Marines" for an expedition against Trujillo, but the State Department prevailed on the principal backer (who had agreed to advance $50,000) "to defer his participation."[105] After the presidential transition, prodded by frequent complaints from Dominican diplomats, Welles kept tabs on some exiles through the FBI and reminded others to obey the U.S. neutrality laws in effect against military intrigues.[106] He listened to the political refugees who came to see him at the State Department, but always with the understanding that he could do nothing to help them and might have to hinder them if they broke any laws.[107]

Dominican diplomatic efforts were effective in impeding the exiles' invasion plans, but they had less impact on the information campaign waged by Trujillo's enemies abroad. The well-connected Angel Morales, a former Dominican minister to the United States, was especially prolific in providing stories to the American press and letters to bankers and public officials, denouncing Trujillo. The *New York Herald Tribune* published his long attack on Trujillo's continuation in power on Dominican election day, 16 May 1934, under the headline "Trujillo Kills Off Opposition—No One Dares Contest Today's Election, Exiles Declare."[108] The article drew a quick response from Joseph E. Davies, chief organizer of the "Dominican lobby" developing in the United States, refuting the charges and affirming Trujillo's character.[109] Exile propagandists were also busy in Havana (where the radical A.B.C. movement was a model for organization), San Juan (where

*El Imparcial* printed a five-part series on the abuse of Oscar Michelena), and Caracas (where a "League for Dominican Liberation" formed at the newspaper *El Universal*).[110] Trujillo agitated for government action to censor the exiles in their respective havens and pressed for their extradition on prosecutions entered against them in absentia.

Trujillo also resorted to violence against the most outspoken of his detractors abroad. The assassination of Sergio Bencosme (whom a gunman apparently mistook for Angel Morales) in New York in April 1935, escalated the conflict between Trujillo and the exiles.[111] The incident foreshadowed the New York abduction and murder of Jesús de Galíndez by Trujillo two decades later, although the events had different results. The 1956 Galíndez case, involving the killing of one of Trujillo's most articulate critics, led to a U.S. congressional inquiry and, because it also involved the murder of an American pilot who assisted the killers, helped precipitate a diplomatic rupture with the United States.[112] The Bencosme murder spurred Angel Morales, who had dodged the assassin's bullet, to intensify his commotion against Trujillo, and led Cordell Hull to assist Trujillo's efforts to censor the harsh publicity that resulted.

### DICTATORS AND GOOD NEIGHBORS AT THE MOVIES

Morales took his story to a powerful new medium, the newsreel *March of Time,* established in February 1935 by Henry Luce as a film counterpart to his successful weekly magazine, *Time. March of Time* circulated at movie theaters for ninety-day runs, sharing the bill with cartoons and features in the popular depression-era diversion of the cinema. By April 1936, more than five thousand theaters in 3,215 American cities screened *March of Time* to an audience of some 12 million people.[113] Prompted by Morales, that month's edition of the newsreel dramatized the Trujillo regime in a piece entitled "An American Dictator."[114] More than any other source, "An American Dictator" summarized and publicized the dirty secrets about the Trujillo regime that complicated public diplomacy with it.

The film followed the career of "the dictatingest dictator who ever dictated" in a series of staged tableaux interspersed with actual footage of parades and ceremonies in the Dominican Republic. It featured all of the most glaring elements of Trujillo's authoritarianism, and it attributed his rise to the Marine occupation. According to the newsreel, Trujillo was "schooled by eight years of devil-dog efficiency" under the Marines, who left him an army and a stockpile of weapons, and as president he "end-lessly . . . plotted to make his army stronger and himself rich." In a vignette showing a state dinner, an actor portraying Trujillo serves "Hitler cocktails, Mussolini salad, and Stalin sauce." "An American Dictator" focused on Tru-jillo's personality cult: the renaming of Santo Domingo as Ciudad Trujillo, the Trujillo name "given to ancient plazas, bridges, avenues, beaches, cafés, and theaters," and the "Dios y Trujillo" sign over Vice-President Peynado's house. A sequence focusing on the exiles demonstrated the influence of Angel Morales in the creation of the film: "Wise Dominicans fled, but last to go was thoughtful Angel Morales, from a long line of Dominican states-men, who took refuge in New York." Following a reenaction of the shoot-ing of Sergio Bencosme, the narration claimed that Morales had "escaped the fate of many prominent enemies of Trujillo, who have been mysteri-ously slain." The final shot was of the gunboat/yacht *Presidente Trujillo* "with steam up" in the Ozama River, "a sure sign of tension and perhaps of sud-den collapse in the tightest little tyranny in the Caribbean."[115]

The film enraged Trujillo and threatened to derail bilateral relations. In a formal letter of protest to Cordell Hull, Dominican Minister Pastoriza located the problem of adverse publicity within the framework of the Good Neighbor policy: "I am convinced that the disruptive campaign by certain sensational newspapers is working powerfully against the brilliant Pan American ideals enunciated in the 'good neighbor policy' by Presi-dent Roosevelt, and it is in view of that conviction [that] I have decided to put on record this new protest."[116] The American financial advisor in the Dominican Republic, William Dunn, thought the film "was holding up the settlement of the debt matter" because it "had caused a great deal of bit-terness" for Trujillo.[117] Dunn and Pastoriza both complained directly to the "film people" of *March of Time,* an effort that Cordell Hull assisted. He told Pastoriza privately that he "would be glad to lay the complaint . . . fully before the suitable officials of the *March of Time* organization."[118] Hull re-leased to the press his reply to Pastoriza, which expressed his "deep regret" over the issue and his hope that it would not hamper "cordial relations" with the Dominican Republic on the eve of the Buenos Aires Peace Con-ference.[119] Radio City Music Hall responded by suspending "An American Dictator" after one showing, and although this action removed the film from the screen in an important venue, it also served to increase publicity of the film's contents.[120] The RKO-Keith Theater in Washington point-edly announced that it would screen an unedited version, prompting the

Dominican minister to complain to Welles, who was probably the least sympathetic man in the city, that the newsreel was a "gross attack" that tried to "make the Dominican people look ridiculous."[121] The "film people" at *March of Time* did not remove the newsreel from general circulation, but "rather had the impression that the Department [of State] was really rather glad that the film had come out."[122] Hull may have publicly "deplored" the damage to the Good Neighbor policy wrought by the film, but his attitude was not widely shared by other U.S. diplomats.[123]

Hull's public expression of sympathy for the Dominican government's protest suggests his recognition of the power of film as a transmitter of ideas. The State Department took little interest in Dominican complaints about critical print journalism, aside from denying any official involvement in it or power to control it, but the potential audience of the *March of Time* made "An American Dictator" a special case.[124] In this instance, fearing that Trujillo's deep resentment of the newsreel might drag down his level of cooperation (which was already a wavering line), Hull gave his vocal support. He may also have used his influence privately, as he told Pastoriza he would, perhaps contributing to the ban at Radio City Music Hall. This act of censorship was significant to the extent that, given the large size and popularity of the space, thousands of New Yorkers did not view the film who otherwise might, considerably reducing its exposure in the city that was the center of the Latin American investment community and of the Dominican expatriate population. Moreover, the event shows that Trujillo interpreted the Good Neighbor policy as a pledge of public support for him, and considered any unfavorable depiction of his rule in the U.S. media to be contrary to friendly relations. Trujillo was especially angry over the *March of Time* because of the wide audience it reached, prompting Cordell Hull to act in support of his sensitive neighbor.

Hull himself starred in a *March of Time* production commissioned by the State Department two years later, a film that encapsulated the public relations effort of the Good Neighbor policy. *Uncle Sam: The Good Neighbor* traced the professionalization of the Foreign Service under Hull, "an ardent man of peace" who was said to judge each diplomat on "his performance as a good neighbor." The focus of the film was Latin America, because "no more vital problem faces the U.S. State Department today, than developing the friendship of the nation's next-door neighbors." Accordingly, the State Department's new Division of American Republics "vigorously pushed" the Good Neighbor policy, assuring the "twenty-one neighbors to the south" that "their sovereignty will be respected and, if necessary, even defended." Already the "fabulously wealthy" markets of the hemisphere had been "invaded" by the commerce of dictatorships, said the narration, while scenes of Italian, Japanese, and German ships and goods (including a Spanish translation of *Mein Kampf*) spilled past. In a cameo appearance, Sumner Welles warned that "the future of all of us . . . may necessarily depend upon our continued solidarity." The film closed with an image of a German newspaper bearing Hull's picture, held aloft by a swastika-emblazoned arm, and with Hull's voice saying that the basic choice facing Latin America was between "violence" and "justice." *Uncle Sam: The Good Neighbor* won a special Academy Award in 1938.[125]

The film sums up the central contradiction of the Good Neighbor policy, which was at the heart of the problem of relations with the Trujillo regime. The premise of the policy was that the sovereignty of all twenty-one "neighbors" was assured. The increasingly urgent object of the policy was to foster "solidarity" against the inroads of "dictatorship" and to support the choice of "justice" over "violence." But where systems such as Trujillo's came to power, "dictatorship" and "violence" prevailed on the local level and prospered behind walls of sovereignty. When this happened, the Roosevelt administration did not single out specific "neighbors" for public censure, but amplified the general appeals for amity that accompanied its calls for inter-American consultation, trade, and cultural exchange. The State Department kept bilateral relations with dictatorships out of public forums when they could, but not at the cost of alienating such regimes and losing their cooperation in achieving inter-American goals. Trujillo's foreign policy sought public acclaim and approval wherever possible, however, and his government cooperated in only the noisiest ways. Concern for how the other neighbors would view close ties with Trujillo prevented the State Department from embracing him, although it also motivated such efforts as Hull's to mute criticism of his regime. Notwithstanding the secretary of state's declarations after the *March of Time* incident, the personal attitudes of most other diplomats involved with Dominican affairs ranged from icy to courteously ambivalent, depending on the extent of their knowledge of Trujillo's rule.

In response, Trujillo engaged in a range of strategies to generate praise, enlist support, and claim recognition for his part in the Good Neighbor policy, satisfactions that Washington seemed so unwilling to grant him. Trujillo's public relations served to increase the points of engagement between his regime and the United States, extending into areas beyond the influence of the State Department and strengthening the autonomy of the Dominican Republic. Trujillo's concerted effort to present himself and his regime to the world, and to craft an independent foreign policy, followed four interrelated approaches: publicity, the "Dominican lobby," symbols, and mimicry.

## PUBLICITY

As a counterpart to his agitation against critical journalism and exile propaganda abroad, Trujillo spent heavily on increasing favorable publicity. Beginning before his first inauguration, Dominican expenditures for this purpose were initially devoted to stimulating tourism and attracting investment, with the Dominican consulate in New York directing the effort. A onetime publication in magazine format called *Santo Domingo* was produced in New York in July 1930, containing articles by Sumner Welles ("Santo Domingo, an Ideal Winter Resort for the American Tourist") and Henry Clay Foster, promoter of the American "residential park" at Boca Chica beach near the capital ("Santo Domingo for Pleasure").[126] After the creation of the "Dominican Chamber of Commerce of the United States" in June 1934, the consulate began to publish a promotional magazine on a regular basis. The first edition, called *The Dominican Republic Actually,* featured a full-page portrait photograph of Trujillo in tuxedo and presidential sash, with a caption assuring readers that he "has maintained absolute peace as an indispensable requisite to national aggrandizement, and consequently has opened the gates to foreign capital." [127] Subsequent issues, with the title shortened to *The Dominican Republic,* featured the activities of the Dominican Chamber of Commerce, coverage of new public works, encouragement of tourism, and frequent tributes to Trujillo and his diplomacy.[128] The magazine was the foundation for the regime's "scientifically organized" publicity abroad, which Trujillo said was geared to achieve "the greatest respect and the most absolute international consideration" for the country and to help make Santo Domingo "an irresistibly attractive tourist center." [129]

In 1935, Trujillo recruited two Hearst newspaper reporters to come to the Dominican Republic on "a 'good will' mission, with a view to correcting mistaken impressions in the United States regarding President Trujillo's personality and administration." Payment for the journalists came from the "recently increased appropriation for publicity abroad" voted by the Dominican Congress, which also financed the publication of the resulting special supplement to the *Washington Herald* and seventy-five thousand copies of a Spanish-language version.[130] One of the reporters, Laurence de Besault, became a fixture in Dominican public relations for the next few years, becoming the first in a long series of paid publicists for Trujillo. A self-described "ambassador of good will between the United States and Latin American nations," de Besault's tactics for soliciting contributions from foreign businessmen came "very close to constituting blackmail."[131] De Besault's newspaper tribute to Trujillo was called the "most nauseating, boot-licking performance I have ever read" by Oswald Garrison Villard of *The Nation* in his own account of visiting the Dominican Republic in 1937.[132] Dominican diplomats posted in Latin American capitals also contacted newspapers and disseminated pamphlets about Trujillo's government and his "renovation" of the Dominican Republic.[133] In the wake of the *March of Times* debacle, the Dominican Foreign Ministry contracted two American filmmakers to produce a promotional film on the Dominican Republic as well, although they apparently failed to complete the project.[134]

## THE "DOMINICAN LOBBY"

A group of pro-Trujillo businessmen, legislators, and paid advocates constituted a kind of "Dominican lobby" in the United States, with Joseph E. Davies at the center. Davies signed a four-year contract to be Trujillo's counsel in the United States in May 1933, and he quickly proved his skill as a negotiator in the FBPC talks, as a lobbyist, and as a spokesman for the regime.[135] He wrote letters to newspapers and the State Department refuting Angel Morales's election-day charges in 1934. To counter unsympathetic coverage of Trujillo's second inauguration, his associate Major Oliver Newman went to Santo Domingo to "supply the Associated Press with correspondence" about the event.[136] His law office also looked into the federal mail statutes, searching for ways to bar anti-Trujillo materials from the U.S. postal system, on the grounds that they tended to incite assassination.[137]

Beyond these "spin control" initiatives, Davies sought to convince his friends in business and government of Trujillo's abilities and the promise of the Dominican Republic. His *Memorial* extolling the progress of the regime, handsomely bound and nearly two hundred pages long, went to fifty of his "friends in the financial world," some of whom he later took on "joy-rides" along the Dominican coast in his yacht *Sea Cloud*, trying to interest them in financing an ambitious national bank plan for the country.[138] Davies and his wife, the heiress Marjorie Meriweather Post, were also at the center of Washington social life, allowing the lobbyist to promote Dominican interests in very influential circles.[139] For instance, at a New Year's banquet for a hundred and fifty people in 1936 (including Assistant Secretary of State Walton Moore), Dominican Minister Andrés Pastoriza was one of only two foreign diplomats present.[140] Pastoriza spent time at Davies's summer retreat in upstate New York, Camp Topridge, and ordered Dominican rum for Davies to use in his efforts to lubricate potential members of the growing Dominican lobby.[141] Davies also distributed Dominican cigars and bound volumes of photos of Dominican public works to influential people like Roosevelt.[142] His most marketable advantage was access to people at the highest levels of the State Department, whose names he dropped; visiting Ciudad Trujillo aboard *Sea Cloud* in January 1936, Davies raised Schoenfeld's eyebrows by saying "he had discussed his plans for this country [the Dominican Republic] with 'Sumner' and 'Cordell.' "[143]

While Davies took the lead in courting financiers and high officials of the executive branch, Trujillo focused his efforts on visitors to the Dominican Republic, including Congressmen, Senators, educators, and journalists. One prominent member of the Dominican lobby, Dominican Chamber of Commerce President H. Murray-Jacoby, described the treatment accorded Trujillo's guests: "Visitors from the United States have been overwhelmed with kindness and consideration, often too much for their own good."[144] Visiting congressmen, reported a U.S. diplomat, were "wined, dined, and fêted, sometimes until six in the morning."[145] A VIP coming to Santo Domingo could expect to be the guest of honor at a series of luncheons, receptions, banquets, and dances; he and his family might spend a few days at one of Trujillo's mansions or take a cruise on the combination yacht and warship *Presidente Trujillo;* and he was certain to be greeted and accompanied everywhere by various officials of the regime.[146] The honors bestowed on influential visitors frequently included those shown Nicholas Murray Butler, president of Columbia University, in February 1937: induction into the Order of Duarte and ritual examination of the purported remains of Christopher Columbus in the cathedral.[147]

The visit of North Carolina Senator Robert Reynolds in 1935 captures the dual reality of the Dominican Republic, like a vast Potemkin village where the clean streets and new buildings mask a violent political system. Reynolds and his family traveled from Haiti to the Dominican border, where "high functionaries" of the government met them and escorted them on a grand tour to Santo Domingo via Santiago. The festivities staged for them in the capital included a dance where the senator's daughter was the guest of honor.[148] Reynolds also attended a "Civic Review," where he felt he had been exhibited to the crowd as an incarnation of U.S. approval of Trujillo, and he subsequently sought accommodations at the U.S. legation rather than be the dictator's house guest. While in the legation, Reynolds received a letter signed by "The Association of Young Patriots [and] the Mothers, Sisters, Sons." Addressed to him personally, the note described the "dark and dismal cells" at the Marine-built Nigua Prison, where "doctors, former Rectors of the University, professors of all branches of learning, are like corpses," held as political prisoners. "You have been entertained in a manner which will have impressed you," the letter acknowledged, but it related the entertainment to the brutality of the regime: "Do not let yourself be deceived by the lights which dazzle your eyes, they are paid for by the oppressed people, do not let yourself be misled by the champagne they offer you, it is the blood of my people, the tears of mothers."[149] Reynolds did not join the Dominican lobby in Washington after his return.

Trujillo had mixed success in courting favor with visitors, depending on the extent to which they discerned, or credited, the connection between the regime's material progress and its political authoritarianism. Some visitors rejected Trujillo's blandishments outright. Although the *Presidente Trujillo* was dispatched for "the exclusive purpose of transporting Senator [William] King and his family" to the Dominican Republic, where he was elaborately fêted, the senator later wrote a critical account of Trujillo for *La Prensa* of New York.[150] But Trujillo was generally effective at swaying the opinions of his guests, even those, like Oswald Garrison Villard of *The Nation,* who were predisposed against him. A week in the Dominican Republic did not change Villard's perception that Trujillo ran "a political dictatorship," but he was nevertheless "impressed with the evidences of order and material progress" there, which he attributed "to the vigor of President Trujillo's personality and the discipline" he had imposed.[151] Villard still compared Trujillo to Hitler in his article about the visit, but also indicated approval of Trujillo's achievements and respect for his being a "colored" leader.[152]

Trujillo had his greatest success with the members of a congressional delegation that visited in 1939. Senator Theodore Green and Representatives Hamilton Fish, Robert Mouton, and Matthew Merritt traveled with an entourage of reporters from the AP, UPI, and INS wire services, Paramount News newsreel, NBC radio, the magazines *Time, Life,* and *Fortune,* and the *New York World Telegram.* They returned with the view that the Dominican Republic under Trujillo was a "fine little republic."[153] Senator Green of Rhode Island was something of a kindred spirit of the macho Trujillo (at age seventy Green spurned the Senate gymnasium as being for "sissies"), a critic of the State Department, and a member of the Senate Foreign Relations Committee. He addressed a joint session of the Dominican legislature on the subject of improved bilateral relations.[154] Green subsequently joined the efforts of the Dominican lobby. Together with Nicholas Murray Butler, cofounder of the Institute of International Education with Stephen Duggan, the father of Assistant Secretary of State Laurence Duggan, he pressed the State Department for an invitation to Washington for Trujillo.[155] Representative Hamilton Fish, from FDR's home region and the ranking Republican on the House Foreign Affairs Committee, had been criticizing the Trujillo regime since 1934, especially after the Haitian massacre in 1937 (the subject of the following chapter).[156] Even so, his visit to Ciudad Trujillo just a year later converted Fish into a vocal supporter of Trujillo and an important member of the Dominican lobby. His change of heart was accelerated by another of Trujillo's tactics in cultivating allies: bribery. In addition to being "lavishly entertained" with his delegation, Fish received $25,000 in "oil speculation" money from Trujillo, who had hired a "protégé" of Fish, George Djamgaroff, to be "Director of Propaganda" in the United States for $50,000 (a sum he may have split with Fish).[157] When Trujillo's trip to Washington was finally arranged by the Marine Corps in July 1939, Representative Fish was the principal speaker at a banquet for Trujillo at the Pan-American Union, where Fish referred to the general as the "creator of a golden age."[158] The extent of Trujillo's bribery of the Dominican lobby is difficult to estimate, but it was reportedly great.[159]

SYMBOLS

In order to project the "renovated" Dominican Republic to a wider audience than those who visited the country, Trujillo adopted, elaborated, and promoted symbols that other target groups could accept, thereby establishing a connection with them. These unifying symbols usually had to do with construction projects, real or imagined, in the Dominican Republic. The most enduring of these symbols was the *Faro de Colón,* or Columbus

Lighthouse, which General Receiver William Pulliam had first proposed in 1914.[160] Framed as a symbol of inter-American cooperation, the project was initiated at the Pan-American Conference in Santiago, Chile, in 1923, where the American republics agreed to contribute to its construction. The U.S. Congress approved the measure and appropriated $800,000 to build the lighthouse in 1929.[161] The onset of the depression stalled progress on the *Faro,* and most contributing nations, including the United States, delayed payment. But the plan had important allies, including Sumner Welles and Leo Rowe, president of the Pan-American Union, and Trujillo embraced it when he came to power. Not only would the monument focus attention on the historical attractions in colonial Santo Domingo (the heart of Trujillo's promotion of tourism and the only district left intact by the San Zenón hurricane), it also provided a vehicle for exhibiting his reconstruction of the city to those unable or unwilling to visit. Despite continued State Department opposition to U.S. government financing, several diplomats who were otherwise wholly unsympathetic to the Trujillo regime supported the lighthouse cause. The project gained momentum with their backing and with the continued involvement of the Pan-American Union.[162] The architects Frank Lloyd Wright, Eliel Saarinen, and Horacio Acosta y Lara constituted an "International Jury" that judged a design contest for the lighthouse in October 1931, selecting the Scottish architect J. L. Gleave as the winner for his idea of a gigantic recumbent cross.[163] He was awarded $10,000 at the Second Conference on the *Faro* in Rio de Janeiro the next year, where Tulio Cestero, minister to Argentina, was the Dominican delegate. Cestero also corresponded frequently with Pulliam and Rowe and distributed copies of a Dominican publication on Columbus and Trujillo to interested parties.[164]

The proceedings of the Montevideo Conference in 1933 included resolutions requesting the Pan-American Union to continue its support of the *Faro* and another "reminding" the republics to pay their "quotas" to finance it. One of the "miscellaneous conclusions" of the meeting "reiterated" the inter-American approval given in 1923.[165] But the continued financial straits of the hemisphere intervened, and the Columbus Memorial Lighthouse Committee of the Pan-American Union declined to "request contributions from the Governments" in 1934.[166] Two new "executive committees" now appeared to solicit funds for the project. Trujillo appointed a Dominican version that included two prominent members of the American Colony, Pulliam and the National City Bank manager J. E. Wheeler.[167] Sumner Welles advocated an American version to raise private donations in the

United States, and after enlisting the aid of Cordell Hull and overcoming opposition from Assistant Secretary of State Walton Moore, he obtained Roosevelt's approval.[168]

In 1937, Welles and Leo Rowe pressed Roosevelt to broadcast a message acknowledging the "generosity of the Dominican Government" in contributing land for the Columbus Lighthouse in a prime location near the mouth of the Ozama River. The message called the *Faro* "a reminder to the nations of this continent of their essential unity of ideals, of interest and of purpose."[169] Roosevelt issued a message citing the "definite form" being taken by the project, and in January 1938 Laurence Duggan of the State Department attended the Columbus Lighthouse Executive Committee meeting in New York, offering government encouragement but not financial support. World War II intervened to delay, but not derail, further consideration of the *Faro,* although Trujillo's "director of propaganda," George Djamgaroff, suggested that it could be constructed as an antifascist gesture.[170] The cornerstone of the monument was laid during a ceremony in 1944, part of the year-long commemoration of the Dominican Centennial that simultaneously glorified Trujillo's nationalism and personalism.[171] The new president of the Pan-American Union, Pedro de Alba, and a papal delegate gave speeches extolling the hemispheric solidarity symbolized by the *Faro;* its cornerstone read "Era de Trujillo, 1944."[172]

In the promotion of the lighthouse, depictions of Gleave's modern design were linked with the material "renovation" of the Dominican Republic carried out by Trujillo. The monument was central to his future plans for Ciudad Trujillo as a tourist destination and hub of commerce, as well as an evocation of the long history of Santo Domingo. Linking these two nationalist themes was the figure of Columbus, whose reputed remains reposed at the ancient cathedral. The tomb was a mandatory stop on every visitor's tour of the city, and VIPs were treated to a close inspection of the box (which Trujillo would open) containing what was left of the Admiral.[173] The cult of the remains of Columbus was also one of the strongest ties between U.S. and Dominican officials during the 1930s. The Columbus Memorial Lighthouse, conceived by Pulliam and backed by Welles, was planned as the final resting place for Columbus, increasing its significance as a monument to the shared heritage of the Americas.

The Dominican Pavilion at the 1939 World's Fair in New York also portrayed the "Land Columbus Loved" with the theme "Ciudad Trujillo: Past and Present." One section of the exhibit depicted colonial Santo Domingo, while the other was arranged like the fuselage of a plane, with windows where visitors could see aerial views of the modern city and the *Faro*.[174] Trujillo, like Roosevelt, seized on the World's Fair itself as a symbol to be shared with the global community of nations. Roosevelt had dedicated the event to "the spirit" of the Good Neighbor policy in his speech at the laying of the fair's cornerstone in June 1938, advising "the other nations here today" to follow the course that "has proven so successful in the Western Hemisphere."[175] The elaborate Dominican Pavilion was both a tangible demonstration of the Trujillo regime's agreement with the sentiment and, with a bust of Trujillo dominating its foyer, a visual tribute to the republic's leader.

The interconnected symbols of the *Faro* and Columbus invoked inter-American ideals and placed them in a Dominican context, whereas the symbol of George Washington did the same for the principle of sovereignty. Washington's Birthday was an occasion to call for close bilateral relations on equal terms, based on the mutual independence of the United States and the Dominican Republic, and to associate Washington with Latin American liberation from colonialism. This rhetoric contrasted the Marine occupation, which violated Dominican sovereignty, with the present relationship, in which Trujillo's "friendly gesture" of celebrating Washington's Birthday was the spontaneous act of an autonomous statesman representing the country he had liberated. The use of Washington as a symbol reached its height on the celebration of his birthday in February 1936, when the coastal road in Ciudad Trujillo, the *Malecón,* was renamed Avenida George Washington. The government ordered five hundred U.S. flags for use at the event, which included the unveiling of an obelisk in the center of the road (it looked like the Washington Monument but was dedicated to Trujillo) and a round of banquets and receptions.[176] The largest of the entertainments took place at the U.S. legation, with a guest list of nearly five hundred people. Minister Schoenfeld had paid for previous, smaller receptions on Washington's Birthday out of his own pocket, but to his "intense surprise" the State Department allocated special funds on this occasion to allow him to reciprocate for Trujillo's lavish observance of the holiday.[177] Most of the event took place outside the modest legation, which would not occupy "an adequate" building until 1939, and Schoenfeld was grateful it did not rain that day.[178] Thereafter, visitors to Ciudad Trujillo could not help but note that the name of the scenic coastal drive was Avenida George Washington, a fact that was frequently cited by the Dominican lobby as proof of Trujillo's affinity for the United States.

## MIMICRY

The symbolic trinity of Dominican foreign relations—Columbus, Washington, and Trujillo—unified the ideas of inter-American fraternity, bilateral amity with the United States, and Dominican national sovereignty. The conflation of these themes continued in Trujillo's construction of the Good Neighbor policy and in the depiction of his relationship with Roosevelt. His public acceptance of U.S. leadership, and of the personal leadership of Roosevelt, has led to the conclusion that Trujillo was "a willing servant of United States governmental and financial interests."[179] But Trujillo's mimicry of U.S. diplomatic and political projects was not an abdication of independent action: it was an assertion of the sovereign nation's right to choose among options and to put its imprint on the option of its choice through the act of choosing. Trujillo's mimicry of the Good Neighbor policy and of Franklin Roosevelt bears out the analysis of the postcolonial theorist Homi Bhabha, that "mimicry emerges as one of the most elusive and effective strategies of colonial power and knowledge." Focusing on the "difference that is almost the same, but not quite" that separates the mimic from the model, Bhabha asserts that "the discourse of mimicry is constructed around an ambivalence; in order to be effective, mimicry must continually produce its slippage, its excess, its difference." This ambivalence was generated by the authoritarianism of Trujillo's regime (despite its façade of constitutional democracy) and by his inter-American grandstanding (a personalist version of solidarity with American aims). The "difference" implicit in Trujillo's emulation of U.S. policy prevented his cooperation from being particularly useful or desirable in the eyes of the State Department. His actions in this regard, like pushing an unwelcome American League of Nations proposal at successive inter-American conferences and nominating Roosevelt for the Nobel Peace Prize, originated in what Bhabha calls the "area between mimicry and mockery, where the reforming, civilizing mission is threatened by the displacing gaze of its disciplinary double."[180] Stated simply, when the dictator with the Marine pedigree repeated the rhetoric of the Good Neighbor policy, the same words seemed to mean different things.

Trujillo integrated Roosevelt's definition of a "good neighbor," one who "respects himself and, because he does, respects the rights of others," into his political discourse soon after the 1933 Pan-American Day speech that contained the phrase. He praised the new "policy of cooperation and mutual respect between the great North American democracy and the Latin Republics of America" in an interview in *Listín Diario* two weeks later. He called himself a "collaborator in universal peace" on the anniversary of his inauguration in August 1933, and he reiterated his intention "to cultivate relations of affectionate reciprocity on the basis of mutual respect" with neighboring nations in a speech in the provincial capital of Azua in December.[181] But with the debt negotiations stalled, the Dominican delegates to the Montevideo Inter-American Conference that year "emphatically denounced United States intervention."[182] Nor was cooperation from the Dominican Republic a sure thing when Roosevelt called the Buenos Aires Peace Conference in January 1936. In response to Roosevelt's letter inviting Dominican participation, Trujillo proposed that the close inter-American ties encouraged by the Good Neighbor policy be formalized in a League of American Nations.[183] He had described the idea in a statement the previous July, saying that he "cherished the idea" for "all the peoples of our continent, [to create] a League of American Nations, more effective than the present League of Nations, because our destiny is a common destiny."[184] Roosevelt and Hull hoped to establish an organ of hemispheric consultation and some enforcement machinery at the conference, but the League of American Nations plan went further than they intended to go and originated with a leader they had not embraced, so they gave no encouragement to Trujillo.[185] The Colombian delegation, however, seconded the motion when it was made by the Dominicans at Buenos Aires, and so the proposal was debated by the full conference.[186] Cordell Hull and the powerful Argentine Foreign Minister Carlos Saavedra Lamas led the successful fight to postpone the measure until the next inter-American conference, on the grounds that it was "not sufficiently ripe for its immediate consideration."[187]

Dominican diplomats "throughout the hemisphere" tried to "stimulate support" in preparation for the reintroduction of the League of American Nations proposal, now a "joint Dominican-Colombian project," at the Lima Conference in December 1938.[188] R. Henry Norweb, the U.S. minister in Ciudad Trujillo since October 1937, led the U.S. diplomatic contingent with Cordell Hull. He commented that "the obvious intention" of the League of American Nations campaign was for the Dominican Republic to "play a role in formulating Pan American ideals," although he also thought Trujillo hoped to recoup "any prestige abroad he feels he may have lost as a result of the Haitian incident," meaning the massacre of thousands in 1937.[189] Dominican press coverage of the Buenos Aires Conference gave the impression that the League initiative conferred "a transcendent power" on the Dominican delegation, as Vice-President Peynado described it. Reintroducing the measure brought a number of special diplomatic missions to Ciudad Trujillo in the months before the Lima Conference.[190] The U.S. delegation again opposed the plan, which would bring a "far-reaching change in inter-American relations," contending that it was "in conflict" with "United States policy and legislation," and again it was rebuffed.[191] Trujillo's plan for a formal organization comprising the American republics, one with greater powers than the Pan-American Union, eventually took shape in 1948 with the creation of the Organization of American States, although Trujillo was not credited with the idea. The OAS would later impose the economic and diplomatic sanctions that contributed to his downfall in 1961.

Trujillo's mimicry of the Good Neighbor policy interfered with its creator's own agenda at Buenos Aires, a conference that Roosevelt had called and that he personally attended, and then again at the Lima Conference. Trujillo's too-effusive imitation of inter-Americanism extended to Roosevelt and his family, who were the objects of his frequent personal attentions. Trujillo elevated his own status as a statesman by eliciting cordial exchanges with the U.S. president, framing them in personal terms whenever possible. Trujillo initiated these individual relations soon after Roosevelt's inauguration, sending an autographed photograph of himself to the White House with General George Richards, one of his friends in the U.S. Marine Corps. Although the Protocol Division at the State Department emphasized the impropriety of reciprocating, Roosevelt autographed a photograph of himself to send to "My good neighbor Señor General Doctor Rafael Leonidas Trujillo Molina, President of the Dominican Republic."[192] Trujillo then nominated Roosevelt for the Nobel Peace Prize for his declaration of the Good Neighbor policy, calling his inaugural address an "epoch-making message" that would provide "a firm basis to universal peace."[193] Two years later, the Dominican legislature nominated Trujillo himself for the Peace Prize for his border treaty with Haitian President Stenio Vincent, news of which he triumphantly wired to Roosevelt; and in 1939 the dictator created a "Trujillo Peace Prize" that the U.S. legation thought would be given to Roosevelt or Hull "in order to obtain certain specific favors from the American Government."[194] Trujillo styled his agricultural policy, which included government-planned "grange" communities, as a "Dominican New

Deal," and he drew a parallel between his momentum toward a third term and Roosevelt's.[195]

Learning of Roosevelt's passion for stamp collecting, Trujillo developed an interest in philately and sought to bring the symbols of Dominican foreign policy to FDR's attention through commemorative stamps. Minister Pastoriza gave Roosevelt a complete set of Dominican stamps when he presented his credentials at the White House in February 1936. He then sent Roosevelt an eight-stamp commemorative issue in honor of the Avenida George Washington.[196] Later issues featured the sesquicentennial of the U.S. Constitution and the planned Columbus Lighthouse.[197] Roosevelt himself communicated through the medium of the postage stamp in 1940, when an issue commemorating the fiftieth anniversary of the Pan-American Union appeared, bearing the inscription he had suggested: "A Hemisphere of Good Neighbors."[198] Although Roosevelt declined Trujillo's offers to "deign to be his guest in his humble Mansion" (the closest he got was a fishing trip to Samaná Bay), First Lady Eleanor Roosevelt made a refueling stop there in 1934 and was met at the San Pedro de Macorís airport by Trujillo and his wife.[199] The event dominated the first edition of the Dominican *Boletín de Relaciones Exteriores* [Bulletin of Foreign Relations], which printed the letters exchanged by Trujillo and Roosevelt about the First Lady's "happy visit."[200] James Roosevelt, the president's son, also visited in 1938, and was given the Order of Duarte in appreciation.[201]

FDR did take a personal interest in the fate of the wreck of the USS *Memphis,* the rusting hulk on the rocks of Santo Domingo that served as a perpetual symbol of U.S. "gunboat diplomacy" in the Dominican Republic. The Dominican press regularly drew attention to the rusting cruiser in editorials denouncing the neocolonial experience of occupation, a practice that continued under Trujillo. The *Memphis* became even more noticeable with the modernization of the capital city during the early Trujillo regime; the new seaside road known as Avenida George Washington, with its obelisk, was planned to extend past the wreck. Until the completion of the road, the *Memphis* loomed beyond right field of the baseball stadium, reminding spectators of the unhappy past every time a left-handed hitter pulled the ball. The American Colony raised money to improve the coastal character of the city, with funds being set aside for a bust of George Washington (which was to be placed along the avenue named for him, since the obelisk honored Trujillo) and for removal of the eyesore of the *Memphis.*[202] When Roosevelt learned that the hulk still reposed where it had when he was assistant secretary of the navy, he expedited its removal, perhaps understanding the negative symbolic power it retained.[203]

Despite a steady stream of hints concerning his desire to visit the United States, Trujillo was unable to elicit the support of Roosevelt or anyone in the State Department to secure an invitation. Tulio Cestero, the Dominican delegate to the Montevideo Conference, announced to Cordell Hull that Trujillo expected to visit the United States after the election of May 1934, although Hull had "in no remote sense" considered "inviting him."[204] Trujillo would not follow up on his oft-stated intention to travel to Washington, however, "unless he was sure before-hand of a welcome," and no such guarantee was forthcoming from the Roosevelt administration.[205] Joseph Davies suggested a trip to Palm Beach, Florida, "to have conferences with American industrialists" in 1935, but again the stated travel plans fell through.[206] And so it went for the next four and a half years, as the State Department fended off Trujillo's clearly stated wish to cement close ties with the United States by coming to its capital. Testing the actual consequences of the Good Neighbor policy, then, Trujillo found very little of the reciprocity he expected. Despite his strenuous performance as a "good neighbor," diplomats discomfited by his dictatorship held him at arm's length and defeated his proposal for a regional organization. It remained for Trujillo's allies in the U.S. Marine Corps, abetted by the civilian "Dominican lobby," to arrange Trujillo's first visit to the United States in 1939, a subject considered in later chapters.

## MUSSOLINI AND THE BARLETTA INCIDENT

Not only did the State Department fail to reciprocate Trujillo's public expressions of amity, but when Benito Mussolini threatened to send the Italian Navy to the Dominican Republic in May 1935, the United States refused to enforce the Monroe Doctrine. The conflict between the two dictators was unexpected, given Trujillo's long identification with the fascist leader. Mussolini's Italy awarded Trujillo the first foreign decoration in what would become his vast collection of medals, in January 1929.[207] British Minister Galienne reported in March 1930 that Trujillo "apparently viewed himself as the prospective Dominican Mussolini."[208] Also, one of the self-promotional pamphlets published during Trujillo's first term in office examined the "Mussolini-Trujillo parallel."[209]

Trouble between them began when the honorary Italian consul, Amadeo

Barletta, clashing with Trujillo over his attempt to monopolize the Dominican tobacco industry, was jailed on "trumped up" charges of conspiracy in April 1935.[210] Barletta was president of the Dominican Tobacco Company, more than half of which was owned in the United States, and also ran the General Motors dealership in Santo Domingo.[211] Trujillo's takeover of the tobacco industry had been one of the "controversies" listed for Welles in August 1934, but his treatment of Barletta, who was held for six weeks "in a revolting condition of dirt and discomfort" at the infamous Nigua Prison, caused an international incident.[212] Coming on the heels of the torture, imprisonment, and property loss endured by Oscar Michelena, the abuse of another prominent foreign citizen by the Dominican authorities jarred the American Colony and the U.S. diplomatic mission as well. Schoenfeld reflected that Barletta's case "betrayed most of the brutality that is associated with the Spanish inquisition—and much more stupidity."[213]

Learning that Barletta had been jailed, the Italian government ordered its nearest ranking diplomat, Minister to Cuba Antonio Maccario, to fly to the Dominican Republic to demand the consul's release. Maccario was "so incensed at the refusal of the Dominican authorities even to let him see" Barletta that he asked Schoenfeld "what his attitude would be in the event of the despatch of an Italian warship." British Minister Alexander Paterson reported that "the American Minister refused to be drawn and evaded the question by asking, 'Have you one ready?', there being probably no such vessel nearer [than] the Mediterranean."[214] Frustrated by Trujillo's intransigence, Maccario suggested to Schoenfeld that, since the United States was "'responsible' for the state of affairs" under the dictatorship, Rome should talk directly to Washington about the problem.[215] Of course, the Good Neighbor policy disavowed such responsibility, so Mussolini would have to deal with Trujillo directly.

The possibility of Italian naval action began to look less remote by mid-May 1935, after Barletta had been in prison for six weeks. At that juncture, Cordell Hull warned Dominican Minister Rafael Brache that unless the Italian consul was freed, Italy "might well resort to drastic measures, such as sending not one battleship but several battleships to the Dominican Republic, in which case the Dominican Government could hardly look for any sympathy from the United States." Hull said he hoped Trujillo would not "lag behind in the effort in which every one of the other American states were loyally working and cooperating," that of "the 'good neighbor.'"[216] A front-page story in the New York Times two days later carried the headline "Italy Threatens Santo Domingo . . . Delay Angers Mussolini." The report carried Italian Ambassador Augusto Rosso's statement that his country "may find it necessary to send a warship," together with the State Department's view that such action "would probably not be viewed with concern."[217] Trujillo released Barletta soon afterward, although Brache explained that the release was not owing to fear of Italian reprisals but because Trujillo "had been profoundly touched" by Hull's "friendly and considerate plea" for clemency (which is how Brache described the meeting at which Hull threatened him with an Italian fleet).[218] The British minister reported the affair differently, saying that Maccario had finally set the deadline for Barletta's release at noon, 21 May, and Trujillo complied at fifteen minutes to the hour. First Trujillo made Barletta sign a letter "drafted by the President's entourage," admitting the existence of a conspiracy, then he "hypocritically embraced" the prisoner in his office.[219] Needing a scapegoat for Barletta's horrendous and well-publicized treatment, Trujillo sacked his foreign minister, Arturo Logroño, replacing him with Elías Brache, brother of the Dominican minister in Washington. The Italian threat of force, and Hull's acquiescence in it, had apparently worked.

Italian Minister Maccario told Schoenfeld that the "energetic action" of the United States "had saved the Trujillo administration."[220] But the Dominican desk officer at the State Department, J. F. McGurk, pointed out the limited utility of "hauling Brache up on the carpet in the Department," because when "such a government" as Trujillo's "becomes convinced that no armed force will be used, diplomatic pressure of that kind becomes ineffective." McGurk himself, whose job acquainted him well with the legation reports detailing Trujillo's outrages, "had sort of hoped" that Mussolini would intervene, perhaps forcing the United States to do something about the regime.[221] He still felt that way ten years later, when he became U.S. ambassador in Ciudad Trujillo. Although the Good Neighbor policy made such intervention unlikely, it was also unlikely that the State Department would side with Trujillo against a third party in defense of his authoritarianism. Trujillo discovered that State Department solidarity with dictators had distinct limitations.

Roosevelt and Trujillo both sought to influence "the mobilized public opinion of the Pan-American family of nations," as *The Nation*'s Ernest Gruening phrased it, but with very different agendas in mind.[222] Trujillo's main concern was the depiction of his government and its relations with both the United States and Latin America. His foreign policy was oriented toward suppressing negative reviews and generating positive reflections of the Era of Trujillo everywhere, with the goal of enlarging the presence of the Dominican Republic and its leader in the international public eye. Two buildings devoted to the advancement of that cause in the United States testify to its success. In Washington, the Dominican legation moved into a four-story mansion, complete with a turret and two loggias, a structure larger than the quarters of the U.S. legation in Ciudad Trujillo.[223] And the large, modern Dominican Pavilion at the 1939 New York World's Fair conveyed the complex of ideas that were Trujillo's message to the world, focusing on the "new fatherland" that he was building on the foundations of Columbian grandeur and Pan-American esprit. In the English-language edition of his biography of Trujillo, Abelardo Nanita concluded in 1939 that the Dominican leader had "passed beyond our frontiers and is now known and discussed in other countries and continents, detracted or defended by a larger number of writers of world repute . . . [more] than any other statesman or personality in Spanish America."[224]

Roosevelt had a more general main concern: communicating the Good Neighbor policy's dual message of nonintervention and friendly reciprocity. He had success spreading the "good neighbor" slogan and its supporting rhetoric, but in specific bilateral cases the meaning of "reciprocity" was subject to conflicting interpretations. Such a disagreement over what were the benefits of the Good Neighbor policy prevented the Dominican Republic and the United States from improving relations before the eve of World War II. Ernest Gruening evoked "the mobilized public opinion" of the American republics as part of his moral argument against close relations with "Dictator Trujillo," but the message of nonintervention central to the Good Neighbor policy would not permit such public criticism from the Roosevelt administration. Yet reciprocity did not necessarily mean vocal approval of dictators, either. British Minister Paterson summarized this U.S. policy quandary after "a large military parade" and baseball tournament kicked off the "pro re-elección Trujillo" campaign in June 1937. "Such manifestations" of the general's control, "coupled with the obligations incidental to the 'good neighbour' policy," might "cause the American authorities sufficient embarrassment to induce them to refrain from any serious" opposition to him, judged Paterson, even though Trujillo was "a thorn in the side of American interests."[225] The activist, personalist and, it shall be seen, viciously racist foreign policy of the Trujillo regime made such a neither-nor stance a difficult one to maintain for the Roosevelt administration, which was forced to reconcile Trujillo's acts of violence with the larger goals of hemispheric solidarity. The Good Neighbor policy's response to the Haitian massacre of 1937 is a prime example of the compromises with the Trujillo regime that resulted.

◆

# CHAPTER FIVE

Genocide Next Door:

The Haitian Massacre of 1937 and the

Sosua Jewish Refugee Settlement

In October 1937, the Dominican Army systematically massacred thousands of Haitians resident in the Dominican Republic. As the Roosevelt administration soon realized, the Dominican authorities had carried out a kind of genocide with "ruthless efficiency," apparently at the personal instigation of Rafael Trujillo.[1] Although estimates of the duration of the massacre and its death toll vary widely, it seems likely that twelve thousand Haitians died during at least a week of violence throughout the country.[2]

The Haitian massacre threatened to damage the Roosevelt administration's Good Neighbor policy toward Latin America by calling attention to dictatorship in the Caribbean area, where a generation of consolidated authoritarian regimes developed in the wake of U.S. intervention and the Great Depression. The carnage focused global attention on Trujillo, the strongest of the region's strongmen, whose brutality invited comparisons with Hitler and Mussolini. In fact, the event was part of the worldwide paroxysm of racist, nationalist violence from 1937 to 1945 that included the Rape of Nanking, China, by the Japanese Army (which began two months after the killings in the Dominican Republic) and the genocide of European Jewry by Nazi Germany. Trujillo's attempt to obliterate Haitian ethnicity within his borders was a Caribbean manifestation of the brand of militarism that precipitated World War II, but one that occurred within the zone of U.S. hegemony. The subsequent diplomatic standoff between the Dominican Republic and Haiti threatened to undo the work of the Good Neighbor policy in promoting inter-American cooperation.

The Good Neighbor policy had changed the tactics but not the objectives of U.S. foreign policy in the American republics, substituting the carrot for

the stick in eliciting cooperation. Stable military leaders, though not preferred, were assumed to prepare the ground for cultivating U.S. commercial
and strategic interests in their respective bailiwicks. Good Neighbor programs, which included regional consultation, loans, and military assistance,
tended in turn to strengthen the regimes.[3] But as the case of Rafael Trujillo
demonstrates, the dictators proved difficult, often impossible, to control.
Their ability to manipulate U.S. diplomacy for their own goals, and in fact
to set the agenda of inter-American relations, has been underestimated.
The Haitian massacre of 1937 is the most graphic example of the inability
of the United States to keep "puppet" strongmen on the string.[4]

The Roosevelt administration succeeded, however, in shaping the aftermath of the Haitian massacre into a seeming victory for the cooperative
Pan-American spirit it promoted with the term "good neighbor." This accomplishment demonstrates an unseemly variant to what Irwin I. Gellman
has called the "massive public relations effort" that was the "most funda-
mental innovation" of the Good Neighbor policy.[5] Seeking some unobtru-
sive resolution to the crisis, the Roosevelt administration abstained from
public judgments against Trujillo and advocated a settlement through international mediation. But Trujillo would not cooperate with multilateral
efforts to investigate and adjudicate the dispute, opting instead to pay a
cash indemnity to Haiti without admitting that the killings had even taken
place. Nevertheless, the Roosevelt administration cited this resolution as
a success for Pan-Americanism and the Good Neighbor policy. Trujillo's
international image, which the dictator took pains to promote, was none-
theless damaged by the massacre. To prove to the world that he was not a
"miniature Hitler," Trujillo offered to accept into the Dominican Republic a hundred thousand Jewish refugees from Germany and Austria. He
donated a parcel of land for the creation of a refugee colony and was re-
warded by well-publicized and uncritical praise from Roosevelt and other
refugee advocates. Trujillo then reneged on his sweeping offer to accept a
hundred thousand refugees; ultimately, only a few hundred Jews settled at
the Sosua refugee settlement.

## ON THE BORDER

The roots of the massacre lay in the markedly different societies sharing the
island of Hispaniola. Their relations have been tense and often violent. But
despite the recurring conflict, the arid, mountainous frontier has only im-

perfectly separated the Spanish-speaking Dominican population from the Creole-speaking Haitian population. By the 1930s, there was a large Haitian presence in the Dominican Republic, composed of two groups. One group was the predominantly male brigades of *braceros,* or agricultural workers, who contracted to work on the sugarcane plantations in the south and east. The seasonal migration of these workers began in the early twentieth century, regulated by the Dominican government for the benefit of the sugar companies, many of which were American-owned. The other, more firmly rooted group included families of workers, smallholders, and entrepreneurs established in the north and west along the border with Haiti. Many of these people were Dominican by birth, but culturally and ethnically Haitian.[6] Over the course of years, these independent immigrants and their progeny, who tended to be darker-skinned than the Dominican inhabitants, established a bicultural identity for the border provinces of the Dominican Republic.

The Dominican nationalism promoted by Trujillo emphasized Hispanic culture and demonized Haitian, African-derived culture. This ideology focused on Haiti's nineteenth century invasions and occupations of the eastern half of the island, and associated Dominican independence with the recurring effort to drive out Haitians. Despite past wars and war scares, the evidence of Dominican nationality remained less discernible in the west, where many inhabitants spoke Haitian Creole, practiced the African religions of *vodun* and *santería,* and circulated the Haitian gourde instead of the official legal tender, which was the U.S. dollar. Trujillo sought to "nationalize" this region by clarifying the boundary with Haiti and imposing on the eastern side of the border the kind of Dominican society imagined from the perspective of the capital. Trujillo's frontier policy was to change the racial and cultural composition of the area to more closely resemble the self-consciously Hispanic population farther east.[7]

Rafael Trujillo began to assert his control over the poorly demarcated frontier and the Haitian population in the Dominican Republic soon after taking power. His primary objective was to formalize the border itself, a process initiated by a 1929 treaty between Trujillo's predecessor, Horacio Vásquez, and President Louis Borno of Haiti, whose country was under U.S. Marine occupation until 1934. The 1929 treaty set up a mixed commission to determine the boundary between the two countries, but did not prevent occasional clashes and the threat of war during the first years of Trujillo's regime.[8] In October 1933, Trujillo traded border-town visits with his Haitian counterpart, President Stenio Vincent. Negotiations over the boundary and Haitian labor migration continued for the next three years, punctuated by Trujillo's visit to Port-au-Prince in November 1934 and Vincent's to Santo Domingo in February 1935. The talks ended in March 1936 with the signing of a boundary treaty, whereby the Dominican Republic yielded a strip of land in return for an unambiguous line on the map.[9] The U.S. legation considered the treaty to be the "major achievement" of the Trujillo regime to that point.[10] The University of Santo Domingo nominated Trujillo and Vincent for the Nobel Peace Prize, sending a petition to the Norwegian Parliament signed by members of the faculty, including past and future foreign ministers (Arturo Logroño and Julio Ortega Frier) and two future presidents (Jacinto Peynado and Manuel de Jesús Troncoso de la Concha).[11] Trujillo triumphantly wired news of the nomination to Roosevelt (who himself annually nominated Cordell Hull for the award to keep up the secretary's morale).[12]

Trujillo also sought to reduce the number of Haitians on his side of the border. He imposed a quota on the percentage of non-Dominican sugar workers that an estate could employ and deported Haitians who could not produce papers establishing their place of birth and nationality. The American-owned estates, supported by the legation, protested the quota on Haitian workers, and it was annually rescinded until 1937. That year, the Dominican government held firm in allowing only 40 percent of the workers on these estates to be Haitian; 70 percent Haitian labor had been permitted previously.[13] At the same time, eight to ten thousand black workers from the British West Indies were affected by new employment rules stipulating that 70 percent of sugar workers in the country had to be Dominican, encoded in the "Law for the Dominicanization of Labor."[14] It is unclear how many Haitian immigrants were rounded up and sent to Haiti under Law 1343, or how many found their way back into the Dominican Republic, but the new border seems to have remained nearly as permeable as the old one.[15] The restrictions came at the same time as similar legislation in Cuba against Haitian cane cutters, whose repatriation added to the problems facing depression-era Haiti. The United States also removed Mexican agricultural laborers from its territory during this period, further weakening its moral authority on the question of ethnic discrimination.[16] As a corollary to his effort to expel black Haitians from the frontier, Trujillo attempted to recruit white immigrants from Puerto Rico. He wrote to Roosevelt offering to take some of the "excess population" from that island

and interested Secretary of the Interior Harold Ickes in the project.[17] The Dominican minister in Washington, Andrés Pastoriza, repeated Trujillo's "firm inclination to supply land for establishing *colonias*" of Puerto Ricans less than a month before the massacre began.[18]

That this policy was not succeeding became clear to Trujillo during August and September 1937, when he toured the route of the "international highway" being built along the border. This firsthand inspection of the least "Dominican" part of the republic apparently convinced him to take drastic action against the Haitians, although the assault may have been planned in advance and then set in motion by Trujillo's order. Trujillo himself was one-quarter Haitian, from his maternal grandmother, and his uncle was coauthor of a book on the frontier, so he was not new to the issues of Dominican and Haitian nationality and territory.[19] Whether the massacre was spontaneous or premeditated, the dictator stated his intention to eradicate the Haitian presence once and for all at "a dance given in his honor" in Dajabón on the night of 2 October 1937.[20]

## THE HAITIAN MASSACRE

During the next week, Trujillo's forces attacked Haitians across much of the country. The army did not target those Haitians resident in the sugar colonies; but all of those found outside the cane fields, even Haitians who had lived in the Dominican Republic for many years or who were Dominican citizens by birth, they seized and killed.[21] Even M'sie, the Haitian gardener at the U.S. legation, "was one of the ones who apparently disappeared."[22]

Although the news emerged slowly from the frontier region of Hispaniola, the catalog of atrocities committed during the Haitian massacre was revealed to American diplomats, journalists, and the general public over the course of the following months. They learned that Haitians had been rounded up by Dominican soldiers and slaughtered en masse. The soldiers mainly used machetes, to convey the impression that local civilians had murdered the Haitians in their midst, although in some instances they were not so careful about appearances: they killed one group of Haitians in a courtyard between government buildings in the city of Santiago, and forced more than a thousand others off the pier at the port of Montecristi to drown. Many of the survivors who fled across the border to Haiti had seen their entire families murdered, the adults hacked to death with machetes or strangled, the children dashed against rocks or tree trunks.[23]

The death toll continued to mount for months after the massacre itself, during "a particularly cold and wet winter in the north of Haiti." One observer reported that the survivors "were destitute, sleeping on the ground in the bush. Many were suffering from wounds, as well as hunger and bereavement." By February 1938, "a great number of the refugees had died of exposure, malaria, and influenza. A great number, despairing of relief, had wandered off into the hills."[24] These unfortunates were among the first of millions of "displaced persons" of the World War II era, victimized by the racial violence that would characterize the next eight years of world history, dying painfully after being expelled from their homes. Any accurate calculation of the body count resulting from the Haitian massacre must include them, increasing the figure well beyond the number of dead conservatively estimated in November 1937 by British diplomats and Dominican government officials, who thought perhaps five thousand had perished at the hands of the Dominican military in early October.[25]

The new U.S. minister to the Dominican Republic, R. Henry Norweb, presented his credentials to Trujillo at the dictator's mansion in San Cristóbal just as the massacre was drawing to a close on 8 October 1937. In one of his first interviews with Dominican Secretary of Justice Julio Ortega Frier, Norweb inquired about the violence against Haitians. Ortega Frier, soon to be appointed foreign minister, "coolly asserted that the Haitians were leaving the Dominican Republic 'alive or dead.' "[26] Ortega Frier's comments confirmed Norweb's suspicion that the murders had been carried out "apparently with the approval of President Trujillo." Sumner Welles brought Norweb's dispatch on the "Slaughter of Haitians on [the] Northwest Frontier" to Roosevelt's attention on 19 October. Welles observed that President Vincent of Haiti had "behaved with an extraordinary measure of prudence" in the affair, which had thus far been kept out of the press.[27]

Roosevelt had several reasons to be concerned with this development and to proceed cautiously in treating it. The bloody animosity between the nations was "endangering the success of our good neighbor policy with special reference to the Caribbean," judged the new minister to Haiti, Ferdinand Mayer.[28] The threat of war between the two countries became increasingly tangible in the following weeks. Haitian Foreign Minister Georges Léger forwarded to Welles a telegram from President Vincent in Port-au-Prince, saying: "We are afraid here of an attack at any moment."[29] Minister Mayer also pointed out that the Trujillo dictatorship was of "the same ruthless character as that in Germany, Italy and Russia."[30] Trujillo's mimicry of Hitler's style of leadership was an alarming development; he had begun wearing a greatcoat and jackboots (unusual attire for the tropics) and had recently mandated that members of the Partido Dominicano, the only legal political party, greet each other with a kind of "Sieg Heil" salute instead of the usual handshake.[31] Minister Mayer advocated "putting Trujillo in his place" with "firmness and strength."[32] But Trujillo was a potential ally in the unfolding effort to erect a "Fortress America" against European fascism, and it was not in the administration's strategic interests to take a hard line against him, even though he seemed to be developing a Caribbean brand of the same ideology.[33] Instead, the massacre was treated as an opportunity to demonstrate the efficacy of hemispheric mediation and the Good Neighbor policy.

### THE U.S. RESPONSE

The State Department's first act in response to the massacre was to recall Minister Norweb from the Havana Radio Conference, convened to promote radio links in the Americas, and send him back to his post in Ciudad Trujillo.[34] The fact that Norweb, an amateur radio operator, had left for the conference at all is an indication of the shallow depth of his concern about the massacre, so long as it remained unpublicized.[35] But Sumner Welles made it clear to Dominican Minister Andrés Pastoriza that Norweb's "sudden return" was "at the express desire" of President Roosevelt, who wanted to send "his personal message" to Trujillo in that way.[36] Welles also announced to the press that Norweb was returning, indicating that there was "considerable concern" at the State Department over the "wholesale killing" on the border.[37]

At a press conference on 9 November, a reporter asked Roosevelt if he was "giving personal attention to the Haiti-Dominican trouble." With characteristic ambiguity, the president replied, "Yes and no. I am familiar with it as it goes on." He downplayed the fact that he had met personally with Minister Mayer before the conference and claimed that his meeting with Haitian Foreign Minister Léger scheduled for the next day would be a "tea visit" unrelated to the massacre.[38] In fact, the guests at the White House the following afternoon did avoid discussion of political affairs.[39] Even so, Dominican Minister Pastoriza responded the next day by criticizing the "unusual" interest shown by the U.S. government in what he termed a local incident and complained that such attention was contrary to inter-

American principles.[40] In a press conference of his own, Sumner Welles averred that the United States was vitally interested in hemispheric peace "on the grounds of the 'good neighbor' policy and the inter-American declaration adopted at the Buenos Aires peace conference, which asserts that any menace to the peace of the American continent is a matter of concern to each American republic."[41] Although the Dominican government asserted that it had not mobilized troops, and that it considered the "frontier incident without importance," the *New York Times* reported that the Dominican Army was massing at the border. In the midst of this charged atmosphere, the Roosevelt administration let it be known that it was "ready to help if [an] invitation is received."[42]

## THE HAITIAN AND DOMINICAN RESPONSES

Haitian President Vincent was reluctant to issue such an invitation for mediation. He feared that the Spanish-speaking nations of the hemisphere were opposed to Haiti and thought Trujillo's response would be violent were he to "lose face" with his Latin American peers in an arbitration procedure with Haiti.[43] The Dominican armed forces were much more powerful than the Haitian, and the potential for military disaster in the event of a war weakened Vincent's position. Minister Mayer felt "a certain sympathy for the Haitian point of view," which was that the United States "would not come to her assistance and save her from being overrun if Trujillo should carry out what doubtless have been continuous underground threats of what he would do if the Haitians did not settle with him directly." All in all, said Mayer, "these Haitians . . . have a real inferiority complex with regard to Trujillo."[44] The Haitians were correct in assuming that the United States would use no force on their behalf, but would be confined to "moral suasion and nothing else." As Welles wrote to Mayer, there would be no "visits of our naval vessels or gestures of that character," lest charges of intervention disrupt "continental unity."[45]

Haiti had been the most diplomatically isolated country in the hemisphere since the slave revolt that led to its independence in 1804, and the Haitians had no allies to call on for help should fighting break out with Trujillo's modern army and new air force.[46] Trujillo had promised to initiate a "judicial investigation" into the killings, but the chances of this being an impartial review were slim.[47] The man in charge of the inquiry would be the newly appointed acting foreign minister, Julio Ortega Frier, who was known to be "personally dedicated to a strong anti-Haitian policy."[48] He had made that obvious during an acrimonious session with Franklin Atwood, the U.S. chargé d'affaires during Norweb's absence at the radio conference, when "he thumped the desk and vehemently announced that if he had a rifle he would like to shoot some Haitians himself."[49] Haitian Foreign Minister Léger told Sumner Welles that any investigation conducted by Ortega Frier would be "a whitewashing." Léger thought the best option for the Haitian government would be to request the good offices of Cuba, Mexico, and the United States as mediators, despite the risk of rejection by what might be unsympathetic third parties. Welles advised him to go ahead with that plan.[50] Vincent accordingly cabled Roosevelt on 12 November asking his services as a mediator, and Roosevelt, invoking "the spirit displayed by all the American Republics in the Conference at Buenos Aires," agreed. Mexico and Cuba followed suit.[51]

Although Trujillo had said that he would welcome the counsel of the United States, the Dominican government asserted that the Haitian request for good offices "had come as an unwelcome surprise."[52] Minister Norweb, who had taken part in what a Dominican witness considered a "very cordial and satisfactory" visit with Trujillo soon after returning to his post, reminded Trujillo that his refusal to comply with the procedure "would aggravate the already widespread unfavorable publicity" of the massacre.[53] Roosevelt followed up with a telegram (published in its entirety in the *New York Times*) expressing his confidence that "the proposal for mediation would be welcomed" by the Dominican Republic.[54] In response, Trujillo characterized the murders as just another minor squabble "between Dominican and Haitian *campesinos*," no different from "the many that have occurred since 1844," when the Haitian occupation ended and Dominican independence began. He defined the problem as an internal affair involving illegal Haitian aliens, not subject to outside mediation.[55] While Roosevelt emphasized the part of the Good Neighbor policy that called for collective mitigation of conflicts within the community of American states, Trujillo stressed the other side of the same policy: the sanctity of each nation's sovereignty.

Employing this broad definition of what constituted interference in Dominican internal affairs, Trujillo protested American scrutiny of the massacre. He accused Chargé d'Affaires Franklin Atwood of giving "grossly exaggerated and distorted versions of the alleged atrocities" during Norweb's absence in Havana.[56] The Dominican Foreign Ministry complained that Atwood was "provoking strong feelings against the Dominican Government and trying to mobilize the Diplomatic Corps in order to provoke scandalous investigations" into the events on the frontier.[57] Asked to investigate this charge upon returning to his post, Norweb sided with Trujillo, even though Atwood's accounts were understatements of the actual events. Atwood, Norweb said, had "left himself open to being used," apparently meaning by the Haitian government, as a result of "incautious . . . unguarded conversations" concerning the massacre. Norweb, taking his cue from the State Department, preferred ameliorative diplomacy to disclosure of the atrocities. He decided that Atwood had become "a blunt tool" for the purpose of negotiation, and replaced him.[58] Trujillo had succeeded in removing one source of diplomatic agitation from the Dominican capital; he had already assured the silence of another potential critic in the U.S. capital. Haitian Minister Elie Lescot had been on Trujillo's payroll since his days as Haitian minister to the Dominican Republic. As might be expected, he kept a low profile during the controversy. Lescot later cooperated with Trujillo to destabilize Vincent's regime (with the help of General Démosthène Calixte, the Marine-trained former head of the Garde d'Haiti living in exile in the Dominican Republic) and was elected president himself in 1941. After their falling out, Trujillo publicized their damning correspondence, hastening Lescot's downfall in January 1946.[59]

## "TO PRESERVE OUR RACIAL SUPERIORITY"

Dominican Minister Andrés Pastoriza looked for common ground with the State Department. Pastoriza, educated in the United States and entering his third year at the Dominican legation, was an experienced observer of American social conditions and class attitudes. Gauging the circumstances of race relations in the United States and the likely perspective of the elite white diplomats he knew, Pastoriza suggested a different tack for Trujillo to take in his response to the offer of mediation. He thought the response should emphasize that "illegal Haitian penetration seriously obstructed the Dominican Government's aim to improve the low Dominican standard of living; to defend the clean, traditional customs of our citizens; to protect Dominican property on the frontier from Haitian bandits; and to preserve our racial superiority over them."[60]

Pastoriza believed that an "intelligent and discrete" explanation of these justifications would "incline the American people to our sympathy."[61] Pastoriza "amply expressed" the racial causes of the frontier bloodshed to Cordell Hull when they met on 23 November. He refused the offer of mediation and "insisted that the State Department conform with the Pan-American treaties and the proper nature of good offices which cannot proceed except in the presence of a legal question."[62] Hull replied that he was "extremely sorry" to see "the splendid progress" of inter-Americanism threatened by the conflict in Hispaniola. Hull said he had "long considered President Trujillo as one of the biggest men" in Latin America, "a big, broad-guaged man" who should offer better leadership for peace. The secretary listed his acts of friendship toward the Dominican Republic: he had gone to "great pains" to suppress the unfavorable *March of Time* newsreel; "had striven real hard" for a higher sugar quota; was "most anxious to cooperate" with the Dominican debt situation; and had "never lost an opportunity to show friendly interest in President Trujillo." Hull exhorted Pastoriza to accept mediation without further delay, advising the minister of the wisdom of extinguishing a fire while the flames are still low.[63]

Sumner Welles, who had known Pastoriza since the 1920s and could speak to him "personally as an old friend," was less patient than Hull with the Dominican stance.[64] In a conference with Pastoriza and Manuel de Jesús Troncoso de la Concha, a "special envoy" recently arrived from Ciudad Trujillo, Welles accused the Dominicans of dodging Vincent's demand for mediation.[65] Although Welles made his point, that meeting was dominated by Troncoso de la Concha; he spoke for two and a half hours, "expressing his hatred and that shared by his fellow countrymen for the Haitians."[66] Pastoriza, discerning the reluctance on the part of Cuba, Mexico, and the United States to involve themselves too deeply, advocated an informal meeting with the mediators. He hoped to convince them to put the pressure back on the Haitian government to accept the results of the Dominican investigation and arrive at a direct, bilateral agreement to settle the affair. This plan had the support of the Mexican ambassador, Pastoriza reported.[67] Now he proposed the same course of action to Welles, who reluctantly agreed on the condition that the meeting be held secretly.[68] Hull agreed more readily three days later.[69]

The meeting took place during the first week of December. Sumner Welles represented the United States in two days of talks at the Mexican embassy in Washington.[70] After hearing both sides of the story, the representatives of the mediating governments agreed that, since the incident had taken on an "international aspect," a commission should go to Hispaniola to investigate and prepare a report. The Dominican government, which had never formally agreed to mediation, gave no answer for eight days, then declined. Rebuffed again, the mediators then recommended that the Haitian government invoke the existing inter-American arbitration pacts, the Gondra Treaty of 1923 and the Convention of Conciliation of 1929, and essentially take Trujillo to court.[71] Mexican Ambassador Francisco Castillo Nájera confided to Pastoriza and Troncoso de la Concha that Haiti was on the verge of breaking relations with the Dominican Republic, an event that would be a disaster for Dominican foreign relations, and had been dissuaded only through the intercession of Welles. The State Department also had proof that the Dominican Army had carried out the massacre, said Castillo, although Welles had remained silent on that subject.[72] He advised the Dominican diplomats to accept arbitration without further delay in order to head off a crisis.

But Trujillo told an Associated Press reporter that "his mind was made up" and that he "would not budge" from his position. He "refused to use the terms 'good offices,' 'mediation' or 'friendly service,' each time correcting [the reporter's] use of such phraseology by calling it 'intervention.' " He accused Welles of "encouraging the other nations to take a hand in a matter which did not concern them," and he was quoted as saying that "if Welles were out of the picture I would settle this matter in fifteen minutes." He declared his willingness to "go up in one final blaze of glory," telling visiting U.S. Senator David Walsh in Spanish, "Before permitting that—'intervention'—I am going to set fire to the whole country."[73]

## GENOCIDE IN THE PUBLIC EYE

As Trujillo stalled, commentary on the Haitian massacre gained greater circulation in the press and the U.S. House of Representatives. *The Nation* called Trujillo a "miniature Hitler" and called for the State Department to conduct its own investigation and to sever ties with the dictator.[74] *Life* magazine ran photos of Trujillo and his victims with an article entitled "The U.S. Is Invited to Arbitrate a Massacre in Its Front Garden." The issue featured a Japanese Imperial Army soldier on the cover ("Fatalist with a Machine Gun") and contained several pages of coverage on atrocities in China, and on Hitler's youth program.[75] Representative Hamilton Fish of New York called the Haitian massacre "the most outrageous atrocity that has ever been perpetrated on the American continent."[76] Trujillo fought back with a full-page disclaimer, "published at considerable expense as an advertisement in the *New York Times* and *Washington Post*," claiming that the border incident was a skirmish between farmers and squatters.[77] The statement cited Dominican government census calculations showing that only 105 Haitians had died. A news report published in the same edition put the death toll at 8,000.[78]

Haiti's invocation of the Gondra and Conciliation treaties and the spate of bad press forced Trujillo's hand, at least temporarily. British Minister Paterson thought "the Dominican Government had entirely overlooked the existence of the Gondra Treaty, the procedure under which hardly seems very much different from the mediation to which they objected with so much verbosity," and now they had to go along with it or "increase by opposition the odium" for Trujillo already felt "in the United States and perhaps also in Latin America."[79] In order to avoid the appearance of guilt, Trujillo had to agree publicly to arbitration, which he did on 19 December.[80] He added a voluntary element to his acquiescence by offering an "Anti-War Pledge" to President Stenio Vincent as a "Christmas gesture."[81] Vincent declined the pledge, perhaps because his flaccid reaction to the massacre had stirred accusations in Haiti that he was "leagued" with Trujillo, and indeed his government was beginning to look "pretty wobbly."[82] The threat of a general strike in Haiti loomed on the day Trujillo accepted arbitration; Vincent strengthened his rhetoric in response, denouncing Trujillo's "mass murder" of his countrymen.[83]

Roosevelt, on the other hand, issued public congratulations to Trujillo for accepting the arbitration procedure.[84] Under the terms of the arbitration treaty, the matter would be investigated by a commission comprising four members, two nominated by Haiti and two by the Dominican Republic. Both countries named an American as one of their represntatives (Hoffman Philip for Haiti and Donald Richberg, a partner of Trujillo's lobbyist Joseph Davies, for the Dominican Republic), but these men were to act in a private capacity and had no affiliation with the State Department.[85] The Roosevelt administration seemed relieved that its "good offices" were no longer required and that its brief official connection with the controversy had ended. Sumner Welles emphasized to the secretary of the National Association for the Advancement of Colored People, Walter White, that the Roosevelt administration had washed its hands of the affair: "The United States Government has no connection with the commission and is without authority or intention with respect to the Haitian-Dominican controversy."[86]

As Welles's response to White suggests, the interest of African-American organizations in the massacre was without effect. In fact, Pastoriza believed that the attention paid to the event at the National Negro Congress in New York (December 1937) "could be beneficial to our case, because the racial division here is so marked, any hostile activity by the negro organizations could gain us the sympathy of the other race. So far we have seen no coverage whatsoever in the white press about this meeting."[87]

International pressure and publicity soon waned, allowing Trujillo to evade the consequences of the arbitration agreement. He offered to pay $750,000 to Haiti to settle the affair immediately, without an investigation by the arbitrators, and Vincent agreed.[88] This agreement was the result of "parallel discussions" by Haitian and Dominican diplomats in Washington and Port-au-Prince, and it was presented as "a *fait accompli*" to the arbitrators, who met at the Pan-American Union on 31 January 1938 to call the case officially closed. Minister Mayer in Haiti concluded that "fright plus venality" motivated the Haitians to conclude the settlement, which he thought would result in them "losing Pan American sympathy and gaining nothing substantially" from the Dominican Republic. He confided to Welles his belief that "these lads," the Haitians, "still have that perfect genius for making a mess of things."[89] British Minister Paterson in Ciudad Trujillo concurred that "the conduct of the Dominicans has been outrageous, and they practically got away with it, largely owing to the supineness of the Haytians. They have even managed to escape with a payment of $750,000 — or an average per Haytian killed of $150."[90]

Franklin Roosevelt responded with a public statement of congratulations to Trujillo and Vincent that credited the Gondra and Conciliation treaties with the settlement. The agreement, said Roosevelt, was "added proof, if such had been needed, that the peaceful solution of international controversies has become the established practice of this hemisphere."[91] He ignored the fact that Trujillo had rejected formal mediation and that no independent investigation of the massacre had been conducted. The irony was not lost on *The Nation:*

> Washington's main concern has been to prevent war between the two countries, and that is understandable. But what of its announced determination to prevent the growth of fascism in the Western Hemisphere? . . . A thorough official investigation by the mediators that identified and indicted the murderers of the 10,000 would have an

excellent effect on the little Hitlers of South and Central America. Instead Trujillo is now in a position to whitewash a major crime—with the concurrence of all "good neighbors."[92]

In the case of the Haitian massacre, Good Neighbor diplomacy meant not protesting the destruction of what one Dominican diplomat labeled a "miserable proletariat" of dark-skinned "pariahs."[93] The final U.S. legation account of the massacre claimed, one year later, that "no such ordered and cold blooded extermination of human beings had been known [in Latin America] since the days of the Conquest," yet Trujillo's punishment for the crime was confined to a dose of bad press.[94] The legation described it as "a bitter lesson" in public relations for Trujillo, who was said to have "little publicity sense."[95] But the resident U.S. diplomats underestimated Trujillo's resourcefulness and political dexterity, which enabled him to repair the public relations damage wrought by the Haitian massacre.

Trujillo's efforts to recoup his international reputation took several forms. First he appropriated $250,000 "to spend on improving the attitude of the press."[96] This effort bore quick results abroad, with favorable articles running in newspapers in Belgium and France.[97] The public relations specialist Robert M. Field signed a two-year deal with the Dominican government "to discourage and overcome adverse and unfriendly propaganda and to inspire and encourage friendly and constructive relations" with the United States.[98] He had his hands full with this task and turned for assistance to "a true friend . . . devoted to" Trujillo, meaning Joseph E. Davies. Davies accompanied Field on his visit to William Chenery, editor of *Collier's*, to object to his publication of Quentin Reynolds's "severely critical" account of the Haitian massacre in January 1938.[99]

Trujillo also repealed several laws that curtailed political freedom, hoping to remove "the stigma of dictatorship" that marked his regime.[100] He invited the chairwoman of the Inter-American Commission of Women to Ciudad Trujillo and promised to recommend equal suffrage for Dominican women.[101] Most important was his decision not to be a candidate in the elections of May 1938. It is significant that his speech to that effect was reprinted as a pamphlet in English.[102] Although this action was calculated as evidence that Trujillo was not a dictator for life, but a man "anxious to give up the burdens of office," it was carried out in a very transparent fashion.[103] Minister Norweb reported that Trujillo treated his successor, Jacinto Peynado, like a "well-trained house dog."[104] Legation reports also referred to Peynado as a "rubber stamp Head of State," and Sumner Welles thought Trujillo's relinquishment of power was a "comedy."[105] Peynado was "the most ignored figure" at his own inauguration.[106] Long renowned for the neon "Dios y Trujillo" sign on the roof of his house, the first noticeable action Peynado took after his transition from sinecure to presidency was to increase the size of the sign.[107] Soon afterward, he promoted Trujillo's nine-year-old son to the rank of general.[108] Peynado's vice-president was Manuel de Jesús Troncoso de la Concha, who had lectured Welles on the Dominicans' hatred for the Haitians; he became president when Peynado died in February 1940.

One element missing from Trujillo's efforts to repair the damage of the Haitian massacre was any expression of remorse. His new minister to Haiti exchanged "extraordinary" speeches with President Vincent upon presentation of his credentials. U.S. Minister Mayer was astonished by their words: "Rarely has profound antipathy between two countries been so thinly veiled at such a ceremony."[109] In May 1938, Trujillo himself delivered a speech during which he ripped the microphone from its pedestal and extemporized that he had been the only Dominican with the "inflexibility of will" to "confront" the "Haitian question."[110] Even the cash indemnity which was the basis of the Haitian peace settlement was not paid in full. In September 1939, Trujillo sent an agent to Haiti with a $250,000 draft on his personal account and $25,000 in "palm oil" to offer President Vincent a quick, quiet cash payment in lieu of the full half million dollars still outstanding, which Vincent accepted. Despite the "dubious circumstances" of the cash settlement and the "scandalized" reaction in Haiti, U.S. Minister Norweb was glad to be rid of the "five-cornered headache" of the indemnity.[111] The payment gave Trujillo his opportunity to mend fences with Haiti. He and Vincent met on the border to exchange "cordial embraces" in front of a platoon of photographers, engaging in what Norweb called a " 'forgive and forget' publicity show."[112]

Despite the carnage of the Haitian massacre, observers in the U.S. armed services continued to praise Trujillo for his maintenance of order. A visiting Naval Intelligence Division attaché believed the explanation offered by government officials he met, who claimed that Quentin Reynolds (author of the detailed article on the massacre in *Collier's* magazine) had fabricated the massacre after trying to blackmail Trujillo.[113] When Trujillo refused to pay Reynolds $10,000, the officer reported, Reynolds made up horrible details about murdered Haitians.[114] The Dominican Republic had its own breed of Holocaust deniers.

## "TRUJILLO, THE LIBERATOR!"

Trujillo seized on a value-laden issue, that of Jewish refugees from Hitler's Third Reich, as his most effective means of scouring his soiled reputation. In the spring of 1938, Franklin Roosevelt began showing interest in the plight of European refugees. Sumner Welles pointed out to the president that the problem would require "the cooperation of all interested Governments," not just the United States. Although the United States traditionally had been a haven for the oppressed when "land was cheap or free," Welles noted that the depression had changed the situation, and immigrants would now be a "burden."[115] His opposition to easing the restrictions against Jewish newcomers reflected the strong current of anti-Semitism that had long existed in the State Department. The climate of prejudice was such that Secretary of State Cordell Hull concealed his own wife's Jewish ethnicity out of concern that it would destroy his political career.[116] In response to the worsening repression, Roosevelt initiated a conference on the refugee problem to be convened at Evian, France, in July 1938, to determine which countries would be willing to accept exiles from Germany and Austria.

Trujillo used the Evian Conference to portray himself as a humanitarian leader, sending his brother Virgilio as a delegate to deliver a speech praising Roosevelt and to announce that the Dominican Republic would open its doors to Jewish immigrants. At the first meeting of the Intergovernmental Committee on Political Refugees in London the following month, he made the offer more specific: the Dominican Republic would accept a hundred thousand refugees.[117]

The idea of settling Jewish refugees in the Dominican Republic was not a new one. Latin American expert Samuel Guy Inman had visited Santo Domingo in February 1935, to ask about such a possibility, and in January 1937 Dr. Howard Blake had come on behalf of the American Jewish Congress for the same reason. Trujillo expressed interest in the plan, especially after Blake pointed out some of the potential benefits that would accrue to Trujillo: "Trujillo, the Emancipator! Trujillo, the Liberator! . . . Who would be the first to buy your tobacco? The Jews! Your coffee? The Jews! Everything that you can export? The everlastingly grateful Jew!"[118]

Jewish immigration would also tie in with Trujillo's "ruthless demographic policy," which Laurence Duggan of the State Department judged to be "the root" of the Haitian massacre.[119] Trujillo continued to be interested in attracting light-skinned immigrants to replace Haitian and West Indian laborers in his country, and he asked the Roosevelt administration to loan him a team of immigration experts to draft a law that would "facilitate 'neo-white' immigration."[120] Cordell Hull honored Trujillo's request and sent two Labor Department officials to conduct a study and suggest legislation.[121] They stayed in the Dominican Republic for a year, helping to draft a racist immigration law.[122] Trujillo also invited refugees from the Spanish Civil War as part of the same initiative.[123] Jewish immigration was even more attractive than Puerto Rican and Spanish, however, since it promised to ingratiate Trujillo with Roosevelt and with the participants in the Intergovernmental Committee on Political Refugees.

The U.S. legation in Ciudad Trujillo was highly skeptical of Trujillo's offer to settle as many as a hundred thousand Jewish exiles. It reported that, in the four months after the offer was made in London, the Dominican government had approved only twenty out of two thousand visa applications from Jewish refugees.[124] Despite Trujillo's guarantees, the legation believed he would "be willing to take in only a handful of carefully selected immigrants whose services will be of particular value."[125] Secretary of Legation Robert Mills McClintock discerned that "the participation of the Dominican Republic on [the intergovernmental] committee . . . was largely an attempt on the part of General Trujillo to make a show of cooperating in a policy sponsored by the United States."[126] Despite the legation's unfavorable judgments, Roosevelt decided to pursue the possibility of the Dominican Republic becoming a "supplemental Jewish homeland."[127] Welles "discouraged" Haiti's simultaneous offer to accommodate fifty thousand refugees.[128]

THE SOSUA REFUGEE SETTLEMENT

In the spring of 1939, Roosevelt's Advisory Committee on Political Refugees sent "a mission of technical experts" named by Isaiah Bowman, president of Johns Hopkins University, "to study the possibilities of refugee colonization in the Dominican Republic."[129] Roosevelt envisioned an "experimental settlement by carefully selected and supervised pioneering groups along Civilian Conservation Corps lines," and the technical mission recommended this plan after six weeks of study in the Dominican

Republic.[130] The mission was "given active assistance by the Dominican Government" in its survey of potential locations for a refugee colony. Roosevelt's advisory committee responded favorably to the prospects, and it entrusted negotiations with Trujillo to James Rosenberg, formerly head of Agro-Joint, a refugee organization that settled Russian Jews in Crimea after World War I.[131] Rosenberg formed the Dominican Republic Settlement Association (DORSA) to coordinate the effort and deal directly with Trujillo, who had begun to appear apprehensive that "Jews would overrun the country."[132] Foremost on Trujillo's mind at his first meeting with Rosenberg (held in Washington during October 1939) was his hope that Roosevelt would make a statement extolling Dominican generosity. Urged by Rosenberg to "pay proper tribute" to Trujillo, Roosevelt agreed to deliver a statement praising Trujillo two days later.[133] The Intergovernmental Committee on Political Refugees also commended Trujillo, although it persisted in its error of calling the Dominican Republic "Dominica."[134] A week later, Rosenberg gave a luncheon honoring Trujillo that was attended by Assistant Secretary of State Adolph Berle and several officials of the refugee committees, and he publicized it with a press release.[135]

The subsequent establishment of the Sosua refugee settlement was a public relations coup for Rafael Trujillo.[136] After DORSA concluded its agreement with the Dominican government, the *New York Herald Tribune* printed Rosenberg's cable of "praise to Trujillo" almost verbatim.[137] Rosenberg also coordinated press releases and worked with Paramount News to produce a newsreel and short film about the "amazingly human story" of Sosua. The films made about Sosua downplayed the Jewish ethnicity of its population, calling it a "non-sectarian venture" with "settlers drawn from Europe's heterogeneous stocks."[138] Even *The Nation,* which usually took the lead in criticizing Trujillo, praised the advent of Sosua, possibly because its new editor, Freda Kirchway, was a friend of Rosenberg.[139] Roosevelt himself declared that the establishment of Sosua "marks concrete progress in the realization of the Evian [Conference refugee] program."[140] Only the Yiddish press in New York was apprehensive about the project.[141]

But the refugees came in dribbles, not in waves. The Sosua colony never reached a population of more than several hundred Jewish inhabitants at any point, and those who came experienced privations that belied the glowing language of the DORSA publicity.[142] Few people outside the U.S. legation noticed when Trujillo suspended visas to all refugees except for those committed to Sosua.[143] In fact, James Rosenberg was instrumental in limiting immigration to those "under the DORSA contract . . . no matter how much money they are able to provide, and no matter what excellent people they are."[144] Ironically, the settlement's rigorous selectivity in some ways resembled the discrimination that Jews faced in Europe; in refusing entry to an applicant in Berlin, Rosenberg regretted that "the Settlement is for young and strong people."[145]

Sosua remained an anomalous showcase of humanitarianism exhibited to the world against a backdrop of repression. Visiting the area in summer 1940, the U.S. minister found "it difficult to believe that a group of white settlers will be able to fare any better than the Dominican peasant through working with their hands in the fields under the tropical sun."[146] The settlement of 235 Jewish refugees in Sosua by 1941 received nearly as much press as the murder of untold thousands of Haitians that had motivated it.[147] There were still only about 500 refugees living there in 1944, few with agricultural backgrounds, and the U.S. ambassador thought the "long-term prospects for the colony are not encouraging." All but 100 of the immigrants lived in barracks in the section of Sosua known as "El Batey," ironically named for the quarters occupied by Haitian cane cutters on a sugar plantation.[148]

## CONCLUSIONS

The conjunction between the Haitian massacre and the Sosua refugee settlement demonstrates how Roosevelt's Good Neighbor policy could reconfigure the violence and cynicism of Caribbean dictatorships to fit under the rubric of Pan-American solidarity. In this scenario, selective use of publicity portrayed Trujillo as a cooperative member of the inter-American community and a savior of Jewish refugees, images that implied success for both Good Neighbor diplomacy and Roosevelt's international refugee initiatives. By playing down and to some extent concealing, the genocidal offensive against Haitians and the failure of the Sosua settlement, the Roosevelt administration not only avoided a diplomatic rupture with the Dominican Republic, it furthered the cause of regional solidarity just when the impending war in Europe underlined its importance. This remarkably dexterous manipulation of the events masked two unattractive truths about U.S. foreign relations.

First, the reliance on dictators to attain the traditional U.S. goals of stability and cooperation in Latin America meant having to ignore those instances when the strongmen themselves incited unrest and conflict. Their inclination to pursue agendas disruptive of regional harmony or threatening to U.S. hegemony tested the flexibility of the Good Neighbor policy. The extent to which the policy was altered to meet and absorb the Haitian massacre highlights the paradoxical nature of the Roosevelt administration's relations with intolerant military regimes. In this case, Trujillo violently achieved his "ruthless demographic policy," inviting war with Haiti and disdaining the Good Neighbor policy, and in turn was praised by Roosevelt for his neighborly spirit and was loaned a team of immigration experts. He then reaped a bumper crop of good will for the empty gesture to Jewish refugees known as the Sosua settlement. Converting the substance of these actions to something useful for U.S. interests required Roosevelt's talent for public relations alchemy. Along the way, Trujillo had demonstrated his own abilities as a "spin doctor." His regime sustained relatively minor damage in the realm of foreign and public relations because of his understanding of the media, his employment of personal influence in the highest circles of American government, and his references to national sovereignty (a central tenet of the Good Neighbor policy) as an argument to counteract international pressure.

Second, the ability of Roosevelt and Trujillo to transform the Haitian massacre and the Sosua settlement into diplomatic victories was partly owing to the racial and ethnic parameters of the issue. Dominican Minister Andrés Pastoriza correctly discerned that general apathy toward the murdered Haitians was the likely reaction of State Department officials and the "white press." Outrage was expressed in cables by a few diplomats on both sides of the border in Hispaniola, in articles by a few journalists like Quentin Reynolds, and in speeches by a few northern congressmen like Hamilton Fish, but otherwise interest in the massacre was fleeting.[149] The official Dominican version of events, which hinged on racial fears and claims of self-defense, seems to have found considerable acceptance in the United States, although for a country unable to pass an antilynching law this might not be too surprising. Nor should the lack of scrutiny into the pitifully small number of Jewish refugees allowed to come to Sosua be unexpected, given the anti-Semitism prominent in U.S. government circles.

The Dominican version of the event was restated in an article on the Sosua settlement published in the *New York Times* in February 1940, and implicitly linked the issues of Haitian and Jewish residence in the Dominican Republic. The account noted that "the olive-skinned Dominicans are outnumbered, three million to one and a half million, by the black and mulatto Haitians. [The Dominicans] are mostly of Spanish blood, with slight Indian and Negro strains." The "old enmity" between the two cultures was said to have "flared up in 1937, when thousands of Haitian squatters were killed and driven out of the Dominican Republic."[150] The "black and mulatto" Haitians living on the eastern side of the border were thus defined as outsiders threatening to demographically inundate the "outnumbered" Dominicans. But the Dominican Republic, home to an "olive-skinned" population, was depicted as a congenial place of refuge for the Jews. As in other accounts of Sosua, the small number of settlers and the criteria for their admission were not emphasized. With the United States having declined to increase its own admission of Jewish refugees, the guilt-assuaging symbolism of the Sosua settlement made better copy than its unimpressive reality. The Roosevelt administration seems to have accepted, if not vocalized, the newspaper's construction of events; namely, that the Haitian massacre was regrettable but understandable, and the Sosua settlement was a gift from an unlikely benefactor where the issue of Jewish refugees, if not the refugees themselves, could conveniently be placed.

Rafael Trujillo posed for this inauguration portrait in the Parisian gold braid he wore for his August 1930 "coronation." (Box 200-DD, RG 208-PU, Still Photography Division, National Archives, Washington, D.C.)

This panorama of the city of Santo Domingo was taken at about the time it became Ciudad Trujillo, in January 1936. The view was to the east toward the Ozama River and port; in the right foreground one can see the hulk of the U.S. Navy cruiser *Memphis,* wrecked by a tidal wave at the time of the 1916 U.S. Marine invasion. Avenida George Washington was under construction along the coast. (Photo contained in Pulliam to Welles, January–August 1936, Folder 14, Box 147, Welles Papers, Franklin D. Roosevelt Presidential Library, Hyde Park, N.Y.)

This scaled-down replica of the Washington Memorial was situated in the center of Avenida George Washington. The accompanying photo of the city was taken from the top of the obelisk, dedicated in honor of Trujillo during the elaborate Washington's Birthday celebrations of February 1936. (Photo contained in Pulliam to Welles, January–August 1936, Folder 14, Box 147, Welles Papers, Franklin D. Roosevelt Presidential Library, Hyde Park, N.Y.)

*President Trujillo inaugurating Avenida George Washington, Santo Domingo, Feb. 22, 1936*

At the inauguration of Avenida George Washington and the Trujillo obelisk, Minister H. F. Arthur Schoenfeld stood in his wool morning coat and striped pants, surrounded by Dominican military brass, while President Trujillo read a speech evoking Pan-American ideals. To mark the occasion, the minister and his wife hosted a Washington's Birthday reception for five hundred guests at their small official residence.

Arthur and Aïda Schoenfeld also attended mass rallies convened by Trujillo, known as *revistas cívicas,* or "Civic Reviews"; these were organized by the Partido Dominicano, the only legal political party, and were attended by tens of thousands of Dominicans. At this rally near Santo Domingo in March 1933, Trujillo led a long cavalcade through the heart of the throng toward the reviewing stand, where the U.S. minister and other dignitaries awaited the beginning of speeches. Trujillo is visible on his horse at the head of the column, saluting in a straw boater hat.

Trujillo welcomed Eleanor Roosevelt during her brief visit to the water airport in San Pedro de Macorís in March 1934, when her Pan American Airways "Clipper" to Puerto Rico stopped to refuel. Always alert to such opportunities to court the favor of a VIP, especially anyone with the magical surname "Roosevelt," Trujillo hosted an official luncheon that the First Lady could not refuse. Trujillo's wife Bienvenida, whom Aïda Schoenfeld befriended and taught bridge, stood beside him.

Other influential people came by sea. Most notable of these was Trujillo's power-ful lobbyist, Joseph Davies, and his wife, the former Marjorie Meriweather Post, aboard their yacht *Sea Cloud,* which required a crew of seventy-two to sail. For this photo, taken in Samaná Bay in March 1936, Trujillo and Mrs. Davies posed with Arthur Schoenfeld (*far right*) and Dominican Foreign Minister Roberto Despradel (*far left*). The girl is Betty Hutton, the future wife of Trujillo's diplomat, sidekick, and erstwhile son-in-law Porfirio Rubirosa.

The American Colony in Ciudad Trujillo posed for this Christmas photo in 1936. This group of the most prominent expatriate U.S. citizens in the capital were attending a holiday reception offered by General Receiver of Dominican Customs William Pulliam, who, as a resident for most of the time since 1907, had earned the title "Dean of the American Colony." The photographer placed the host in the second row (*wearing bow tie*), flanked by his wife on his left and Aïda Schoenfeld on his right, and near the U.S. minister (*in double-breasted jacket*). The guests included other diplomats, the managers of banks, sugar estates, the electric company, and the brewery, and their wives.

The American Colony also included numerous children, some of whom attended this costume birthday party in 1936. Aïda Schoenfeld helped to establish a school for Anglo-American children, an improvement on correspondence schooling. During World War II, U.S. Ambassador Avra Warren sent his son to the Haina Military Academy, Trujillo's alma mater, established by the U.S. Marines in 1919.

Social life in Ciudad Trujillo revolved around its private clubs, none more prominent than the Santo Domingo Country Club, "El Country Club," founded during
the Marine occupation. Members of the American Colony and the Dominican *alto
mundo,* or high society, dominated its membership rolls. As president of the club,
Minister Schoenfeld was expected to organize festivities for Trujillo's birthday,
along with the presidents of the other clubs in the capital. The Santo Domingo
Country Club (which did not change its name along with the city) had a golf
course and a new, fresco-decorated bar, constructed the year Mrs. Schoenfeld took
this picture. (All from photograph album of the Schoenfeld family, 1931–37, private
collection.)

The main street of the Sosua Jewish Refugee Settlement appeared in the Paramount News film *Sosua: Haven in the Caribbean* (1941), produced as part of Trujillo's public relations campaign to recoup his international prestige after the Haitian massacre of 1937. (Photo from Paramount News, 20 February 1941, v. 41, no. 51, *Sosua: Haven in the Caribbean*, Paramount Pictures, National Archives, Washington, D.C.)

Although Trujillo offered to accept a hundred thousand refugees from Nazi Germany, only some hundreds were permitted to enter the country and settle at Sosua, where most lived in barracks in a section of town known as "El Batey," named after the plantation quarters occupied by Haitian cane cutters. Publicity for the settlement played down the Jewish ethnicity of the refugees and highlighted the natural beauty of the 26,000-acre coastal tract donated for the project by Trujillo. (Photo from Paramount News, 20 February 1941, v. 41, no. 51; *Sosua: Haven in the Caribbean,* Paramount Pictures, National Archives, Washington, D.C.)

Soldiers of the Dominican National Army lined Avenida United States Marine Corps in their jodhpurs and field hats (remnants of the Marine occupation) when the road running along Puerto Trujillo on the Ozama River received that name in February 1939. U.S. troops marched in a parade that day, and the battleship *Texas* and a squadron of Marine aircraft performed war maneuvers for the crowd. (RG 127-G-51D515010, Still Photography Division, National Archives, Washington, D.C.)

General William Upshur, USMC, wore his dress whites and a row of medals to take part in the Avenida USMC festivities, along with U.S. Minister Henry Norweb (*left*) and Dominican Foreign Minister Arturo Despradel (*right*). First Secretary Eugene Hinkle, who befriended the Axis diplomats in Ciudad Trujillo while acting as chief of mission in spring 1940, stood behind Upshur. Hinkle's style of mustache as well as his name were reminiscent of Hitler, as Charlie Chaplin showed in his performance as Adenoid Hynkel in *The Great Dictator* (1940). (RG 127-G-51D528567, Still Photography Division, National Archives, Washington, D.C.)

Trujillo supplied this official wartime photograph to the new U.S. Office of War
Information, established to publicize the war effort, in 1942, the year he was re-
inaugurated (twice) as president. He carries a U.S. Marine sword and wears an
assortment of his military decorations. Trujillo sent an autographed copy of an
earlier version of his official portrait to Franklin Roosevelt, who reciprocated with
a photo of himself he inscribed "To my Good Neighbor, General Doctor Rafael
Leonidas Trujillo Molina, President of the Dominican Republic." (Box 200-DD-2,
RG 208-PU, Still Photography Division, National Archives, Washington, D.C.)

The first Dominican ambassador to the United States, Jesús María Troncoso (*second from right*), beamed at Franklin Roosevelt in the Oval Office in May 1943, when he and the ministers of Haiti and four Central American nations presented their upgraded credentials. Increased diplomatic contact was a hallmark of the Good Neighbor policy declared by Roosevelt, who beamed back for the cameras at this White House photo opportunity. The United States also elevated its Dominican mission to embassy status in 1943, with the diplomatic staff increasing from just a few, circa 1930, to more than forty, including several military attachés to provide advice and arms to the Dominican military. (Box 175-0-1, RG 208-PU, Still Photography Division, National Archives, Washington, D.C.)

The film actress María Montez is shown receiving the Order of Trujillo from the dictator's daughter Flor de Oro, first secretary of the Dominican embassy in Washington, at a ceremony in New York in October 1943. The press release announcing the occasion cited the actress's good effect on friendly relations between the United States and the Dominican Republic, relations that were advanced on movie screens, at gala events like the awarding of a medal, and in government corridors. (Box 138-Z, RG 208-PU, Still Photography Division, National Archives, Washington, D.C.)

# CHAPTER SIX

# Gold Braid and Striped Pants:
## The Culture of Foreign Relations in
## the Dominican Republic

Two cultural spheres characterized foreign relations with the United States in the Dominican Republic during the Trujillo regime. One was the world of the military, which included U.S. Marine and Navy officers who made occasional visits to the realm of their protégé, the Generalísimo. The other cultural sphere was that of the international Diplomatic Corps, the Cuerpo Diplomático y Consular, the most prominent among whom was the head of the U.S. diplomatic mission in Santo Domingo/Ciudad Trujillo. Those wearing the gold braid of high military rank and those wearing the striped pants of formal cutaway morning suits had differing experiences and points of engagement with the "court" of the dictator, the ever-shifting circle of supporters who constituted both the national government and the "high society," or *alto mundo,* of the capital. The extent to which these individuals shared values, vocabularies, symbols, and even wardrobes helped determine the tenor of relations between the nations.

### DIPLOMATS AND OFFICERS

This approach examines the cultural forms of diplomacy shared by representatives of the United States and the Dominican Republic between Trujillo's rise and his regime's full integration into a hemispheric military alliance with the United States during World War II. Its primary concern is the changing cultural content and meaning of the interaction between the North American metropolis, which during this period attempted to redefine the terms of its hegemony in the region through the Good Neighbor policy, and the emerging Dominican nation, which the consolidated

Trujillo regime similarly redefined. This chapter will examine the proto-
cols and rituals acted out by the inhabitants of Santo Domingo's military
and diplomatic spheres, especially during state occasions and "good will"
visits by U.S. Navy vessels, to demonstrate the multiplicity and importance
of social and organizational cultures in relations between states and within
the process of state formation.[1]

"Diplomacy," often portrayed as a unified and rational expression of
national political will, was incrementally determined by sets of institutional actors who competed both internationally and intragovernmentally.[2]
Individuals within formal, "total" institutions like the military and the
diplomatic ranks share identities, priorities, and modes of distinction that
amount to separate cultures, which they perpetuate by political means in
bureaucratic struggles with each other over power and prestige.[3] In the case
of the Dominican Republic, competing factions included the quasi-official
"court" around Rafael Trujillo, the staff of the American legation and members of the "American Colony" in Santo Domingo/Ciudad Trujillo, and the
bloc of Trujillo supporters in the U.S. armed services. Each faction operated
in its own cultural milieu and pursued different agendas which together
generated the "relations" that this study attempts to disentangle, define, and
evaluate. At times, the institutional cultures that shaped actors of different
nationalities (particularly the military cultures of the U.S. Marine Corps
and the Dominican Army) bore greater similarity to each other than to
the values of other actors of the same nationality but different institutional
backgrounds. In such instances, divisions of language and nationality were
mediated by associations of discourse, shared symbols, and modes of dress
and comportment. It is important to consider these factors in attempting
to trace the lines of influence along which "bilateral" relationships proceed.

The involvement of foreigners in the elaborate and well-publicized
events through which Rafael Trujillo defined his version of Dominican
nationhood was bound up in that definition, which required strong external references to underscore the transition of the Dominican Republic
from colonial domination to full sovereignty. The members of the Cuerpo
Diplomático, especially the representatives of the most recent colonial
power, the United States, dramatized that transition through their sometimes unwilling integration into Trujillo's official circle during numerous
public events celebrating the grandeur and autonomy of Trujillo's reign.
His regime, like the "court" of a *Carnaval* queen, placed the "ambassadors"

in prominent display to signify the approval of the nations they represented and also required their personal deference.[4]

The foreign military officers who visited Ciudad Trujillo served a similar function, the participation of U.S. Navy and Marine Corps representatives being most highly valued by Trujillo. The naval vessel is the most potent symbol in relations between the United States and the Caribbean, and although "gunboat diplomacy" pejoratively connotes U.S. intervention and domination in the republics of the Greater Antilles and Central America, gunboats have conveyed a variety of messages to Caribbean leaders, whose interpretations of those messages have been similarly varied. Although interwar U.S. policy in the region has generally been summarized as the replacement of aggressive "gunboat diplomacy" with ameliorative "Good Neighbor" relations in the early 1930s, the active participation of naval vessels and Marine Corps representatives in communicating that shift has mostly been ignored.[5] Especially as the threat of war became imminent, the "Good Neighbor" frequently arrived in the ports of potential regional allies aboard a gunboat.[6]

The symbolic power of a cruiser or battleship making a "good will" visit was a resource to be tapped and channeled by Trujillo, as well, often to the discomfiture of U.S. diplomats on the scene. As State Department ambivalence toward the region's dictators deepened, and as the contrasting urgency to erect a Fortress America against fascism intensified in the late 1930s, Navy and Marine officers took on a greater share of the diplomatic task. Their success in creating a regional alliance that included the strongmen of the Caribbean was owing in part to the military culture they shared with (in fact, had taught to) such leaders as Trujillo and Anastasio Somoza of Nicaragua. Presiding over the "new palace of the Interior, Police, War, and Marine," Trujillo was "in his favorite atmosphere, that of the military world," reported Minister Schoenfeld after an appointment with him.[7] In contrast, the appeal of the cosmopolitan diplomatic culture did not resonate as deeply with Trujillo, although his appropriation of the prestige and symbols of the Cuerpo Diplomático reinforced Dominican national sovereignty.

The cultural milieus of the U.S. Foreign Service and the U.S. Navy and Marine Corps came into conflict around the person of Rafael Trujillo. Rivalry between these branches of the foreign policy establishment was keen in the Caribbean region, with diplomats insisting on the ancillary role of gunboats and admirals vocally disapproving of the diplomats' frequent, bothersome calls for intervention.[8] Nowhere had intervention been more thorough than in the Dominican Republic, where the Navy Department exercised complete control and transformed the face of the country during the eight-year occupation. U.S. Navy and Marine officers who had apprenticed in the military government respected the accomplishments of its most lasting creation: President Trujillo. U.S. diplomats, on the other hand, disapproved Trujillo's brutal means of control and scoffed at his social background and at the excesses of his personalistic government rituals. This variance translated to a debate over how closely Trujillo would be embraced by the United States, often argued in the terms of those state rituals which were so predominate in the foreign relations of the Trujillo regime.

NAVY AND STATE

This debate over the how and where of relations with the Dominican Republic was symptomatic of a broader contest between the Navy and State departments over the how and where of foreign relations generally. Rivalry between admirals and ambassadors was nothing new, owing to the close functional relationship between ships and statesmen in projecting the country's presence around the world. Navy and State were harnessed together in this enterprise, but they did not always pull in the same direction. The Navy and its dependent Marine Corps were said to serve together as the "handmaiden" of "the architecture and objectives of American foreign policy," which originated at the State Department.[9] Implementation of national policy was the duty of diplomats stationed in foreign ports and capitals, who had the power of the Navy, symbolic and real, behind them. The art of "showing the flag" on naval visits to port cities was an especially useful policy tool for the United States during the nineteenth century, when it was a large nation with an active commerce and a small navy.[10] In times of trouble, isolated American ministers and consuls could call on the itinerant warships of the far-flung American squadrons to back their policies and protect the local American colony. But there was also a contending tradition in the naval officer corps of acting as diplomats on their own volition and carrying out epochal diplomatic missions without help from the State Department.[11]

This institutional contest intensified in the 1920s and 1930s as a result of self-conscious professionalization programs in the Navy, the Foreign Service, and the increasingly autonomous Marine Corps.[12] As the case of the Dominican Republic shows, these three services developed different conceptions of the proper design and agenda of foreign relations, with the military branches discarding their traditional ancillary role. The occupation of the Dominican Republic, along with other "colonial small wars" and experiments in governance in Haiti and Nicaragua, provided an important proving ground for the Marine Corps, helping it to survive as a force during the period of disarmament following the First World War, and to diversify into aviation and the early forms of counterinsurgency training.[13] Marine officers pointed with pride to having earned their "diplomatic spurs" during the Caribbean occupations, and they saw nothing amiss in maintaining their institutional and personal ties with military leaders in the region.[14] Naval officers who had been "gunboat diplomats" during the period also valued the experience from a professional standpoint.[15] They called for a more prominent role for the Navy in foreign relations, vying openly with blue-blooded diplomats. This contest was outlined by Rear Admiral Harry S. Knapp, former military governor of Santo Domingo, in a 1923 speech to the Naval War College:

> It can scarcely be claimed that the life experience of the naval officer is a broadening one in the way of general culture in literary and intellectual pursuits. But it is broadening in the practical matter of international affairs and a knowledge of foreign peoples. . . . Can it be believed that the average experienced senior officer—and only to such would the opportunity be apt to come—is any less fitted for diplomatic action than some citizen (in many instances chosen largely because his fortune is sufficient to bear the expense of representing the government abroad) whose previous experience in diplomatic life has been no whit greater than the officer's own?[16]

The following year, the belated professionalization of the State Department began in earnest with the passage of the Rogers Act to expand and update the Foreign Service. Adopting a selective recruiting process and instituting an extended apprenticeship "in diplomatic life," the Foreign Service tried to counteract criticisms, like Knapp's, that the average diplomat was just "some citizen" with deep pockets. But the mystique of the worldly and refined diplomat was still at the heart of the Foreign Service, much of it based on the same cultural distinctions "in the way of literary and intellectual pursuits" that men like Knapp dismissed as superfluous to "the practical matter of international affairs and a knowledge of foreign peoples."[17] The professionalization of American diplomats accelerated rapidly during the Roosevelt administration, and the Foreign Service expanded to represent the country in three hundred fifty cities by 1938. This institutional development was portrayed to the public in the film *Uncle Sam — The Good Neighbor,* commissioned by the State Department and released that year. Opening with a montage of exotic locales and the image of a Foreign Service officer and his wife greeting guests in a receiving line, the film explained that the diplomat's "most important job is to make friends for his country." In response to the global problems of the 1930s, the Roosevelt administration had been "building up a trained and skilled diplomatic service" of "handpicked men," the movie explained, accepting only twenty-five out of a thousand. After "tasting routine" for a time in a consular appointment, the rising Foreign Service officer "studies diplomatic procedure and the art of protocol" at the State Department's "post-graduate school." The film illustrated the career of a diplomat in a series of tableaux, one of them showing a consul conferring with a naval officer on the evacuation of a threatened American colony, leaving little doubt as to which of the two was calling the shots.[18] The cultural and jurisdictional friction between the diplomatic and military services was further intensified in the Dominican Republic because of the nature and the foreign policy of the Trujillo regime.

The diplomats, who were extensively choreographed in the pageantry of *trujillismo,* frequently opposed U.S. participation in such legitimizing public displays of affection. Specifically, they opposed naval visits to Santo Domingo/Ciudad Trujillo and Trujillo's desire to visit Washington. For most of the 1930s they were successful in this dual effort; naval visits were few during the early years of Trujillo's rule, and his persistent solicitations of an invitation to Washington were rebuffed. But as the danger of war in Europe became imminent in the later part of the decade, the criteria of the Good Neighbor policy in selecting allies loosened, and Caribbean leaders with fascist proclivities were actively wooed into the alliance against their European counterparts. Naval visits became an important role for the Caribbean Special Service Squadron, which previously had been concerned mainly with responding to distress calls from U.S. diplomats in Central America and Cuba, and Ciudad Trujillo became a frequent stop. State Department objections to Trujillo visiting Washington also were overcome by insistence from his Marine mentors that they be allowed to reciprocate his generous hospitality to visiting Navy and Marine officers. He made the first of many visits to the United States in 1939, and was entertained in the capital almost exclusively by military men at military events and spaces. The military relationship between the two countries subsequently flourished during the Second World War. Latent disapproval of Trujillo within the State Department would resurface as the war waned, when Trujillo was denied arms purchases partly because of the undemocratic nature of his rule and partly because he had offended an American diplomat at a state dinner. Thereafter, Trujillo often portrayed diplomats as traitors to the Pan-American cause, but extolled U.S. military men as good neighbors. The roots of this dichotomy can be traced to the early years of the Trujillo regime.

## THE "HOST SOCIETY"

The Diplomatic Corps was prominent in the high society, or *alto mundo*, of Santo Domingo before Trujillo seized power in 1930. Under Horacio Vásquez and during the tense interregnum of Rafael Estrella Ureña, diplomats were prestigious decorations at state functions, which were the highlights of social life in the Dominican capital. Part of the tension of this period was owing to the social snubbing of President-Elect Trujillo at the galas preceding his own inauguration. His name was pointedly omitted from *Listín Diario*'s account of the reception held for the Cuerpo Diplomático at the presidential mansion just two nights before his swearing-in: "as elegant a party as there ever has been," in honor of the diplomats and "those elements among the *alto mundo* in this Capital to whom invitations circulated." That edition of the paper carried photos five columns wide of the ministers of Cuba and the United States, wearing morning suits, and those of Argentina, France, and Spain, wearing full military regalia with plumed bicorn hats, standing on the steps of the presidential mansion as they arrived for the party.[19] Trujillo's social climbing had been noticed and discouraged by foreign diplomats during the previous year. British Minister W. H. Galienne reported in December 1929 that Trujillo "tries to usurp a position as a Cabinet Minister, and it is no uncommon occurrence to see him try to insert a chair for himself at official functions, so that he will be placed with the Cabinet, above the Diplomatic Body." The Diplomatic Corps collectively chose to ignore Trujillo's invitation to a "grandiose banquet" for himself a week after his election in May 1930.[20] Trujillo and his cohort were not considered part of Dominican high society, and so were disdained both by the "distinguidas damas y cabelleros" of the Dominican elite and by blue-blood diplomats like the Bostonian John Moors Cabot, who had characterized the political struggles of the February revolution as a class conflict pitting those owning waistcoats, the incumbents, against those without, who led the coup.[21]

After having taken the oath of office, however, Trujillo gradually gained control of the instruments of culture, as he already possessed the instrument of power, the National Army. The rituals of his inauguration day included a prominent role for the military, beginning with the Military Band and the First Battalion marching through the streets of the old city in the morning, then a full program of military drills by infantry, cavalry, and transportation units staged at the hippodrome for Trujillo's review, then finally the movement of these troops, eight hundred strong, down Avenida 27 de Febrero (the date both of Dominican independence and the Revolution of 1930) to Parque Colón in the center of the city. Having demonstrated the foundation of his rule, Trujillo turned in subsequent days to asserting his control over the Cuerpo Diplomatico and the *alto mundo*. One of Trujillo's first official functions, held a few days after his inauguration, was a repeat of Estrella Ureña's reception for the Diplomatic Corps and high society of the city. It, too, took place at the executive mansion, formerly the General Receivership during the occupation and now known as the "Presidential Palace" in the *trujillista* nomenclature of sovereign grandeur. *Listín Diario* noted that not one of the foreign representatives was absent from "la brillante fiesta," and it placed the name of U.S. Minister Charles B. Curtis first among the hundreds of guests listed in the coverage. The reception was followed by a banquet at the Palacio del Ayuntamiento [Palace of the City Council] where Trujillo was the center of attention, unlike the reception of the previous week. The guests drank "President Cocktails" and the members of the Cuerpo Diplomático were seated around Trujillo at the central table, although Curtis was inexplicably absent from the evening's festivities.[22] He made up for his absence by hosting "an intimate dinner" for Trujillo at the U.S. legation the following week.[23] Curtis had apparently dictated the times and places of his personal contact with the new leader, but this latitude grew increasingly constricted over the following months. At future events like Dominican Independence Day and the awarding of Trujillo's first foreign medal, the integration of the Cuerpo Diplomático into the military precise orchestration of state functions was complete. The arrival of groups of Dominican dignitaries was choreographed down to the minutest details with the diplomats in their hot woolen monkey suits always prominent among them.

Minister Curtis had been vocally opposed to Trujillo's candidacy and election, and he was known to be deeply sympathetic to the well-born Estrella Ureña and contemptuous of Trujillo's background, but he still had the responsibility of carrying out normal relations with the new government. Such was the case as well with Curtis's successors, most of whom developed a measure of contempt as a by-product of their familiarity with Trujillo's brutal rule. This responsibility was multiplied by the other roles expected of the chief of the U.S. mission: periodic service as the "dean" of the Diplomatic Corps and as president of El Country Club.

The dean, or *decano,* of the Cuerpo Diplomático was expected to be its spokesman, mainly as a proposer of toasts at the banquets and receptions that were the theater of foreign relations under Trujillo. The title was held by the senior diplomat in the Cuerpo, which included no full ambassadors and only a handful of ministers along with lesser chargés d'affaires and consuls, and it devolved rapidly to the U.S. chief of mission.[24] As formal occasions came to resemble precision-drill exercises, the importance of the dean as leader (and shepherd) of the assembled diplomats increased; and as it became apparent that the president could not, as his Marine mentor Colonel Cutts phrased it, "separate the official from the personal," the wording of toasts that invoked the good health and prosperity of both the nation and its leader also gained in importance.[25]

More important from a social and cultural standpoint was the central role of the U.S. minister at El Country Club, focal point of the American Colony in the Dominican Republic. The U.S. diplomats and their wives were automatically high-ranking members of the American Colony in the capital, a group that also included businessmen involved in the sugar industry, banking, the electric company, and transportation firms, as well as their wives and children. About one hundred Americans lived in the capital, and another two hundred or so resided elsewhere in the country, estimated Minister Schoenfeld in 1937.[26] His wife, Aïda, found it to be "a very pleasant life" in the city, where "there were nice people—Dominicans and Canadians and Americans, British, French—a little bit of everything."[27]

Schoenfeld's successor, Henry Norweb, had been minister in La Paz, Bolivia, and was disappointed that his transfer sent him to Ciudad Trujillo, instead of to San José, Costa Rica. Welles consoled him with two points likely to register with a career diplomat: "the Legation in Santo Domingo [Welles was slow to accept 'Ciudad Trujillo'] is infinitely more important than San José," and he would encounter there a "nucleus of cultured and agreeable Dominicans whom you will like."[28] Norweb was born in England and moved to Cleveland, Ohio, when he was thirteen years old; he later attended Harvard, joining the Foreign Service in 1917. He had spent years at the U.S. embassies in Paris, Tokyo, and The Hague, and despite Welles's assurances that the Dominican post was important, he still felt "like a clown doing little tricks" in a corner of the vast circus tent of world affairs, finding "Colony gossip" to be "the A-1 sauce of our daily life."[29] The foreign *colonias*—American, Spanish, Italian, and Syrian—were prominent in the social life of the city, with Casa de España and El Country Club being comparable to the upper-class Club Unión as centers for cultural relations between the expatriates and the host society. Trujillo's destruction in 1936 of the Club Unión, bastion of the old *capitaleño* elite, and his subsequent establishment of the *trujillista* Club Juventud, strengthened his hold on the cultural identity of the city.

The government also expected visible support from the foreign enclaves and foreign-owned businesses, and such obeisance was duly provided on Trujillo's inauguration day. The triumphal arches that decorated the city that day were erected by the Spanish, Italian, Syrian, and Chinese colonies and by the Eastern Sugar Association and the electric company, as well as by the two important hotels in town, Colón and Fausto, which were frequently the scenes of the "sumptuous banquets" punctuating social and official life in the capital. Among the city's clubs, El Country Club was the primary point of engagement for the American Colony, U.S. diplomats, and Trujillo's "court"; in this liquor-lubricated, cultural realm, the real work of diplomacy went forward. At the time of Trujillo's inauguration, Curtis had room at the old legation building for only a small dinner for the new president, but "el aristocrático Country Club" had the resources to throw "a glowing white ball" in his honor a few nights later. The social calendar of the capital, like the official one, was dominated by the figure of Trujillo, to whom the Country Club paid frequent homage. As president of the Country Club, the U.S. minister was expected to serve on Trujillo's Comité de Festejos pro-Natálico y Onomástico [Committee on Birthday and Nameday Festivities], along with the presidents of Club Unión, Casa de España, Club Nosotros, and Centro Sirio.[30] The Country Club was rebuilt and expanded in 1935, with "a most elaborate new bar including oil frescoes on the wall," thus increasing its attraction over the U.S. legation as a venue for interactions with the "host society."[31]

The financial resources of the U.S. legation were meager in the early years of Trujillo's rule, posing a number of challenges for its personnel. For one thing, the State Department budget had been cut by 25 percent in 1932, with the result that salaries and allowances for diplomats in the field were deeply reduced.[32] The budget of the U.S. legation in Santo Domingo was also strained by the need to keep up with the Trujillo regime, both socially and with respect to transportation. In the summer of 1932, Trujillo moved his entire government operation to the Cibao for special sessions, and Minister Schoenfeld found himself without the means to follow. He was advised by his supervisors in Washington to avail himself of "occasions on which he will be offered a ride by Dominican officials," athough they recognized that "the legation's prestige obviously would suffer . . . should he have to depend entirely on the kindness of other people for his transportation," and eventually some money was allocated for his travel costs.[33] Cultural events held at the legation, such as the Fourth of July and Washington's Birthday, were necessarily small, and cut into the personal funds of the minister.

The increasing budget of the newly professionalized Foreign Service changed the situation in 1936, when Schoenfeld received funding for the legation's lavish reception on Washington's Birthday. The expense was necessitated by Trujillo's Avenida George Washington extravaganza, which obliged the U.S. mission to reciprocate in some grand manner or risk insulting the regime.[34] With a $1,000 "representation allowance" thereafter, the minister was better able to attend to the three main duties of "representation," as explained by Schoenfeld in 1937: "attendance at official and semi-official functions; entertainment; and active participation" in the American Colony. "Due to the peculiarity of local conditions," he observed, "a diplomatic agent would have but slight personal relations with [Dominican officials] unless he entertains and cultivates them at his own residence, thus necessitating many luncheons, dinners, etc."[35]

By that time, the search was under way for a site on which to build a larger legation building (to replace the one where more than two visitors had to be squeezed in "with a shoehorn") as well as a new residence for the minister.[36] The result was an "imposing" new edifice, completed in 1939, "far superior to those of any other missions in the capital and in fact superior to any Government structure in the Dominican Republic."[37] The amenities of the new building increased the autonomy of U.S. diplomats in relation to Trujillo, who had said he considered the U.S. legation to be "an extension of his own house."[38]

Although Trujillo probably intended his comment about the legation being "his house" as a compliment, it must have been an unsettling thought for diplomats who felt manipulated by their expected participation in events that "turned out to be more political in character than international or social." U.S. diplomats made sardonic references to their public treatment from Trujillo, who once gave Schoenfeld an *abrazo* (hug) "for the edification of the crowd in the street" and who used the Diplomatic Corps as a "decorative backdrop" at distasteful ceremonies, such as the dedication of public works built with forced labor and named for Trujillo.[39] The ministers of Mexico and Argentina were also upset over their involvement in official functions that doubled as campaign events for Trujillo's reelection.[40]

### "ALL OF OUR ELEGANT PARTIES"

The conflation of the political, international, and social during the Trujillo regime is apparent in the Dominican press coverage of official entertainments. The accounts of these events detailed the elements of the cultural sphere of the capital, focusing on the dress, decorations, cuisine, music, discourse, and membership of the new *alto mundo* as defined by Trujillo. Front-page headlines trumpeted news of the latest "refined" or "splendid" reception and banquet, with the full dress ("traje de toda gala") of the president and his general staff described in fashion-show prose. For instance, at a Hotel Fausto bash on the occasion of Trujillo's return from Santiago in July 1931, the "social splendor" included decor designed by the director of the National Archives, "one of the most cultured elements" in the city, featuring the flags of all "países amigos" (nation-friends), a classical music program played by the Banda Militar, and a French menu including "Consommé President." The guests and the band then removed to El Country Club for a dance party.[41] The accounts often included the texts of toasts offered to Trujillo and invariably long columns listing everyone on the guest list in order of their government capacity, with cabinet secretaries, diplomats, and generals first. Trujillo's practice of shuffling individuals into and out of government posts was therefore reflected in their social standing as well, because their status in his official circle translated directly to the *alto mundo*.

The lead sentence of *Listín Diario*'s front-page story covering a reception in May 1937 demonstrates the extent to which fantasy came to characterize the image of the Trujillo regime and its foreign relations:

> The very elegant reception hall of the National Palace, the splendid and always marvelous Terrace of the Secretary of Foreign Relations, under whose ceiling of the thousand and one nights (*miliunanochesca*) love has so many times been woven with the mesh of happiness, was adorned yesterday evening, from five to seven, to receive our beautiful and elegant women, ambassadors of joy, who, honored invitees at all of our elegant parties, promenaded with aristocratic bearing through those salons, miracles of light in the madness of an afternoon of music, of perfume, of luxury, of the exquisite, and of emotions, becoming one with the beauty of the light.[42]

The article goes on to characterize the National Palace as a place "where everything abounds and nothing is lacking." The culture of foreign relations was presented to the Dominican public as something straight out of *The Arabian Nights,* populated by actual foreign envoys and by feminine "ambassadors of joy" and endowed with an inexhaustible font of champagne and "exquisite punch."

Another insight into the diplomatic sphere in the Dominican capital comes from the experience of Arthur Schoenfeld's wife, Aïda, who lived there with her husband and various of her six children for six months of every year during the five years "Turo" served as minister. This was an unusually long diplomatic assignment by Foreign Service standards, and the task of relating with equanimity to the Trujillo regime was delicate and taxing. Both Arthur and Aïda had a wide repertoire of diplomatic skills to draw upon, however, as British Minister Paterson pointed out: Minister Schoenfeld was a "good linguist," speaking French, Spanish, and German fluently, and Mrs. Schoenfeld was "very popular and a woman of considerable charm."[43] She recounted that Trujillo was "very happy when he realized" that she spoke Spanish, and her name, Aïda, was serendipitous: Trujillo had named his son Ramfis after a character in the Verdi opera (*Aïda,* 1871). Trujillo "didn't seem to object" when she would "call him 'El Jefecito' to his face, which was rather impertinent." Despite her bold use of this diminutive nickname for the dictator, she recognized the power the president wielded over her family and Dominican society: "we were under his jurisdiction, really."

There were many manifestations of this fact evident in the diplomatic life-style the Schoenfelds led, where point of protocol took on mortal significance and Trujillo's sexual domination of the elite was inescapable. One of her strongest impressions of the president was of "dancing with him one night somewhere in some party" and realizing he had a gun under his tuxedo, whereupon he stopped to show her that he actually had two. He always had a coterie of "henchmen," as well, sometimes as many as "fifteen or twenty making a semi-circle around him." To the minister's wife fell the sensitive task of entertaining Trujillo at formal dinners at the official residence, involving up to twenty-four people (the number that could fit around the table in the dining room). Trujillo sat at the head of the table, with Mrs. Schoenfeld to his right, and a Chinese butler served the food prepared by a Chinese chef. The "whole place was surrounded by guards with machine guns . . . and searchlights on us" when the president came to dinner. It was at such an affair that Oscar Michelena ran afoul of Trujillo, leading to his torture and incarceration. Michelena and his wife Teté, "a very good friend" of Aïda Schoenfeld, "were always known to be late at everything," and they showed up that night after the soup course, which Trujillo accepted "very graciously, but he didn't say very much." When the guests had departed, Arthur Schoenfeld told his wife, "I bet Mich is going to lose his job, having arrived late," which happened two weeks later, "and everybody put it down to the fact that he'd kept the President waiting, which he wouldn't stand for. Trujillo was very much of a military man."

Aïda may have influenced her husband's perception of the Dominican leaders with whom he conducted official business, offering the sharp observations of a hostess after these evenings with Trujillo and the members of his inner circle. Nearly fifty years later she could relate with detail her thoughts during a dinner party at her home, when she "couldn't help but notice" that Foreign Minister Arturo Logroño, a short man who weighed more than three hundred pounds, consumed four dinner rolls and put a fifth in his pocket. She charitably ascribed his action mentally to the fact that his wife was absent, "pregnant with her umpteenth child," and he might be taking it home to her. But since the rolls "were all buttered inside," she worried that "his very spick and span white linen suit" would not fare well in transit. Would it have been possible for Arthur Schoenfeld to make his next demarche to the foreign minister without thinking of this scene, and letting the humor and muted contempt it inspired color his attitude toward the obese official?

The question of which woman would accompany Trujillo to social events "was always a big to-do because he had umpteen mistresses . . . a couple of them so-called society."[44] The president's love life was entangled with the culture of the capital and with Dominican foreign relations, as well, prompting a British observer to comment that "the Generalissimo has a certain robust Tudor quality; his private life seems no less colourful and his statesmanship no less flexible and rigorous than those of Henry VIII (as performed by Mr. Charles Laughton a few years ago)!"[45] Mrs. Schoenfeld befriended Trujillo's wife Bienvenida (his second wife, the first being "just a peasant woman and he got rid of her very early") and taught her to play bridge, then watched as Trujillo divorced her while she was in Europe (the dictator employed a new law which permitted a man to abandon a wife who does not produce a child in five years after marriage). He subsequently "married one of his favorite mistresses, who had been a Cuban cabaret dancer," María Martínez. She was the mother of his only son and "was quite white . . . which Bienvenida had not been."[46]

Trujillo's period of estrangement from Bienvenida took its toll socially, since he had no one to perform the role of first lady and so was "unable to entertain socially the foreign representatives" to his second inauguration in August 1934. Before Stenio Vincent's visit to Santo Domingo brought another wave of social events, Trujillo fixed the problem with a law declaring the mother of the president to be acting first lady in his wife's absence.[47] After divorcing Bienvenida, Trujillo kept her as a mistress (she belatedly began to bear children), and despite consecrating his third marriage, he showed off new women at social events in Ciudad Trujillo. Mrs. Schoenfeld met one of the most famous of these, the 1937 *Carnaval* queen Lina Lovatón, "at a party one night [and] she showed me this beautiful diamond bracelet" he had given her, causing the minister's wife to reflect that Trujillo "must spend an awful lot of money on all these different women." Such was the unavoidable (and probably the intended) conclusion of anyone who attended events in the Dominican "court"; that is, anyone who noticed jewelry and picked up on the *chismes,* or hot gossip, about the president's love life.[48] Aïda certainly did, and so must have her husband through her, if he did not on his own. Minister Schoenfeld would not include items about Lina Lovatón's seduction in his official dispatches, but he may have thought about her diamonds when he protested the improvident spending of Trujillo's government.

Like so many who met Trujillo, Aïda Schoenfeld concluded that, in his case, clothes came very close to making the man. She knew of his humble personal origins, how "the Marines thought he seemed like a very sharp fellow and [how] they promoted him" to power in the army, and she met his parents, noting that "both of them were quite dark in color." Even so, she found that his personal style nearly neutralized his questionable social and racial status. "If you didn't realize his background, you'd really be quite impressed with the way he looked. Of course, he was always extremely well-groomed and very gracious and so on. But he was a real devil, that one!"[49] It took someone who had lived "under his jurisdiction," who had friends victimized by his cruelty, to see past Trujillo's "impressive" façade and make this critical judgment. Herein lay the difference between the diplomatic and military perspectives on his regime.

U.S. diplomats in the Dominican Republic struggled to assert their influence over what they perceived as an undesirable system of government and a problematic leader, without notable success. They took solace mainly in their prominence in the "modest but normally pleasant social life of Santo Domingo."[50] Lacking more tangible criteria for judging their effectiveness, the diplomats staked out their social turf in the capital and defended it against their military rivals, whose common experience with Trujillo gave them considerably greater leverage and influence with him. After prolonged daily exposure to the Trujillo regime, the diplomats perceived both ruthlessness and macabre humor in the Trujillo regime. But this was not the case with those military officers who had personal experience in the Dominican Republic during the occupation, who compared the state of affairs then with the order imposed under Trujillo, and who saw nothing humorous or repellent about it. On a number of cultural and functional levels the military men saw eye-to-eye with Trujillo, and their approval of his efficient means of governance was spontaneous.

### GENERAL TRUJILLO AND MAJOR WATSON

Trujillo's training at the Haina Military Academy and the Officers' School of the Northern District imparted to him the lessons of the Marine occupation: to construct public works, keep public spaces clean, and extinguish opposition. On a more personal level, Trujillo absorbed with great alacrity the Marine style of dress and comportment, earning his highest marks in the categories of "military bearing," "cleanliness of person and uniform," and "way of wearing uniforms and care of same."[51] These criteria of Marine approval were reflected in descriptions of Trujillo by his most productive biographer, Abelardo Nanita: "He is fastidiously careful of his person. Always clean, always tidy, well groomed, well tailored. He dresses with elegance and simplicity. His neckties are famous. His wardrobe could be envied by many a prince."[52] The evaluator who awarded Trujillo "excellent" ratings in looking the part of the soldier was Captain Thomas Watson, USMC, who rose to the rank of Lieutenant Colonel in the Guardia/Policía during eight years in the Dominican Republic and was instrumental in the Marine training program. Watson, a career officer from rural Iowa, made a reputation fighting the Dominican *gavilleros* as commander of the Forty-fourth Marine Infantry Company in 1916. Watson spent a good deal of his time during the Marine occupation inspecting the personnel and facilities of the Dominican armed forces, emphasizing the Marine Corps criteria of cleanliness and orderliness.[53] Watson subsequently entered the Guardia himself, serving first as recruiting officer and then as major inspector after 1920.[54] He received high marks himself from Brigadier General Harry Lee during the military professionalization campaign in the early 1920s, and he requested extensions of his tour of duty in 1922 and 1923.[55] During that time, he formed a close friendship with Trujillo, his star student, who was less than a year older than him. When the San Zenón hurricane struck, Trujillo officially requested the services of his mentor during the emergency; Watson's return to the Dominican Republic in September 1930 inaugurated the dispute between the diplomatic and military approaches to Trujillo.[56]

Watson, now a major in the Marine Corps, arrived in the midst of the personal imbroglio between Minister Charles B. Curtis and Trujillo, which the hurricane relief effort had served to intensify. In the weeks and months following the disaster, Watson maintained a delicate working relationship with both men in his twin capacities as naval attaché and director of hospitals and food, "extending the greasy mitt in the approved diplomatique manner."[57] But his sympathies were clearly with the man he had helped to train, as he confided in letters to Marine associates in Washington and occupied Haiti. At the outset, Watson reported to Brigadier General J. T. Myers, Trujillo had put himself back under his former superior's command, telling Watson: "I am now the Lieutenant and you are the President." Watson avoided getting into the expected "row" with Curtis by giving him "a little back scratching," and lunched with Trujillo daily, spending "a couple of hours at that time talking over old times."[58] He admitted he was "having more fun than a monkey with flees [*sic*]," diving into every aspect of civil and military administration, and dabbling in politics as well. "About every day I think of some other job I can take over and of course it is all right with T.," he wrote to Colonel Richard Cutts "the last one is the attempt on my part to mold public opinion along the right line. . . . Tomorrow I will see the newspaper men."[59] His movements thereafter were covered closely by the Dominican press: he took a *Chicago Daily News* correspondent (who arrived via Haiti with an introduction from Cutts) to visit Trujillo's birthplace; he distributed food and blankets to orphans; and his presence at all manner of social functions was reported as prominently as that of the U.S. minister.[60] The British minister called Watson the "Dominican food dictator," reported that "his exaggerated idea of his own importance as the right-hand man of a President is slightly ludicrous," and prophesied that "he will undoubtedly become a thorn in the side of the American Minister."[61]

Long after the crisis of disaster relief had passed, Watson stayed on in Santo Domingo as naval attaché, even though the Dominican Navy was "largely nonexistent."[62] He was technically a U.S. government employee assigned to the legation, but his office was in the National Palace and he lived in a house owned by the Dominican government "almost on the threshold of the President's residence" in "the 'compound' surrounding the presidential mansion."[63] In an indication of how drastically the sources of U.S. influence on the Dominican Republic had changed in a decade, Watson moved into the same "chalet" (on the grounds of the old Receivership building) that Sumner Welles had occupied in 1922 while negotiating the end of the Marine occupation.[64] From that base, Watson coordinated with his Marine contacts and members of the Dominican lobby in trying to gain the most important items on Trujillo's foreign policy agenda: a loan, favorable publicity, and arms and airplanes. Watson worked at cross-purposes to the U.S. legation on each of these counts, but he did so with such discretion that Curtis continued to praise "his very good influence" on Trujillo and to recommend that his service in the country be extended, while at the same time Watson harshly denounced the minister in correspondence and conversation with influential U.S. citizens.[65] For instance, at a dinner for the members of the Wadsworth Commission during their inspection visit after the 1930 hurricane, Elliot Wadsworth asked Watson what the Marines thought of the State Department; Watson replied that he was unable to comment, but later he let Wadsworth know privately "that we were sent to correct blunders of diplomats."[66] Invited to Puerto Rico the following month by Governor Theodore Roosevelt Jr., Watson told his host that "it would be better for me to have an old woman on the job" than Curtis, who lacked the "force of character to up hold the prestige of the US." Governor Roosevelt pledged to "go to the Secretary of State and if necessary direct to the President" to lobby for a Marine training mission for the Dominican Republic, and said he would report back to Watson "in care of Trujillo" so Curtis would not find out.[67]

Watson also kept in close touch with representatives of the three New York firms that had showed interest in a loan (Lee, Higginson; Ulen and Co.; and J. G. White) and arranged their accommodations when they visited Santo Domingo, although the deals he helped to foster were nixed by State.[68] Some of these same bankers were also active in the Dominican lobby and aided Trujillo's efforts to repair bad publicity in the United States. Judge Otto Schoenrich, author of *Santo Domingo: A Country with a Future,* exerted pressure on the editor of the *Baltimore Sun* to discontinue Drew Pearson's articles attacking the Trujillo regime.[69] M. D. Carrel of Ulen and Co., mindful that such "publicity isn't doing the bankers any good in their efforts to arrange for financing," recommended that Trujillo hire "an expert press agent here—to give the papers *helpful facts.*"[70] The new Dominican Chamber of Commerce in New York became just such a conduit of favorable information, assisted by men like Schoenrich and Carrel, both of whom also lobbied in Washington on Trujillo's and Watson's behalf.[71] Watson also had a penchant, as he put it, to "stick my nose into the running of the army a whole lot and in many other things that are none of my business."[72] He and Cutts advised Trujillo on what kind of arms and airplanes to purchase and cautioned him that "any money . . . for armament and equipment must not appear as such, or for that purpose," lest the State Department disapprove the sales.[73] In this way, Trujillo acquired his first airplanes and several small lots of rifles and equipment from the United States.[74] Watson and Cutts also helped Trujillo buy rifles from Spain.[75]

Although Watson's wife and children joined him in Santo Domingo and the family took a prominent part in the social life of the capital, the members of the American Colony in Santo Domingo complained that he was ineffective in "requesting punishment" for Dominican officers who had abused them, and it was reported that his sentiments were "all for the army."[76] Where Watson finally ran into problems with Curtis, however, was over the protocol of visits to the Dominican Republic by a pair of Roosevelts. In March 1931, Eleanor Roosevelt passed through Santo Domingo on a Pan American Airways flight and was met at the airport by a delegation including Watson but not Curtis, who was not informed of her brief visit. Watson tried to arrange an informal dinner for her when she passed through again a few days later, this time including the U.S. minister in the plans, but the damage had been done and "a mass of petty jealousies" replaced the trust that Curtis had previously held for his naval attaché.[77] Watson also took the lead in entertaining Governor Theodore Roosevelt Jr., with whom he'd been in frequent personal contact, ten days later.[78] Roosevelt, deeply enmeshed in the Dominican lobby by this time, had a number of issues to discuss with Trujillo and Watson that he did not want to share with Curtis, so he asked Watson to arrange a second, secret visit to the country that would allow such a conference. The chance came when Roosevelt was en route to Washington in May 1931; he met with Trujillo and Watson at the airport without the knowledge of the legation. Although the brief stay was not reported in the press, Curtis found out and was furious.[79] At the same time, Watson alienated William Pulliam, the general receiver as well as "Dean of the American Colony," by refusing to follow the guest policy and payment procedure of the Santo Domingo Country Club, leading to an ugly public scene between the two.[80] Pulliam complained that Watson was a "blatant rough neck type" and agitated for his removal, as did Curtis.[81] Watson's office of naval attaché was abolished in July, and Watson left the country at the request of the State Department in early August, leaving a bad taste for Marines in the mouths of American diplomats. The State Department also transferred Charles Curtis from Santo Domingo to San Salvador in July, a move that Governor Roosevelt claimed to have brought about.[82]

"THE MEMORY OF THE MARINES"

When Trujillo asked that the U.S. military mission to the Dominican Republic be resumed in 1932, the State Department drew on its experience with Watson in denying the request. "In view of President Trujillo's close affiliations with the Marine Corps, his tendency would be to rely on officers of that organization for guidance and support, instead of being guided by the American Minister and the Financial Adviser."[83]

After the Roosevelt administration came into office the following year, Trujillo employed an alternative to these unsympathetic diplomatic channels in attempting to reestablish the military mission. He asked a visiting Marine officer, Brigadier General George Richards (who was also a friend of Watson), to convey an "oral message" to the new president. Richards had first met Trujillo in 1926 and had received from him a ceremonial Dominican Army sword identical to the sword of the Marine Corps. The meaning of the gift was clear: "We cherish the memory of the Marines," explained Colonel Trujillo's messenger, "and we have adopted your sword as our sword."[84] Richards agreed to be Trujillo's messenger in 1933, going to the Oval Office to tell Franklin Roosevelt personally of Trujillo's "affection" for the Marine Corps. Richards wrote back to Trujillo that his affection for the Marines was shared by Roosevelt, who was an avid naval historian.[85] Trujillo then sent his request for a military mission to Roosevelt's relative, Assistant Secretary of the Navy Henry Latrobe Roosevelt (a recent visitor to the Dominican Republic), who conveyed the request to the president (who had previously served as assistant secretary of the Navy himself). Trujillo asked to have Watson returned, and President Roosevelt agreed.[86] Secretary of the Navy Claude Swanson subsequently announced that Watson and Lieutenant Gregon Williams, USMC (another close friend of Trujillo, who had served in his Guardia company) would be detailed to Santo Domingo, doing so without consulting anyone in the State Department's Division of Latin American Affairs.[87] The Foreign Policy Association protested to Roosevelt, reminding him that the presence of a Marine mission would be used by the dictator "to strengthen his position in the midst of widespread opposition."[88] Assistant Secretary of State Jefferson Caffery also reiterated the State Department's concern, first raised by Watson's cozy relations with Trujillo, that the position held by the diplomats in Santo Domingo was vulnerable to that of Trujillo's Marine comrades.[89] To Trujillo's chagrin, the military mission was belatedly scratched, and the Navy Department's fait accompli was defeated for the moment.[90] The position of naval attaché was eventually returned to the U.S. legation in the Dominican Republic in 1940, after the momentum of foreign relations had shifted in favor of the military approach.

In the meantime, Trujillo settled for the services of another of his former Marine associates, Charles McLaughlin, who had come to the Dominican Republic in 1917 as a sergeant in the occupation forces, then had remained in the country for a time after the Marine withdrawal before returning to civilian life in the United States. McLaughlin was working at a Cleveland steel company in October 1930 when he learned that Watson was back in Santo Domingo "in charge of relief work," so he wrote asking for help in getting a job with Trujillo.[91] Watson secured a position as an "efficiency engineer" for McLaughlin, his "former trusty helper" during the occupation, who then joined him in the Dominican Republic in December.[92] Soon after his arrival, McLaughlin became manager of the national railroad, beginning a lucrative second career; he later named a gold mine after Watson's wife.[93] After Watson's departure in August 1931, McLaughlin donned the Marine look-alike jodhpurs and ranger hat of the Dominican Army and fulfilled the same right-hand-man functions that Watson had, an embodiment of the military culture that Trujillo shared with the U.S. Marine Corps.[94] Robert Crassweller described him as "a man who moved . . . within a changeless nimbus of brine and bootcamp."[95] McLaughlin was Trujillo's military surrogate, his messenger, his companion on foreign jaunts. Rising to the rank of colonel, he became Trujillo's "trouble shooter," controlling all army purchases and "quietly getting rich," and he was credited with "help[ing] Trujillo to Americanize the Dominican Republic" in a wartime Naval Intelligence report. But the real control of the relationship was in Trujillo's hands; McLaughlin was in his employer's personal debt for the house he lived in, and Trujillo's brother Héctor was informally engaged to McLaughlin's daughter Alma. Although McLaughlin was married to a Dominican woman who "was not too white, herself," his "sensitivity on the 'color angle'" prevented him from approving a marriage between his "Dutch-looking blonde" daughter and Héctor, better known as "Negro," who had "rather pronounced negroid features."[96] His attempts "to leave the employ of the President" and return to the United States with his daughter were unsuccessful, though, and instead he became a Dominican citizen in 1956. Alma McLaughlin finally married Héctor Trujillo in 1959.[97]

### "GOOD WILL" GUNBOATS

Visits from U.S. military men to the Dominican Republic were few during the early years of Trujillo's tenure. The USS *Sacramento* made the first call to Santo Domingo after the 1930 revolution, arriving in June, when Trujillo was president-elect. The brief visit was notable mainly for the opportunity it afforded the press to compare it with the same cruiser's call in 1916, when it came to bombard Puerto Plata, and for the 23–1 drubbing of the ship's baseball squad by the Dominican Army's "Estrellas [Stars] Dominicanas" team in front of a large crowd. It was two years before another naval vessel called, this time the *Raleigh* with Assistant Navy Secretary H. L. Roosevelt aboard. Trujillo honored Roosevelt with a gesture that would become a regular feature in the itineraries of visiting dignitaries: that of removing

and opening the box in the National Cathedral containing the reputed remains of Columbus.[98] Mostly, though, the State Department opposed such
visits, furthering the dispute with the Navy Department over who would
take the lead in relations with the Caribbean republics.

The principal purpose of the U.S. Navy's Special Service Squadron,
the Caribbean contingent created in 1920, was in doubt under the Good
Neighbor policy, which claimed to abandon the interventionism that the
squadron had been formed to serve. By 1933 the force had declined to four
old vessels, and although the Cuban revolution that year briefly revived
the interventionist role of the squadron, which swelled to forty-four vessels on patrol in Cuban waters between September 1933 and May 1934, its
role was disputed within the Roosevelt administration. Rear Admiral C. S.
Freeman, commander of the squadron, complained in 1934 that "the cultivating of friendly relations by foreign cruising . . . has been rendered
difficult . . . by the attitude of the Department of State in regard to visiting
the countries of Latin-America. Repeated efforts to break down the ban
on such visits have proved unsuccessful." Freeman sought to redefine the
squadron in terms of Roosevelt's new policy:

> The announcement and cultivation of the "good neighbor" policy . . .
> suggest an opportune time for any change in the status of the Special
> Service Squadron that may be determined. . . . [T]he original mission
> of the Special Service Squadron, which contains no suggestion of a
> policy of interference or intervention, has never fully been developed.
> There is implicit in this mission the policy of the "good neighbor."
> The failure fully to develop this mission lies not with the Navy De-
> partment, but in the impossibility of securing the acquiescence of the
> Department of State in a policy of foreign cruising in Latin-America.[99]

The following year, Freeman reported that the Navy Department had
"succeeded in breaking down the ban that undoubtedly had developed in
regard to visits to foreign ports in Latin-America," considering it "one of
the outstanding accomplishments of the year, irrespective of the manner
in which it was brought about."[100] As his wording suggests, there was no
formal change in State Department policy toward naval "good will" visits
in the Caribbean; the ships just started coming. Not until 1938 was a Liaison
Committee established between the departments to coordinate the timing
and message of such events.[101]

Even then, the men in striped pants were fifth wheels in the whirl of events prompted by the arrival of a naval vessel at the mouth of the Ozama River. Squadron Commander G. J. Meyers observed that "the promotion of friendly relations with the republics of Latin-America calls for 'show,'" and although it is evident that Trujillo agreed, the diplomats continued to obstruct the cultural ties that bound the dictator with the military visitors who began to arrive with frequency in the late 1930s.[102] The first inclusion of the Dominican Republic in a "good will" cruise after the resumption of such visits came in May 1937, when Rear Admiral Yancey S. Williams arrived on the flagship of the Special Service Squadron, the cruiser *Omaha,* largest ship ever to visit the port. Previous naval visits had been brief and took place without elaborate ceremony, but this visit was a conscious effort on the part of both the U.S. Navy and the Dominican government to change the symbolic meaning of the gunboat in the context of their relations. *Listín Diario* asserted that, because of Trujillo, there was no cause for "alarm" at the visit of a U.S. warship and, in fact, that under his rule there was "nothing to fear from anyone." Roosevelt had corrected the "errors of other epochs," assured the paper, so a naval presence that previously would have "merited hostile attitudes" would instead be celebrated, "thanks to Roosevelt and Trujillo, as a fiesta."[103] But the State Department refused Trujillo's request for a contingent of *Omaha*'s Marines to take part in a joint military parade with the Dominican Army.[104] The Marine rifle squad was not prevented from facing and besting the Dominican Army marksmen, and liberty parties of bluejackets were allowed to circulate through the city and proceed to the Boca Chica beach enclave to be hosted by the American Colony. But the most graphic evidence of "la política confraternización panamericana" would have been the cooperation of the U.S. troops in the kind of military spectacle that was dear to Trujillo and central to his reformulation of Dominican nationhood, and this the diplomats denied. The offended Trujillo did not attend the "radiant" reception for the *Omaha*'s officers at the National Palace after the parade, and he made himself scarce during the rest of the cruiser's four-day stay in port. Denied the participation of the sailors and Marines, who were the "personification and incarnation" of the new relationship, Trujillo withdrew his own physical presence from the numerous scheduled events.[105]

In the wake of Trujillo's boycott, the legation recommended that naval visits be suspended "until this country has a Chief Executive who has sufficient culture" to receive dignified guests, and the Division of American Republics concurred that "naval visits to Ciudad Trujillo should be avoided for some time to come."[106] But the military men did not take it so hard. Lieutenant Colonel Robert Blake, USMC, reported his favorable impressions of the visit: "In the three countries visited where American military and naval forces had in the past been stationed for sufficient length of time to permit mutual understanding and friendship to develop, the cordiality of the reception accorded the Squadron was most gratifying. . . . At Managua and Ciudad Trujillo the reception turned into a regular home-coming celebration."

Admiral Williams was similarly uncritical in his reports. He had been aboard the USS *Memphis* in 1916 when the cruiser was washed up and wrecked on the rocky shoreline of the city, and he remembered the hazards of entering the Ozama River in those days, when it was impossible to moor anywhere close to the west bank. He was impressed by the extensive harbor improvements completed by Trujillo—now the *Omaha* could dock alongside the General Receivership directly below Fortaleza Ozama—and he complimented the work to several Dominican officials.[107]

Like Williams, many of the military visitors had personal recollections of the undeveloped state of Santo Domingo in the days of the occupation. For a naval officer, the quality of port facilities is a paramount consideration in judging the merits of a civilization; and for a Marine the cleanliness and orderliness of a place are similarly central in his evaluation. For such men, the physical achievements of the Trujillo regime outweighed any other consideration.[108] The resident diplomats, on the other hand, counted the cost of the regime's oppression and the dictator's self-obsession against the value of the order and development he had fostered.

Visiting military men without previous experience in the country were unable to compare the status quo under Trujillo with conditions under the Marines or after the hurricane, but they drew on the same criteria of order and infrastructure to evaluate what they saw. Rear Admiral Ford A. Todd visited Ciudad Trujillo with the new cruiser USS *Philadelphia* in October 1938, to follow up on Trujillo's "180-degree turn" toward the United States at the time of the Munich Conference. Todd completed a "strenuous" round of calls, "ostentatious entertainment," and sight-seeing, impressing U.S. Minister Norweb as "one of the best diplomatists" he had met among naval officers, despite his having arrived without a single Spanish-speaking officer on board to help him communicate with Trujillo, who spoke little English.[109]

Admiral Todd reported his visit in the language of military approval.

Crediting Trujillo with rebuilding the city after "the great hurricane of 1930," he cited the new harbor, paved roads, public works, fortifications, and "improvement of the army" as the major achievements. He noted Trujillo's self-aggrandizement in changing the city's name and erecting the obelisk to himself on Avenida George Washington, but considered it an element of Trujillo's "genius and foresightedness" to erect his "own memorial" before he died, in the manner of the pharaohs. Todd also applied the criteria of the transnational military ideal in judging Trujillo the man. His favorable appraisal began with an excellent first impression based on his "meticulously neat and well groomed" appearance and his "fine military bearing," as if he were being reviewed on the parade ground at the Haina Military Academy. Predisposed to accept what he was told by a man so imbued with military culture, Todd reported Trujillo's "sincere desire to uphold democracy" and pointed to Avenida George Washington and the unfinished "Avenue U.S. Marines" as evidence that Trujillo was "a very loyal and grateful friend of those whom he admires and who have helped him." In his parting words to Todd, Trujillo referred to Franklin Roosevelt's fishing-and-poker cruise earlier in the year aboard the *Philadelphia,* when FDR had visited Samaná Bay and exchanged radio messages with Trujillo. Trujillo told Todd that "he hoped President Roosevelt would always remember that the fishing was good in Dominican waters," leaving Todd unable to "tell whether he was speaking literally or allegorically."[110]

A poem entitled "The Grand Reception to the Benefactor of the Fatherland on the Cruiser *Philadelphia*" later appeared in an anthology of verse about Trujillo and his regime. After an opening stanza recounting how the ship unfurled the Dominican flag ("the insignia of the great Dominican"), fired a salute, and launched its planes in Trujillo's honor, the poem expounded on the significance of the handshake between Todd ("the valiant mariner") and Trujillo ("the hero"). "The friendship of the two countries shined in that human contact" between the admiral and the Generalísimo, while the Dominican and American flags, "tied together" by the touch of the two men's skin, flew among the twenty-one flags of "free America . . . under a sky of peace."[111]

The past personal experience in the Dominican Republic of individuals in the Department of State, on the other hand, tended to be unpleasant. Some of Sumner Welles's friends from the 1920s were exiles from Trujillo or victims of his torture, as were some of the elite friends of more recent American diplomats. The group of State Department officials who had spent time in the country since 1930 (and others who had simply kept tabs on developments there)—including John Moors Cabot and J. F. McGurk, who had become important figures in the new Division of American Republics—openly opposed Trujillo. This disapproving cohort advocated a hard line against the dictator, but the rise of European fascism and the impending need to cobble together some kind of hemispheric defense arrangement ran counter to their efforts. The creation of the Standing Liaison Committee in late 1938 forced the State Department to come to terms with the Navy and War departments over the courtship of regional allies.

After years of internecine squabbling over the propriety, nature, and content of visits by U.S. ships and planes to the American republics, the Joint Secretariat of the Liaison Committee, composed of representatives from each department, sat down to lay out some guidelines. Selden Chapin of the State Department cited "the heavy and apparently inescapable 'entertainment expenses'" incurred by Foreign Service officers, naval officers, and host governments as a result of these visits, but he agreed with his military counterparts in the secretariat that semantics might offer a solution. "Official" visits with all the trimmings would be limited to one per year per country in the interest of economy, they advised, but "in the interest of our general policy" unofficial visits by sea and air would be increased and would "become routine in character." The Liaison Committee enumerated the benefits of frequent military calls: "an unostentatious but regular display of naval and air force" would be "a constant reminder of the strength and greatness of the United States"; it would strengthen bilateral relations "through the cultivation of social intercourse between the American and local officers and officials"; and it would lend "support and solidarity" to each "local American colony." The committee recognized that the term "informal visit" had lost its meaning in places like Ciudad Trujillo, where military visitors were swept up in *trujillista* displays regardless of the "official" or "unofficial" status of their presence.

Now the U.S. "good will" effort in the Caribbean republics would concentrate on an annual "visit of courtesy," paid by an admiral aboard the largest vessel available, during which there would be a full range of scheduled social and athletic events. The Liaison Committee recommended bilingual officers and a company of enlisted men with "a *good* ship's baseball team, rifle team, et cetera," and "most important of all . . . a good band and orchestra."[112] Welles continued to resist this kind of benevolent gunboat diplomacy, preferring his good neighbors to come calling in striped pants, not gold braid, as the armed services took the lead in lining up the available allies in the region. A Naval Intelligence report advocated naval and air visits for that purpose in April 1939, making particular reference to Welles: "In the highs of our present trend in South America, instead of desparing [sic] because of Well's [sic] pedicular [sic] policy, it is all the more important that we bend new effort towards preparing liaison men for the future."[113] In the case of the Dominican Republic, the new efforts for liaison were extensions of the military tradition and outlook that so many American officers shared with Trujillo, and those efforts were reciprocated in kind by him. This collaboration was acted out in ways still substantially dictated by Trujillo, whose employment of cultural symbolism gained new expression in the festivals of preparedness and solidarity staged during 1939 and 1940.

AVENIDA USMC

Trujillo announced that the road running along the new quays on the Ozama River would be renamed Avenida United States Marine Corps, ostensibly as a tribute to the Marines' relief efforts after the 1930 hurricane, and in February 1939 he requested a U.S. naval vessel and a squadron of aircraft to take part in the ceremonies. The commandant of the Marine Corps at the time was Major General James Breckinridge, Trujillo's commanding officer during the guerrilla wars in the eastern Dominican Republic in 1919–20. He dispatched thirty-six Marine aircraft under the command of General William Upshur to rendezvous with the battleship *Texas* and "represent him and the officers and men of the U.S. Marine Corps . . . to express their deep appreciation and thanks for this tribute to our Corps; for the sentiments which caused you to give our name to one of the principal avenues of this historic city." This time the diplomats were not asked for permission before a "parade battalion with band and colors" went ashore to march in the "post of honor" with "a large detachment of the Dominican Army." Trujillo was a passenger aboard the *Texas* the next morning as it went through a series of maneuvers with the Marine aircraft squadron staging a mock attack. The ship's captain considered Trujillo to be "obviously a man of first rate ability," and he found Ciudad Trujillo to be "clean and exceptionally well regulated and policed." In this case, not only were the officers fêted at a National Palace reception, but five hundred U.S. enlisted men came ashore for a dinner of "pig, plantain, and beer" hosted by the Dominican Army Command.[114]

Perhaps the most telling episode that occurred during the USS *Texas* festivities was when the U.S. officers visited Trujillo aboard the *Presidente Trujillo,* his combination yacht and warship. Trujillo showed them the jeweled sword and gold scabbard of the late-nineteenth-century dictator Ulises Heureaux, and commented that they were from "the days when the Dominican Republic was ruled by a black man and not by a mulatto like myself." In its report of this moment, the legation cited the episode as an indication of Trujillo's "increasing self-assurance and realization of mastery," since at other times he presented himself as a white man and was known to wear whitening makeup.[115] Still, his use of whitening cosmetics continued into the last years of his rule, and in the *alto mundo* his color consciousness was apparently unabated. A likelier explanation was that Trujillo felt himself to be among "old friends," to borrow a phrase from General William Upshur's speech at the Avenida USMC ceremony the day before.[116] Despite the notorious bigotry of the Marines during the occupation, Trujillo's military colleagues looked at more than just complexion in estimating his worth, placing value on the symbols of power that he acquired and displayed with considerable martial flair, like the sword of Heureaux and military decorations.[117] A British legation report captured this dynamic between racial and cultural judgments in its description of Trujillo: "In appearance he is slightly mulatto, but this is off-set by a good military bearing."[118]

A few days after this incident another military ritual took place, at which Upshur and the other officers witnessed the conferral of one of the scores of medals that Trujillo accrued in his lifetime. The Diplomatic Corps played an important role in the conferral of medals awarded by foreign governments, and the awarding country's chief of mission was one of the focal points of an otherwise martial ceremony. For instance, when Trujillo received France's Legion of Honor in August 1931, it was invested on him by the French chargé on "the new army parade ground [and] made the occasion for a great military display . . . attended [by] all the members of the diplomatic and consular bodies [with] a parade lasting over three hours on a very hot day." The French diplomat spoke "bitterly" of having to play his part in the steamy spectacle, since the award had been obtained without the French legation's approval through the efforts of the Dominican minister in Paris, who promised tariff concessions that proved to be illegal under the terms of the U.S.-Dominican Convention of 1924. The State Department intervened to prevent the Dominican Republic from lowering duties on such French imports as perfume, but Trujillo still got his medal.[119] At the Avenida

George Washington festivities held at the Country Club in 1936, William Pulliam teased a visiting dignitary who was there to confer an award on Trujillo, saying there were already enough "decorations to cover the whole front of his coat," so he would have to pin the medal on the back.[120]

Trujillo also gave military awards, routinely conferring medals on U.S. officers and other VIPs who visited his capital. But here again the State Department played an obstructionist role. The medals could be given to U.S. officers, but then they had to be surrendered to the State Department, which held the awards until the recipient left government service.[121]

## TRUJILLO'S FIRST VISIT TO THE UNITED STATES

For years, Trujillo and every U.S. ally he could muster had tried to arrange for him to come to the United States, but every effort had been quashed by disapproving diplomats who had knowledge of his regime. After the success of the *Texas*/Avenida USMC festivities, however, Marine Commandant Breckinridge led a campaign, assisted by General Upshur and now-Colonel Thomas Watson, to overcome the State Department's resistance to a visit to Washington by Trujillo.[122] With these "high officers in the USMC urging General Trujillo to come to the U.S. in order to repay his numerous hospitalities to them," State Department opposition faded.[123] Sumner Welles continued to insist that there was "no thought on the part of the Federal Government of extending him any official invitation to visit Washington," but the military authorities had the prerogative to entertain Trujillo in his capacity as head of the Dominican armed forces, should he travel to the United States on his own.[124] Breckinridge and Upshur were assisted in their efforts to pave their protégé's way to Washington by congressional members of the Dominican lobby, all of whom had been on visits of their own to Ciudad Trujillo and who pressured the State Department to cooperate. Representative Hamilton Fish of New York warned that Trujillo was contemplating a visit to Nazi Germany, a trip that could be forestalled by offering Trujillo military courtesies in Washington.[125] Senator Theodore F. Green of Rhode Island noted that "a similar way was found of entertaining General Baptista [sic] of Cuba" without State having to issue a formal invitation.[126] Senator David Walsh of Massachusetts, who had visited Trujillo two months after the Haitian massacre, also chimed in. Walsh, chairman of the Naval Affairs Committee, received Roosevelt's assurances in late May 1939 that Breckinridge and Army Chief of Staff George Marshall would host Trujillo if he came to Washington, although his invitation to the United States would come from the New York World's Fair authorities, not the State Department or the Marine Corps.[127]

This decision to roll out the khaki carpet for Trujillo came about as a result of the network of supporters that Trujillo had cultivated among military men and legislators. They determined that, regardless of the attitude of the State Department and the U.S. legation, Trujillo would come to Washington and be accorded the martial pomp and ceremony (and the social emoluments) that had configured so much of the relationship between the two countries in Ciudad Trujillo. *Time* magazine judged the arrangement a "squeeze play" on the part of Trujillo, "the little brown bandit," who was jealous of "the parade of other Latin American strong-men to Washington: Cuba's Batista, Nicaragua's Somoza, Brazil's Aranha and Monreira."[128] Trujillo had indeed forced the issue by announcing his intention to visit the New York World's Fair (with its elaborate Dominican Pavilion), but the "squeeze play" worked only because his American allies helped him to pull it off.

As a result, Trujillo was entertained by those whom Norweb called "his friends in the Marine Corps," who were showing themselves to be much better neighbors than the chilly diplomatic crowd, during the dictator's first visit to the United States in July 1939. Although the sudden death of Secretary of the Navy Claude Swanson caused the cancellation of many of the dinners and military reviews that had been scheduled, Trujillo's visit to such sites as Quantico Marine Base and the Tomb of the Unknown Soldier (a version of which he later erected in Ciudad Trujillo) went forward, as did a dinner hosted by Senator Green at the Capitol and a reception at the Pan-American Union.[129] Paradoxically, Trujillo did not come to Washington in the full-dress uniform and bicorn hat that he wore when entertaining military visitors to his country, even though he was coming in his capacity as Generalísimo, the highest-ranking Dominican officer, and not as president, having left that office the year before. Instead, seeking to project the image of a civilian statesman, he wore a modest suit and a straw boater at every stop on his itinerary, and at events like the Marine parade at Quantico he was the only individual not in uniform. The Marine connection was simply transmitted through his two tall military aides, who were continually at his back; these officers wore the familiar jodhpurs of the Marine-inspired Dominican Army.[130] Trujillo's stay in Washington also included informal meetings, sans photographic coverage, with Franklin Roosevelt and Cordell

Hull. They talked about the Dominican debt negotiations (which Trujillo stressed) and continental defense (which Hull and Roosevelt stressed) but concluded no agreements. The *Washington Post* judged correctly that in conferring with "the strong man of Santo Domingo," the Roosevelt administration hoped "to draw his West Indian state more closely into incipient plans for joint hemisphere defense," but Trujillo maintained that "the anachronistic Dominican-American Convention of 1924" could "hardly be reconciled with the new continental spirit."[131] The issues of debt and defense could be resolved only in tandem, as the following chapter will relate.

Trujillo next traveled from Washington to New York, where the martial flavor of his visit continued with a full-dress parade and a twenty-one-gun salute at the U.S. Military Academy at West Point. Trujillo also received twenty-one guns at the World's Fair during a ceremony at the Dominican Pavilion, where a bust of himself dominated the entrance. Some were not glad to see him. Mayor Fiorello La Guardia refused to have his photo taken with Trujillo; a small group of protesters picketed his arrival; and Heywood Broun brought up the Haitian massacre in his column in the *New York World-Telegram*: "The murdered men and women at our doorsteps were Negroes of Haiti. The persecuted folk of Germany are Jewish. And it seems that such things can be overlooked by certain statesmen."[132] But these rebuffs were offset by the dictator's welcome from the Dominican lobby in New York. Trujillo was the guest of honor at a dinner at the Biltmore Hotel hosted by U.S. Representative Fish, whose toast to him as "a builder greater than all the Spanish Conquistadors together" was drunk by a roomful of wealthy supporters and reported to the press.[133] Fish's toast was only the most hyperbolic of the many kudos for Trujillo that were generated during his visit by a variety of Americans outside the official policy-making apparatus of the executive branch; and these individuals' actions shaped relations with the Trujillo regime in ways disapproved by many within that apparatus. The reviews and receptions in Washington and New York were reported in great detail in stories and photographs throughout the Dominican press, coverage which demonstrated that Trujillo had the approval and cooperation of American generals, legislators, and bankers (if not too many diplomats) and which served to "strengthen his hold on the republic."[134] Whether taking place on the parade ground or in the banquet hall, these cultural manifestations of Trujillo's ties with influential Americans were both personal and political, growing out of individual relationships and together constituting an ad hoc diplomacy within which professional diplomats were noticeably absent.

## "OLD COMRADES IN ARMS"

In the course of the following year, as Fortress America was erected against the European threat, the ties between Trujillo and the U.S. military grew stronger through the increased exchange of visits and compliments. In January 1940, Trujillo asked to visit the Puerto Rican island of Culebra during U.S. Navy maneuvers so that he might "renew associations with his old comrades in arms." Once again the State Department was opposed, but was finessed into approval when the admiral in command of the exercises informally invited Trujillo "to take a little trip and wander over there" in his yacht.[135] Trujillo was greeted by a twenty-one-gun salute from the U.S. Atlantic Fleet, which displayed the Dominican flag. When informed by the omnipresent McLaughlin that he was the first foreigner to be accorded such an honor, Trujillo replied: "I am not a foreigner; I am a Continental American." These words were reported to the Navy Department by Lieutenant John A. Butler, who had recently been appointed as naval attaché in Ciudad Trujillo, fulfilling Trujillo's long-held desire for a continuous official U.S. military representative in his capital and, as the Dominican Ministry of Foreign Relations put it, "cementing even closer the bonds of friendship" between the two nations.[136] After the maneuvers at Culebra, Trujillo was flown back to Ciudad Trujillo in a Navy plane in the company of two of his Marine associates from the occupation days, upon whom he then conferred military decorations.[137] Foreign Minister Arturo Despradel wrote to his counterpart Cordell Hull to express the "profound and sincere gratitude of the Dominican Government and people" for the honors shown Trujillo at Culebra, calling them "the highest and most authentic representation of national sentiments" and a demonstration of "the ideal of Panamerican solidarity."[138] That ideal, which was at the heart of the Good Neighbor policy, had not been conveyed well by the diplomats but was communicated clearly by the military through an invitation, a salute, and personal camaraderie.

At the Havana Conference in July 1940 and again a month later in staff talks with U.S. military representatives in Ciudad Trujillo, General Trujillo offered "the land, the sea, the air, and the men of the Dominican Republic—including the blood of the Dominicans themselves" for the defense of the hemisphere.[139] This was, as one historian has put it, "an amazing offer. It was virtually a blank check. . . . [T]he U.S. obtained the right to use bases in a number of other nations, but never on such favorable terms as those granted by the Dominican Republic."[140] These talks and the defense arrangements of World War II will be examined in the following chapter, but it should be noted here that the propinquity of the U.S. military to the Trujillo regime gained greater functional significance as a result of the war: U.S. weapons, equipment, and liaison officers began to flow in addition to Good Neighbor rhetoric and Marine esprit. Diplomats with an aversion to Trujillo had to console themselves as Roosevelt did on the subject of allying with dictators; sometimes it is necessary to "hold hands with the devil," went the proverb cited by FDR.[141] But the planners of military preparedness needed no such rationalization to enlist Trujillo in their cause in 1940. The War Plans Division was clear in its endorsement of Trujillo that summer, characterizing him as "intelligent, energetic, forceful and progressive. Because of these qualities the Dominican Republic is the best governed country in the West Indies."[142]

Back in Washington in September to sign the Hull-Trujillo Treaty terminating U.S. control of Dominican customshouses (also considered in the next chapter), Trujillo hosted a luncheon for Chief of Staff, General George C. Marshall, who toasted the "more intimate bonds" between the nations of the hemisphere as "one splendid result" of the "tragic and cataclysmic developments" in Europe. Extolling Trujillo's "wholehearted cooperation . . . in the problem of Hemisphere defense," Marshall concluded by saying: "I speak for all the officers present when I say, 'I hope you come often.'"[143] The strategic urgency of "drawing together" a defensive bloc of nations, as Marshall said, had been greatly facilitated in the case of the Dominican Republic by the shared military and cultural outlook of Trujillo and the U.S. architects of Fortress America.

## AMBASSADOR WARREN AND AMBASSADOR BRIGGS

Two wartime diplomats, Avra Warren and Ellis O. Briggs, sharply diverged in their attitudes toward the Trujillo regime. Their differing relations with the government were carried out through their involvement in the cultural tableaux of Trujillo-worship: parades, receptions, dinners. In both cases, personal relations influenced the diplomats' attitudes toward the regime and the American military and became intertwined with the political relationship between the countries. As a result, Avra Warren presided over the closest Dominican–American relations in history, manifested by his prominent social presence. Ellis O. Briggs, on the other hand, initiated the sourest moment in bilateral relations since the Marine occupation, which he acted out at public events.

Avra Warren presented his credentials to Trujillo on the Fourth of July 1942. The new minister had come up through the consular ranks of the Foreign Service, rather than through the diplomatic side like his predecessors, most of whom were Harvard alumni (he was a Marylander and a graduate of Johns Hopkins). His most recent position at State had been three years as chief of the Visa Division, and he had little personal knowledge of what had been going on in Ciudad Trujillo, where he now arrived to take up his first appointment as chief of mission. The Dominican government made a special effort in 1942 to celebrate the Independence Day of its ally in the war, staging a parade of soldiers and students on Avenida George Washington, and Warren hosted a reception for six hundred fifty "persons prominent in the social and political life of the country," crowding them all into his official residence.[144] Warren's photograph was printed with Trujillo's and Roosevelt's on the front page of *Listín Diario* the next day.[145] Upgraded to the level of ambassador in September 1943, Warren threw himself and the resources of his mission, now housed at an impressive embassy building with a staff four times larger than that of the 1930s, into the accelerated, and increasingly martial, social whirl of Ciudad Trujillo. His reports revealed no self-consciousness about the role he played in the nationalist, personalist spectacles of the Trujillo regime. He seemed rather to enjoy the attention and entertainment that came with the job, and he did not dwell on the authoritarian aspects of the government to which he was accredited.[146] Warren aligned his policies closely with the American military, empowered the military attachés on his staff (now three in number, not counting pilots and mechanics), and participated unflinchingly in the calendar of the *trujillista* state. He also delighted in the social intrigues of the Cuerpo Diplomático, intrigues that in some ways doubled as the political life of the capital. He was an old friend of Haitian Minister André Chevalier, who had been appointed to his post because he was a second cousin to both Trujillo and Minister of the Interior and Police Teódulo Piña Chevalier. Chevalier was also an old friend of the Argentine chargé, who Warren said was "the town gossip of this circle" and liked to "stir up trouble in the Corps."

A good example of how foreign relations in the Dominican Republic were molded by personal relationships occurred in October 1942, when the Argentine diplomat tried to find another chief of mission who would join him to "voice an irritation over Trujillo's appeal to the Americas" to declare war on the Axis. His ability to find a diplomat to second Argentina's position was predicated on the personalities involved and their social roles:

> He got nowhere with the Brazilian who is Dean of the Corps because he, too, is a very careful person. Neither did he with the Englishman who is cautious and one of my close friends. He did not bring in the Vichy Frenchman because he is in the dog house here anyway. So he fastened on Garland, the Peruvian Minister, whom you know. Garland is the most popular member of the Corps. They entertain frequently and well, he and his wife find time for bridge every afternoon and evening and both of them have so much personal charm that everybody likes them.[147]

The affable Peruvian agreed to bring the matter up with Trujillo, but ended up getting "a spanking" from El Jefe when he did. Trujillo warned the Argentine to stop his "rumor mongering" or get thrown out of the country, because he "was not going to let the Diplomatic Corps here get out of hand."[148] There was no disharmony between Trujillo and Warren, however, during the latter's two years in the country. Warren even took the unusual step of placing his son in the Dominican Military Academy at Haina.[149]

Ellis O. Briggs replaced Warren in June 1944. Briggs had grown up in Maine and attended Dartmouth College, retaining the acerbic tone and worldview of the Down-Easter stereotype. He arrived in the midst of the Dominican centennial year, with its profusion of civic spectacles and other reasons to dress up. He endured the three-hour "Victory in Europe" parade after D day with the rest of the Diplomatic Corps in their "striped trousers, cutaway coats, and high hats," which were "as appropriate for the ardent Caribbean summer" as "horse blankets." Trujillo wore "one of his gaudiest uniforms" as the diplomats "grouped around him while unnumerable photographs were taken." Briggs rejected the dress code before the next civic occasion, this one to celebrate the Dominican contribution to the Allied war effort:

> More sartorial splendor for the *Benefactor*, and more sartorial roughage for the diplomats. Contemplating these portents and the advantage

that might accrue to the dictator from another meretricious display of diplomats-in-the-pocket, I sent word to the Chief of Protocol that the American ambassador would be pleased to attend the projected cele-bration in a white suit and Panama hat or, should that not be consid-ered suitable, to be represented at the parade by an attaché in uniform. Since President Trujillo needed the personal presence of the American envoy to add verisimilitude to the flexing of his patriotic muscles, the white suit was tolerated—and it created a sensation. . . . Trujillo was not amused . . . by my sartorial declaration of independence.[150]

The challenge posed by the new ambassador to the culture of foreign re-lations under the Trujillo regime merged with his disdain for its politics. Instead of a cheerful narrative of the Fourth of July festivities in 1944, Briggs filed a report denouncing Trujillo's "cynical disregard" for "liberty, justice, and democracy," his "colossal vanity," and his "personal enrichment" through the regime. He recommended that the U.S. government "should decline to endorse Trujillo's dictatorship," and he behaved as if that were already his personal policy.[151]

Briggs made little effort to conceal his contempt for the marathon cele-bration of the Dominican Centennial in 1944 (which he considered an expensive distraction from the Allied war effort), and he protested U.S. military visits and arms deliveries to the Dominican Republic. Unlike War-ren before him, who had had nothing unkind to say about the American Colony's proliferating expressions of support for the Trujillo regime, Briggs demanded complete "non-participation by American companies and citi-zens in the political affairs of the Dominican Republic," which were difficult to differentiate from the social affairs of Ciudad Trujillo. He personally re-buked the managers of the American-owned brewery and the electric com-pany for sponsoring a resolution calling for Trujillo's reelection.[152] Coming so soon after the affectionate Warren, Briggs's hostility was palpable in the reviewing stand and at the banquet table, and was intended to communi-cate, in a public pantomime of personal disdain, a national change of heart on the question of dictatorship.

Trujillo's response was a *coup de protocol* on the occasion of a state dinner offered by Foreign Minister Manuel Arturo Peña Batlle in honor of Assis-tant Secretary of State Nelson Rockefeller, coordinator of Roosevelt's Office of Inter-American Affairs, during his visit to Ciudad Trujillo in November 1944. While Rockefeller was seated at the head table with Trujillo, Ambassador Briggs was relegated to a minor place at a "floor table" in the banquet hall, a gesture that had particular potency given the intertwined cultural and political modalities of the Trujillo regime.[153] Briggs interpreted the gesture as an insult to the president of the United States, whom he as ambassador embodied, worsening his personal and official relations with Trujillo. Also emblematic of the difference between Warren and Briggs was what the latter called "the brandy incident" in his memoirs. Warren had left half a case of Carlos Primero brandy, Trujillo's exclusive drink, at the U.S. embassy for Briggs to use in entertaining the general. Told that Trujillo "expected wherever he went to have a new bottle . . . opened in his presence," Briggs insulted him on his second visit to the embassy by serving him from the same bottle opened for him on his first. Briggs recalled this slight as "the most satisfying of my personal tilts with President Trujillo."[154]

But Trujillo had the support of Rockefeller, who became assistant secretary of state the month following his visit to the Dominican Republic, and of Warren, whom Rockefeller brought in as chief of the Division of American Republics. "They fired me," recounted Briggs, whose pro forma resignation to Roosevelt after his reelection was the only one accepted out of all the chiefs of mission in the U.S. Foreign Service. But Briggs returned to a position of power in the State Department in late 1945, when Spruille Braden replaced Rockefeller as assistant secretary and tried to initiate a policy against Latin American dictators. Braden was coming from his post as U.S. ambassador to Argentina, where he had been dramatically unfriendly to Juan and Eva Perón. Briggs had served under Braden when the latter was ambassador to Cuba. While posted in Havana together, Briggs and Braden had maintained contacts with the growing Dominican exile movement there (these exiles were organizing to invade their neighboring homeland and overthrow Trujillo). Briggs now returned to Washington to serve as Braden's assistant. With these two in the posts recently occupied by Rockefeller and Warren, State Department relations with Latin American dictators cooled, most noticeably with regard to Perón and Trujillo, who were the personal nemeses of Braden and Briggs. U.S. representation in the Dominican Republic continued to be chilly under the new ambassador, J. F. McGurk, who had been the State Department "desk officer" for the Dominican Republic and chief of the Division of American Republics, and who was a longtime opponent of the Trujillo regime. He continued the pattern of official ambivalence and personal distaste established by Briggs vis-à-vis the Trujillo regime.[155] The following chapter will return to the antidictatorial policy of Braden and Briggs and their conflict with the U.S. military over the close wartime relationship with the Dominican Republic.

## "THE CULTURE OF THE SOLDIER"

The military relationship between the two countries involved weapons and training, as we shall see, but like the bilateral political relationship, it was also ingrained in the public life of the Trujillo regime. The culture of foreign relations in wartime Ciudad Trujillo was increasingly martial, with social and strategic concerns overlapping in the persons of American military visitors and resident attachés, who were bound up in the gala expressions of patriotic and inter-American sentiment following Pearl Harbor. The Trujillo regime cultivated an omnibus *cultura militar* in the armed forces and in Dominican society during the war years; this "military culture" simultaneously nourished and drew strength from ties to the U.S. military. Thus the lead editorial in the February 1942 issue of *Revista Militar* declared that Trujillo was "not satisfied" with the perfection of the army from "the military point of view," but now wanted to develop "the culture of the soldier." The leading role of the army "from the cultural point of view" in the "social evolution" of the country had to be recognized, and from now on the Generalísimo would concentrate on the "social factor" of the military. One of the first steps he took in this direction was to found a Military Club, housed in a "modern building" with the new Officers' Theater.

To illustrate further what was meant by the term "military culture" in the title of the *Revista Militar* editorial, the same issue carried a story under the prominent headline "Cocktail Party." This story reported a gathering at the home of Lieutenant Colonel David R. Kerr, who had arrived to fill the newly created position of U.S. military attaché. The forms of cultural transmission adopted by military "liaison" during the war are portrayed in the account, composed in the same breathless prose style as newspaper reporting about Trujillo's *alto mundo*. "The buffet was splendid. Exquisite liquors and the finest wines delighted those invited; and when the night closed its broach of sloe, and the light of the winking stars fled before the dawn, the echo of the last woman's laugh died away to become a memory of this fiesta of North American gentility."[156] Kerr's party also featured the familiar guest list from Dominican high society, mixing military men, government officials, diplomats of several countries, and "the most select" members of the American Colony. Thrown to express the "frank confraternity" between the American and Dominican militaries, the party was a demonstration of bilateral cooperation acted out in the form of martial camaraderie and social exclusivity. Although formal negotiations and agreements are the bones of diplomatic relations between nations, these are fleshed out by events like Kerr's party. Trujillo's "military culture" was to a large extent cocktail culture, where social and political relationships flowed together.

Liquor was an enduring element of the cultural relations between the countries, going back to the Marine occupation, when one of the few elements of the Progressive agenda not imported under the military government was the prohibition of alcohol. Rum flowed freely on the "Isle of Boozodoo," as the Dominican Republic was dubbed by the U.S. naval officer Constantine M. Perkins at a "get together dinner of College Men" in Santo Domingo in 1921:

> Have you ever had a vision
>    Of an island far away
> Free from blight of Prohibition?—
>    Would you like to go and stay?—
> Island of our ardent fancies
>    Void of life's vicissitudes;
> Isle where "bacardi" enhances
>    Generous Nature's lavish moods;[157]

This element perhaps partly explains the rush of ex-occupiers to seek positions in the Dominican Army under Trujillo, "as if it is a foreign legion," as Major Watson commented.[158] It may also explain some of the fondness of military visitors to stop in the Dominican Republic when they went on boozey "good will" cruises, or "champagning around the Caribbean," as Colonel Blake called his tour with the Special Service Squadron.[159] Ambassador Avra Warren's party ethos was particularly enthusiastic, helping to account for his popularity with the regime and his relations with American military men.[160] A sense of fraternity and nostalgia amplified by alcohol connects the "Isle of Boozodoo" experience of the Marine occupation, with its bleary insouciance, to the culture of foreign relations under Trujillo, with its "cocktail party" style of military interaction. Liquor was among the primary elements of inter-American spirit in both Ciudad Trujillo and Washington. The following epilogue follows this strand beyond the Second World War in one final example of military-cultural relations.

Acting on General Marshall's wish that he would "come often" to the United States, Trujillo made several postwar visits to Washington. During his visit in 1952, Trujillo was entertained at a cocktail party at the home of Admiral Milton "Mary" Miles in Chevy Chase, Maryland. Miles was director of Pan-American affairs and naval missions in the War Department and senior naval delegate to the Inter-American Defense Board. Miles and Trujillo hit it off at the party, and the following year the admiral and his wife accepted Trujillo's invitation to visit the Dominican Republic. "Don Rafael," as Admiral and Mrs. Miles called him, was back in the United States again (this time signing a military-assistance treaty with John Foster Dulles) when they arrived for their visit, but they were treated as "a member of his family" during their stay. Miles's photo album of their time in the Dominican Republic is a catalog of exactly what impressed the admiral about the Generalísimo's efficient rule. Miles took photos of new "modern markets," the shining new firehouse in the capital, and the shipshape naval air station outside of town. The album is also a graphic depiction of the intensely personal nature of Trujillo's relations with "Tío María," as Trujillo called "Mary" Miles, and is suggestive of the intimate terms he enjoyed with U.S. military representatives, but rarely with State Department personnel. The Mileses recorded their days at Trujillo's beach house, at the Villa Altagracia mountain resort, and in the Presidential Suite of the recently completed Hotel Jaragua, where Mrs. Miles was surrounded by "flowers, cakes, the attention paid to royalty." The couple visited Trujillo's favorite house, Las Caobas, outside San Cristóbal, where their tour included the dictator's bedroom and even his closet. There the admiral stood amid rows of Trujillo's uniforms and jackboots, his personal vault of gold braid. Far from feeling embarrassment or derision, Admiral Miles was moved to photograph the scene and include it in his album along with his shots of brand-new buildings and luxurious accommodations. When the phone rang it was Trujillo calling from New York to make certain that every possible convenience was afforded to his good friend "Tío María."[161] In contrast, after Assistant Secretary of State John Moors Cabot, who had been first secretary in Santo Domingo during the February 1930 revolution, also visited Ciudad Trujillo in 1953, he was attacked in the Dominican press as a communist sympathizer.[162]

There was little formal coordination of approaches toward the Dominican Republic on the part of American officials wearing gold braid and those wearing striped pants during the Good Neighbor policy, and little semblance of the unified national policy that any construction of "bilateral" relations assumes. The two groups described by this sartorial metonymy offered two very different faces to the Dominican Republic. "Striped pants" members of the Diplomatic Corps tended to be distant and correct, and often reproving. Concerned primarily with the financial entanglements of the republic, which Trujillo was determined to administer himself, and the harsh nature of his rule, which Trujillo found to be effective in establishing the order and efficiency he valued, the diplomats were mainly unimpressed. On a personal level, those attached to the U.S. legation experienced the expropriation of their professional culture, its symbols and cosmopolitan demeanor, into state rituals that they derided as charades. Their reports on Trujillo's personalistic and nationalistic pageantry tended to be contemptuous and condescending, and they sent clippings of Dominican press coverage of such events highlighted for the "amusement" of their colleagues at Foggy Bottom. How well, then, could these men perform their parts in the public staging of Trujillo's regime, what Norweb derided as "the antics of this island nation"?[163] Could they conceal their personal attitudes at the social and political gatherings where their attendance was symbolic of genial bilateral relations, and therefore mandatory? The lack of common ground between them and Trujillo must have made this a very difficult role to play.

"Gold braid" military visitors did not have to be actors. Most of these Marine and Navy officers had some personal experience in the Dominican Republic, either during the occupation or after the San Zenón hurricane. During their infrequent stays in the country they observed changes of a sort they admired: new port facilities, cleaner streets, more police, sharper drills by the army, new public buildings and services, and one of the most important streets in town named for the Marine Corps! These physical and behavioral improvements had been carried out by a leader they approved of, in fact had trained, who shared their criteria of progress, their comportment, and such symbols as uniforms, medals, and weaponry. Their reports about him and his governance were favorable, and their behavior during his public rituals and social gatherings must have been natural and congenial, reflecting their personal opinions of what they saw. Their participation facilitated the continuation of the imperial link between the two countries, albeit on Trujillo's terms.[164]

The second general conclusion, then, is that Trujillo's efforts to create and publicly depict a new Dominican nation are inseparable from his reinterpretation of all references to the colonial past. Dominican statehood under Trujillo was defined over and against those powers that had in the past controlled the country, directly or indirectly: Spain, France, Great Britain, the papacy, Haiti, and especially the United States. This is the source of the great symbolic importance and social prominence of the Cuerpo Diplomático and its American leaders, and to a lesser extent the foreign "colonies," and the reason why their lockstep integration into the "stagecraft" of the Trujillo regime was necessary.[165] The appropriation and Dominicanization of the many related symbols of external influence during the Era of Trujillo conditioned relations with the United States on a cultural level and point to the dominant role of the dictator in orchestrating the relationship. El Country Club, long the exclusive preserve of foreigners, became another venue for paying homage to Trujillo and, by association, his nation. The continental cuisine served at the many splendid receptions was nationalized and personalized, with menus including "Sauce Dominicaine" and "Consommé President."[166] Foreign steamship lines and Pan American Airways made more frequent stops in the growing city, and therefore hosted more frequent entertainments for its *alto mundo*. The stranded wreck of the *Memphis*, symbolic of intervention, was demonized, its "belly . . . a cave of rats," allowing other gunboats to be depicted as arks bringing *el buen vecino* (the good neighbor).[167] Other artifacts of occupation were integrated into the Dominican armed forces, such as the jodhpurs they retained as their own after the Marine Corps discarded them; the Banda Militar, the capital's dance band before the establishment of "La Orquesta Presidente"; and baseball teams, who always beat the visiting squads from the U.S. ships. In the cultural forms through which foreign relations between the United States and the Dominican Republic were acted out, what began as mimicry became mastery in the process of the consolidation of Trujillo's dictatorship and the Dominican state.

⬥

# CHAPTER SEVEN

Fortress America, Fortaleza Trujillo:
The Hull-Trujillo Treaty and the
Second World War

The overall aim of Roosevelt's Latin American policy in the late 1930s was
to strengthen the defenses of the Western Hemisphere in response to the
growing conflict in Europe and Asia.[1] The onset of the Second World War
transformed the Good Neighbor policy from a rhetorical device to a set of
inter-American organizations established for the defense and economic development of the region. The Roosevelt administration devised new means
of improving Latin American diplomacy in the late 1930s and early 1940s,
including governmental instruments of military, financial, and cultural aid,
which served the strategic imperative of strengthening "Fortress America."
The organizational apparatus of the wartime Good Neighbor policy included committees for military liaison; the Lend-Lease Program, which
distributed military supplies and hardware; the Export-Import Bank, which
extended credits for government projects; and the Office of the Coordinator of Inter-American Affairs, which fostered cultural ties through movies,
publications, and student exchanges.[2] Roosevelt's efforts to "give them
[Latin Americans] a share" were in response to the threat of fascist economic
penetration and "Fifth Column" insurgencies to the south, with the Panama
Canal and its approaches always the most important area of concern.[3]

The Dominican Republic's position on the Mona Passage, one of the two
main shipping lanes to the Panama Canal, put it in the same category of
strategic importance as Haiti and Cuba, which flank the Windward Passage.
Soon after the war began in September 1939, Colonel Frank Knox (about
to be named secretary of the navy) emphasized publicly that the United
States would have to "make the Caribbean an American lake" to defend
the hemisphere.[4] The active cooperation of the strategically located states

in the region was a prerequisite for national security. "As *neutrals* in case of conflict they would be a very serious impediment" to the cause, and "as *enemies* they would be a great potential danger," judged a military intelligence report in 1940.[5] The transformation of the Good Neighbor policy into an active alliance with Latin America was energetically pursued in the case of the Dominican Republic, which was a salient of Fortress America that could easily be strengthened if Trujillo agreed. The fact that Trujillo seemed to be ready at times for a dalliance with the Third Reich also invigorated the Roosevelt administration's pursuit of closer ties with the Dominican Republic, despite the fascist trappings of the regime.

Bumpy problems like the U.S.-Dominican Convention of 1924 were finally smoothed over by the same forces that erected defensive walls around the Americas. The administration implemented military coordination with the Trujillo regime, inaugurated a campaign against fascist influence, and arranged the final removal of the U.S. Receivership of Dominican Customs—all as part of the expanded and purposeful wartime version of the Good Neighbor policy. As a result, the relationship between the two countries went on a wartime footing from which it never clearly emerged. This development also occurred in other military regimes in Latin America that were considered reliable allies during World War II, and then were seen as bastions against communism during the Cold War. The Good Neighbor policy, under which U.S. diplomats had maintained uneffusive (and at times even embarrassed) relations with dictators, changed into a full regional alliance, under which new forms of defensive and economic assistance actively fostered such regimes.

## THE "SORE THUMB" OF THE GOOD NEIGHBOR POLICY

Throughout the decade of the 1930s, the Convention of 1924 had been an impediment to Good Neighbor diplomacy with the Dominican Republic. The moratorium arranged in 1931 and the Foreign Bondholders Protective Council Agreement of 1934 were stopgap measures that did not remove the Receivership, which was one of the last interventionist organizations maintained by the United States in Latin America. The collection of Dominican customs by officials of the U.S. government was an infringement of Dominican sovereignty, a fact recognized in both capitals. As the Good Neighbor policy developed, similar manifestations of U.S. hegemony elsewhere in Latin America were removed: the Haitian occupation ended, the

Platt Amendment to the Cuban Constitution was abrogated, and Mexican oil rights were gradually surrendered. Only the Receivership in the Dominican Republic remained, a focal point for charges of intervention from the community of nations invoked by the Good Neighbor policy.

The U.S. government was increasingly prepared to heal what Cordell Hull called the "sore thumb" of the Good Neighbor policy.[6] This brought about a tripartite bureaucratic battle between the FBPC, hard-liners in the State Department, and the more defense-minded individuals in Franklin Roosevelt's circle of advisors. Those advisors, especially Secretary of the Treasury Henry Morgenthau Jr., considered the problem of Latin American debt defaults to be insignificant, an unnecessary impediment to the greater goal of hemispheric unity against the Nazi threat. They believed the FBPC had been too conservative in clearing defaulted loans from the path of the Good Neighbor policy, and they pushed successfully for a more active and expeditious role on the part of the U.S. government. Sumner Welles and his allies in the State Department had always supported the FBPC's practice of striking hard bargains, and they had begun pressuring defaulted Latin American nations for repayment in the late 1930s. Morgenthau challenged these hard-liners, and his views were accepted by Roosevelt. The losing party in this policy conflict was the FBPC. Always an anomalous quasi-public organization, the FBPC had no bureaucratic power base from which to press its increasingly outdated views, and the council lost its role in U.S. foreign policy when Roosevelt decided to press for quick bond-default settlements. The winner was Rafael Trujillo, who finally gained control of the Dominican purse strings on his own terms.

Representatives of the Dominican government clamored against the Convention of 1924 even as the FBPC Agreement put it back in force in September 1934. Dominican Minister of Finance Rafael Brache visited Welles to lodge the perceptive complaint that the customs arrangement was an "anachronism" that should be replaced by a "defensive alliance."[7] Brache, who soon resumed his old post as minister to Washington, and Joseph Davies, the central figure in the Dominican lobby, met with Undersecretary of State William Phillips in February 1935 to register Trujillo's protests against the intrusive nature of the convention. They also informed Phillips that the Dominican government was proceeding independently in an effort to establish a Dominican national bank. A national bank had been founded in Haiti the previous year as part of the comprehensive debt settlement with the United States; now the Dominican government focused on such a solution for its own financial woes.[8] Joseph Davies encouraged the plan and sought the assistance of his banking contacts in New York to secure a debt-settling loan that would also support a national bank.[9]

Sumner Welles prepared to meet the Dominican initiative head-on. He considered the 1934 FBPC Agreement to be a sound arrangement and favored the perpetuation of his "pet" convention as the guarantor of Dominican debt payments. To arm himself for the ensuing battle with Davies and Brache, Welles asked J. F. McGurk, one of the most strident critics of Trujillo in the State Department, to draft a memo detailing Trujillo's defiance of the Convention of 1924, with specific attention to how "the interests of American concerns are being prejudiced."[10] McGurk did a very thorough job in compiling a litany of Dominican "violations and contemplated violations" of the convention, but the memo was not yet ready when Brache came to Washington to meet with Welles.[11] Brache had just completed his mission into New York's financial circles with Davies, and in his first meeting with Welles he related "in utmost detail" a national bank plan that would involve abrogation of the Convention of 1924.[12] But when the Dominican minister called again two days later, Welles had McGurk's list of violations in hand. He bluntly informed Brache that Trujillo's flouting of Article III of the convention, the article that forbade unapproved increases in the Dominican debt, precluded State Department cooperation on any other point.[13]

Welles had several allies in his opposition to the Dominican proposal. First was the U.S. legation staff, especially the financial wizard James Gantenbein, who submitted a critical report on the Dominican "fiscal situation." Gantenbein informed Welles that it was "the reasoned opinion of well-informed foreign businessmen in Santo Domingo that a National Bank operated under the control of the present government would have every chance of failure within a short time." In denouncing the idea, Gantenbein cited "the dishonest and incompetent administration" of other government monopolies and submitted figures showing that, since 1930, Dominican expenditures for the military had increased 44 percent; for public works, 65 percent; and for the salary and expenses of the president, 275 percent.[14] Welles issued a commendation to Gantenbein for his memo, which concluded that the Convention of 1924 should not be "relaxed" in any way.[15] The FBPC also lined up behind Welles. Francis White of the council leadership received a visit from Brache, who told him that "governments do not now treat commitments the way they used to do, and that international agreements have not the same sanctity as formerly." This statement is indicative of Trujillo's interpretation of the Good Neighbor policy, and White's reply is equally illustrative of the FBPC's belief that existing contracts limited Roosevelt's freedom of action: "The Council feels that there is not the slightest shadow of a doubt that this Convention is legally binding between the two governments . . . [which] should live up to their obligations just as much as individuals and even more so, that any other basis would mean the breakdown of our whole civilization if contracts and pledged words are to be mere scraps of paper and meaningless."[16] White related this conversation immediately to Hull and also expressed the FBPC's strenuous opposition to the national bank plan.[17]

In the meantime, the FBPC Agreement of 1934 hung in limbo. Although signed and sealed by the Dominican government and the FBPC, and supported by the State Department, the implementation of the agreement remained an issue. The fiscal agents for the Dominican debt (Guaranty Trust) "required instructions from some source—it did not matter from whom, whether it be the Dominican government, the American government, or the FBPC" to begin applying payments from the Dominican government to amortization.[18] But the FBPC did not have any legal status in the matter, and the State Department, as always, wanted to keep the negotiations from being identified with the U.S. government. That left Trujillo, who was in no hurry to enact the agreement, free to push his national bank plan throughout 1935 while Guaranty Trust grew "restive" over the delay.[19] Francis White of the FBPC prepared the groundwork for getting the bondholders' approval of the agreement, but he could not follow up until the Dominican government acted.[20] Sumner Welles prodded the Dominican government to issue the "appropriate instructions," but he failed to move Trujillo.[21]

Joseph Davies, who negotiated the agreement, now was working to undermine it. He counseled Trujillo against acting on the agreement and sequestered himself in the Adirondacks while the angry bondholders threatened to reject FBPC representation unless payment on their Dominican bonds resumed.[22] Davies was closely involved with the Dominican national bank plan and had floated plans for a development corporation to Trujillo and "friends of his in the financial world." The corporation would refinance the Dominican debt, manage the national bank, make a private loan to the

Dominican government from U.S. sources, and "retain the substance" of the customs receivership "while eliminating the 'political implications.'"[23] Davies courted potential investors with "joy-rides" along the Dominican coast on his enormous yacht, *Sea Cloud;*[24] he also enlisted the support of some of the U.S. business concerns in the republic.[25] Welles, the student of Dominican history, "reminded" Davies that the bank plan resembled the "monopolistic corporation" attempted by "the dictator Heureaux" in the 1890s, which was "disastrous" for the country and the investors alike.[26] To keep the idea of a development corporation alive, Davies had to prevent the FBPC Agreement from being confirmed. He gave the FBPC false assurances that Trujillo wanted "to go through with the plan, [to] clean it up now," but nothing had been accomplished when 1936 ended.[27]

### "THIS CASE MUST BE SOLVED"

Cordell Hull broke this particular stalemate in February 1937, perhaps persuaded by Davies. Roosevelt appointed Davies ambassador to the Soviet Union, and Davies left in December 1936 after a large farewell dinner at the Mayflower Hotel where, with Dominican Minister Andrés Pastoriza and the Soviet ambassador being the only diplomats in attendance, he toasted Roosevelt, Stalin, and Trujillo.[28] Soon after Davies's arrival in Moscow, Pastoriza wrote to him "at the request of President Trujillo, to beg you not to forget, when you write to your good friend Secretary of State Hull," to urge the removal of the convention. Pastoriza had a ready line of inter-American reasoning for Davies to use: "It would be advisable, when you treat this question with Secretary Hull, to point out that the case of the Dominican Republic is the only pending solution in the Good Neighbor Policy which President Roosevelt so thoroughly and admirably advocates; and that consequently, this case must be solved before the Policy can exist entirely without exception or partiality."[29] Whether Davies wrote to Hull is uncertain, but the encouraging tone of Hull's subsequent note indicates that he was beginning to agree that the matter "must be solved." Hull attested to the "considerate attitude" that the United States had long maintained toward the Dominican Republic, omitting mention of Sumner Welles's tough stance on the subject of budgetary control the year before, and asserted that the State Department had "refrained from the strict and legalistic interpretation" of the convention "upon which it might have insisted." After alluding to the "very definite responsibility" of the U.S. government toward the bondholders, Hull cheered Trujillo with the following unprecedented expression of discomfort with the state of U.S.-Dominican relations:

> Provided these acquired interests of the bondholders are respected, this government has no interest in continuing the present provisions of the Convention of 1924, nor the general receivership as a treaty entity. On the contrary, in accordance with its policy of refraining from any form of activity involving participation by it, even through treaty rights, in the domestic concerns of the other American republics, the government of the United States would welcome the opportunity of relinquishing the obligations which it assumed under the terms of the Convention of 1924.[30]

Hull's note prompted the Dominican government to demonstrate its cooperation by implementing the FBPC Agreement. This action was less risky for Trujillo after Hull stated his low opinion of the convention, a fact not lost on some observers in the State Department. Selden Chapin, for instance, saw an "ethical inconsistency" in the State Department's entertaining a revision of the convention at the same time the FBPC plan revived it.[31]

Hull's subsequent proposal for "modifying" the convention included an end to U.S. supervision of the Dominican budget and tariff, but retained the essence of the 1924 treaty: customs collection and debt management by U.S. citizens.[32] Trujillo, who had long believed that the treaty should be "abrogated without further ado," rejected the compromise and steeled himself instead to achieve complete sovereignty for Dominican finances.[33] He bent the ear of James Roosevelt on the subject during the latter's tour of the Dominican Republic in February 1938. Trujillo maintained that Colonel Roosevelt's father should, "in pursuance of the Good Neighbor Policy," scrap the convention.[34] General Receiver William Pulliam wrote to his friend Schoenfeld, who had left his post in Ciudad Trujillo, about the increased heat he was feeling from the Dominican government's criticism of his receivership, as Trujillo prepared to step down from the presidency in 1938. "Street talk is very persistent that as a grand finale Trujillo plans to build a fire under *la pobre Convención y Receptoria* [the poor convention and Receivership]; of course the agitation is on just as in your time, but now the steam is being turned on."[35] Foreign Minister Julio Ortega Frier unleashed a diplomatic broadside on the subject at the State Department in May 1938. The memo described first how the Convention of 1924 was an act of intervention "incompatible" with the resolutions adopted at the Buenos Aires Conference in 1936. Having asserted the "uselessness" of the convention, and having noted (with a deft reversal of State Department logic) that the bondholders had not approved the 1924 treaty, the memo declared the treaty invalid.[36] Most interested State Department officials bristled with indignation over the tone and contentions of the note. Selden Chapin referred to its wording as "thinly veiled insolence," and Legal Advisor Green Hackworth penciled "nonsense" in its margin.[37] Sumner Welles shot back a fiery formal response, registering his "complete surprise" that the Dominican government "would seriously advance" such contentions.[38]

Cordell Hull, however, was rattled by the Dominican threat of unilateral abrogation of the treaty. He wanted both notes, Welles's and Ortega's, to be withdrawn. Trujillo responded that he would agree to do so only if he had "some assurances of success" in his campaign to end the receivership; otherwise, he preferred to publish the notes.[39] At this point, the irrepressible Ortega launched another missive denouncing the convention, and Trujillo saw the opportunity to make the foreign minister the scapegoat of the acrimony in order to pursue Hull's spirit of accommodation. Trujillo let Welles know that he was "exceedingly indignant" about Ortega's notes, which "did not represent Trujillo's desires or wishes," and he fired the foreign minister.[40] Both sides withdrew their notes and beat a diplomatic retreat, but Trujillo had accomplished more than a return to the status quo ante. Secretary Hull had once again glimpsed the specter of unilateral action by the Dominican Republic and had been forced to consider the repercussions. As a result, the episode strengthened his desire to be rid of the "existing difficulty" of the customs receivership.

The new U.S. minister, Henry Norweb, rejected the likely reasons why the U.S. government might want to abolish the receivership. He did not think it should be abolished as a quid pro quo for "military concessions [and] facilities" on Dominican soil, or as a "gesture of good neighborliness in the interest of inter-American solidarity." Norweb believed that the military priorities of the United States were served by the General Receivership, which would be there to keep Trujillo in line, and that those priorities superseded the goals of "military concessions" and "inter-American solidarity."[41] He was wrong. The course of action Norweb dismissed was exactly the one the Roosevelt administration would follow, for exactly the same reasons he rejected.

ACTING ON THE "ANCIENT FRAUDS"

The State Department still referred frequently to the role of the FBPC, but increasingly excluded the council from the debt negotiations. The story of the FBPC's fall demonstrates the changing priorities of U.S. Latin American policy during the late 1930s, as the emphasis shifted conclusively from regard for private interests to the need for a unified hemispheric front; the FBPC declined as the idea of Fortress America prevailed. Whereas the FBPC had been created to serve the needs of the Good Neighbor policy, the Good Neighbor policy was now strengthened to serve the needs of national security and global strategy. The council's loss of status was apparent to its president, Reuben Clark. In April 1937, he put his mounting frustration over the lack of support from the State Department into words addressed to Herbert Feis, whose brainchild the FBPC had been:

> I wonder if you men in the Department of State really appreciate in what a perfectly helpless position the Council is in in its negotiations with debtor governments. . . . We poor fellows sit here absolutely naked of prestige or potential coercive power. . . . I repeat that I wonder whether you men in the Department—you with your relatively unlimited resources, your representatives in every country, your prestige and your potential power—do realize what a helpless, unarmed, impotent organization this Council is.[42]

The FBPC may have been weak and isolated, but its approach was increasingly strident and unyielding. The council had been created, after all, to play hardball with debtor governments so that the slow-pitch game played by the Good Neighbor team would seem that much friendlier in comparison. During 1938 and early 1939, however, the FBPC drove a harder bargain than ever before. Francis White asked for a duty on Brazilian and Colombian coffee to force those governments into a more cooperative mood, a measure which the free-trading Hull would not consider.[43] The Colombian minister complained about the FBPC's attitude, especially that of White, who had bluntly accused the Colombian government of bad faith.[44] Nor was the FBPC's ire reserved for Latin America; Herbert Feis characterized the FBPC statement on Yugoslavia as "vicious," and he urged White to change the council's tone before the State Department had to differ publicly with it.[45] Feis concluded that "the demanding and rigid attitude taken by the Council" was becoming a problem.[46]

Roosevelt's softened financial policy left Francis White, Clark's successor as FBPC president, feeling alienated. His loyalty was to the bondholders, not to the " 'good neighbors' who believe in selling out the United States," and he denounced the "pious talk" of Cordell Hull. He was not without supporters at the State Department, however, especially Sumner Welles. Early in 1939, Welles began calling for payment of defaulted debts and was threatening to withhold possible economic assistance from nations that would not repay.[47] White was elated by Welles's message to Peru, that the United States would not "play Santa Claus" unless the "old debt" was serviced.[48]

Welles immediately ran into stern opposition from Secretary of the Treasury Henry Morgenthau Jr. and his ally, Secretary of the Interior Harold Ickes. These two intimate advisors to Roosevelt counseled him that economic assistance to Latin America was a useful way to prevent Nazi inroads into the hemisphere. Accordingly, Roosevelt requested $500 million for Export-Import Bank loans mostly to Latin America, and he dismissed the problem of defaults with severe language: "Ancient frauds of the 1920's should not interfere with new sound loans under consideration."[49] The State Department tried to hold up loans to Colombia, which had been in default for years, but Morgenthau stepped in again. Feis told the deflated White that when the complaints came in from the bondholders, he would "send them all to Mr. Morgenthau to answer."[50]

Roosevelt and Morgenthau exerted great pressure on the State Department to settle the problems of old defaulted loans quickly, and both criticized the FBPC in the press in October 1939. Asked if outstanding Latin American debts "were an obstacle to the good neighbor program," Roosevelt replied that "of course he favored scaling down this debt, the matter going back to 1933 when the Administration gave its blessing to the FBPC." He added that "members of the council had been working along and he did not think they had got very far," and he concluded with the comment that he was "rather disappointed with their operations."[51] Morgenthau was less tactful in stating his opinion of the FBPC: "What have they done? No money has passed and I'd like to know of any settlement." Morgenthau said that the federal government would begin direct negotiations with Latin American countries to set a " 'pattern' for cleaning up Latin American finances."[52]

Roosevelt "personally designated" a committee consisting of Morgenthau, Welles, and Jesse Jones of the Reconstruction Finance Corporation "to deal with the subject of debt defaults of the other American republics." It was established under the newly created Interdepartmental Committee on Cooperation with the American Republics, which included representatives from twenty-two government agencies and was chaired by Welles.[53] The committee would act on Roosevelt's sudden urgency to resolve old private debts, which had produced acrimony, and would establish in their place intergovernmental debts, which were designed to produce allegiance. Welles set aside his personal opinion on the subject and presented the FBPC with an ultimatum on behalf of the U.S. government: "If the FBPC continues to expect our help and active interest, they will have to abide by our recommendations as to policy." In the case of Brazil, the State Department "virtually coerced" Francis White to accept the final settlement, opening the doors for $19 million in Export-Import loans. In the case of Colombia, the hasty settlement "smacked somewhat of a double-cross to the bondholders," said FBPC Vice-President Dana Munro.[54] This shift in policy led Minister Norweb in Ciudad Trujillo to observe that "the State Department is being pushed more and more out of the international financial problems" in favor of Morgenthau and Jones, the probable overseers of the new Inter-American Bank. Norweb noticed that Economic Advisor Herbert Feis, whose FBPC had lost step entirely with the pace of the Good Neighbor policy, "was being more or less left out of these matters."[55] A settlement with the Dominican Republic could not be far behind.

The alphabet soup of draft proposals for a Dominican national bank cooked up by the negotiators during the spring of 1940 resulted in Draft X, which everyone involved deemed an equitable solution. They decided that a "fiscal representative," who would be appointed by Trujillo from a list of nominees submitted by Roosevelt, would replace the general receiver of Dominican customs, a procedure that resolved the major issue of debt supervision. Pastoriza took the document to Trujillo for his approval in May, but he returned to Washington from the Dominican capital with bad news. Trujillo had insisted on an abrogation of the Convention of 1924, not simply a tactful replacement of it.[56] This was an affront to the State Department, and the indignant assistant secretary, Laurence Duggan, was ready to give up, telling Welles (who had come to depend on Duggan's assistance in Latin American policy), "I think we can rest on our oars for awhile."[57] But Welles was now a man with a mission. Welles knew that Trujillo was depositing millions in personal accounts in U.S. banks, and that the Dominican government was entirely, unquestionably solvent, but he also knew that solvency and debt service were no longer the issues. Defense was.[58]

## "FLIRTATIONS" WITH THE AXIS

The military courtship of Trujillo was allowed to flourish in its variety of forms in 1939 when the Roosevelt administration committed itself to war preparedness. The administration did not seek written defense agreements from the Caribbean republics for more than a year, not until the summer of 1940, but in the meantime it cultivated informal ties with Trujillo through the Marines. The USS *Texas* visit to the Avenida USMC commemoration in February 1939 had a notably warming effect on relations between the two countries' armed forces. Trujillo professed his readiness for military cooperation even before Roosevelt set the public tone for hemispheric defense with his Pan-American Day speech, 14 April 1939, on "the American peace." "We are prepared to maintain it, and to defend it to the fullest extent of our strength. . . . Our will to peace can be as powerful as our will to mutual defense."[59] Trujillo had said as much to ten members of the House of Representatives Subcommittee on Naval Affairs who visited the Dominican Republic in early April, saying that "harbor and other facilities" in the country "were at the unlimited disposal of the United States."[60] He also announced to the American press his desire to build air and naval bases in the Dominican Republic that would be at U.S. disposal.[61]

At the same time, however, Trujillo demonstrated that he was "capable of flirtations" with the fascist states of Europe.[62] In 1938, Trujillo had welcomed a German naval visit to Ciudad Trujillo with "social and official pleasantries," and he gave permission for the German battleship *Schlesien* and its escort oil tanker to visit Samaná Bay.[63] In response to the presence of a German warship in that strategic anchorage, Roosevelt asked Welles to "please expedite" sending a U.S. Navy destroyer to the bay at the same time.[64] The USS *Mugford* steamed over from the naval base at Guantánamo Bay and was greeted by Charles McLaughlin, the former Marine now serving as a lieutenant colonel in the Dominican Army, and a contingent of four English-speaking Dominican officers. McLaughlin hosted the German and American officers at a dance at the City Clubhouse in Sánchez, then accompanied the American officers on board the *Schlesien* the next day for a lunch hosted by the German captain, a lunch that was also attended by the British and German consuls and the mayor of Sánchez. Movies of Mussolini's trip to Germany and German Navy maneuvers were screened for the luncheon guests, as they had been "in all ports visited" by the battleship. The *Mugford* had been the first American warship to visit Samaná "in quite some time whereas German and French ships have been there almost yearly," reported its captain, but thereafter the U.S. Navy paid closer attention to the area.[65] The cruiser *Philadelphia* surveyed the bay and visited the capital in October 1938, and "Fleet Problem Twenty," the naval maneuvers that tested Caribbean defense in early 1939, used Samaná with Trujillo's permission.[66] A dozen warships in the company of the aircraft carrier USS *Langley* conducted exercises there, with aircraft "flying over the bay and adjacent Dominican territory."[67]

Despite Trujillo's offer to let the United States "take over" Samaná Bay "and keep a vessel there all the time," other aspects of his international policy toward Germany and Italy undermined the credibility of such pledges.[68] The German Horn Line steamship company initiated regular service to Santo Domingo in 1936, linking Germany with San Juan and Jamaica.[69] The "Dominican-German Scientific Institute" established in 1938 with a staff of German scientists, worried American observers, who suspected it was for the purpose of setting up "a Nazi colony."[70] Although the institute was subsequently ousted by the Dominican government, the U.S. legation discounted "much of the supposed anti-Nazi activity" of the Trujillo regime as "dumb show and noise" put on to please the United States, which had shown it "was eager to see evidence of anti-Nazi feeling in the American Republics."[71] Even during 1939, when Trujillo was paid in the currency of respect and attention during his visit to Washington, he kept the Americans guessing about his true allegiance. Trujillo displayed three books on his desk for visiting diplomats to see: biographies of Franklin Roosevelt and Adolf Hitler, and a volume on life in the Soviet Union. Observers at the legation and in the State Department discerned and discussed the fascistic elements of the Trujillo regime, such as the "Trujillo Salute," the Partido Dominicano, and the boot-stomping participation of the military in frequent nationalist displays. In addition to these outward manifestations, the civic ideology of the Trujillo regime was disturbing. The *Cartilla cívica para el pueblo dominicano* [Civic Primer for the Dominican People] was "disseminated to every school child in his country, and taught in the schools." Diplomats noted uneasily that the "Civic Primer" taught that "a sick person has nothing to offer and gives nothing except pain."[72] Schoolchildren at all levels learned "military discipline and military exercises" beginning during Trujillo's first term.[73]

In August 1939, when Dr. Hans Felix Rohrecke joined the Cuerpo Diplomático, Hitler had thereby fulfilled Trujillo's "long-cherished desire" to host a fully accredited minister from the Third Reich. Trujillo had dispatched a minister to Berlin in June 1935, and he had sent his daughter Flor de Oro and her husband Porfirio Rubirosa, a dashing protegé of Trujillo, to serve at the post the following year.[74] In 1938, Trujillo appointed a prominent figure, the former minister to the United States Roberto Despradel, to be chief of mission in Germany; Roberto's brother Arturo had replaced Ortega Frier as foreign minister earlier in the year, becoming the only "ideological fascist" in the cabinet.[75] Roberto Despradel presented his credentials at Hitler's Alpine retreat near Berchtesgaden in November.[76] British Minister Paterson reported that Rohrecke's appointment to Ciudad Trujillo the following year "was in the guise of reciprocity for that of a Dominican Minister at Berlin, [but] was doubtless designed mainly to exploit the generally credited pro-Nazi and anti-American sympathies of the Trujillo regime."[77] Dominican Foreign Minister Arturo Logroño had signaled as much to the German consul back in 1935, when he compared Trujillo to Hitler and himself to Joseph Goebbels.[78] The new German minister "had ample means and time at his disposal, [and] was able to entertain lavishly and travel freely about the country." A minister from Mussolini's Italy, which had forgiven the Barletta incident, also resided in Ciudad Trujillo: Commendatore Mario Porta, who arrived in October 1937, the month of the Haitian massacre. Porta was "the best-paid head of mission" in the Diplomatic Corps, and "he and his [English] wife entertain lavishly and are to all intents and purposes members of the Anglo-American community." With the outbreak of the Second World War in September 1939, a month after Rohrecke's arrival, the presence of the Axis diplomats took on greater significance. Porta disrupted the Diplomatic Corps by becoming "personally hostile" to the British minister, "to the point of avoiding the usual exchange of salutations on public occasions." His wife, though English, "became by her defeatist talk a most insidious anti-British propagandist, especially amongst American women." Rohrecke "attained some success amongst all classes of Dominicans—and especially the army which was impressed by German successes." Minister Paterson judged that "American isolationism smoothed his way."[79]

The outbreak of the Second World War also brought the danger of German submarine operations in the Caribbean.[80] In October 1939, a Dominican Coast Guard cutter sank in a collision with a French destroyer amid rumors that the cutter had been engaged in a refueling operation for German subs near Samaná Bay.[81] The French were convinced that such was the case, and they seized a Dominican merchant steamer at Martinique in reprisal.[82] The State Department made no public comment, but Assistant Secretary of State Adolph A. Berle made quiet inquiries to the Division of American Republics after receiving further reports of "oil movements" to German submarines at sea in the vicinity of the Dominican Republic.[83] At the same time, Trujillo "shied away" from issuing the blanket permission for naval and air visits to the Dominican Republic that he had tendered earlier in the year.[84] At a ceremony awarding an Italian prince the Order of Duarte in February 1940, Trujillo denounced American "financial intervention" in the form of the lingering customs receivership, which he called "a formidable barrier to a policy of true cooperation" with the United States.[85]

British Minister Paterson was even more disturbed by "the ultra-neutral atmosphere of the U.S. Legation" between February 1940 (when Norweb departed) and June (when Robert Scotten presented his credentials as minister). During that time, the chargé d'affaires was Eugene Hinkle, "in part of German descent," whose behavior toward Rohrecke and Porta was of "almost open pro-Nazi sympathy," said Paterson. Considering the significance of social behavior in the culture of foreign relations in the Dominican Republic during the Trujillo regime, Hinkle's actions seem to merit Paterson's denunciation. Hinkle, the son of a millionaire steel magnate, gave a dinner in honor of the two Axis ministers less than a week after the German invasion of Norway on 23 February 1940, and even "when the U.S. official attitude had moved a long way from isolation, [he] dined at the Italian Legation on the day following President Roosevelt's 'stab in the back' utterance" of 10 June, denouncing Italy's declaration of war on France. These dinners were "marks of attention which could not fail to be noted by the Dominican authorities." Paterson attributed the neutral stance of the Dominican press toward the war—a stance dictated by the government—to Hinkle's friendly treatment of the German and Italian diplomats. The U.S. Legation also "set a bad example" for the American Colony, because "the swollen size of the Legation staff, now numbering forty, makes it, with the families of its members, a predominant element" in the expatriate community, and these people were expected to follow the lead of the acting chief of mission. The situation ended later in June, when Minister Robert McGregor Scotten arrived and "put an end to overt expressions" of amity for the Axis ministers.[86] Charlie Chaplin's film *The Great Dictator* (1940) came to Ciudad Trujillo the following February, seven months after Eugene Hinkle's departure, and some in the audience at the Teatro Rialto were probably reminded of him by Chaplin's satire of Hitler, a character named

"Adenoid Hynkel."[87] If so, perhaps the scene in the movie most reminiscent for them of Hinkle's controversial tenure as chargé was the hilarious dinner party scene, featuring Hynkel, his Göring-like army chief (who resembled Rohrecke, a "large, florid German type"), and the Italian envoy.[88]

Robert Scotten was the same age as Trujillo, forty-eight and, like most U.S. diplomats, he was a product of Ivy League schools and Anglophilia. He held the pro-Allied, antifascist views of his superiors in the White House and the State Department, whose policy was increasingly tilted in favor of the British cause, although British Minister Paterson criticized the new chief of mission because he "preferred the golf course" to "the details of the work of his post." German Minister Rohrecke contributed to his own loss of influence by publishing an open letter in *La Nación* soon after Scotten's arrival, in which he thanked the many Dominicans who had congratulated him on the blitzkrieg. Scotten immediately "induced" the Dominican government to "administer a public rebuke" to Rohrecke, and thereafter *La Nación* supported the Allied cause in print, even employing Spanish Republican writers who angered Rohrecke and Porta with their "repeated lampooning of their masters."[89] Rohrecke and Porta could not have been thrilled by the popularity of *The Great Dictator* either, a film that skewered the fascist bombast and racist arrogance of their governments, traits that were also characteristic of the government to which they were accredited. It is somewhat surprising that Trujillo approved exhibition of the film in the Dominican Republic in the first place, given its withering denunciation of dictatorship. There were eerie similarities between Chaplin's 1940 film and the 1936 *March of Time* newsreel "An American Dictator," especially the dinner party scenes: in one there is a hysterical, deathly pale Adenoid Hynkel shrieking at his guests; in the other, there is an actor in pancake makeup as a mustache-twirling Trujillo, murdering his guests. The newsreel, of course, was banned in the Dominican Republic, but not the film. Perhaps Trujillo failed to see the resemblance between his regime and that of Chaplin's Hynkel in "Tomania" and, therefore, it never occurred to him to suppress *The Great Dictator.* Or perhaps it did, but he decided that to ban a movie calling for human freedom and dignity against political oppression could damage his public and foreign relations. "However great his admiration for Herr Hitler," Trujillo was careful not "to provoke the United States by any overt act of pro-Nazism."[90]

The increased U.S. naval visitation to the Dominican Republic during 1939 and 1940 was partly in response to Trujillo's dalliance with the Axis powers. More tangible benefits for Trujillo were also forthcoming from the U.S. military during this period. Trujillo obtained Coast Guard cutters at bargain prices, beginning the flow of military goods from the United States to the Dominican armed forces, although the State Department continued to refuse permission for Trujillo to buy rifles in the United States. Trujillo also welcomed the long-sought appointment of a naval attaché (a Marine officer) to his government in February 1940—and, later, a military attaché—establishing direct U.S. military liaison with the Dominican government.[91] Weapons transfers and staff interaction would become dominant elements in relations between the two countries during and after World War II, as the Dominican Republic was fortified with Lend-Lease arms and airplanes, and the Inter-American Defense Board and Standing Liaison Committee were created to coordinate the Fortress America alliance.

The Export-Import Bank was also added to the diplomatic repertoire of the Good Neighbor policy at this time, offering credits to Latin American governments to stimulate inter-American trade. Despite the efforts of the FBPC, Herbert Feis, and certain members of Congress to prevent Export-Import money from going to nations in default, all Latin American nations were eligible for Roosevelt's "rich-uncle-ism," including the Dominican Republic.[92] In March 1940, the Dominican government requested funding for projects "chiefly for municipal embellishments," and although there was some opposition in the Division of American Republics, the Export-Import Bank favored the allocation.[93] The Bank approved $2 million in credits in June 1940, carefully leaving the impression that more would be forthcoming if the Dominican government agreed to a foreign debt settlement.[94]

## MILITARY STAFF TALKS

In June 1940, the Roosevelt administration finally took Trujillo up on his standing offer to join forces, an offer that Minister Pastoriza had reiterated in a letter to Hull in December 1939.[95] The "exploratory conversations" and "staff conversations" that followed in June and August 1940 were part of a hemisphere-wide effort on the part of the Joint Army and Navy Planning Committee "to obtain Military Cooperation with the American Republics."[96] The Joint Planning Committee dispatched Lieutenant Colonel Norman Randolph, USA, and Colonel Pedro A. del Valle, USMC, to Cuba, Haiti, and the Dominican Republic to sound out "the ability and willingness of each country to cooperate with the United States" in hemisphere defense.

Del Valle, who was Puerto Rican, was particularly well qualified for this errand. He had served with the Marine occupation of the Dominican Republic in 1916, with the Garde d'Haiti in the late 1920s, and as squadron marine officer with the Special Service Squadron in Havana at the time of Fulgencio Batista's rise to power in 1933.[97] He was also a friend of Colonel Thomas Watson, who continued to work on Trujillo's behalf and even to visit him in secret during this period.[98] The talks with Trujillo focused on airfields, and resulted in an oral agreement for broad military cooperation.[99] "The Generalissimo reiterated again and again that Santo Domingo was 100% with the United States insofar as concerns the necessary measures of hemisphere defense," reported Scotten.[100] The staff talks themselves were not publicized in the Dominican Republic, but "the idea of forming a powerful military alliance between the nations of Continental America" was praised under a banner headline ("Political Change in All of America") in *Listín Diario* soon afterward.[101] Trujillo followed up with his offer of "the land, the sea, the air, and the men of the Dominican Republic," announced by Foreign Minister Arturo Despradel at the Havana Conference in late July.[102] In the meantime, Pan American Airways undertook the development of the airport at Santo Domingo, acting "as the agent" of the U.S. government, which paid for the improvements.[103]

A second U.S. military staff mission to the three Antillean republics arrived in Ciudad Trujillo in time for Restoration Day, 16 August 1940, one of the two most important Dominican national holidays. Marking the restoration of Dominican sovereignty at the end of the Spanish recolonization of 1861–65, the occasion had often been taken by Trujillo in the past to lambaste intervention in general and the Marine occupation of 1916–24 in particular. At the 1940 celebration, however, Trujillo delivered what Scotten judged to be "the most friendly" speech he had ever made about the United States.[104] In anticipation of the next day's talks with the two U.S. military representatives, the point of the address was to prepare "the Dominican people for any defense arrangements which may be made with the U.S.," indicating Trujillo's "willingness to cooperate fully in such a program."[105]

The U.S. "liaison officers," Commander Rufus King of the Navy and Lieutenant Colonel Arthur Harris of the Army, were accompanied to the Presidential Palace the following morning by Scotten and the naval attaché, Captain John A. Butler, USMC. After introductions to Trujillo, who was attended by Pastoriza and Colonel McLaughlin, the U.S. delegation submitted a prepared statement to him reprising "the preliminary conversations" of June which had resulted in the general defense agreement and the plans to develop the Santo Domingo airport under the name of Pan American Airways. The statement explained that the present talks were to ascertain "the requirements of the Dominican Republic for adequate defense" against a "non-American state" and to outline "the broad strategical problem" posed by Germany. Trujillo replied that the Dominican armed forces were sufficient to suppress "any internal (5th Column) attack," and he assured King and Harris "that he would not hesitate to use concentration camps in the suppression of non-American activities." He then repeated the offer of full assistance announced previously at the Havana Conference, "including the blood of the Dominicans themselves," and said he "would prefer to let the United States determine" what military assistance he required.

Lieutenant Colonel Harris "found it difficult to reply" because "he was so impressed with the Generalísimo's magnanimous attitude," but he managed to add that it was "the least he could do" to help Trujillo compose a list of weapons for the United States to supply. Harris's list included the shipment of rifles that the State Department had been holding up (4,500 Springfield "thirty aught six" models), along with an assorted gross of machine guns.[106] He "recommended that the arms be made available" to Trujillo as "a fitting reward for his fine spirit of cooperation." In return, Trujillo gave Harris and King a list of harbors and airfields in the Dominican Republic, placing "all the facilities and resources of the country . . . unreservedly at the disposal" of the American armed forces.[107]

## THE HULL-TRUJILLO TREATY

The State Department also contributed to the flurry of personal diplomacy that took place in Ciudad Trujillo during the summer of 1940, as they pushed for an agreement to end the customs receivership. Hull took the opportunity of Scotten's arrival in June to send Trujillo his "personal regards" and best wishes for "a speedy recovery" from his bout with anthrax, and he followed up by sending a shipment of medicine and detailing a Navy doctor to examine the Generalísimo.[108] Welles then suggested that a special representative go to Santo Domingo to "thrash out" the issue of the debt in Trujillo's presence.[109] "Knowing as I do the Dominican psychology in this regard," Welles explained to Scotten, it would be "expedient for the negotiations" to appoint a "high-ranking official" for the talks rather than the first-time U.S. minister, who was just establishing his "social position" in the capital.[110] Trujillo was "in entire agreement" with the move, so Hugh Wilson, former ambassador to Germany, was appointed as special representative to the Dominican Republic (he was the first U.S. envoy to the country appointed with the rank of ambassador).[111]

Hugh Wilson arrived in Ciudad Trujillo the day after the bilateral military-staff talks of 17 August 1940. Wilson's prestigious mission, coming on the heels of the military agreement and the Export-Import Bank allocation, broke the long impasse over the Convention of 1924. Within a week, Wilson and Trujillo agreed on a new convention that would abolish the U.S. Receivership of Dominican Customs. They retained the basic form of Draft X, which had been on the table since June, with its provisions for a bank depository and a fiscal representative to oversee payment of the debt.[112] The Foreign Bondholders Protective Council was written out of the final draft, however, which designated a "representative of the holders of the 1922 and 1926 bonds" as the fiscal representative rather than a "representative of the FBPC."[113] Wilson stayed in the Dominican Republic until early September, attending luncheons and galas, and was still being fêted after Trujillo departed for a leisurely trip via Florida to Washington to sign the treaty they drafted.[114]

Trujillo stopped to see Hull a few days before the signing ceremony and "was profuse in every way in his professions of friendship and cooperation."[115] The Trujillo-Hull Treaty, as the Convention of 1940 was known in the Dominican Republic, was signed in Hull's office on 24 September 1940 and was celebrated as a national holiday in the Dominican Republic.[116] The State Department announcement of the treaty claimed the inauguration of "a new era" in U.S.-Dominican relations, calling the accord "an additional step in the development and coordination of the Good Neighbor Policy."[117] Trujillo returned to the Dominican Republic on 20 October, which was celebrated as another national holiday. Trujillo began the day with an address to a joint session of the Congress, where "he reviewed the importance to the Dominican Republic of the recovery of its sovereignty" and "praised the facilities which had been given him in Washington and the interest shown by President Roosevelt and Secretary Hull in the negotiations." He "emphasized the special nature of relations" between the two countries, which he said was based on the importance of "the route to the Panama Canal," and his peroration invoked "the defense of the hemisphere and democratic traditions" in declaring Dominican opposition to "the ambition of conquest" threatening to bring "war to these shores."[118]

Twenty-five thousand people from all over the country—"representatives of all the large foreign colonies, industries, unions and political subdivisions"—participated in a "March of Victory" in the afternoon of 20 October. The American Colony's delegation, including "over 100 leading business men, occupied a prominent place" in the procession, halting for the American and Dominican national anthems when they reached the reviewing stand. Minister Scotten thought the name "March of Victory" was "badly chosen," because it could imply "a diplomatic defeat" on the part of the United States, but he comforted himself that his own participation (no other member of the Diplomatic Corps had been invited) and that of the American Colony "dispelled any misunderstanding" on that score.[119] Of course, the incorporation of so many Americans into a ceremony that, Scotten admitted, was "marked by a spirit of national pride" could easily be interpreted the other way, as visible evidence that Trújillo really was calling the shots now in the bilateral relationship. Generalísimo Doctor Trujillo, Benefactor of the Fatherland, also added another title to his heraldic moniker as a result of the Convention of 1940: "Restorer of the Financial Independence of the Republic."[120]

Since Roosevelt's Good Neighbor relations with the Dominican Republic were always conducted with the intention of improving the image of the United States throughout Latin America, the State Department closely monitored the reactions of other nations to the Hull-Trujillo Treaty. The results were encouraging. Rio de Janeiro's *Correio da Manha* called it "a new achievement of the policy of peace, justice, and good will . . . one more good lesson to be learned from America."[121] The *Diario de Centro América* of Guatemala saw it as "tangible evidence of the new North American policy towards the nations of the continent."[122] Other Latin American journals followed suit, as did editorial comment in many U.S. papers.[123] The *New York Times* took the words right out of Roosevelt's mouth: "The new agreement records the determination of the United States to abide by the implications of the Good Neighbor policy, and to build its relations with other American countries on a basis of equality rather than one of domination."[124]

Cordell Hull's role in bringing about the treaty made him the literal image of the Good Neighbor in the Dominican Republic. "Pictures [of Hull] by the thousands" were distributed around the country by the government in the early 1940s, finding their way into "some of the most remote villages in the interior," and a street in Ciudad Trujillo was named Avenida Cordell Hull. Later in the decade, a large Trujillo-Hull monument would be erected on the waterfront *Malecón* in the capital.[125] Sumner Welles, usually regarded as the principal architect of the Good Neighbor policy, was instead denounced by the Trujillo regime for his association with exiles.[126]

Although Welles had been instrumental in finally bringing about a settlement ending the customs receivership, especially by involving Hugh Wilson as a special ambassador, his heart was still not in it. In a conversation with the bondholder Frank Vedder about the Hull-Trujillo Treaty, Welles recounted the story of a Dominican woman he met while he was serving with the Dawes Commission. She had a plan to go into the fishery business, to buy some boats and drill holes in their hulls to fish through: small holes for small fish, big holes for big fish. Welles applied the analogy to "the various projects" of the Dominican government for debt resolution, which he said were "just as fantastic as this woman's schemes."[127] Unable to shed his latent disdain for non-elite Dominicans, Welles did not admit the success that many of Trujillo's "projects" had already enjoyed, including the infrastructure development that military visitors admired and the settlement of the foreign debt on terms favorable to the Dominican Republic. Nor did Welles foresee Trujillo's success in simultaneously building up his armed forces and paying off the remaining foreign bonds over the next seven years, accomplishments facilitated by the new military and financial ties with the United States.

The Hull-Trujillo Treaty cleared the way for such ties to proliferate. Minister Pastoriza requested another Export-Import Bank loan on the day the treaty draft was initialed.[128] In December 1940, the bank allocated $4 million for road and hotel construction in the Dominican Republic. The modern La Jaragua hotel in Ciudad Trujillo was built with this money, supplanting the old city hotels, Fausto and Colón, as the preferred entertainment venue of the Trujillo regime. The bank claimed that the loan "had nothing to do" with the Hull-Trujillo Treaty, but the loan and the agreement were intertwined with the defense arrangement in constituting a new kind of Good Neighbor policy in the Dominican Republic in 1940.[129] This version cut through the long-standing moral tension between nonintervention and approval of dictatorships, a tension that had nurtured State Department opposition to ties with Trujillo, and instead fully embraced his regime for the sake of regional defense.

That the Hull-Trujillo Treaty and regional defense were linked in the new wartime Good Neighbor policy was implied in Hull's announcement of the agreement on 7 September 1940, which he revealed at the same time as the epochal "destroyers-for-bases," which brought British military facilities in the hemisphere under U.S. control. The end of the U.S. Receivership and the acquisition of eight new bastions for Fortress America were extolled together in Hull's statement stressing "effective cooperation [and] common defense" in the hemisphere.[130] Within a month, the Pan-American foreign ministers's meeting at the Panama Conference declared a *cordon sanitaire* around the Americas extending hundreds of miles into international waters. Franklin Roosevelt followed up on this "Declaration of Panama" in a landmark speech at Dayton, Ohio, on 12 October, in which he sounded a new urgency on the theme of continental defense.[131] Less than a week later, Minister Scotten in Ciudad Trujillo was requested "to obtain from the Dominican authorities a signed statement" verifying the oral agreement on defense reached at the staff talks of August 1940. The Dominican government complied immediately.[132]

## THE END OF THE RECEIVERSHIP

The Hull-Trujillo Treaty led to a final parting between the Roosevelt administration and the FBPC.[133] The council's falling out with government policy was apparent after Roosevelt's and Morgenthau's public attack on the FBPC's record in late 1939, but the final parting of the ways between the FBPC and the State Department, "the subject of one of the most deliberate and gravest debates the Council ever had," was over the Hull-Trujillo Treaty.[134] Francis White, now president of the council, did not receive a copy of the treaty until the day before Hull and Trujillo were to sign it. He went to the State Department the next day, apparently unaware that the signatories were meeting for the ceremony in Hull's office.[135] After reading the news of the signing the following morning in the newspaper, White returned to the State Department to ask Laurence Duggan if the report was true.[136] Told that it was, White telephoned Arthur Burke of Guaranty Trust, the fiscal agent for the Dominican bonds, who told him he "knew nothing about the treaty except what he had seen in the paper."[137] Then White called an official of National City Bank, specified as the depository for Dominican revenues in the new treaty, who also knew only "what he had seen in the press."[138] The fact that neither the old fiscal agent nor the new depository had been kept informed by the State Department concerning the last stage of negotiations is indicative of the forcefulness and haste of Good Neighbor diplomacy toward debtor nations during 1940.

Francis White finally saw Hull at the State Department on 7 November 1940, a month after the treaty was signed. Hull arranged for White to be briefed first by most of the State Department officials involved with the treaty negotiations, including Ambassador Hugh Wilson, Assistant Secretary of State Laurence Duggan, and Legal Advisor Green Hackworth.[139] Wilson told White that the removal of the customs receivership was necessary partly because "this remnant of American intervention had seriously embarrassed the Department in successfully carrying out its policy of friendship and understanding with the other American republics." Moreover, Wilson said that hemispheric preparedness necessitated Dominican cooperation, and that with "the termination of the Customs Receivership, there would be removed a difficult and irritating obstacle to the success of the policy of hemispheric solidarity." Duggan predicted that "the Dominican Republic would become a more cooperative debtor" as a result of the Hull-Trujillo Treaty, and Hackworth said he feared a total default on the $15 million Dominican debt unless the treaty gave the Dominican Republic "a shot in the arm."[140] White next met with Hull, who recapitulated all of the points made earlier by his subordinates. The Convention of 1924 and the Mexican oil controversy, said Hull, were the last two "sore thumbs" that "stuck up" from the Good Neighbor policy. He told White he had had "one hell of a time" keeping the Latin American community from adopting a resolution against the Convention of 1924 at the Havana Conference, and he stressed the importance of lining up the hemisphere in a defensive alliance. Hull promised to send White a letter setting forth the State Department's position, but said that "the effect on national defense" could not be put into writing. If the letter did not convince White to side with State, Hull said, he could protest at the Senate ratification hearing and there would be "no hard feelings."[141]

White would have his day at the Senate Foreign Relations Committee hearings, but not before the State Department laid its own case before the group. On 27 November, Green Hackworth borrowed some of Trujillo's rhetoric and told the senators that the customs receivership had been "a thorn in the side of the Dominican government for a long period of time," but now the U.S. government was "getting away from the idea of wielding a big stick over the heads of those people."[142] He cited the favorable Latin American press commentary on the proposed treaty. Senator Arthur Vandenburg, with a letter of protest from White before him, asked about Roosevelt's 1933 statement that the U.S. government had no power to change such debt arrangements; and Hackworth's assistant, Harold Finley (who had accompanied Hugh Wilson to Ciudad Trujillo), replied that "times change and international agreements become outmoded. Our first obligation in the conduct of foreign policy is toward the public interest and secondarily, in this case, toward the bondholders."[143]

The senators seemed confused about the role of the FBPC, or even about what it was. Senator Theodore Green, a prominent member of the Dominican lobby, questioned why the FBPC had any standing at all in the matter.[144] The senators learned more about the FBPC the following week, when Francis White testified. He claimed that the average bondholder of Dominican securities was a common, sometimes impoverished, American citizen holding less than $500 in bonds, and he argued that the debt arrangement could not be legally altered without the permission of the bondholders.[145] Senator Green, who was the most vocal supporter of the treaty, sharply challenged White, saying that the State Department, representing the interests of the entire American polity, was in a better position to decide policy than the FBPC, the "protector" of a tiny and self-interested minority.[146] Harold Finley then returned to testify to the senators off the record that Cordell Hull "feared that Trujillo would throw [the customs receiver] out of the country," as he had threatened to do in 1938. Finley said that a "stiff note" from Hull prevented unilateral action then, but he could not guarantee what might happen if the treaty were not ratified.[147] As the committee hearings adjourned, Vandenburg continued to oppose the Hull-Trujillo Treaty as "a breach of faith" to the bondholders, notwithstanding the efforts of Representative Hamilton Fish of the Dominican lobby to "soften [him] up" on that score.[148]

During the floor debate, Theodore Green got to the heart of the argument in favor of ratification of the Hull-Trujillo Treaty. Green read into the record Trujillo's statement of military alliance, which he said "was the first substantial offer of cooperation and aid by any of the American republics."[149] Secretary Hull may have resisted putting the military angle into writing for Francis White, but Green knew what kind of reasoning would play in Congress, and he was free to express the link between regional defense and the end of the U.S. Receivership of Dominican Customs.

The Senate duly ratified the Hull-Trujillo Treaty on 14 February 1941. The next day the customs offices returned to Dominican control, and thirty-six years of U.S. Receivership records were boxed and shipped to Washington. Trujillo learned of the ratification as he stayed at the Waldorf

Astoria in New York City. He had discovered that he liked very much "to mingle in the society of Senators and Congressmen," and he had come back to the United States for a three-month hiatus.[150]

The FBPC was not officially informed of the dismantling of the Receivership and its replacement by National City Bank as depository until six weeks later.[151] The day the notice from the State Department arrived, Reuben Clark wrote Francis White suggesting that the defeated organization "shrink" to a skeleton operation, and that it not allow itself "to be made the 'goat'" for policies it strenuously condemned.[152] Dana Munro complained to White that "the whole arrangement for the service of the bonds would become little more than a joke."[153] As Export-Import Bank money and new armaments flowed into the Dominican Republic, as Rafael Trujillo began spending longer periods of time enjoying his vast wealth on vacations to the United States, Francis White commiserated with Munro, his fellow refugee from the Hoover administration. "This whole Dominican matter," he said, "is a travesty."[154]

The U.S. Receivership of Dominican Customs, with its control of the nation's commercial entrepôts and its veto power over the national budget, had stood in tangible, visible opposition to the Good Neighbor policy. Until its removal, U.S. efforts to reformulate regional relations on the basis of respect for the national autonomy of the Latin American republics would be incomplete. Why, then, did it take until 1941 to heal the "sore thumb" of the Good Neighbor policy? The reasons for this long delay are best explained by an interpretation that emphasizes the bureaucratic parameters of the issue, which were greatly complicated by the bankruptcy of the Dominican Republic. Policy makers in both the Hoover and Roosevelt administrations found it difficult to reconcile public policy with private debts, even though those debts had been incurred through the agency of the Marine occupation. Dominican Minister Roberto Despradel had been impatient for Cordell Hull to make "technicalities harmonize with policy," but the architects of the Good Neighbor policy found this to be easier said than done.[155] While trying to remodel the structure of U.S. policy, they realized that the previous tenants, the bondholders, were still on the premises and could not be made to leave quietly. Their solution was to give the work to a subcontractor, the Foreign Bondholders Protective Council.

The improvisation of this anomalous bureaucracy perpetuated rather than resolved the problem of the customs receivership and the Dominican foreign debt. Although the FBPC was effective as a buffer between the

State Department on one hand and both the Dominican government and the holders of its bonds on the other, the council confused the dynamics of the situation considerably. First, because Roosevelt staffed the FBPC with Hoover administration diplomats who believed civilization rested on the sanctity of contracts, it was not an easily manipulated organization. Second, because he suspended the FBPC in a legal limbo between government authority and private advocacy, the organization was not clearly accountable to anyone. Instead, everyone involved in the dispute tried to shape the FBPC to suit their own perceptions of its role.

Differing views of the FBPC's mission were especially apparent in the U.S. government. Roosevelt and Hull wanted the council to be a vehicle transporting the debt problem away from Washington, but Sumner Welles and his allies in the State Department used the FBPC to defend the Convention of 1924 in the Dominican Republic, mainly by providing damaging information about Trujillo's financial record. The staff of the U.S. legation provided the dirt on the dictatorship but complained that the U.S. government, not the FBPC, was responsible for collecting the Dominican debt. Lack of coordination between these different axes of the diplomatic bureaucracy impeded the full implementation of the Good Neighbor policy in the case of the Dominican Republic. The addition of the FBPC to this set of institutional actors slowed the integration and adoption of nonintervention as the criterion of U.S.-Dominican relations and helped perpetuate U.S. financial control through the imperialist receivership. The acrimony generated by the protracted debt negotiations of the 1930s was among the three main reasons for what José Antonio Osorio Lizarazo called *The Birth and Growth of Anti-Trujillism in America,* the title of his 1958 book. He blamed three groups for the problems in U.S.-Dominican relations: "the sugar interests" (meaning the U.S. companies pushed out by Trujillo); "the professional revolution-mongers" (meaning the exiles and their allies in the media); and "the bond-holders." [156]

The sword that cut this legal, bureaucratic, and interventionist knot was the same one forged by the Roosevelt administration to defend the hemisphere in the late 1930s. As early as February 1937, Dominican Minister Pastoriza had advocated replacing the "anachronism" of the U.S. Receivership with a "defensive alliance" with his country, a course of action brought into being by the unfolding global war. The bondholders' interests were outweighed by the national interests outlined by U.S. Minister Norweb in 1939: "military concessions" from Trujillo and the furtherance of "good neighborliness" and "inter-American solidarity." In the case of the Dominican Republic, the Good Neighbor policy did not make the transition from rhetoric to action until the catalyst of world conflict was added. Then, the Roosevelt administration discarded the FBPC and expedited the conclusion of the Hull-Trujillo Treaty to remove the last bad wood of intervention, replacing it with the stout timber of military cooperation. The subsequent construction of Fortaleza Trujillo as a bastion of Fortress America proved to be very durable.

## TWO INAUGURATIONS, TWO EMBASSIES

In comparison with the vast scale of the overall U.S. war effort, the assistance given to the Dominican Republic in the form of weapons, supplies, and expertise was minuscule. The Lend-Lease Act, which authorized arms and equipment transfers to "any country whose defense the President deems vital to the defense of the United States," was initially funded at $7 billion in March 1941.[157] Of this unprecedented arsenal, the Dominican share consisted of a dozen coastal patrol boats, nineteen airplanes, three thousand old Enfield rifles without ammunition, and some equipment for general use (medical kits and items of Marine apparel, like field hats and fabric for uniforms).[158] But this limited wartime aid influenced the Trujillo regime and helped it to accelerate the pervasive militarization of the country first set in motion by the Marine occupation. This process was expressed metaphorically with the expansion of the ancient Fortaleza Ozama in the heart of old Santo Domingo. This fortress had been the fulcrum of many Dominican wars and the headquarters of the U.S. Marines during the occupation, and it now continued as the ceremonial home of the Dominican military. The bastion was enlarged and renamed Fortaleza Trujillo in 1941, just as the public campaign for defense of the hemisphere was reaching a crescendo and as new sources of weaponry were becoming available to the Dominican Republic through Lend-Lease. The rechristening of the fort corresponded to the larger effort to reshape the entire country on the ideals of nationalism and military might and to portray an increasingly muscular version of Dominican sovereignty to audiences both domestic and international. The wartime experience of the Dominican Republic set the stage for Trujillo's postwar buildup of the Dominican armed forces, which far outstripped the expectations of Trujillo's erstwhile American military advisors and contributed to the instability of the Caribbean area.

With the arrangements for regional defense in place and his Lend-Lease wish list in the pipeline, Trujillo kept up his end of the bargain when the Japanese attacked Pearl Harbor on 7 December 1941, promptly joining the United States in declaring war against the Axis powers.[159] The two best vessels of the Dominican merchant marine, named *San Rafael* and *Presidente Trujillo,* were sunk by German submarines during May 1942, as submarine warfare intensified in the western Atlantic and claimed more than one hundred ships in the Caribbean that month.[160] The pressing need for coastal patrols and submarine tracking in the Caribbean speeded the allocation of nineteen Lend-Lease airplanes and a U.S. Naval Aviation Mission of fifteen fliers, trainers, and technicians to the Dominican Republic.[161] Although the "Arsenal of Democracy" could spare no more rifles and bullets for Trujillo's forces, airplanes were of far greater interest and potential use for the Dominican Republic and became the most important aspect of wartime assistance from the United States.[162]

The war also brought new airport facilities to Santo Domingo, where Pan American Airways expanded Miraflores Airport with U.S. government underwriting. Although American aviation experts agreed that the airfield at the Consuelo sugar estate, amid cane fields, was a safer location for military aircraft than Miraflores, just two miles from the center of Ciudad Trujillo, Trujillo insisted that the construction money go to the capital's airport "for political reasons."[163] Some of the most important events in Dominican public life during the years of the Second World War, occasions that combined the politics and culture of the regime, took place at the city's modern urban airport. Both of Trujillo's two inaugurations during the year 1942, when he resumed the presidency after his one-term hiatus, involved the airport and American airmen. His first, "emergency" inauguration coincided with the opening of the improved Miraflores Airport on 10 May and with the commencement of "the new Interamerican Air Service." Held on the broad tarmac with thousands in attendance, the event "eclipse[d] anything in the history of the Capital as regards political demonstrations." The day's activities served to "reaffirm and endorse" the previous dozen years of Trujillo's rule, judged Minister Robert Scotten, as well as to indicate the participants' "unreserved support" for his resumption of the presidency. "It is for this reason that the opening of the airport on this day, and the capital made of the presence of the diplomatic corps in the reviewing stand had at least potential significance."[164] Several U.S. Army and Navy officers who "were simply passing through" and who claimed ignorance of Trujillo's swearing-in were listed in the press among the dignitaries in attendance at the official ceremonies.

Trujillo's second inauguration of 1942 took place on the date that he had made customary, Restoration Day, 16 August. On that occasion, Lieutenant General Frank Maxwell Andrews, head of the Army Caribbean Defense Command based in the Panama Canal Zone and an eminent military aviator, made a "sudden arrival" with Major General James A. Collins and six staff officers on the day of the inauguration; they stayed overnight. Minister Avra Warren, who had arrived in July, reported the surprise to the State Department:

> President Trujillo was gratified at this visit and went to particular pains to show courtesies to these officers. They were met at the airport by two generals and a detachment of troops who rendered honors, and were conducted by the President himself to two of the ceremonies held that day. The presence of these high-ranking American officers in field uniform in the midst of the formally dressed Dominican and Latin American dignitaries was, in my opinion, one of the most fortunate features of the past week.[165]

Andrews made just the one visit to the Dominican Republic, but his preference for "direct action" concerning military liaison with Caribbean governments (cutting through the diplomatic channels dictated "by custom and also by orders"), and his praise for Trujillo's "beautification" of the capital, quickly endeared him to Trujillo.[166] After Andrews was killed in an airplane crash in 1944, Trujillo announced that Miraflores would be renamed for him.[167] The Dominican Centennial celebrations of 1944, which lasted ten days and included special diplomatic delegations from twenty-two countries, commenced with the inauguration of "Lieutenant General Andrews Airfield" on Pan-American Aviation Day, 22 February. Other major events attended by the entire Trujillo retinue and a mob of special envoys included the unveiling of the Trujillo-Hull Treaty Monument on Avenida George Washington and the laying of the Columbus Lighthouse cornerstone.[168]

Relations between the two countries took on many new facets during the war years, especially in 1943. During that year, diplomatic representation in both capitals rose to embassy status, with Jesús María Troncoso becoming the first Dominican ambassador to the United States in April. Four Central American nations and Haiti simultaneously upgraded their diplomatic representation to the embassy level, providing a Good Neighbor photo opportunity for FDR.[169] Trujillo's oldest child, Flor de Oro, became first secretary of the Dominican embassy and something of a celebrity. In October she awarded the Order of Trujillo and the Order of Duarte to the film star María Montez, a Dominican, "for her efforts toward promoting friendly relations" between the United States and "her native land."[170] Also in 1943, Undersecretary of State Sumner Welles was forced to resign from the State Department as the result of a homosexual scandal, removing the most vocal and powerful opponent of the Trujillo dictatorship from government.[171] The new force in U.S. Latin American policy was Nelson Rockefeller, grandson of the founder of Standard Oil Company and a Republican from New York, whom Roosevelt appointed to coordinate the administration's cultural overtures to the region. Rockefeller's office ordered the creation of "cultural coordination committees" at each of the diplomatic missions in Latin America. In Ciudad Trujillo, Rockefeller's friend Avra Warren devoted a room in the embassy for the weekly meetings, where the committee members (the first through third secretaries of the embassy) and their staff of three (including an "executive secretary" devoted full-time to committee work) planned the Dominican version of the Good Neighbor policy's cultural campaign. Their chosen instruments included films, posters, pamphlets, English teaching projects, maps of the two countries, and a Pan-American Day essay contest. The most active member of the committee after its formation in 1943 was Third Secretary of the Embassy W. Tapley Bennett, a future ambassador to the Dominican Republic.[172]

## THE MILITARY AID DEBATE

The military footing of inter-American relations during 1943 increased Trujillo's contact with U.S. military and diplomatic representatives, and the cultural manifestations of close wartime relations abounded during Warren's tenure as chief of mission in Ciudad Trujillo (his term lasted until April 1944). Warren apparently shared the respect for Trujillo's material accomplishments expressed by so many U.S. generals and admirals, and he delegated complete authority for Lend-Lease acquisitions to the embassy's naval attaché, Colonel Joe W. Smith, USMC.[173] After leaving the Dominican Republic, Warren became ambassador to Panama, the most important part of the region from a strategic perspective, where he formed a close association with Lieutenant General George H. Brett, head of the Caribbean Defense Command after Andrews's death.

In the wake of Warren's warm stay came Ellis O. Briggs, whose bitter distaste for the Trujillo regime developed rapidly. Briggs admitted the importance of "the security of the Caribbean" during 1942, when "a German attack on the New World was a real possibility," so he did not criticize the "past collaboration" with the Trujillo regime. But the crisis was long over, he claimed upon his arrival in July 1944, and it was time for an honest "stock-taking" of U.S. policy toward the dictatorship, "because the small Caribbean countries and our relations with them constitute a sort of show-window through which our inter-American relations are carefully examined by other—and more important—nations with which we are dealing."[174] Briggs objected to the flow of Lend-Lease matériel, especially aircraft, into the country. Colonel Smith, the naval attaché, went to Florida to arrange the delivery of six airplanes in July 1944 "without any reference whatever to the Embassy" and kept Briggs in the dark (as he had Warren) about the amount of Lend-Lease equipment already delivered. Briggs complained that the threat of submarine incursions was past, leaving "no justification" for arming the regime, and he protested the influence of Lieutenant General Brett of the Caribbean Defense Command.[175] Briggs's opposition revived the intragovernmental rivalry between the diplomats and the military over the direction of Dominican relations.

General Brett visited Ciudad Trujillo on three days' notice in July 1944, coming to invite Dominican officers to the Army Service Schools in Panama and to offer a U.S. Military Mission to the Dominican Republic. Brett's reception at Lieutenant General Andrews Airfield dominated the front page of *La Nación,* as it did when he returned on a visit four weeks later, this time with two days' notice to the embassy, but with elaborate planning by the Trujillo regime.[176] This time Brett brought Ambassador Warren with him from Panama, and Puerto Rico's Governor Rexford Guy Tugwell was also in attendance. As before, Brett and Trujillo discussed liaison and aviation projects without including Ambassador Briggs, who did not learn of the proposed Dominican national airline until he read about it in the Panama Canal Zone *Star and Herald.* The article, "General Brett Sees Dominican Air Progress," related how Brett and Warren "were strongly impressed by the evidences of progressive reform" in the "up-and-coming country," where "rapid development of air transportation" was predicted by Brett. Brett's back-to-back visits prompted another strong protest from Briggs, who urged the State Department to "re-assert its authority" in "the Caribbean republics," where military representatives had seized the initiative. "If my interpretation of the views of our military is correct, they regard President Trujillo and his Government with great favor, which they often make no effort to disguise. They are inclined to view Trujillo's many substantial achievements—maintenance of order, 'making the Dominicans work,' et cetera—as indicating that Trujillo is operating the best possible government in the best of all possible Caribbean worlds."[177]

Briggs recommended action on many of the long-standing grievances that diplomats in the Caribbean harbored toward their military rivals: unauthorized visits, conferrals of foreign decorations, public statements of support for dictators, and free agency by military attachés. He conjured up many of the old demons that plagued the Good Neighbor policy, especially the basic contradiction of aiding the dictators next door for the sake of fighting other dictators overseas.

This lament was familiar to many in the State Department, who listened sympathetically and concurred. John Moors Cabot was most vocal in support of Briggs's indignant analysis of the Trujillo regime, an analysis that echoed his own from fourteen years earlier. He said that "the friendship between Trujillo and our military men" began before he "seized power" (right before Cabot's eyes) in 1930, and had since "given a distorted impression of our policy to the public."[178] The State Department subsequently resumed its prewar policy of obstructing most weapons deliveries to the Dominican Republic. No more Lend-Lease airplanes arrived after Briggs registered his opposition, although Trujillo was granted export licenses for the two transport planes he had asked Brett to obtain for the new commercial airline. Like the first planes purchased in the United States, these commercial aircraft were disguised warplanes, in this case the first bombers in the Dominican Air Force.[179]

Cordell Hull, Trujillo's best hope for cooperation in the Roosevelt administration for more than a decade, retired from the State Department in November 1944. The following April, President Roosevelt himself died, calling into question whether the Good Neighbor policy would, or could, exist without him. The answer to that question depended on one's view of what it meant to be a "good neighbor," which in turn had to do with the issue of arms sales. There was strong disagreement on this point in the new Truman administration, which wrestled with the morality and expediency of supporting dictatorships with military aid after the end of the war. Although Ellis Briggs lost his ambassadorial post in Ciudad Trujillo after his run-in with Nelson Rockefeller, his successor, Joseph F. McGurk, was no better neighbor to the dictator than Briggs had been. McGurk was from Paterson, New Jersey, the rare diplomat with neither a college education nor a wife to assist in the social side of relations with the host society. He was serving as first secretary of the legation in neighboring Haiti when the 1930 revolution took place in Santo Domingo, and he had closely monitored events in the Dominican Republic since, first as Dominican "desk officer" and most recently as chief of the Division of American Republics. He shared the contempt Briggs felt for the dictatorship; both the departing and the arriving ambassador to the Dominican Republic belonged to a coalescing antidictatorial camp in the State Department that would soon gain the upper hand in Latin American policy. McGurk arrived just as Roosevelt died, and had to delay the presentation of his credentials until after the nine-day national period of mourning declared by the Dominican government.[180] Then he picked up where Briggs left off, opposing arms shipments to the regime. Although McGurk had waited more than three decades for his first post as chief of mission, his stay in the Dominican Republic was brief; he contracted malaria and had to leave in October 1945, just as the diplomatic offensive against regimes like Trujillo's was gaining momentum in Washington. As part of the strategy to cold-shoulder dictators, no replacement for McGurk arrived in the Dominican capital for almost a year.

In late November 1945, Dominican Ambassador Emilio García Godoy went to see President Truman at the White House. García Godoy, a former newspaper publisher and "longtime friend" of Trujillo, had been at his post for eleven months. He was familiar with Washington, having served at the Dominican legation as first secretary and counselor from 1934 to 1938, and he had gone on to be minister in Haiti and Cuba. He became a diplomat upon Trujillo's invitation, and thereafter "life became a whirl of gay social activities, exciting new friends, interesting places and subtle diplomacy" for the Dominican ambassador, although now he was tense and fearful of imminent removal by Trujillo.[181] Hoping to improve relations with the United States by using familiar tactics, he had hosted a "gay social activity" at the Dominican embassy the month before in honor of two key members of the Senate Foreign Relations Committee, Chairman Thomas Connally of Texas and Arthur Vandenberg of Michigan.[182] Now he engaged in some "subtle diplomacy" with Truman.

Beginning his talk with Truman on a familiar theme, García Godoy extolled the regime's efforts to develop the region bordering Haiti, the scene of "difficult moments in the past." This probably played well with the man who read his reports back in Ciudad Trujillo, Foreign Minister Manuel Arturo Peña Batlle, who was becoming the leading intellectual apologist for the Haitian massacre as a patriotic defense of the Dominican nation.[183] García Godoy reprised Trujillo's main complaint about the Good Neighbor policy—that Sumner Welles had been out to get him—and his highest praise for it, that Cordell Hull had been truly a good neighbor, as the treaty ending the customs receivership, recently dubbed the "Treaty of Financial Liberation," had clearly shown. He brought Truman a copy of a recent telegram he had elicited from Hull, which had been prominently publicized in the Dominican press, in which the former secretary of state referred to Trujillo as a "splendid President." Throughout the exchange, the agitated ambassador had to parry the caustic remarks of the new assistant secretary of state for American Republic Affairs, Spruille Braden. Braden was the best-known opponent of Latin American dictatorship since his opposition to Juan Perón in Argentina had put him on the cover of *Time* magazine earlier in November. The magazine also attacked Trujillo as the "gaudiest dictator" in the issue that was on the newsstands at the time of the Dominican ambassador's White House visit.[184] García Godoy's purpose in arranging the meeting was to counteract Braden's influence on Truman and to gain favor with Braden himself. The Dominican ambassador denied to the president that Trujillo was a dictator, whatever he may have heard, and assured him that Trujillo had only fond thoughts for Braden and Briggs, whatever mistaken impressions they may have received. Before leaving, García Godoy asked Braden to bring his wife to the dinner at the Dominican embassy scheduled in their honor for the next night, but Braden gave no response.[185] Nevertheless, the *Washington Post* society section announced the next day that García Godoy would "entertain" the assistant secretary.[186]

Despite García Godoy's efforts to entertain and explain his way to improved relations with the Truman administration, Spruille Braden launched his harshest attack on Trujillo a month after the meeting in the White House. Braden definitively severed the military pipeline to the Trujillo regime and delivered a stinging public rebuke to go with it. In denying Trujillo's request for a shipment of ammunition, Braden issued an aide-mémoire that made explicit the ambivalence felt by most diplomats who had had anything to do with the Trujillo regime: "The Government and people of the United States necessarily have a warmer friendship for and a greater desire to cooperate with those governments which rest upon periodically and freely expressed consent of the governed. This Government has over the past years observed the situation in the Dominican Republic and has been unable to perceive that democratic principles have been observed there in theory or in practice."[187]

This statement signaled the end of the wartime alliance to Trujillo and to all interested parties in the United States, where Braden's aide-mémoire circulated widely. But Trujillo's proponents in the military, the Congress, and the Dominican lobby continued to offer praise and cooperation to him, offsetting the intensified hostility toward his regime that had been building in the State Department since 1930. The limited scope of Braden's influence in the matter was indicated by the view from the Dominican Republic, where his aide-mémoire was not revealed until 1953.[188] The tightly controlled Dominican press printed nothing about Braden's new interpretation of the Good Neighbor policy, but García Godoy's dinner for the senators and his telegram from Cordell Hull, "always a loyal and active friend of our country," received front-page coverage.[189]

## WITH FRIENDS LIKE THESE . . .

Braden's righteous refusal to allow Trujillo to purchase U.S. arms marked the beginning of Trujillo's quest for military self-sufficiency. Over the next three years, Trujillo built the most powerful air force in the region on the foundation left by Lend-Lease, mainly by smuggling airplanes out of the United States without export licenses and buying others on the booming international arms market. By 1948 he had about a hundred and forty planes, including two smuggled B-17 "Flying Fortress" bombers, operating from eleven air bases around the country. This air power kept neighboring Haiti in a near-constant war scare beginning in 1943 (five of the new airfields were on or near the Haitian border) and menaced the anti-Trujillo governments in Cuba, Costa Rica, Guatemala, and Venezuela.[190] Frustrated by the trickle of arms and ammunition available in the United States and on the international market, Trujillo also established a modern weapons arsenal near his hometown in 1947, which produced high-quality "San Cristóbal" rifles and other guns and munitions. This buildup was partly in response to the threat of invasions organized by exiles and mercenaries in Cuba and Guatemala, but it was also the culmination of another aspect of the larger, ongoing drive toward sovereignty engineered by Trujillo.[191] Having regained "financial independence" with the 1940 Hull-Trujillo Treaty and the retirement of the foreign debt in 1947, and having established political autonomy at the expense of the State Department at home and in the inter-American arena, Trujillo now stood on his own in military terms as well.

The strategic considerations of the Cold War and Trujillo's success in buying the arms he needed elsewhere brought to an end the antidictatorial policy of Braden and Briggs, who had also cut off arms sales to the military governments of Haiti, Nicaragua, Honduras, Argentina, Bolivia, and Paraguay. President Harry S. Truman was "of the opinion that striped pants are trying to run South America," and in 1947 he sided with Secretary of State George C. Marshall on the question of sending arms to such regimes as Trujillo's. General Marshall, whose toast to Trujillo in 1940 had evoked the twin themes of strategic cooperation and personal visitation, believed that "Pan-American solidarity" was in essence a "military need."[192] This was impossible to achieve while the State Department impeded all military contact. In Trujillo's case, Braden even tried to prevent the U.S. Army Band from playing at the Dominican embassy, telling General Dwight Eisenhower that it would be "inopportune and undesirable." The concert took place anyway, although Braden and Briggs declined to attend.[193] By the time Braden and Briggs lost the debate over democracy and dictatorship, there were few weapons to spare for Latin America, but there was no scarcity of social emoluments to promote the military relationship: drinking, backslapping, parading, and showing off weapons.

Thereafter, Braden and Briggs became the Trujillo regime's symbols for everything that was wrong in the relationship between the two nations, and the Dominican press and government officials continued to attack them long after military cooperation with the United States was firmly reestablished.[194] After 1947, the U.S. government approved export licenses and offered direct military aid for aircraft purchases; established a missile-tracking station in the country; routinized naval visits; and, in 1953, concluded a Military Assistance Program agreement with Trujillo. It was on his trip to Washington to sign the latter document that Trujillo befriended Admiral Milton "Mary" Miles, who later toured his closet (see Chapter 6 above).

The objections that Braden and Briggs raised on the issue of support for dictatorships were drowned out in the clamor against communism and the related search for Cold War allies in the 1950s, just as the campaign for preparedness against fascism in the late 1930s had muted the arguments of Sumner Welles and his circle on the same issue. Even as a 1953 U.S. embassy report from Ciudad Trujillo defined the dictator's "progressive megalomania" as an "illness," stating that "his basic policies derive from compulsions to improve his international reputation," the military relationship with him continued to prosper, as it had during the Marine occupation and the Second World War. As he had done throughout the entire period, however, Trujillo acted for his own advantage at every juncture, professing allegiance to the United States at one moment and "gringo-baiting" the next, and lashing out with violence at his enemies wherever they were.[195] The advantages of having Trujillo as a "favored friend," as Ellis Briggs derisively termed the military relationship, were countered by the liabilities of close public ties with a despotism of Byzantine proportions.[196] The Good Neighbor policy left unresolved the tension between the advantages dictatorship seemed to offer with regard to order, progress, and regional defense coordination and the liabilities of such regimes with regard to morality, publicity, and U.S. leadership in inter-American affairs.

# CHAPTER EIGHT

# The Good Neighbor Policy
# and Dictatorship

The defeat of America's enemies at the end of World War II prompted a reevaluation of the country's friends. Dictators who had been allies against fascism came under fresh scrutiny in the wake of the crisis, as the necessity of "holding hands with the devil" faded along with the flames in Berlin and Tokyo. At the State Department, Spruille Braden and Ellis O. Briggs tapped fifteen years of ethical discomfort as they denounced the wartime alliance with Latin America's strongmen, singling out Trujillo for special opprobrium. But this moment of ascendancy for democracy as the guiding criterion of the Good Neighbor policy was brief, ending when another erstwhile ally, Joseph Stalin, became the next great threat to the hemisphere's security. As the denouement of World War II became the preface to the Cold War, the feeling that U.S. national security was at risk endured in the government and dictated the end of the State Department's anti-dictatorial stance. Like allies against fascism in the late 1930s, allies against communism would be enlisted wherever they were found.

## AFTER THE WAR

Rafael Trujillo waited out this postbellum soul-searching in a position of strength, behind physical and rhetorical defenses built up during fifteen years in power. In response to the Braden/Briggs offensive against him, he lifted the ban on political dissent, invited opposition parties to form, and eased the repression of organized labor. But he also continued to excoriate Braden and Briggs as communists who stabbed good neighbors in the back, and he took his arms business elsewhere. When anticommunism replaced anti-*caudillismo* as the basis for State Department Latin American policy in 1947, Trujillo returned to the status of an ally. Official U.S. disapproval had made it more difficult for Trujillo to obtain arms and may have weakened his stability by encouraging invasion attempts by Dominican exiles and their allies, but now these threats ended. Political parties and labor activism had flourished during Trujillo's "interlude of tolerance," which the Braden/Briggs policy helped to prompt, but these were crushed when U.S. pressure stopped. To those who had formed unions and opposition parties, it seemed as if the reforms had been decoys all along to draw out passive opponents of the regime.[1] Trujillo's international leverage increased again with the resumption of weapons sales by the United States, a renewed "liaison" relationship with the U.S. military, and the creation of the Organization of American States (a point of pride for the longtime promoter . of a League of American Nations). These developments at the end of the 1940s provided Trujillo with further means to protect his realm. Military ties with the nearby superpower supplied new hardware and the knowledge to use it, and generally conveyed strength by association through multiplied naval visits and personal relations between the officer corps of the two countries. After its formation at the Bogotá Conference in 1948, the OAS quickly became a forum where charges of American intervention in the internal affairs of the member states found a sympathetic audience. Even dictatorial states like the Dominican Republic, the target of increasing criticism from the new democracies of the Caribbean region, qualified for protection under this principle. "Nonintervention" was defined differently by different leaders, however. Trujillo frequently evoked nonintervention against official expressions of disapproval from abroad, and he clamored against the activities of Dominican exiles on the same grounds.

During the second fifteen years of his rule, Trujillo attained new levels of expression in the three dominant elements of his regime: repression, self-aggrandizement, and militarism. Opponents of dictatorship highlighted these characteristics in condemning Trujillo, while those with a different Cold War perspective saw repression as stability and saw militarism as strength, attributes required to oppose communism. Whatever one's interpretation of his actions, Trujillo grew noisier and more violent during the second half of his long tenure, exacerbating the main reasons why he had been a difficult neighbor from the start. These factors are at the heart of the basic dilemma that the United States has always faced in conducting relations with dictatorships. The repression and militarism of authoritarian systems make them morally repugnant to deal with, while refusing to deal with such governments seldom serves U.S. commercial or strategic interests. Quiet, nonjudgmental relations are difficult to maintain with dignity.

Trujillo's repression of all opposition following the brief period of political freedoms doused the rising expectations of optimistic Dominicans and underscored the caprice of his authority. The *trujillista* state pushed all members of Dominican society even deeper into their roles as supporters of the New Fatherland and of El Benefactor, restoring the usual domestic quietude of the Era of Trujillo. Hopes for an invasion of the country by a force of exiles and sympathizers faded in 1947 when Cuba, under diplomatic pressure from Trujillo, disbanded the multinational "Caribbean Legion" forming at Cayo Confites. A remnant of this group collected in Guatemala and attempted a landing on the north coast of the Dominican Republic two years later, but Trujillo's air and coastal defenses easily destroyed the only plane to make it to Luperón, the invasion site.

In addition to possessing complete authority at home and capable deterrents against external threats, Trujillo sought to control his image abroad by increasing the violence against his critics. As in the case of Sergio Bencosme and others during the 1930s, Trujillo's system of repression reached across national boundaries to strike at exiles like the labor leader Mauricio Báez, assassinated in Cuba in 1950. Dominican relations with the United States were badly damaged by the twin murders in 1955 of Jesús de Galíndez and Gerald Murphy. Trujillo was anxious to suppress a comprehensive study of his regime that Galíndez had written, and Murphy was the American pilot who flew the airplane transporting Galíndez after he was kidnapped off the streets of New York. Murphy was killed to guarantee his silence about the crime he had witnessed, triggering an investigation headed by the Murphy family's congressional representative, Charles Porter of Oregon. This controversy simmered on for years, churning up anti-Trujillo sentiment in the United States and adding to the regional agitation against dictatorship. Resentment against Trujillo, the most eminent strongman of them all, boiled over in June 1960 when his agents tried to assassinate his most persistent enemy, President Rómulo Betancourt of Venezuela, with a car bomb. Betancourt survived but was badly burned. This outrage prompted the Organization of American States to set aside the rule of nonintervention and vote for sanctions against the Dominican Republic, the first time such collective action was taken. Isolated from the community of neighboring nations but determined to stifle the faintest breath of opposition in the Dominican Republic, Trujillo lashed out at the Catholic Church and terrorized whatever opposition tried to form against him, actions that accelerated the cycle of international disdain for his government.

In addition to the Trujillo regime's repression, the dictator's self-aggrandizement contributed to the current of international scorn directed against him in the 1950s. Civic adulation of El Benefactor continued apace during the decade, with the same goal of achieving international status that had been set early in his rule. The details of Trujillo's personalism, simultaneously malevolent and ludicrous to many outside observers, had always provided compelling copy for critical journalism and diplomats' dispatches. But Trujillo's foreign relations were geared to exhibit the material progress and sovereignty of the Dominican Republic to as many people as possible. Such events as the 1955 World Peace Fair in Ciudad Trujillo were intended to attract a wider pool of visitors to the Dominican Republic than ever before. The fair, celebrated in conjunction with the twenty-fifth year of "La Era de Trujillo," generated a dizzying array of physical and rhetorical homages to *trujillismo,* further melding the man together with the Dominican state and bringing the astonishing scale of Trujillo's megalomania to a larger foreign audience. The public culture and diplomacy of the regime were designed to embellish an international image that was already both tasteless and threatening in its authoritarian excesses.

The Trujillo family's travels abroad also displayed the decadence of their rule to communities otherwise insulated from Caribbean politics. The numerous Trujillos enjoyed their vast wealth in such diverse American and European venues as cattle auctions, polo grounds, and the finest hotels. The enrichment of the Trujillo family came at the expense of the national economy, which in the most important sectors was virtually synonymous with the Trujillo fortune, especially foreign sugar holdings, which Trujillo systematically absorbed.[2] Critical accounts of his dictatorship frequently cited the long list of business monopolies enjoyed by the Trujillos.

Another element of the Trujillo regime that complicated U.S. relations was the rapid buildup of the Dominican military after the world war. Trujillo's modern air force, army, navy and armory made him one of the most powerful actors in the region. Dominican militarism menaced the neighborhood, especially Haiti next door and the democracies in power at various times in Cuba, Guatemala, Costa Rica, and Venezuela. Trujillo acted on his own in the international arms market to amass much of this might during the postwar rupture in U.S. military assistance. But State Department hostility to right-wing dictatorship was subsumed by the Manichaean worldview of anticommunism. The Cold War alliance of the "free" nations against the conspiracy of communism grew directly from the wartime alliance against fascism and its "fifth columns" in the Western Hemisphere, and carried with it many of the lessons learned about military liaison, tactical planning, and technical standardization. The military-assistance groups sent out by the Pentagon during the Eisenhower administration served these ends throughout Latin America. The Dominican Republic hosted a tracking station for the U.S. missile program and in turn received a great deal of help in developing its air force. But Trujillo balked at taking directions from the U.S. military mission concerning the kind and number of aircraft to acquire, continuing to shop for equipment and advice wherever there was a seller and assembling a vast fleet of fighters and bombers. Many observers in the United States noted that Dominican military capability was far greater than what was required for national defense, pointing out that the likeliest targets for Trujillo's excessive firepower were not communist guerrillas but the neighboring states of the "Free World." The State Department acted several times in the post-Braden era to impede Trujillo's military buildup, while the Pentagon continued to deliver war matériel and emotional support to the regime until 1958, when Trujillo expelled the U.S. military mission.

### "ANY AMERICAN ABROAD"

How was Rafael Trujillo able to achieve his international stature and leverage when so many policy makers in the State Department opposed him? The United States had been the dominant power in the hemisphere since the turn of the century, and its government had asserted its particular hegemony in the Caribbean region in a variety of diplomatic, economic, and military ways. Even after Franklin Roosevelt swore off the habits of intervention, the U.S. presence in the region exerted a powerful force on the governments of the neighboring republics. Still, the State Department's constitutional authority over U.S. foreign policy does not always give it the power to shape the gravitational forces at work in every set of bilateral relations. The diplomats involved in the process of policy formulation and implementation are only one factor of a complicated equation determining the affinity between two nations, a fact that Trujillo understood and acted on. He solicited, purchased, and sometimes coerced other sources of support having the power to influence relations with the United States, including the Marine Corps, the Dominican lobby, the American Colony, and various communications media. The "foreign policy" of the United States may have been debated and defined at the State Department, but the full spectrum of U.S. "relations" with the Trujillo regime frequently overlapped and contradicted the official line. This translated to a far greater quantity of weapons and kind words going to the Dominican Republic than many in Foggy Bottom approved of, and contributed to the false perception that Trujillo was a pliable client of a coherent U.S. policy.

Rear Admiral Harry S. Knapp, who commanded the 1916 invasion and occupation of the Dominican Republic, espoused this inclusive view of American diplomacy in an address to the Naval War College in 1923:

> The officers and men of the Navy are in a very real sense doing diplomatic work daily in so far as they meet foreigners—doing it well or ill as they represent well or ill American standards. Any American abroad is representative in a way they cannot escape if they would. The diplomacy they exercise in routine daily life will be unconscious. It will not be in the way of outstanding incidents, nor recorded in international archives, but each act touching a foreigner will be an infinitesimal element of the sum total of our foreign relations, as the individual drops of water make the ocean.[3]

Knapp's notion of the unwitting diplomat, of each individual contributing his or her set of personal foreign relations to the undifferentiated mass of national foreign relations, presents a much more complicated picture of how nations interact than historians have generally acknowledged. In this construction, foreign policy fragments at the level of implementation, which occupies a greater social and cultural expanse than the traditional paradigm of diplomacy would admit. The basic idea of international relations, of how governments communicate, leans heavily on a fragile synecdoche—the ranking diplomat in each foreign country *is* the state; he embodies it and speaks for it. In Knapp's view, every American embodies and speaks for the state; taken together, the actions and "unconscious" attitudes of these individuals constitute the nation's diplomacy. It follows that each foreign country encounters and responds to a unique configuration of words and deeds from many U.S. citizens with greater or lesser influence over how the United States is perceived in that locale. Diplomats may usually have loud voices among them, but they can be drowned out by soldiers, lobbyists, businessmen, and journalists.

Where foreign relations take place between individuals, pride and personality play important roles. This is especially true in relations with dictators, for whom *L'état c'est moi* can be a much sturdier metaphor than for diplomats "representing" the United States. Knapp's assertion that the tone of foreign relations resonates with the "unconscious" demeanor of each de facto diplomat also underlines the importance of pride and personality. Considerations of personal respect and prestige were often paramount in determining the tenor of the relationships between Trujillo and the North Americans who came into contact with him. If "relations" with the Dominican Republic are taken to mean the aggregate of these interpersonal interactions, then the identity of the "good neighbors" in the picture is ambiguous, because many who had the official responsibility to implement the policy of that name clashed with Trujillo, while others with no official standing embraced him. One of the first to embrace him, Colonel Richard Cutts of the U.S. Marines, commented that the general was "unable to separate the personal from the political," as if that were Trujillo's particular failing. But Cutts himself was guided by his personal evaluation of Trujillo when he decided to assist the new Dominican president to buy weapons in defiance of the State Department, and upon closer inspection it is difficult to find any actor on the stage of U.S.-Dominican relations whose personal and political actions were clearly divisible. In fact, the two are intertwined to the point of sameness in the context of foreign relations: individuals scrutinize each other's personal actions for their political content, and political actions are shaped by the personality of the individuals who carry them out.

Partly for this reason, the axes of diplomacy oriented in Washington and implemented "in the field" are difficult to align. Issues that loom large to diplomats in the field, matters having to do with the social setting of the "host society," may not enter into anyone's consideration in Washington. Diplomats to the Trujillo regime discovered that "a moderate degree of good nature in diplomatic (and other) relations" was taken "also to signify easy acceptance of the Dominican standpoint" in bilateral issues, which made it difficult to know how to behave or how to bring up "awkward matters" with Trujillo without becoming the object of "one of his sulky phases."[4]

The situation of implementing "policy" is further complicated by the intercultural, intrabureaucratic rivalries between and among the many military, diplomatic, commercial, and journalistic organizations involved. In

this light, the notion that there are only two axes of bilateral foreign relations—one in each capital—is insufficient. There would seem instead to be
multiple lines of influence emanating from each country, connecting like-
minded individuals, each sometimes aligning with the other in unexpected
and, from the perspective of the State Department, unintended ways. As
we have seen in the case of the Dominican Republic, the axis connecting
U.S. military men aligned more closely with the axis connecting Dominican military men than it did with the official U.S. diplomatic axis. Trujillo
also subtly coerced the American Colony into aligning with the regime,
and he projected his own favorable press coverage abroad to contradict the
criticism of his regime produced by other journalists and by the Dominican
exiles. Moreover, Trujillo organized a mix of American politicians, investors, and educators—referred to in this book as the "Dominican lobby"—to
exert influence on his behalf. The individuals forming these lines of influence were oriented to different criteria of judging Trujillo and U.S. policy
toward his regime. They disagreed about exactly what a good neighbor
should be in the particular circumstances of the Dominican Republic.

These factors provided Trujillo with considerable leverage in dealing
with the United States. He chose aspects of the Good Neighbor policy (like
nonintervention and mutual respect for sovereignty) and of the American military culture (like discipline and infrastructural development) that
benefited him, but he rejected the assumption that he would accept U.S.
leadership where his interests diverged. Trujillo chose his own friends and
ways of using power, as well, which Minister Norweb described after finding him in "a debonair mood" in 1938, surrounded by his favorite things:
"One of his military airplanes was busy shooting off machine gun salvos
over his head, American Senators in the zealous guard of our newspaper
friend were getting off the weekly steamer, a high official of the Marine
Corps, Lt. Col. Watson, was lodged under his roof, the Dominican political situation was as usual under iron control and the principal thing on
his mind was a large fiesta he intends to give this weekend at Santiago
where an irrigation ditch—benefiting his own private lands—will be inaugurated with the resounding name of the 'Flume Trujillo.'"[5] His political
and personal agenda revolved around establishing a Dominican nationalism
in his own image—literally constructed in the form of public works bearing his name—and building a military force to guard and symbolize the
new Dominican state within and beyond its borders. These achievements
impressed a number of Americans who employed the criteria of material

progress, civil order, and national stability. But Trujillo's pursuit of adulation, which was part and parcel to these efforts, offended many of the diplomats, whose views on the dictatorship were formed by their extended interaction with its leader and their personal familiarity with his venality and brutality. And Trujillo's personal enrichment threatened the businessmen of the American Colony, who operated the U.S.-owned sugar estates and utilities that he coveted and eventually appropriated. The face of the "good neighbor" toward the Trujillo regime was a collage of features, then, with new ones being pasted on over the old ones as individuals came and went. Many groups were represented in the fractured visage of U.S. "policy" toward Trujillo: the reproving diplomats "in the field," the nervous American Colony, the inquistive visiting journalists, and the congenial Marines. Trujillo was left to interpret the ambiguous image for himself.

The face of Dominican foreign policy was more unified, dominated as it was by Trujillo, although the dictator had his own Janus-like characteristics that made him inscrutable to many observers. That group included his own diplomats, whose tenure in office was very uncertain owing to the likelihood of their becoming scapegoats for the dictator's foreign relations problems. The position of foreign minister proved particularly vulnerable, and eight different men held the position during Cordell Hull's years in office. The position of Dominican minister in Washington was less shaky, although Rafael Brache went directly from his mission into exile, and Andrés Pastoriza once informed the U.S. government he was about to be replaced, only to stay at his post for another three years. Their work in Washington was redoubled by members of the Dominican lobby, whose membership was similarly in flux. Whoever represented the Dominican government, minister or lobbyist, did so at the pleasure and according to the strict dictates of the dictator, who promoted or purged the members of his cabinet and diplomatic service as it suited him. The U.S. system of policy formation and diplomacy does not allow such streamlining, because there are many who presume to speak for the nation.

Trujillo vigorously manipulated the multiple, irreconcilable factions in the United States who interested themselves in the Dominican Republic, in most cases seizing the initiative in relations between the two nations. The same can be said of Trujillo's exertions within the Pan-American community that he and Roosevelt both tirelessly evoked in their pronouncements. In relations with his neighbors, Trujillo tried to form his own coalitions of support in other countries in order to offset the efforts of his opponents abroad. The essence of the Trujillo regime's regional relations was captured on the cover of *Trujillo: Little Caesar of the Caribbean,* an exposé by the exile Germán Ornes published in 1958. On that cover a cartoon rendition of Trujillo, dressed in a toga, towers over the Antilles. In his hands are the strings leading to small marionettes in togas, one labeled for each of the neighboring states: Haiti, Cuba, Puerto Rico, and the United States. From the American strategic perspective, the Trujillo regime was a reliable bulwark in any given regional alliance, whether against fascism or communism. But from the perspective of the Caribbean republics that Dominican militarism threatened, Trujillo was not controlled from the United States, but pulled the strings himself, often with painful results for those who opposed him.

## SUPPORT FOR DICTATORS AND "RESPECT FOR FORCE"

U.S. relations with dictatorships anywhere have to contend with the basic issues of moral ambivalence and national interest, issues that are subject to multiple interpretations and evaluations. These knotty problems were greatly complicated in the case of the Trujillo regime by the ambiguous legacy of the 1916–24 U.S. intervention in the Dominican Republic. The Marine occupation and Trujillo's government were indelibly identified with each other, whether they were viewed with patriotic pride or seen as national scandals. This fact pushed the opposing views on the dictatorship farther apart, driving the wedge of national responsibility between the usual factors in the debate over relations with dictators: i.e., morality versus practicality. If Trujillo was too repugnant to deal with, then the United States bore at least some of the blame. If Dominican stability made him practical to deal with, then the United States shared at least some of the credit.

These contradictory conclusions about the value of order and the shame of dictatorship are not confined to the particular set of circumstances pertaining to the Trujillo regime and the Good Neighbor policy. Wherever the United States has shaped events by military means, the same kernel of contention sticks in the national craw. The Wilsonian tactic of imposing Marine-trained constabularies was only the most thorough form of armed intervention. The military diplomacy of training and liaison, an approach that became a global strategy of the United States in the postwar era, began in the 1920s and 1930s in the Caribbean national guards. A U.S. Army study concluded in 1943 that the Dominican version "was bound later to play into the hands of a dictator," and although such a result was unintended and widely denounced, not everyone saw it as a bad thing.[6] Strategic considerations and racist assumptions have inclined many to favor the rule of strongmen in Latin America ever since, and many of the fragmented attitudes and actions called "U.S. foreign relations" stem from these opinions.

In numerous cases since Rafael Trujillo's graduation from Haina Military Academy, American military organizations and intelligence agencies have transmitted the tactics of counterinsurgency and the culture of the elite warrior to the armed forces of the region through training and liaison, often carried out against the wishes or without the knowledge of diplomats "in the field" in the American republics. Sometimes a jingoist, racist, or anticommunist ambassador has thrown his support behind the use of force—e.g., John Peurifoy, ambassador to Guatemala during the CIA-assisted coup of 1954—but the support or opposition of U.S. diplomats has become largely superfluous. U.S. soldiers and agents often proceed alone in their tutelage of military protegés around the region. The Trujillo regime is one of the earliest cases demonstrating this twentieth-century trend in U.S. foreign relations. In the confused field of bilateral contact between nations, where the pertinent officials of the State Department and members of the Foreign Service are but one bureaucratic group among many, the warriors have jostled their way to the front of the pack.

The diplomats who formulated the Good Neighbor policy surrendered the field to the military approach by remaining largely passive concerning the ethical dilemmas posed by dictatorships. Even Sumner Welles, coauthor of the Good Neighbor policy and nemesis of the Trujillo regime, was unable to impede the military confraternity that developed in the 1930s on the foundation laid during the Marine occupation. This relationship perpetuated the identification between the United States and the Trujillo regime on public stages in both Washington and Ciudad Trujillo, and it reinforced Trujillo's national and internal security with material and logistical assistance. Furthermore, the U.S. military version of Good Neighbor relations with the Trujillo regime, exemplified by the backdoor tactics of Major (later Lieutenant General) Thomas Watson and Colonel Joe W. Smith, helped establish the precedent for military patronage of neighboring authoritarians. Finally, the case of Trujillo also helped to establish the pattern wherein the recipients of U.S. military aid and training employ them indiscriminately, often against their own neighbors and innocent citizens. The misdirection of military assistance was embodied in the figure of Marine Lieutenant Leland P. Johnston, naval attaché to the U.S. embassy in Ciudad

Trujillo from 1943 to 1946. He resigned from the Corps in 1947 to go to work for Trujillo, smuggling arms and plotting against the liberal president Ramón Grau San Martín of Cuba.[7]

The justification for supporting Latin American dictators is rooted in the enduring notion that order among nonwhite people can be maintained only by strong discipline. A *Marine Corps Gazette* article, "Indoctrination of Latin-American Service," made this point in 1920: "The Dominican is himself indoctrinated with one thing—respect for FORCE. I do not mean to say that a brutal application of force is all that he understands or respects, but I do most emphatically say that to gain his respect one must have and exert the strong hand in dealing with him."[8] The author, Lieutenant Colonel Henry C. Davis, USMC, went on to state the corollary to this construction of effective relations with Latin America, a corollary that dismisses the later rationale of the Good Neighbor policy: "The attempt to gain his confidence by hand-shaking is the old method he knows and has no faith in. He does not want to be patted on the back and told he is an equal. He has had a master his entire life; he recognizes the necessity of a master, and he wants a master. He prefers to have a just one, but he prefers any kind to the hand-shaking, back-patting politician in whom he has no faith and less confidence."[9] Such reasoning, bound up in the doctrine of military training for Latin American officers, explains the doctrine's harsh methods and willingness to employ them without reference to the wishes of "hand-shaking politicians." Even diplomats opposed to the Trujillo dictatorship, and to Latin American authoritarianism in general, had low expectations for democracy among people whom Ellis Briggs said were "just out of the palm trees."[10]

After twenty-eight years of working primarily with the Marines and the U.S. Air Force, Trujillo eventually came to a parting of the ways with his military colleagues in the United States. His abuse of foreigners, within the expatriate communities and abroad, called attention to his record of cruelty and changed his relationship with the United States. The murders of Galíndez and Murphy, not to mention the attempted assassination of Betancourt, opened a torrent of cold water into the "ocean" of foreign relations with Trujillo, which had grown tepid from martial fervor. The chronic abuse of the Dominican population never caused enough indignation in the United States to threaten the survival of the military system that inflicted it. When the victims were foreigners, however, then many new voices in the din of bilateral relations demanded an account of the executive branch's handling of the apparent murderers. The U.S. Congress and the Organization of American States investigated the Trujillo regime, and the news media ran unfavorable stories about the dictator. The Eisenhower and Kennedy administrations dabbled with Central Intelligence Agency aid to Trujillo's enemies, who eventually succeeded in assassinating him, at great cost to nearly everyone involved, in May 1961.[11]

As the Good Neighbor policy toward the Trujillo regime demonstrates, there are military approaches to Caribbean relations other than intervention. The U.S. presence in the Caribbean has more often taken a different form of "gunboat diplomacy" than the coercive practice intended by the phrase, one in which the gunboats make the "good will" rounds of the Caribbean like gray cruise liners. The original Special Service Squadron was as concerned with the showmanship and revelry of military relations as it was with the potential for trouble in the American republics. Other operational units since then have emphasized the flag-waving, drum-pounding, rum-swilling qualities of naval diplomacy in the Caribbean, where foreign relations are constituted by parades, liberty parties, and officers' receptions. Social camaraderie and public pageantry have been potent expressions of approval for foreign military leaders since the late 1930s, a precedent that also endures in contemporary naval policy. Denying a report that the Guantánamo Bay naval base would be mothballed at the close of the 1994–95 Cuban refugee crisis, the commander of the Atlantic Fleet, Admiral William Flanagan Jr., said that the new "Western Hemispheric group" of sixteen U.S. Navy ships would be based there. The squadron would "take over Caribbean missions" such as "showing the flag in South American ports."[12] In deciding how and to whom the flag will be shown, the "Western Hemispheric group" will exert some of the same influence on the full picture of U.S. relations in the Caribbean that the Special Service Squadron did during the Good Neighbor policy, conveying personal messages that become political, engaging in social rituals that prepare the way for strategic decisions.

It is difficult to see what the benefit of supporting leaders like Trujillo might have been. Defense during World War II and the Cold War has been cited as the national security priority overriding the ethical considerations of teaming up with despicable rulers. Yet contributions to the respective war efforts by these individuals were negligible at best, and in some cases were surely detrimental to the overall cause. The United States never made much use of the facilities constructed in the Dominican Republic, and Trujillo mainly used the airplanes and weapons he acquired to menace his neighbors (especially Haiti) and his own citizens for three decades. But the contradictory arguments on both sides of the issue of the dictator next door—that strongmen provide the stability necessary for growth and democracy, that they stifle growth and democracy by being strongmen—both come up against the problem of implementing change in U.S. relations. The proliferation of organizations and individuals with a stake in "foreign policy" has surrounded and submerged the constitutional model of the State Department. Operating on entirely different frequencies and transmitting from distinct cultural terrain, the assortment of writers, diplomats, soldiers, investors, lobbyists, expatriates, tourists, and advocates are unable to broadcast together because there is no possible common band. In a democratic system, theory may dictate that the hierarchical alignment of the executive branch will boost the power of that single point of transmission, drowning out lesser signals; but in fact the government communicates via an array of spokesmen and symbolic acts, and a multiplicity of other voices and noise reverberate at the point of reception. The organizational apparatus of a dictatorship's diplomacy is clearer, for it admits of less interference between the leader's decision and its implementation. In the case of the Dominican Republic and the Good Neighbor policy, the cacophony of U.S. foreign relations worked to the advantage of Trujillo, who was free to tune in the messages he found most soothing and ignore the bad reception elsewhere on the dial.

NOTES

———————————— ✦ ————————————

ONE   *Dominican History, the United States in the Caribbean,*
*and the Origins of the Good Neighbor Policy*

1   Irving Rouse, *The Tainos: Rise and Decline of the People Who Greeted Columbus* (New Haven, 1992).

2   Lester D. Langley, *America and the Americas: The United States in the Western Hemisphere* (Athens, Ga., 1989), 1–81.

3   Spanish Consul Mariano Alvarez, quoted in Luis Martínez-Fernández, "Caudillos, Annexationism, and the Rivalry between Empires in the Dominican Republic, 1844–1874," *Diplomatic History* (Fall 1993): 571–97. The general outline of Dominican history offered here draws from this article and the following works: Sumner Welles, *Naboth's Vineyard: The Dominican Republic, 1844–1924,* 2 vols. (New York, [1928] 1966); Roberto Cassá, *Historia social y económica de la República Dominicana,* 2 vols. (Santo Domingo, 1981); Harry Hoetink, *The Dominican People, 1850–1900: Notes for a Historical Sociology,* trans. Stephen K. Ault (Baltimore, 1982); David C. MacMichael, "The U.S. and the Dominican Republic, 1871–1940: A Cycle in Caribbean Diplomacy," Ph.D. diss., University of Oregon, 1964.

4   Lester Langley, *Struggle for the American Mediterranean: United States–European Rivalry in the Gulf-Caribbean, 1776–1904* (Athens, Ga., 1976); Robert G. Albion and Jennie Barnes Pope, *Sea Lanes in Wartime: The American Experience, 1775–1942* (New York, 1942); David G. McCullough, *The Path between the Seas: The Creation of the Panama Canal, 1870–1914* (New York, 1977).

5   David Long, *Gold Braid and Foreign Relations* (Annapolis, 1988), 118–50.

6   For the dominance of the Caribbean in American naval strategy, see Robert W. Love Jr., *History of the United States Navy, 1775–1941* (Harrisburg, 1992); Albion and Pope, *Sea Lanes in Wartime;* Donald A. Yerxa, *Admirals and Empire: The United States Navy and the Caribbean, 1898–1945* (Columbia, 1993).

7   Robert E. May, " 'Plenipotentiary in Petticoats': Jane M. Cazneau and American Foreign Policy in the Mid-Nineteenth Century," in *Women and American Foreign Policy: Lobbyists, Critics, and Insiders,* ed. Edward P. Crapol (New York, 1987), 19–44.

8   Hoetink, *The Dominican People,* 106, 97. The estimate of the number of "generals" is Luperón's.

9   René De La Pedraja, *The Rise and Decline of U.S. Merchant Shipping in the Twentieth Century* (New York, 1992), 33–38.

10  Dominican sugar exports to the United States went from a value of about $70,000 in 1870 to $1.3 million in 1885 to more than $3.3 million at the turn of the century. Statistics from U.S. Register of the Treasury, Bureau of the Census, *Foreign Commerce and Navigation of the United States,* annual volumes (Washington, D.C.) 1870–1900.

11  Cyrus Veeser, "Remapping the Caribbean-Private Investment and U.S. Intervention in the Dominican Republic, 1890–1908," Ph.D. diss., Columbia University, 1997.

12  See three works by Richard H. Collin: "The 1904 Detroit Compact: U.S. Naval Diplomacy and Dominican Revolutions," *The Historian* (May 1990): 432–52; *Theodore Roosevelt's Caribbean: The Panama Canal, the Monroe Doctrine, and the Latin American Context* (Baton Rouge, 1990); *Theodore Roosevelt, Culture, Diplomacy, and Expansion: A New View of American Imperialism* (Baton Rouge, 1985). For a study of the elaboration of the American role in and around Panama, see Thomas D. Schoonover, *The United States in Central America, 1869–1911: Episodes of Social Imperialism and Imperial Rivalry in the World System* (Durham, 1991).

13  For the Dominican origins of the Roosevelt Corollary to the Monroe Doctrine and "dollar diplomacy," see Welles, *Naboth's Vineyard,* 601–39; Dana G. Munro, *Intervention and Dollar Diplomacy in the Caribbean, 1900–1921* (Princeton, 1964), 78–111; Scott Nearing and Joseph Freeman, "Dollar Diplomacy," in Paul Drake, ed., *Money Doctors, Foreign Debts, and Economic Reforms in Latin America from the 1890s to the Present* (Wilmington, Del., 1994), 3–25.

14  Hoetink, *The Dominican People,* 177.

15  Bruce Calder, *The Impact of Intervention: The Dominican Republic during the U.S. Occupation of 1916–24* (Austin, 1984), 1–5. The bottom dropped out of Dominican sugar exports to the United States during the last year of the Cáceres administration, hitting a forty-year low in 1910 and remaining down until 1921. Statistics from *Foreign Commerce and Navigation of the United States,* 1901–21.

16  Calder, *The Impact of Intervention,* 5 and n. 7; Munro, *Intervention,* 263–306.

17  Hans Schmidt, *The United States Occupation of Haiti, 1915–34* (New Brunswick, 1973).

18  Lester Langley, *The Banana Wars: An Inner History of American Empire, 1900–34*

(Lexington, 1983); Calder, *The Impact of Intervention,* 5–12; Ivan Musicant, *The Banana Wars: A History of United States Military Intervention in Latin America from the Spanish-American War to the Invasion of Panama* (New York, 1990), 235–84.

19  Calder, *The Impact of Intervention,* 10–19.

20  Ibid., 19–114.

21  Schmidt, *The U.S. Occupation of Haiti;* Robert E. Quirk, *An Affair of Honor: Woodrow Wilson and the Occupation of Veracruz* (Lexington, 1962); Frederick Calhoun, *Power and Principle: Armed Intervention in Wilsonian Foreign Policy* (Kent, Ohio, 1986); Lauren H. Derby, "The Magic of Modernity: Dictatorship and Civic Culture in the Dominican Republic, 1916–62," Ph.D. diss., University of Chicago, 1998 (see the chapter entitled "Teaching Democracy: The U.S. Occupation, 1916–24").

22  Calder, *The Impact of Intervention,* 115–212, 219, 246.

23  Dominican sugar exports to the United States fluctuated wildly during the occupation, bottoming out entirely during 1918, when sales totaled only $7,000. The global sugar market surged in 1921, when the value of Dominican sugar entering the United States exceeded $9 million, although that postwar boom was bracketed by years of less than $100,000 in sugar trade between the countries. Another good year ensued in 1923, with nearly $4 million worth exchanged, before falling off again by some 80 percent during the final year of the Marine presence. Statistics from *Foreign Commerce and Navigation of the United States,* annual volumes 1916–24.

24  At the close of the occupation, twelve of the twenty-one sugar estates in the Dominican Republic were U.S.-owned, comprising 80 percent of the half-million acres under cultivation. Melvin Knight, *The Americans in Santo Domingo* (New York, 1926), 93.

25  Julie Franks, "The Gavilleros of the East: Social Banditry as Political Practice in the Dominican Sugar Region, 1900–24," *Journal of Historical Sociology* (Spring 1995): 158–181.

26  Eric Roorda, "The Cult of the Airplane in the Dominican Republic during the Marine Occupation and the Trujillo Regime, 1919–1961," in *Close Encounters of Empire: Writing the Cultural History of U.S.–Latin American Relations,* ed. Gilbert M. Joseph, Catherine C. LeGrand, and Ricardo D. Salvatore (Durham, 1998), 269–310.

27  Calder, *The Impact of Intervention,* 148–70.

28  For the creation of the Dominican constabulary, see ibid., 54–66. Other sources include Marvin Goldwert, *The Constabulary in the Dominican Republic and Nicaragua: Progeny of the United States Intervention* (Gainesville, 1962); Captain Stephen M. Fuller, USMC, and Graham Cosmas, *The Marines in the Dominican Republic* (Washington, D.C., 1974).

29  *Inquiry into the Occupation and Administration of Haiti and Santo Domingo: Hear-*

*ings before a Select Committee on Haiti and Santo Domingo,* U.S. Senate, 67th Congress, 1st and 2d sessions, 2 vols. (1921 and 1922).

30   Ibid., 183–237.

31   Brigadier General Harry Lee, "Final Report of the Commanding General, Second Brigade, U.S. Marine Corps, Concerning the Activities of the Brigade in the Dominican Republic," 20 September 1924, 16870–766, General Correspondence of the Secretary of the Navy, 1920–29, Record Group 80, National Archives (hereafter RG and NA).

32   Valentina Peguero, "Trujillo and the Military: Organization, Modernization and Control of the Dominican Armed Forces, 1916–1961," Ph.D. diss., Columbia University, 1993, 68–86.

33   Calder, *The Impact of Intervention,* 59–60.

34   Ibid., 221–25.

35   Lee, "Final Report," 9–11; Lieutenant Edward A. Fellowes, "Training Native Troops in Santo Domingo," *Marine Corps Gazette* (December 1923): 215–33.

36   Lee, "Final Report," 12, 17–18, 25, 27.

37   For the general history of the Trujillo regime, see Robert D. Crassweller, *Trujillo: The Life and Times of a Caribbean Dictator* (New York, 1966); Jesús Galíndez Suárez, *La era de Trujillo: Un estudio casuístico de dictadura latinoamericana* (Santiago de Chile, 1956); Howard J. Wiarda, *Dictatorship and Development: The Methods of Control in Trujillo's Dominican Republic* (Gainesville, 1968); Derby, "Magic of Modernity." For Good Neighbor relations with the Trujillo regime, see G. Pope Atkins and Larman C. Wilson, *The United States and the Trujillo Regime* (New Brunswick, 1972); Raymond Pulley, "The United States and the Dominican Republic, 1933–1940," *Caribbean Studies* (October 1965): 22–31; and Earl R. Curry, *Hoover's Dominican Policy and the Origins of the Good Neighbor Policy* (New York, 1979).

38   Crassweller: *Trujillo: Caribbean Dictator,* 26–27.

39   Germán Ornes, *Trujillo: Little Caesar of the Caribbean* (New York, 1958), 30–31.

40   Bernardo Vega, *Trujillo y las fuerzas armadas norteamericanos* (Santo Domingo, 1992), 2–3.

41   Richard Millett and Marvin Soloman, "The Court Martial of Lieutenant Rafael L. Trujillo," *Revista/Review Interamericana* (Fall 1972): 396–404.

42   Peguero, "Trujillo and the Military," 123.

43   Andrés L. Mateo, *Mito y cultura en la era de Trujillo* (Santo Domingo, 1993), 33–48.

44   Fredrick B. Pike, *The United States and Latin America: Myths and Stereotypes of Civilization and Nature* (Austin, 1992), 161–62.

45   John L. Offner, *An Unwanted War: The Diplomacy of the United States and Spain over Cuba, 1895–1898* (Chapel Hill, 1992); John J. Johnson, *Latin America in Caricature* (Austin, 1980), 78–95.

46   Mark Gilderhus, *Pan American Visions: Woodrow Wilson and the Western Hemisphere, 1913–21* (Tucson, 1986), 11; Johnson, *Latin America in Caricature,* 72–119.
47   Gilderhus, *Pan American Visions,* 33–34, 125.
48   Ibid., 73–136.
49   Arthur P. Whitaker, *The Western Hemisphere Idea: Its Rise and Decline* (Ithaca, 1954).
50   For the general history of the Good Neighbor policy, see Fredrick B. Pike, *FDR's Good Neighbor Policy: Sixty Years of Generally Gentle Chaos* (Austin, 1995); Bryce Wood, *The Making of the Good Neighbor Policy* (New York, 1985) and *The Dismantling of the Good Neighbor Policy* (Austin, 1985); Irwin F. Gellman, *Good Neighbor Diplomacy: United States Policies in Latin America, 1933–1945* (Baltimore, 1979); David Green, *The Containment of Latin America* (Chicago, 1971); and Robert Dallek, *FDR and American Foreign Policy, 1932–1945* (New York, 1979).
51   Brian Henderson, "A Musical Comedy of Empire," *Film Quarterly* (Winter 1981–82): 2–16; Pike, *FDR's Good Neighbor Policy,* 102–15.
52   Brenda Gayle Plummer, *Haiti and the United States: The Psychological Moment* (Athens, Ga., 1992), 121–38; Helen Delpar, *The Enormous Vogue of Things Mexican: Cultural Relations between the United States and Mexico, 1920–1935* (Tuscaloosa, 1992); George Black, *The Good Neighbor: How the United States Wrote the History of Central America and the Caribbean* (New York, 1988).
53   Black, *The Good Neighbor,* 67–73; Alfred Charles Richard, *The Hispanic Image on the Silver Screen: An Interpretive Filmography from Silents into Sound* (Westport, Conn., 1992). See also the chapter entitled "Carmen Miranda on My Mind," in Cynthia Enloe, *Bananas, Beaches, and Bases: Making Feminist Sense of International Politics* (London, 1989), 124–47.

TWO    *The Dominican Revolution of 1930 and the Policy of Nonintervention*

1   Minister Charles B. Curtis to Francis White, 16 February 1930, Box 1, Francis White Papers, Milton S. Eisenhower Library, Johns Hopkins University, Baltimore.
2   Curtis to Acting Secretary of State Joseph E. Cotton, 1 March 1930, 839.00 REVOLUTIONS/48, U.S. Department of State, *Foreign Relations of the United States: Diplomatic Papers, 1930* (Washington, D.C., 1945), 5:709 (hereafter FRUS, followed by year and volume).
3   Literature on the Dominican Revolution of 1930 includes Bernardo Vega, *Los Estados Unidos y Trujillo, 1930,* 2 vols. (Santo Domingo, 1986); idem, *El 23 de febrero, o la más anunciada revolución de América* (Santo Domingo, 1989); Mateo, *Mito y cultura,* 67–89; Galíndez, *La era de Trujillo,* 10–19.

4  For the growth of the Dominican Army, see Peguero, "Trujillo and the Military," 229–68.

5  Stimson *Diaries,* 25 November 1930, 10:180–81, Herbert Hoover Presidential Library, West Branch, Iowa.

6  Minister Evan Young to Secretary of State Frank Kellogg, 26 October 1928, in MacMichael, "A Cycle in Caribbean Diplomacy," 625.

7  Ibid., 620–25.

8  Herbert Hoover, *Memoirs,* quoted in Bryce Wood, *The Making of the Good Neighbor Policy* (New York, 1961), 126. Nicaragua, where the Marine occupation was ongoing, was of particular concern.

9  *New York Times,* 17 December 1928, quoted in Wood, *The Making of the Good Neighbor Policy,* 126.

10  Legation First Secretary John Moors Cabot, "The Dominican Reaction towards Present American Policies," 8 July 1929, John Moors Cabot Papers, Sterling Memorial Library, Yale University, New Haven.

11  Cabot's Dispatch 1326, 26 June 1929, Cabot Papers.

12  Cabot, "The Dominican Reaction," 8 July 1929, Cabot Papers.

13  Cabot's Dispatch 1370, 29 July 1929, Cabot Papers.

14  Legation First Secretary Warren McK. Wilson to Kellogg, 13 July 1926; Legation First Secretary Orme Wilson to Assistant Secretary of State Francis White. Both quoted in MacMichael, "A Cycle in Caribbean Diplomacy," 622–23.

15  Young to Secretary of State, 25 December 1929, 839.00/3340, RG 59, NA. Young had "patched up" one "violent quarrel" between Trujillo and the acting president, José Alfonseca, "the very first day" after Vásquez departed. British Minister W. H. Galienne reported that the dispute between Trujillo and Alfonseca "nearly ended in armed conflict." Galienne concurred that Vásquez "intended to be President as long as he lives," but he also thought the president's "star is on the wane." See "Report on Some of the Leading Personalities in the Dominican Republic," October–December 1929, in Kenneth Bourne and D. Cameron Watt, eds., *British Documents on Foreign Affairs: Reports and Papers from the Foreign Office Confidential Print,* Part II, Series D, Latin America, 1914–39 (Bethesda, 1989–92), 6:267, 271.

16  Chargé d'Affaires Cabot to Secretary of State, 10 and 14 January 1930, 839.00/3342–44, RG 59, NA. British Minister Galienne also reported that Vásquez "treats his Secretaries of State like schoolboys." "Report on Leading Personalities," *British Documents,* 6:271.

17  "Memoranda Regarding Revolutionary Movement in Santo Domingo," n.d., FO [Foreign Office] 140/22, Public Record Office, Kew, England (hereafter PRO).

18   Curtis to Cotton, 1 March 1930, 839.00 REVOLUTIONS/48, FRUS 1930, 5:709–17.

19   Cabot wrote his friend Susan Hammond that two cabinet officers with chattering teeth hid beneath his bed at some point during the revolution, although the official reports mention asylum being given only to the president's wife. Cabot to Hammond, 4 March 1930, Cabot Papers. In any event, Secretary Stimson acted to remove the liabilities of diplomatic asylum two years later, when he announced to diplomats "in the field" that only "uninvited fugitives" fleeing from "mob violence" were to be given sanctuary inside U.S. diplomatic buildings. Stimson may have had the Dominican Republic partly in mind when he prefaced the announcement with an allusion to "unsanctioned asylum" in the wake of "recent political disturbances in certain countries." Memo by Stimson, 30 November 1932, Box 1016, Hoover Presidential Papers—Foreign Affairs, Hoover Library.

20   Curtis to Cotton, 1 March 1930, 839.00 REVOLUTIONS/48, FRUS 1930, 5:709–17.

21   Curtis to Cotton, 24 February 1930, 839.00 REVOLUTIONS/6, FRUS 1930, 5:700.

22   Cabot to Susan Hammond, 4 March 1930, Cabot Papers.

23   Curtis to Cotton, 1 March 1930, 839.00 REVOLUTIONS/48, FRUS 1930, 5:710–11.

24   Galienne, despite having "no experience in this type of country," had gauged the situation in the Dominican Republic much more accurately than Curtis and Cabot. He had "sounded a note of warning" in his dispatches "for some months . . . that civil disturbance was imminent," even though "few persons [in Santo Domingo] were of that opinion." Galienne to A. Henderson, 24 February 1930, *British Documents*, 6:303.

25   Curtis to Secretary of State, 24 and 25 February 1930, 839.00 REVOLUTIONS/7 and 8, FRUS 1930, 5:700–701.

26   *New York Times,* 11 March 1933.

27   Cotton to Curtis, 25 February 1930, 839.00 REVOLUTIONS/13, FRUS 1930, 5:701–2.

28   Ibid.

29   *New York Times,* 26 April 1931.

30   Curtis to Cotton, 25 February 1930, 839.00 REVOLUTIONS/14, FRUS 1930, 5:702.

31   *New York Times,* 26 February 1930.

32   "Memoranda Regarding Revolutionary Movements," FO 140/22, PRO.

33   Cotton to Curtis, 26 February 1930, 839.00 REVOLUTIONS/21, FRUS 1930, 5:703–4.

34 Curtis to Cotton, 1 March 1930, 839.00 REVOLUTIONS/48, FRUS 1930, 5:712–14.

35 Cabot to Hammond, 4 March 1930, Cabot Papers.

36 Cotton to Curtis, 27 February 1930, 839.00 REVOLUTIONS/27–28, FRUS 1930, 5:706–7.

37 Curtis to Cotton, 1 March 1930, 839.00 REVOLUTIONS/48, FRUS 1930, 5:714–15.

38 Cabot to Hammond, 25 March 1930, Cabot Papers.

39 Cabot to Hammond, 4 March 1930, Cabot Papers. Ellipses in original.

40 Exchange of cables, Curtis and Cotton, 26 February 1930, 839.00 REVOLUTIONS/20 and 22, FRUS 1930, 5:704–5.

41 Curtis to Cotton, 1 March 1930, 839.00 REVOLUTIONS/48, FRUS 1930, 5:714–17.

42 Cabot to Hammond, 10 March 1930, Cabot Papers.

43 *New York Times*, 2 March 1930.

44 *Boston Herald*, 25 February 1930, contained in Cabot Papers.

45 Secretary of State to Curtis, 26 March 1930, 839.00 REVOLUTIONS/59, RG 59, NA, *Boston Herald*, 3 April 1930; Cotton to Hoover, 29 March 1930, Cabot Papers.

46 Galienne to Henderson, 10 March 1930, *British Documents*, 6:314.

47 Curtis to Cotton, 1 March 1930 REVOLUTIONS/48, FRUS 1930, 5:717.

48 Curtis to Secretary of State, 6 March 1930, 839.00/3356, RG 59, NA.

49 Curtis to Secretary of State, 8 March 1930, 839.00/3358, RG 59, NA.

50 Curtis to Secretary of State, 7 March 1930, 839.00/3357, RG 59, NA.

51 Cabot to Hammond, 4 March 1930, Cabot Papers; Curtis to Secretary of State, 1 June 1930, 839.00 GENERAL CONDITIONS/53, RG 59, NA. British Minister Galienne agreed that the cabinet was "an unimposing array," basing his judgment chiefly on their social backgrounds (*British Documents*, 6:315) while his successor, R. G. Goldie, denounced the same individuals in racist terms. American and British diplomats alike were most scornful of Secretary of State for the Presidency Rafael Vidal, who had met Trujillo while serving a jail sentence for murder and who became prominent in his circle chiefly for editing Trujillo's military magazine, *Revista Militar.* Goldie described Vidal as "a typical negro of particularly repulsive appearance . . . a sexual pervert [and] a known syphilitic, he is chiefly known as a patron of the national sport of cock-fighting." Goldie, "Report on Leading Personalities in the Dominican Republic," 31 December 1930, *British Documents*, 7:299.

52 Curtis to Secretary of State, 7 March 1930, 839.00/3357, RG 59, NA.

53 Curtis to Cotton, 18 March 1930, 839.00/3355, FRUS 1930, 5:717–18.

54 Cotton to Curtis, 18 March 1930, 839.00/3355, FRUS 1930, 5:718–19.

55 Ibid., 5:719.

56   Cutts memo on conversation with Trujillo, 5 April 1930, 839.00/3371, RG 59, NA.

57   Cabot to Hammond, 25 March 1930, Cabot Papers.

58   Cabot personal letter to Scott, 26 March 1930, FW 839.00/3473, RG 59, NA.

59   Curtis to Cotton, 31 March 1930, 839.00 PRESIDENTIAL CAMPAIGNS/10, RG 59, NA.

60   Galienne to Henderson, 10 March 1930, *British Documents*, 6:315.

61   Cabot, "The Dominican Reaction," 8 July 1929, Cabot Papers.

62   Curtis's unfamiliarity with Dominican politics is indicated by his cable referring to the prominent politician Bonetti Burgos as Bonetti Buckhart. Curtis to Cotton, 27 February 1930, 839.00 REVOLUTIONS/23, RG 59, NA.

63   Cabot to Scott, 3 April 1930, Cabot Papers.

64   Curtis to Secretary of State, 19 April 1930, 839.00/3376; 3 May 1930, 839.00 GENERAL CONDITIONS/52, RG 59, NA.

65   Curtis to Secretary of State, 5 April 1930, 839.00/3366, RG 59, NA.

66   Curtis to Secretary of State, 5 April 1930, 839.00/3370, RG 59, NA.

67   *Listín Diario,* 4 May 1930. Other notable incidents of violence were reported 16–18 April and 2, 6 May 1930.

68   Enrique Deschamps to Tulio Cestero, 12 April and 4 May 1930, Archivo Tulio Cestero, Universidad Autónoma de Santo Domingo, D.R.

69   *Listín Diario,* 7 and 14 May 1930.

70   Curtis to Secretary of State, 21 April 1930, 839.00/3383, RG 59, NA.

71   Cabot to Hammond, 20 May 1930, Cabot Papers.

72   U.S. Consul William A. Bickers to Curtis, 24 May 1930, 839.00/3415, RG 59, NA.

73   Morales and an associate found shelter at the home of General Receiver of Dominican Customs William Pulliam, where Trujillo was "ashamed to send for them." From there, Morales went into hiding for ten days before "escaping almost miraculously" to Puerto Rico. Muriel Pulliam to Mathilde Welles, 7 June 1930, Folder 7, Box 147; Angel Morales to Sumner Welles, 21 June 1930, Folder 5, Box 159. Both in Sumner Welles Papers, Franklin D. Roosevelt Presidential Library, Hyde Park, N.Y. (hereafter FDRL).

74   One of the judges, Cabot wrote, came "disguised in a most ludicrous manner as a woman, with a large hat, a shawl, [and] a gray cotton dress, short underneath, his white underwear and men's garters showing. It was a sight for the Gods, but pathetic." Cabot to Susan, 20 May 1930, Cabot Papers; Curtis to Secretary of State, 18 May 1930, 839.00/3407, RG 59, NA; memo of conversation, Acting President Jacinto Peynado with Curtis, 20 May 1930, 839.00/3411, RG 59, NA. British Minister Galienne also mentioned that the president of the court had been "disguised ridiculously as an old woman," and he also reported that General Receiver of Dominican Customs William Pulliam had

secretly harbored vice-presidential candidate Angel Morales at his home after the election. Galienne to Henderson, 19 and 26 May 1930, *British Documents,* 6:361–62.

75  Dana Munro to Cotton, 7 April 1930, 839.00/3366, RG 59, NA.

76  White to Joseph Grew, 7 November 1924, 711.13/65, quoted in Louis Pérez, Jr., *Cuba under the Platt Amendment, 1902–1934* (Pittsburgh, 1986), 256.

77  Stimson Diaries, 13 October 1930, 10:65–66.

78  Stimson *Diaries,* 25 November 1930, 10:180–81.

79  U.S. Department of State press release, 25 April 1931.

80  *New York Times,* 18 May 1930.

81  Cotton to Cameron Forbes, 13 March 1930, 838.00 COMMISSION OF INVESTIGATION/95, FRUS 1930, 203–4.

82  Scott to Munro, 11 April 1930, 839.00/3394, RG 59, NA.

83  Memo by Colonel Richard M. Cutts, USMC, 7 May 1930, 839.00/3398, RG 59, NA.

84  *New York Times,* 11 May 1930.

85  Walter Thurston to Munro, 26 May 1930, 839.00/3414, RG 59, NA.

86  Curtis to Secretary of State, 26 May 1930, 839.00/3414, RG 59, NA.

87  Curtis to Secretary of State, 1 June 1930, 839.00 GENERAL CONDITIONS/53, RG 59, NA.

88  W. H. Galienne to Foreign Secretary Arthur Henderson, 21 July 1930, FO 140/22, PRO.

89  Cabot to Hammond, 10 June 1930, Cabot Papers.

90  Cabot to Hammond, 5 June 1930, Cabot Papers.

91  Cabot to Secretary of State, 16 June 1930, 839.00 REVOLUTIONS/74, FRUS 1930, 5:723–24.

92  Cabot to Hammond, 5 and 17 June 1930, Cabot Papers.

93  *Listín Diario,* 3 and 9 June 1930.

94  *Listín Diario,* 31 May 1930.

95  Cabot to Hammond, 5 June 1930, Cabot Papers.

96  Cabot to Stimson, 28 June 1930, (SC) EF63, RG 80, NA.

97  Report of Commander Harold Train, Squadron One, Fleet Base Force (based in Samaná Bay for Fleet Problem VII) to Chief of Naval Operations, 27 July 1927; Stimson to Navy Secretary Charles Francis Adams, 23 July 1930; Adams to Stimson, 25 July 1930. All in (SC) EF63, RG 80, NA.

98  *Listín Diario,* 27 June 1930.

99  Cabot to Secretary of State, 20 July 1930, 839.01/1, FRUS 1930, 5:725–26.

100  Galienne to Henderson, 21 July 1930, FO 140/22, PRO.

101  Cabot to Secretary of State, 26 July 1930, 839.00/3432, FRUS 1930, 5:726.

102  William Pulliam to Sumner Welles, 6 August 1931, Folder 8, Box 147, Welles Papers, FDRL.

103   Stimson to Hoover, 14 July 1930, Box 983, Hoover Presidential Papers—Foreign Affairs, Hoover Library.

104   Memo of conversation, Minister Manuel de Jesús Galván with Curtis, 22 July 1930, 839.00 REVOLUTIONS/86, RG 59, NA.

105   Cabot to Secretary of State, 23 July 1930, 839.00/3422, RG 59, NA.

106   James Beverly, Governor of Puerto Rico, to Chief of Bureau of Insular Affairs General Parker, 23 July 1930, 839.00 REVOLUTIONS/78; also see correspondence between 7 and 15 August 1930, 839.113/510–12, RG 59, NA.

107   Cabot to Secretary of State, 11 August 1930, 839.00/3438, RG 59, NA.

108   *Listín Diario,* 17 August 1930.

109   Reports of the San Zenón hurricane, 4–8 September 1930, 836.48 1930 Hurricane/I, FRUS 1930, 2:725–32; *New York Times,* 5–7 September 1930.

110   Curtis to Stimson, 4 September 1930, American Legation in Santo Domingo 1930, pt. II, Foreign Service Posts of the Department of State, RG 84, NA.

111   Captain E. H. Petri, USS *Grebe,* to Governor Waldo Evans, Governor of the Virgin Islands, 15 September 1930, H4–9/EF63 (300908), RG 80, NA (hereafter Petri report).

112   Major William B. Sullivan, USMC, to Chief of Naval Operations, report on "Conditions in Santo Domingo City" [hereafter Sullivan report], 10 September 1930, (SC) EF63, RG 80, NA. See also Commander Lucius W. Johnson, Medical Corps, USN, *Report on Relief Work in the Santo Domingo Disaster* (Washington, 1930).

113   Sullivan report.

114   Ibid.

115   Ibid. Watson did come to the Dominican Republic as naval attaché, then became a food administrator, a close advisor to Trujillo, and a rival to Curtis. His tenure in the Dominican Republic will be examined more closely in Chapter 6.

116   Ibid.

117   Petri report.

118   Sullivan report.

119   Petri report.

120   Sullivan report.

121   *Stimson Diaries,* 13 October 1930, 10:64–65.

122   Derby, "Magic of Modernity," chapter entitled "A City of Miracles: Urban Space, Social Dis-ease and the Hurricane of San Zenón." For the *trujillista* interpretation of the hurricane and the rebuilding of the capital, see *La Nueva Patria, suplemento: La reconstrucción, por el Generalísimo Doctor Rafael L. Trujillo Molina, de la ciudad de Santo Domingo de Guzmán, abatida por el ciclón del 3 de septiembre de 1930* (Santo Domingo, 1935).

123   Vice-Consul Elvin Seibert, monthly report, 20 October 1930, 839.00/3446, RG 59, NA.

124   Cabot to Secretary of State, 17 November 1930, 839.00/3451, RG 59, NA.

125   Curtis to Secretary of State, 10 January 1931, 839.00/3461, RG 59, NA.

126   Gerardo to Cestero, 5 February 1931, Archivo Cestero.

127   Stimson Diaries, 3 December 1930, 10:192. At the same time, the unconstitutional actions of the admittedly stable Trujillo regime, like replacing the judges of the Supreme Court, shook the Dominican elite and the foreign business community: "This is a matter which must necessarily be of vital concern to every Dominican citizen of property and to any enterprise within the republic financed by foreigners." British Minister R. G. Goldie to Henderson, 20 February 1931, British Documents, 7:142.

128   Welles to Drew Pearson, 4 and 9 February 1931, Folder 1, Box 160, Welles Papers, FDRL. Welles's role in the politics of publicity is considered further in Chapter 4.

129   Scott to White, 19 February 1931, 839.00/3473, RG 59, NA.

130   Cabot, "Memo Regarding Policies toward the Trujillo Government," 13 March 1931, 839.00/3477, RG 59, NA.

131   Elting E. Morison, Turmoil and Tradition: The Life and Times of Henry L. Stimson (New York, 1960), 307–8.

132   Dozer, Are We Good Neighbors?, 14.

133   Scott to White, 19 February 1931, 839.00/3473, RG 59, NA.


THREE    The Bankrupt Neighbor Policy: Depression Diplomacy and the Foreign Bondholders Protective Council

1    Alexander DeConde, Hoover's Latin American Policy (Palo Alto, 1951), 66–78.

2    Emily S. Rosenberg and Norman L. Rosenberg, "From Colonialism to Professionalism: The Public-Private Dynamic in United States Foreign Financial Advising," in Drake, ed., Money Doctors, 59–83.

3    The Latin American depression was exacerbated by the Smoot-Hawley tariff, a rigidly protectionist measure reluctantly signed into law by Hoover at the outset of his term in office. This tariff, one of the highest in American history, was anathema to the export economies of Latin America. It effectively barred from the U.S. market many of the most important commodities produced in the south and complicated the task of recovery for those nations. For Latin American comment on Smoot-Hawley, see Dozer, Are We Good Neighbors?, 10–15, and Wood, The Making of the Good Neighbor Policy, 128. For the foreign policy of the Hoover administration, see DeConde, Hoover's Latin American Policy; idem, "Herbert Hoover's Good Will Tour," The Historian 12 (1950): 167–81; Robert H. Ferrell, American Diplomacy in the Great Depression:

*Hoover-Stimson Foreign Policy, 1929–1933* (New Haven, 1957); and William Starr Myers, *The Foreign Policies of Herbert Hoover, 1929–1933* (New York, 1940).

4   Some pertinent works on Hoover include Joan Hoff Wilson, *Herbert Hoover, Forgotten Progressive* (Boston, 1975) and George H. Nash, *The Life of Herbert Hoover,* 2 vols. (New York, 1983 and 1988). Also see Hoover's books, *American Individualism* (Garden City, N.Y., 1922) and *American Ideals versus the New Deal* (New York, 1936). For Stimson, see Elting E. Morison, *Turmoil and Tradition: The Life and Times of Henry L. Stimson* (Boston, 1960); Godfrey Hodgson, *The Colonel: The Life and Wars of Henry Stimson, 1867–1950* (New York, 1991).

5   *New York Times,* 21 June 1930.

6   Convention between the United States and the Dominican Republic, 12 June 1924, Treaty Series no. 729, FRUS 1924 (Washington, 1939), 1:631–42.

7   For an exhaustive account of the Dominican foreign debt during the Trujillo regime, see Bernardo Vega, *Trujillo y el control financiero norteamericano* (Santo Domingo, 1990).

8   Hoover's Gridiron Club speech, 13 April 1929, quoted in Myers, *The Foreign Policies of Herbert Hoover,* 42–43; Stimson nationwide address, U.S. Department of State press release, 9 May 1931.

9   White House press release, 6 July 1931, FRUS 1931 (Washington, 1946), 1:163.

10   DeConde, *Hoover's Latin American Policy,* 70.

11   Draft of statement, William R. Castle to Herbert Hoover, 27 June 1931, Hoover Presidential Papers—Foreign Affairs, Box 1018, Hoover Library.

12   The Johnson hearings are printed in *Sale of Foreign Bonds or Securities in the United States: Hearings before the Committee on Finance, U.S. Senate, Pursuant to Senate Resolution 19,* 72d Congress, 1st session (1933). A concise overview of the loan controversy is provided by Joan Hoff Wilson, "A Reevaluation of Hoover's Foreign Policy," in Martin Fausold, ed., *The Hoover Presidency* (Albany, 1974), 76–82.

13   Winthrop R. Scott to Joseph Cotton, 24 April 1930, 839.51/3206, RG 59, NA.

14   Until March 1930, only interest payments on the outstanding bonds were required, but monthly amortization payments were due thereafter. The amount of money needed annually to satisfy the amortization requirement was $1.8 million, whereas interest payments equaled $1.1 million. Chargé d'Affaires Thomas Stafford to Henry L. Stimson, 14 September 1931, 839.51/3487, RG 59, NA.

15   "Report on Economic Conditions in the Dominican Republic," April 1930, Hoover Presidential Papers—Foreign Affairs, Box 983, Hoover Library; Scott to Cotton, 24 April 1930, 839.51/3206, RG 59, NA.

16   Secretary of War Patrick Hurley to Stimson, 6 September 1930, 839.51/3256, RG 59, NA.

17    Dominican Government to Dominican Legation in Washington, 10 September 1930, 839.52/3265, RG 59, NA.

18    Hurley to Stimson, 6 September 1930, 839.51/3256, RG 59, NA.

19    Pulliam to Welles, 2 June 1931, Folder 8, Box 147, Welles Papers, FDRL.

20    Cotton to Minister Charles B. Curtis, 16 September 1930, 839.51/3267, RG 59, NA.

21    Wadsworth report, 13 October 1930, 839.51 Economic Mission/13, RG 59, NA.

22    Dominican Economic Mission to President Herbert Hoover, 31 December 1930, 839.51 Economic Mission/5, RG 59, NA.

23    *Stimson Diaries,* 13 October 1930, 10:64–65.

24    Scott memo of conversation, Dominican Minister Rafael Brache with Stimson, 12 February 1931, 839.51/3360, FRUS 1931, 2:88–90.

25    Ibid., 24 November 1930, 2:175.

26    The involvement of the Marine officers Thomas Watson and Richard Cutts will be considered in greater detail in Chapter 7.

27    Dominican Secretary of Finance Roberto Despradel to Stimson, 20 October 1931, 839.51/3582, FRUS 1931, 2:124–30.

28    The 20 March 1932 edition of the *New York Times* reported that the Dominican budget was again balanced.

29    Stimson to Lee, Higginson, 10 November 1931, 839.51/3632, FRUS 1931, 2:131–35.

30    Minister H. F. Arthur Schoenfeld to Harvey Bundy, 14 November 1931, 839.51/3607, RG 59, NA.

31    Scott memo, 4 March 1932, 839.51/3707, RG 59, NA.

32    Stimson to Schoenfeld, 4 February 1932, 839.51/36772, RG 59, NA.

33    Schoenfeld to Stimson, 5 and 17 February 1932, 839.51/3678 and 3689, RG 59, NA.

34    Scott memo, 7 March 1932, 839.51/3708, RG 59, NA.

35    James Gantenbein, *Financial Questions in Foreign Policy* (New York, 1939), 172; Allen W. Dulles, "The Protection of American Foreign Bondholders," *Foreign Affairs* (April 1932): 3–13.

36    Dick Steward, *Trade and Hemisphere: The Good Neighbor Policy and Reciprocal Trade* (Columbia, 1975), 153.

37    Herbert Feis, *Characters in Crisis: 1933* (Boston, 1966), 266–70. The Hoover administration tried to recruit "eminent men" who were not "stuffed shirts" to constitute a protective committee. John Foster Dulles, "Suggestions Relative to an American Council for Foreign Bondholders," 14 May 1932; Dulles to Norman Davis, 26 June 1932; Pierre Jay to Norman Davis, 18 August 1932, Box 9. All in Papers of Norman Davis, Manuscript Branch, Library of Congress.

38    For Roosevelt's foreign economic relations and the Good Neighbor policy, see

Frederick C. Adams, *Economic Diplomacy: The Export-Import Bank and American Foreign Policy, 1934–39* (Columbia, 1976); Steward, *Trade and Hemisphere;* and Lloyd C. Gardner, *Economic Aspects of New Deal Diplomacy* (Madison, 1964).

39  Feis, *Characters,* 274. Emphasis in original.

40  Ibid., 273. Hull phoned Minister Josephus Daniels in Mexico City to tell him that "we are creating a committee here of big, patriotic citizens" who would soon begin work on the Mexican debt. Hull memo of conversation with Daniels, 22 September 1933, 80.51/844 1/7, and Frank Lowden to William Phillips, 18 December 1933, 800.51/912, FRUS 1933, I:937–39.

41  FBPC certificate of incorporation, Box 20, Francis White Papers, Milton Eisenhower Library, Johns Hopkins University, Baltimore, Md. Former Secretary Stimson congratulated Roosevelt on following through with this Hoover administration initiative (*Stimson Diaries,* 26 October 1933, 13:192).

42  Samuel Guy Inman to Dot Inman, 23 November and 8 December 1933, Box 13, Papers of Samuel Guy Inman, Manuscript Branch, Library of Congress.

43  Cordell Hull, *The Memoirs of Cordell Hull* (New York, 1948), 335–36.

44  Feis, *Characters,* 267.

45  Gellman, *Good Neighbor Diplomacy,* 15.

46  Hull memo, 28 September 1933, 800.51/841, RG 59, NA.

47  J. Herbert Case to Thomas D. Thacher, 7 December 34, Thomas Thacher Papers, Sterling Memorial Library, Yale University, New Haven. The meeting between Case and these business leaders was held on 17 December 1933. Governor Harrison of New York had met with "leading New York bankers" on the same subject on 6 December 1933. Both meetings were held at the New York Federal Reserve Bank.

48  Gantenbein, *Financial Questions,* 172.

49  Frederick W. Marks, *Wind over Sand: The Diplomacy of Franklin Roosevelt* (Athens, Ga., 1988), 29–30; Feis, *Characters,* 270–71.

50  Steward, *Trade and Hemisphere,* 160.

51  Memo of conversation, Special Agent for the Emergency Fund William Dunn with Wilson, 19 June 1933, 839.51/3916, RG 59, NA.

52  Memo of conversation, Joseph Davies with Assistant Secretary Jefferson Caffery, Edwin Wilson, Schoenfeld, and J. F. McGurk, 14 June 1933, 839.51/3915, RG 59, NA.

53  William Phillips memo to Roosevelt, 19 July 1933, OF [Official File] 138, FDRL.

54  Schoenfeld to Phillips, 29 July 1933, Papers of H. F. Arthur Schoenfeld, private collection.

55  First Secretary James E. Brown to Schoenfeld, 14 August 1933, Schoenfeld Papers.

56  Memo of conversation, Dominican Foreign Minister Arturo Logroño with Schoenfeld, 16 January 1934, 839.51/4044, RG 59, NA.

57    William Dunn, "The Early Years of the Trujillo Regime in Santo Domingo," sent to Assistant Secretary of State Spruille Braden, 25 January 1946, 839.00/ 1-2546, RG 59, NA. ·

58    Brown to Acting Secretary of State, 22 June 1933, 839.51A/255, FRUS 1933, 5:638–39; Brown to Schoenfeld, 23 June 1933, Schoenfeld Papers.

59    Memo of conversation, Logroño with Schoenfeld, 19 June 1933, 839.51/3916, RG 59, NA.

60    Pulliam to Welles, 2 June 1930, Folder 8, Box 147; Welles to Federico Velásquez, 20 January 1931, Folder 1, Box 160; Welles to Kent Cooper, General Manager of the Associated Press, 14 April 1930, Folder 4, Box 159. All in Welles Papers, FDRL.

61    Irwin F. Gellman, *Secret Affairs: Franklin Roosevelt, Cordell Hull, and Sumner Welles* (Baltimore, 1995), 56–86, 106–7.

62    Pike, *FDR's Good Neighbor Policy,* 204.

63    Welles memo, 3 August 1933, 839.51/3928, RG 59, NA.

64    Schoenfeld to White, 8 January 1934, Box 4, White Papers.

65    "Policy towards the Dominican Republic," 17 August 1933, FW 839.51/3933, RG 59, NA.

66    Welles wrote to Angel Morales that he could "see no solution" to the Trujillo regime "except through a successful revolution." Welles to Morales, 26 June 1930, Folder 5, Box 159, Welles Papers, FDRL.

67    Pulliam to Welles, 23 June 1931, Folder 8, Box 147; Welles to Rafael Ortiz Arzeno, 10 May 1930; Welles to White, 13 May 1930, Folder 5, Box 159. All in Welles Papers, FDRL.

68    Memo of conversation, Rafael Trujillo with Schoenfeld, 2 September 1933, 839.51/3935, RG 59, NA.

69    Davies "Informal Memo" to Hull, 7 September 1933, OF 138, FDRL.

70    Davies to Senator Key Pittman, included in Davies to Hull, 18 September 1933, 839.51/3949 1/2, RG 59, NA.

71    Davies to Hull, 8 November 1933; Hull to Davies, 18 October 1933. Both in Records of the Foreign Bondholders Protective Council, Pioneer Business Records Service, Brooklyn, N.Y. (hereafter FBPC Records).

72    Draft memo, Hull to Roosevelt, 9 November 1933, 800.51/806, RG 59, NA. Emphasis in original.

73    Presidential press conferences, 6 December 1933, FDRL.

74    Hull circular memo, 3 January 1934, 800.51/a, FRUS 1933, 1:639–40.

75    Phillips to Despradel, 28 November 1933, 839.51/4013, FRUS 1933, 1:667; Phillips to Despradel, 28 November 1933, 839.51/4010 1/2, RG 59, NA.

76    Feis, *Characters,* 267; Dunn to Schoenfeld, 2 April 1934, Schoenfeld Papers. Raymond Stevens, former head of the Federal Trade Commission, was the

first FBPC president, but absences and illness made his a brief tenure. Clark to Roosevelt, 16 March 1934, OF 242-a, FDRL.

77    Memo, Clark's meetings at Department of State, 27 June 1934, FBPC Records.

78    Davies to Hull, 28 April 1934, 839.51/4112, RG 59, NA.

79    Brown to Schoenfeld, 18 June 1934, Schoenfeld Papers.

80    Memo, Clark's meetings at Department of State, 27 June 1934, FBPC Records.

81    Memo of conversation, Clark with Davies, 28 June 1934, FBPC Records; Joseph Davies, *Memorial*, 12 May 1934, FBPC Records.

82    Schoenfeld to McGurk with Gantenbein memo, 7 June 1934, 839.51/4176 1/2, RG 59, NA.

83    Brown to Schoenfeld, 18 June 1934, Schoenfeld Papers.

84    Gantenbein to Schoenfeld, 20 March 1934, Schoenfeld Papers.

85    *La Información*, 3 May 1934.

86    Pike, *FDR's Good Neighbor Policy*, 6.

87    Crassweller, *Trujillo: Caribbean Dictator*, 61–62; Mateo, *Mito y cultura*, 42, 47, 107.

88    Despradel to Hull, 19 June 1934, 839.51/4158, RG 59, NA.

89    Memo of conversation, Clark with Hull and Moore, 27 June 1934, FBPC Records.

90    Columnist Drew Pearson quoted in Gellman, *Secret Affairs*, 50.

91    Memo of conversation, Clark with Davies, 28 June 1934, FBPC Records.

92    Memo of conversation, Clark with Davies, 30 June 1934 FBPC Records.

93    This "history" was an important section of Gantenbein's memo. Memo of conversation, Clark with Davies, 3 July 1934, FBPC Records.

94    Memo of conversation, Clark with Davies, 6 July 1934, FBPC Records.

95    Minutes of FBPC Board of Directors meeting, 25 July 1934, FBPC Records.

96    Hull to Schoenfeld, 12 July 1934, 839.51/4170, RG 59, NA.

97    Outline of Trujillo's relations with the Roosevelt administration, 10 August 1934, 839.00/3797, RG 59, NA.

98    Minutes of FBPC Board of Directors meeting, 25 July 1934, FBPC Records.

99    Minutes of FBPC Executive Committee meeting, 31 July 1934, FBPC Records.

100    *London Times*, 18 August 1934, 800.51/1079, RG 59, NA.

101    *Wall Street Journal* and *New York Herald Tribune*, 18 August 1934. See also 18 August 1934, *Journal of Commerce;* 22 August 1934, *Poor's* Business and Security Service, Box 20, White Papers.

102    Undated, unsigned draft, OF 138, FDRL.

103    Press release from the Dominican legation, 17 August 1934, Box 20, White Papers.

104    *Boletín de Relaciones Exteriores*, July–August 1934, Biblioteca Nacional, Santo Domingo.

105   Schoenfeld to Hull, 22 August 1934, 839.51/4207, RG 59, NA.

106   Ibid.; Schoenfeld to Hull, 18 August 1934, 839.51/4200, RG 59, NA.

107   Welles to Schoenfeld, 16 August 1934, Folder 7, Box 36, Welles Papers, FDRL.

108   Gantenbein memo entitled "Specialized Fiscal Income," 13 November 1934, 839.51/4241, RG 59, NA.

109   Ibid.; Brown to Schoenfeld, 14 September 1934, Schoenfeld Papers.

110   Brown to Schoenfeld, 18 June 1934, Schoenfeld Papers.

FOUR    *What Will the Neighbors Think? Dictatorship and Diplomacy in the Public Eye*

1    Welles to Roosevelt, 7 April 1933, OF 480, FDRL.

2    Welles to Roosevelt, 6 April 1933, OF 480, FDRL.

3    Some of the better treatments of Roosevelt's complex personality are James MacGregor Burns, *Roosevelt: The Lion and the Fox* (New York, 1956); Patrick J. Maney, *The Roosevelt Presence: A Biography of Franklin Delano Roosevelt* (New York, 1992); Frank Friedel, *Franklin D. Roosevelt: A Rendezvous with Destiny* (Boston, 1990); Warren F. Kimball, *The Juggler: Franklin Roosevelt as Wartime Statesman* (Princeton, 1991); and Geoffrey C. Ward, *A First-Class Temperament: The Emergence of Franklin Roosevelt* (New York, 1989).

4    Abelardo Nanita, *Trujillo: A Full-Size Portrait* (Santiago, D.R., 1939), 118.

5    Marks, *Wind over Sand,* 234.

6    Michael Hall, "Sugar and Power: Eisenhower, Kennedy, and the Trujillos, 1958–1962," Ph.D. diss., Ohio University, 1996, 134–43.

7    Legation report, 30 November 1934, 839.00/3822, RG 59, NA.

8    Legation report citing *La Opinión* editorial, 19 January 1937, 839.00/4093.

9    Galíndez, *La era de Trujillo,* 23.

10   Legation report, 11 February 1936, 839.00/3993, RG 59, NA; "Memo on Political and Economic Conditions in the Cibao," 16 March 1936, 839.00/4009, RG 59, NA. Demonstrations in force with the army "to overawe the population of the principal towns" had long been a tactic of the Trujillo regime, going back to December 1931, when Trujillo chartered a German steamer and a steamer from the U.S.-owned La Romana sugar estate to carry fifteen hundred soldiers on a coastal tour culminating in Monte Cristi on the Haitian border. Goldie to Sir John Simon, 14 December 1931, *British Documents,* 8:78.

11   "Unrest in the Cibao," 15 September 1937, 839.00/4136, RG 59, NA.

12   Vega, *Los Estados Unidos y Trujillo, 1930,* 2:652; Crassweller, *Trujillo: Caribbean Dictator,* 94–95.

13   Schoenfeld to Secretary of State, 4 January 1933 and 26 March 1934, 839.00/3623 and 3759, RG 59, NA.

14   Schoenfeld to Secretary of State, 6 December 1933, 839.00/3854, RG 59, NA.
15   "Outline of the First Term of the Trujillo Administration," 10 August 1934, 839.00/3797, RG 59, NA.
16   Schoenfeld to Secretary of State, 22 March 1935, 839.00/3845, RG 59, NA.
17   "Deposition given by Oscar Michelena to First Secretary James Brown," 13 June 1935, 839.00/3931, RG 59, NA.
18   Schoenfeld to Secretary of State, 22 March 1935; Welles memo to Hull, 27 March 1935. Both in 839.00/3845, RG 59, NA.
19   Welles personal letter to Schoenfeld, 2 May 1935, 839.00/3845, RG 59, NA.
20   Hull and Welles telegram to Schoenfeld, 29 May 1935, 839.00/3879, RG 59, NA.
21   Schoenfeld telegrams to Hull and Welles, 5 June 1935, 839.00/3921 and 3922, RG 59, NA.
22   Catherine LeGrand, "Informal Resistance on a Dominican Sugar Estate: The Ozama Sugar Estate during the Trujillo Regime," *Hispanic American Historical Review* (Fall 1995): 555–96.
23   Memo of conversation, Alfredo Ricart with Schoenfeld, 2 May 1935, 839.00/3885, RG 59, NA.
24   Schoenfeld to Secretary of State, 9 April 1936, 839.00/4014, RG 59, NA.
25   "Outline of Seventh Year of the Trujillo Administration," 11 September 1937, 839.00/4135, RG 59, NA.
26   "Outline of the Sixth Year of the Trujillo Administration," 8 August 1936, 839.00/4050, RG 59, NA.
27   Schoenfeld to Secretary of State, 9 April 1934, 839.00/3762, RG 59, NA.
28   *Listín Diario* clipping enclosed in Legation report, 25 September 1934, 839.00/3811, RG 59, NA.
29   *La Opinion,* 29 March 1935, clipping enclosed in Legation report, 2 April 1935, 839.00/3853, RG 59, NA.
30   First Secretary Franklin Atwood to Secretary of State, 6 May 1936, 839.00/4019, RG 59, NA.
31   "Outline of the Eighth Year of the Trujillo Administration," 7 November 1938, 839.00/4209, RG 59, NA. For a description of how Trujillo moved into and dominated logging, peanut production, and mule and truck transportation in the sierra, see Eugenia Georges, *The Making of a Transnational Community: Migration, Development, and Cultural Change in the Dominican Republic* (New York, 1990), 58–78.
32   Donald Edgar reports, 10 and 16 October 1936, 839.00/4067 and 4069, RG 59, NA.
33   Partido Dominicano circular from Bonetti Burgos, quoted in Legation report, 26 March 1937, 839.00/4110, RG 59, NA.
34   Vice-Consul William A. Elders to Eden, 21 November 1936, FO 371/20632, PRO.

35   "Outline of First Term of Trujillo Administration," 10 August 1934, 839.00/
3797, RG 59, NA.

36   A copy of the "Civic Primer" was enclosed with the Legation report of
17 October 1938, 811.3339/52, RG 59, NA.

37   For more on the Partido Dominicano, see Derby, "Magic of Modernity,"
chapter entitled "The Terrors of Public Identity: The Politics of Official Per-
sonhood within the Dominican Party."

38   Schoenfeld to Secretary of State, 30 January 1936, 839.00/3988, RG 59, NA.

39   *La Opinión,* 15 December 1936, quoted in Legation report, 17 December 1936,
839.00/4086, RG 59, NA.

40   Dominican Senate resolution to do so reported by Legation, 10 November
1932, 839.00 TRUJILLO/51, RG 59, NA.

41   "Outline of First Term of Trujillo Administration," 10 August 1934, 839.00/
3797, RG 59, NA.

42   First Secretary James Gantenbein reports, 9 and 16 November 1935, 11 January
1936, 839.00 TRUJILLO/148, 149, and 162, RG 59, NA. Honorifics were not new
with Trujillo (see, e.g., Hoetink, *The Dominican People,* 127, on Heureaux),
but his prolific circle of sycophants took them to new heights of expression.

43   Legation reports, 20 January and 6 February 1934, 839.00/3742, RG 59, NA.

44   *Listín Diario,* 2 November 1935, clipping translated and enclosed in Legation
report, 2 November 1935, 839.001/20, RG 59, NA.

45   Legation report, 29 August 1938, 839.00/4205, RG 59, NA.

46   Juan M. Contin, *Por qué Trujillo es el lema y el emblema de la patria* (Ciudad Trujillo, 1938), 11–14.

47   "Outline of the Fifth Year of the Trujillo Administration," 15 August 1935,
839.00/3951, RG 59, NA.

48   Legation report, including translation of Emilio Jiménez speech at "Civic
Review," 21 January 1933, published in *Listín Diario,* 23 January 1933, 839.00/
3628, RG 59, NA.

49   Legation report with translation of Trujillo's Esperanza speech, published in
*Listín Diario,* 27 January 1936, 839.00/3989, RG 59, NA.

50   First Secretary James Brown report, 27 September 1934, 839.00 TRUJILLO/
132, RG 59, NA.

51   Schoenfeld to Secretary of State, 30 January 1936, 839.00/3988, RG 59, NA.

52   "Outline of the Fifth Year of the Trujillo Administration," 15 August 1935,
839.00/3951, RG 59, NA.

53   Legation report, 4 November 1935, 839.00/3965, RG 59, NA.

54   Crassweller, *Trujillo: Caribbean Dictator,* 274.

55   Memo of conversation, Dominican Foreign Minister Elías Brache with
Schoenfeld, 20 July 1935, 839.014/22, RG 59, NA.

56  Brown report, 28 January 1935, 839.00 TRUJILLO/171, RG 59, NA.

57  Memo of conversation, Logroño with Schoenfeld, 20 January 1935, 839.014/22, RG 59, NA.

58  *New York Times,* 10 January 1936. Prior to his first visit to the United States in 1939, Trujillo sought to have the name changed back "as a gesture of modesty for consumption in countries where his vanity has made him to some extent an object of ridicule and which he may now contemplate visiting"; but neither the press nor the legislature would risk advocating such a move, and the city stayed "Ciudad Trujillo" until after Trujillo's death in 1961. British Minister Alexander Swinton Paterson to British Foreign Minister Anthony Eden, *British Documents,* 20:322.

59  Legation report, 19 September 1936, 839.00/4060, RG 59, NA.

60  Legation report, 2 October 1936, 839.00/4064, RG 59, NA.

61  Ornes, *Little Caesar,* 229.

62  Translation of law naming Parque Ramfis, Brown report, 28 January 1935, 839.00 TRUJILLO/171, RG 59, NA. Also see *La Nueva Patria, suplemento,* and Mateo, *Mito y cultura,* 107–11.

63  *Dominican Republic* magazine, November 1935; *Album de oro de la República Dominicana: Por la unión y confraternidad entre los pueblos de la América Latina, 1936* (Havana, 1936).

64  Legation report, 2 October 1936, 839.00/4064, RG 59, NA.

65  "Outline of the Ninth Year of the Trujillo Administration," 27 September 1939, 839.00/4223, RG 59, NA.

66  Law no. 396, *Gaceta Oficial* no. 4522, 23 November 1932, contained in Legation report, 28 November 1932, 839.00/3614, RG 59, NA.

67  Legation report, 1 May 1935, 839.00/3883, RG 59, NA.

68  Legation report, 1 April 1933, 839.00/3644, RG 59, NA.

69  Legation report, 10 April 1933, 839.00/3651, RG 59, NA.

70  Schoenfeld to Secretary of State, 26 April 1933, 839.00/3657, RG 59, NA. The editor of *La Opinión,* Alvaro Alvarez, was left off the ballot for the Chamber of Deputies in February 1934, as his paper and Sardá's "reversed their previous roles." Legation report, 13 February 1934, 839.00/3753, RG 59, NA.

71  "La Prensa Dominicana" section, *Album de oro de la República Dominicana 1936.* *Listín Diario* again fell out of favor and ceased publication altogether with the surge in newsprint prices in 1942. For Trujillo's conquest of the Dominican press, see José Pérez Sánchez, "La prensa durante los primeros años de Trujillo," *Eme Eme* (July–August 1973).

72  *La Opinión* clipping, 23 February 1935, 839.00 TRUJILLO/172, RG 59, NA.

73  Schoenfeld to Secretary of State, 24 January 1937, 839.00/4125, RG 59, NA.

74  Legation report, 5 September 1936, 839.918/32, RG 59, NA.

75  Fabio Fiallo to Trujillo's uncle, Teódulo Pina Chevalier, reproduced in Bernardo Vega, *Control y represión en la dictadura trujillista* (Santo Domingo, 1986), 23.

76  Bernardo Vega, *Unos desafectos y otros en desgracia: Sufrimientos bajo la dictadura trujillista* (Santo Domingo, 1985), 128.

77  Legation report, 3 August 1931, 839.00/3502, RG 59, NA.

78  Brown to Schoenfeld, 18 June 1934, Schoenfeld Papers.

79  Paterson to Eden, 31 March 1936, "Annual Report, 1935," FO 371/19788, PRO.

80  Curtis to Secretary of State, 26 February 1931, 839.00/3470, RG 59, NA.

81  *Baltimore Sun,* 17–20 February 1931.

82  Curtis to Secretary of State, 6, 10, and 30 May 1931, 839.00/3470, RG 59, NA.

83  Welles to Morales, 15 April 1930; Welles to Kent Cooper, general manager, Associated Press, 14 April 1930; Charles Stephenson Smith, Associated Press, to Welles, 22 April 1930. All in Folder 4, Box 159, Welles Papers, FDRL.

84  Welles to Pearson, 4 and 9 February, with enclosed memos, Folder 1, Box 160, Welles Papers, FDRL.

85  Welles to Federico Velásquez, 23 February 1931, Folder 1, Box 160, Welles Papers, FDRL.

86  U.S. Minister R. Henry Norweb to Welles, 4 April 1939, Folder 16, Box 54, Welles Papers, FDRL.

87  Ornes, *Little Caesar,* 119–20.

88  Charles A. Thomson, "Dictatorship in the Dominican Republic," *Foreign Policy Reports* (15 March 1936): 30–40. Thomson subsequently joined the State Department's Division of Cultural Relations, 1939–44, becoming its chief.

89  Exchange summarized in Legation report, 10 August 1936, 839.00/4052, RG 59, NA.

90  *The Dominican Republic Actually* (January 1934): 3.

91  *Dominican Republic* (November 1934): 5.

92  Legation report, 2 June 1935, 839.00/3926, RG 59, NA.

93  "Report on Leading Personalities," November–December 1929, *British Documents,* 6:269–70.

94  "Outline of the First Term of the Trujillo Administration," 10 August 1934, 839.00/3797, RG 59, NA.

95  Edwin Wilson to Welles, 1 August 1934, enclosing memo, "Controversial Matters with the Dominican Government Affecting American Interests," Folder 5, Box 175, Welles Papers, FDRL.

96  Paterson to Eden, 31 March 1935, "Dominican Republic Annual Report, 1935," FO 371/19788, PRO.

97  "Outline of the Seventh Year of the Trujillo Administration," 11 September, 1937, 839.00/4135, RG 59, NA.

98   Schoenfeld personal letter to J. F. McGurk, 22 June 1934, 839.00/3792.5, RG 59, NA.

99   Legation report, 10 August 1936, 839.00/4052, RG 59, NA.

100  For example, the conferral of the Order of Duarte on Kilbourne and two other sugar executives (*New York Times*, 6 July 1937).

101  Legation report, 25 March 1936, 839.00/4010, RG 59, NA.

102  Schoenfeld to Secretary of State, 19 April 1933, 839.00/3655, RG 59, NA.

103  Memo of conversation, Dominican Minister to Cuba Osvaldo Bazil with Welles, 1 May 1933, 839.00 REVOLUTIONS/124, RG 59, NA.

104  Assistant Attorney General Roy St. Lewis to Stimson, 26 January 1932, 839.00 REVOLUTIONS/95; Chief Special Agent Bannerman to Assistant Secretary of State Harvey Bundy, 4 and 15 March 1932, 839.00 REVOLUTIONS/103.5; unidentified Special Agent to Welles, 12 February 1934, 839.00 REVOLUTIONS/134. All in RG 59, NA.

105  Spencer Phenix to Bundy, 9 February 1932, and Major C. A. Ross, U.S. Army General Staff, to McGurk, 7 March 1933, 839.00 REVOLUTIONS/96.5 and 122, RG 59, NA.

106  Welles to Attorney General, 29 March and 8 July 1937, 839.00 REVOLUTIONS/150 and 152; Welles to Schoenfeld, 6 August 1936, 839.00/4047, RG 59, NA.

107  Welles memo of conversation, 23 January 1936, Folder 5, Box 175, Welles Papers, FDRL.

108  *New York Herald Tribune*, 16 May 1934.

109  Davies wrote to the *Herald Tribune* and to the New York Spanish-language daily *La Prensa* as well as to the State Department. Copies of letters, 18–19 May 1934, caja 6, tomo 179, Archivo General de la Nación, Santo Domingo (hereafter AGN).

110  Schoenfeld telegram to Secretary of State, 5 October 1933, and Legation report, 6 October 1933, 839.00/3694 and 3698; memo of conversation, Dominican Minister Andrés Pastoriza with Hull, 20 May 1936, 839.00/4023; Caracas Legation report, 3 June 1936, 839.00/4028. All in RG 59, NA.

111  *New York Times*, 29 April 1935.

112  Charles O. Porter and Robert J. Alexander, *The Struggle for Democracy in Latin America* (New York, 1961), 142–59; Crassweller, *Trujillo: Caribbean Dictator*, 311–28; "The Galíndez-Murphy Case: A Chronicle of Terror," Edward R. Murrow broadcast on CBS, 20 May 1957.

113  Raymond Fielding, *The March of Time, 1935–1951* (New York, 1978), 138–39, 154.

114  "An American Dictator," *March of Time* (1936), VT 200 MT 2.7, Motion Picture Division, NA.

115  *March of Time* was not the first newsreel banned in the Dominican Repub-

lic. A Casa Pathe film on the Dominican Revolution of 1930 was suppressed from exhibition even before Trujillo's election, perhaps the first instance of his strategy of censorship. Rafael Brache to Elías Brache, 2 May 1930, caja 5, tomo 136, AGN.

116    Pastoriza to Hull, 11 July 1936, 811.4061 MARCH OF TIME/15, FRUS 1936, 5:479.

117    Memo of conversation, William Dunn with Francis White, 28 July 1936, Box 17, White Papers.

118    Memo of conversation, Pastoriza with Hull, 13 July 1936, Box 57, Cordell Hull Papers, Manuscript Branch, Library of Congress; New York Times, 19 July 1936.

119    New York Times, 17 July 1936; Hull to Pastoriza, 811.4061 MARCH OF TIME/17, FRUS 1936, 5:480–81.

120    John T. McManus screen column, New York Times, 19 July 1936.

121    Pastoriza to Welles, 11 and 15 July 1936, with Washington Post clipping enclosed, Folder 5, Box 175, Welles Papers, FDRL.

122    Memo of conversation, Dunn with White, 28 July 1936, Box 17, White Papers.

123    New York Times, 17 July 1936.

124    In only one instance during the 1930s did Trujillo succeed in censoring what was written about him in other countries. That occurred in San Juan in 1938, when Francisco C. Girona, author of Las fechorías del bandolero Trujillo (translated as The Misdeeds of the Bandit Trujillo), was convicted of libel by the Puerto Rican Department of Justice and sentenced to a year in prison. U.S. Minister R. Henry Norweb to Secretary of State, 1 October 1937, 839.00/4140, RG 59, NA; New York Times, 17 January 1938.

125    Uncle Sam: The Good Neighbor, RKO Radio Pictures, 1938 (March of Time), RG 59.18, Motion Picture Division, NA.

126    Listín Diario, 17 July 1930. The publication was modeled on a promotional newspaper called the Santo Domingo Review, which was produced during the Marine occupation and stressed the commercial potential of the Dominican Republic. It had strong connections with the self-promotion of the U.S. military government, including tours for favorably disposed writers. See Calder, The Impact of Intervention.

127    The Dominican Republic Actually (June 1934): 3.

128    The Dominican Chamber of Commerce was headed by H. Murray-Jacoby and included Evan Young, former U.S. minister to the Dominican Republic and vice-president of Pan American Airways, on the board of directors. New York Times, 13 July 1934.

129    Interview with Trujillo in Listín Diario, 17 July 1935, enclosed in Legation report, 17 July 1935, 839.00/3947, RG 59, NA.

130    Gantenbein reports, 24 July 1935 and 14 February 1936, 811.91239/10 and 12, RG 59, NA.

131   Laurence de Besault letter of introduction, undated, OF 1970, FDRL; U.S. Ambassador to Cuba J. Butler Wright to Welles, 13 February 1939, OF 87, FDRL.

132   Oswald Garrison Villard, "Santo Domingo, 1937," *The Nation* (20 March 1937): 323–24.

133   Dominican Minister to Argentina Tulio Cestero, account of diplomatic activities and distribution of "La obra de un renovador" [The Work of a Renovator] and "Los dos años de gobierno del presidente Trujillo," 27 January 1933, Archivo Cestero.

134   Dominican Foreign Minister Ernesto Bonetti Burgos to Pastoriza, 18 December 1936, caja 7 (2), tomo 206, AGN.

135   Davies contract, 2 May 1933, caja 6, tomo 172, AGN.

136   Davies letters to State Department, *New York Herald Tribune,* and *La Prensa* of New York, 18–19 May 1934, caja 6, tomo 172, AGN; Dewitt MacKenzie of the Associated Press informed his agent in Santo Domingo of Newman's special status (Legation report, 8 August 1934, 811.91239/8, RG 59, NA).

137   Seth Richardson to Pastoriza, 19 November and 3 December 1936, caja 7 (2), tomo 202, AGN.

138   Joseph E. Davies, *Memorial,* 12 May 1934, FBPC Records; Schoenfeld to Hull, 16 March 1936, 839.51/4366, RG 59, NA.

139   In 1936, Davies was president of the executive committee of Roosevelt's election campaign and vice-president of the Democratic national campaign. *New York Evening Star,* 9 October 1936, clipping contained in caja 7 (2), tomo 202, AGN.

140   Pastoriza cable to Bonetti Burgos, 31 December 1936, caja 7 (2), tomo 205, AGN.

141   Bonetti Burgos to Chargé Emilio García Godoy, forwarded to Pastoriza, 29 August 1936; Davies to Pastoriza, 10 December 1936. Both in caja 7 (2), tomo 206, AGN.

142   Roosevelt to Davies, 22 December 1936, PPF [President's Personal File] 1381, and sometime in February 1936, OF 138, FDRL. Davies also sent gifts to Trujillo, including a "magnificent portrait" that pleased its subject well. Rafael Brache to Davies, 15 June 1935, caja 7 (1), tomo 187, AGN.

143   Schoenfeld to Welles, 23 January 1936, Folder 10, Box 36, Welles Papers, FDRL.

144   Pamphlet reprint of H. Murray-Jacoby, *Cooperación,* August 1943, 839.001 TRUJILLO/32, RG 59, NA.

145   U.S. Minister R. Henry Norweb to Welles, 25 March 1939, Folder 16, Box 54, Welles Papers, FDRL.

146   See Legation reports for Representative Charles J. Linthicum, 19 July 1932, 033.1139 Linthicum/5; Senator Robert Reynolds, 10 May 1935, 033.1110 Reynolds/17; Senator William H. King, 7 August 1936, 033.1139 King/4. All in RG 59, NA.

147   See the film of the ceremony, "Santo Domingo," 27 February 1937, Universal News, v. 9, R 541, no. 5, Motion Picture Division, NA.

148   Dominican Foreign Minister Arturo Logroño to Rafael Brache, 10 May 1935, caja 7 (1), tomo 187, AGN.

149   "The Association of Young Patriots. The Mothers, Sisters, Sons. And the A.B.C.D." to Reynolds, 9 May 1935, enclosed in Legation report, 10 May 1935, 839.00/3892, RG 59, NA.

150   Bonetti Burgos to García Godoy, 5 August 1936, caja 7 (2), tomo 205, AGN; Richardson to Pastoriza, 16 November 1936, caja 7 (2), tomo 206, AGN.

151   Legation report, 12 February 1937, 811.91239/13, RG 59, NA.

152   Villard, "Santo Domingo, 1937," 323–24.

153   Representative Matthew Mouton to Hull, 18 April 1939, 033.1136/10, RG 59, NA.

154   Legation report, 20 March 1939, 033.1139/9; *Washington Herald* clipping, undated, in PPF 1769, FDRL.

155   Nicholas Murray Butler to Hull, 11 February 1939, and Senator Theodore Green to Assistant Secretary of State Adolph Berle, 10 April 1939, 839.001 TRUJILLO/313 and 320, RG 59, NA.

156   Fish to Roosevelt, 20 February 1934, PPF 4744, FDRL. For an account of Fish's speech, see *New York Times,* 22 December 1937; he also read an article condemning the massacre into the *Congressional Record* in January 1938.

157   *Washington Post,* 20 August 1942; Welles to Roosevelt, 1 July 1942, PPF 6012, FDRL; memo to Secretary of the Treasury Henry Morgenthau from Mr. Gaston, Department of Justice Intelligence Unit, 15 April 1942, *Morgenthau Diaries,* 516:386, FDRL. Also see chapter on "Jamón Pescado [Ham Fish]" in Albert C. Hicks, *Blood in the Streets: The Life and Rule of Trujillo* (New York, 1946), 125–38.

158   "Jamón Pescado," 125–38.

159   Crassweller, *Trujillo: Caribbean Dictator,* 323–25; Rafael Espaillat, *Trujillo: The Last Caesar* (Chicago, 1963), 74–88.

160   Legation report, 16 May 1933, 839.00 TRUJILLO/65, RG 59, NA. Clipping from *New York Times,* 5 July 1914, enclosed with Pulliam to William Manger, Counselor of the Pan-American Union, Columbus Memorial Lighthouse Collection, Columbus Library, Organization of American States, Washington, D.C. (hereafter OAS).

161   *Christopher Columbus Memorial Lighthouse at Santo Domingo: Hearings before the Committee on Foreign Affairs, U.S. House of Representatives,* 70th Congress, 2nd session, 23 January 1929; Hull to Roosevelt, 13 November 1935, OF 781, FDRL.

162   For instance, see James W. Gantenbein, "The Columbus Lighthouse," *American Foreign Service Journal* (August, 1936), reprinted and distributed by the

Pan-American Union, contained in Columbus Memorial Lighthouse Collection, OAS.

163    The Columbus Memorial Lighthouse Collection contains the records of the design competition, including drawings, correspondence, and publicity efforts.

164    Cestero correspondence, 1932–33, concerning distribution of the pamphlet *Trujillo y Colón,* Archivo Cestero. For Pan-American Union publicity, see for example "Periodicals Receiving Photographs of the Columbus Lighthouse Prize Winners," listing forty-four Latin American and fifty-one U.S. publications, 23 March 1932, Columbus Memorial Lighthouse Collection, OAS; for a later version of publicity linking Columbus with tourism and modernization under Trujillo, see John W. White, *The Land Columbus Loved* (Ciudad Trujillo, 1945).

165    Resolutions XX and LXI and "Miscellaneous Conclusions," in *Report on the Results of the Seventh International Conference of the American States at Montevideo, Uruguay,* Washington, D.C., Pan-American Union, 21 February 1934.

166    *Report on the Steps Taken by the Pan-American Union in Fulfillment of the Conventions and Resolutions Adopted at the Seventh International Conference of American States,* Washington, D.C., Pan-American Union, 27 June 1934.

167    *Boletín de Relaciones Exteriores,* July–September 1934, Biblioteca Nacional, Santo Domingo.

168    Undated, unsigned chronology of Columbus Lighthouse memos, 839. 413C72/403, RG 59, NA; Hull to Roosevelt, 13 November 1935, OF 781, FDRL. The new committee, formed in 1936, included Nicholas Murray Butler and Judge Otto Schoenrich, two leaders of the Dominican lobby (Welles memo to Roosevelt, 4 March 1937, OF 781, FDRL). Others who accepted appointments to the committee were Bernard Baruch, Robert Woods Bliss, W. A. Harriman, Thomas Lamont, and the presidents of ITT, American and Foreign Power Company, the National Geographic Society, CBS, International General Electric, and Pan American Airways (J. C. Holmes, Acting Chief of the Division of International Conferences, to Rowe, 1 October 1937, Columbus Memorial Lighthouse Collection, OAS). British Ambassador Paterson reported Trujillo's fear that changing the name of Santo Domingo to Ciudad Trujillo had "prejudiced the success" of the project in other countries that "have no interest in the glorification of Trujillo" (Paterson to Eden, 4 July 1939, *British Documents,* 20:322).

169    Welles memo to Presidential Secretary Stephen Early, 26 July 1937, in *Franklin D. Roosevelt and Foreign Affairs,* 2d series, New York, 1979, 6:201–2; Rowe to Roosevelt, 8 October 1937, OF 781, FDRL. See also the text of the joint Columbus Day radio messages by FDR, Welles, and Trujillo in 1936: "Announcers

Sheet for Broadcast of Presidential Messages on the Columbus Memorial Lighthouse," 12 October 1936; "Remarks to be Delivered . . . Relative to the Columbus Memorial Lighthouse," undated; and "Message of Pan-American Fraternity from Generalissimo Doctor Rafael L. Trujillo Molina," 12 October 1936. All in Columbus Memorial Lighthouse Collection, OAS.

170    Chronology of Columbus Lighthouse memos, undated, 839.413C72/403, RG 59, NA; Welles to Rowe, 8 July 1938, Columbus Memorial Lighthouse Collection, OAS.

171    Derby, "Magic of Modernity," chapter entitled "The Choreography of Consent."

172    Film of *Faro* cornerstone ceremony, March 1944, Universal News outtake, 1688 × 7, Motion Picture Division, NA. The *Faro a Colón* was finally completed in 1989 by the government of the *trujillista* President Joaquín Balaguer, following the 1931 design. See James Ferguson, *The Dominican Republic: Beyond the Lighthouse* (New York, 1992). Its image also appears on the Dominican half-peso coin.

173    Brown to Schoenfeld, 4 August 1933, Schoenfeld Papers. A film of a Columbian ritual ceremony, "Santo Domingo Honors Ashes of Columbus" (1936), shows Trujillo, the archbishop of Ciudad Trujillo, U.S. diplomats, and Dominican military officers at the cathedral, pouring the remains of the Discoverer into a new stone receptacle (Universal News, v. 8, R 510, no. 5, Motion Picture Division, NA). The sarcophagus required three keys to open, one kept by Trujillo, one by the archbishop, and one by the mayor of the capital; but, for visitors with publicity potential, these luminaries could be assembled quickly. Trujillo did so for the travel writer E. Alexander Powell during his Pan American Airways tour of the Caribbean in 1936. It was "one of the most memorable moments" of Powell's life when he "beheld all that is mortal of the Grand Admiral of Spain," and he subsequently wrote a glowing account of the Dominican Republic and its president in *Aerial Odyssey* (New York, 1936), 44–72.

174    *New York Times,* 24 June 1939.

175    *Public Papers and Addresses of Franklin D. Roosevelt,* 1933 (New York, 1941), 7:411–13.

176    *Listín Diario,* 23 February 1936; "Outline of the Sixth Year of the Trujillo Administration," 8 August 1936, 839.00/4050, RG 59, NA.

177    Schoenfeld to Rudolf Schoenfeld, 5 February 1936, Schoenfeld Papers.

178    Legation report, 11 September 1937, 839.00/4135, RG 59, NA; Schoenfeld to Rudolf Schoenfeld, 22 February 1936, Schoenfeld Papers.

179    Raymond Pulley, "The United States and the Dominican Republic: The High Price of Caribbean Stability," *Caribbean Studies* (October 1965): 30.

180    Homi Bhabha, "Of Mimicry and Man: The Ambivalence of Colonial Dis-

course," in Annette Michelson et al., eds., *October: The First Decade, 1976–1986* (Cambridge, 1987): 317–25.

181  Legation reports, 25 April 1933, 839.00/3656; 17 August 1933, 839.415/14; and 20 December 1933, 839.00/3730. All in RG 59, NA.

182  Gellman, *Good Neighbor Diplomacy,* 25.

183  Roosevelt to Trujillo, 30 January 1936, and Trujillo to Roosevelt, 11 February 1936, both in *Boletín de Relaciones Exteriores,* January 1937, Biblioteca Nacional, Santo Domingo.

184  Legation report, 17 July 1935, 839.00/3947, RG 59, NA.

185  Marks, *Wind over Sand,* 239.

186  Samuel Guy Inman to Dott Inman, 15 December 1936, Inman Papers.

187  "Report of the Delegation to the Buenos Aires Conference," FRUS 1936, 1:21. Saavedra Lamas was contemptuous of the Caribbean "Republiquitas," which he regarded as the "mistresses" of the United States, and he opposed "concessions to the[ir] vanity" such as Trujillo's proposal. J. H. Leche to Eden, 20 January 1937, *British Documents,* 16:366.

188  "Outline of the Eighth Year of the Trujillo Administration," 7 November 1938, 839.00/4209, RG 59, NA.

189  Norweb to Secretary of State, 9 March 1938, 710 H Agenda/37, RG 59, NA.

190  Legation report on Peynado's Restoration Day speech, 17 August 1937, 839.032/117; "Outline of the Eighth Year of the Trujillo Administration," 7 November 1938, 839.00/4209. Both in RG 59, NA.

191  "Instructions to the Delegates, Eighth Pan American Conference, Lima," undated, Papers of Adolph A. Berle, FDRL.

192  Presidential Secretary Marvin McIntyre to Protocol Division, 27 March 1933, OF 138, FDRL.

193  Trujillo speech on the third anniversary of his election, translation enclosed in Legation report, 22 May 1933, 839.00/3667, RG 59, NA.

194  Trujillo to Roosevelt, 3 February 1936, OF 138, FDRL; "Outline of the Ninth Year of the Trujillo Administration," 27 September 1939, 839.00/4223, RG 59, NA.

195  "Outline of the Seventh Year of the Trujillo Administration," 11 September 1937, 839.00/4135, RG 59, NA; *Listín Diario* report of a *Brooklyn News* opinion poll regarding Roosevelt's chances for a third term, with the headline "Roosevelt and Trujillo towards a Third Term," enclosed in Legation report, 24 July 1937, 839.00/4126, RG 59, NA. Trujillo withdrew from the election after the Haitian massacre.

196  Pastoriza to Roosevelt, 29 February 1936, OF 138, FDRL.

197  Legation reports, 7 December 1937, 839.713/8, and 3 July 1940, 839.413C72/395, RG 59, NA.

198    Roosevelt to Postmaster General James Farley, 27 December 1939, OF 480, FDRL. The stamp was issued 14 April 1940.

199    See exchange of radio messages between FDR aboard the USS *Philadelphia* and Trujillo, Ms. 48, Walter Woodson Collection, Naval War College, Newport, R.I.; Trujillo to Roosevelt, 26 April 1933, 032 Richards, George/2, RG 59, NA.

200    *Boletín de Relaciones Exteriores,* June 1934, Biblioteca Nacional, Santo Domingo.

201    *New York Times,* 7 February 1939.

202    Pulliam to Welles, 26 February 1937, Folder 1, Box 147, Welles Papers, FDRL.

203    Pulliam to Roosevelt, Roosevelt to Pulliam, n.d., OF 1730, FDRL.

204    Hull to Undersecretary of State William Phillips, 25 December 1933, 839.001 TRUJILLO/89, RG 59, NA.

205    Memo of conversation, Loranzo de Besa [*sic*] with Edwin Wilson, 31 August 1935, 839.001 TRUJILLO/216, RG 59, NA.

206    Legation report, 6 December 1934, 839.001 TRUJILLO/153, RG 59, NA.

207    Ernesto Vega y Pagán, *Military Biography of Generalísimo Rafael Leonidas Trujillo Molina* (Ciudad Trujillo, 1956), 132.

208    Galienne to Henderson, 10 March 1930, *British Documents,* 6:314.

209    Julio César Castro H., *Paralelo (Mussolini-Trujillo)* (Santo Domingo, 1933).

210    *New York Times,* 29 April 1935.

211    Hull telegram to Schoenfeld, 2 May 1935, 339.115 General Motors Export Company/55, RG 59, NA.

212    Paterson to Sir John Simon, 20 April 1935, FO 371/18700, PRO.

213    Schoenfeld to Welles, 22 May 1935, Folder 8, Box 36, Welles Papers, FDRL.

214    Paterson to Simon, 20 April 1935, FO 371/18700, PRO.

215    Schoenfeld to Secretary of State, 23 April 1935, 339.115 General Motors Export Company/33, RG 59, NA.

216    Memo of conversation, Rafael Brache with Hull, 14 May 1935, 339.115 GM Export Co./155, RG 59, NA.

217    *New York Times,* 16 May 1935.

218    Memo of conversation, Brache with Schoenfeld, 27 May 1935, RG 59, NA.

219    Welles to Hull, 17 May 1935, enclosing clipping from *La Opinión,* Folder 5, Box 177, Welles Papers, FDRL; Paterson to Simon, 27 May 1935, FO 371/18700, PRO.

220    Schoenfeld to Secretary of State, 27 May 1935, 839.1561/40, RG 59, NA.

221    Gantenbein to Schoenfeld, 11 July 1935, Schoenfeld Papers.

222    Ernest Gruening, "The Dictatorship in Santo Domingo: A 'Joint Concern,'" *The Nation* (23 May 1934): 583–85.

223    *Dominican Republic,* January 1936.

224    Nanita, *Trujillo: A Full-Size Portrait,* 10.

225    Paterson to Eden, 23 July 1937, *British Documents,* 17:283.

FIVE    *Genocide Next Door: The Haitian Massacre of 1937 and the Sosua Jewish Refugee Settlement*

1   Portions of this chapter appeared in *Diplomatic History* (Summer 1996): 301–19, and are reproduced here with the permission of Blackwell Publishers. Norweb to Secretary of State, 11 October 1937, enclosed in Welles to Roosevelt, 19 October 1937, in *Franklin D. Roosevelt and Foreign Affairs*, 7:121–25. News of the massacre was first reported on 7 October 1937 by the American customs inspector in the Dominican border town of Dajabón and by the U.S. legation in Port-au-Prince, where twelve hundred Haitian refugees were reported to have arrived in the city during the preceding days (738.39/23–24, RG 59, NA).

2   Bernardo Vega, *Trujillo y Haití, 1930–1937* (Santo Domingo, 1988), 1:386–87, lists 54 estimates of the death toll made between 1937 and 1987. These estimates range between five hundred and thirty-five thousand. In the second volume of his study (Santo Domingo, 1995), 342–53, Vega himself accepts a figure of approximately forty-five hundred to five thousand and lists 113 estimates of the number killed.

3   The most thorough critique of the Good Neighbor policy's objectives and its tendency to "entrench" dictators is Green, *The Containment of Latin America*.

4   This thesis supports the contention that the ability of states "to resist external exploitation has been considerably more varied and extensive" than students of U.S. foreign relations have recognized. Thomas J. McCormick, "Something Old, Something New: John Lewis Gaddis's 'New Conceptual Approaches,'" *Diplomatic History* (Summer 1990): 427.

5   Gellman, *Good Neighbor Diplomacy*, 73; Fred Fejes, *Imperialism, Media, and the Good Neighbor* (Norwood, N.J., 1986); Graham White, *FDR and the Press* (Chicago, 1979).

6   For a portrait of the society and culture of the frontier, see Lauren H. Derby, "Haitians, Magic and Money: *Raza* and Society in the Haitian-Dominican Borderlands, 1900–1937," *Comparative Studies in Society and History* (July 1994): 488–526. I am indebted to Dr. Derby for sharing her knowledge of the borderlands and the *matanza* so generously with me.

7   See ibid. and Lauren H. Derby and Richard Turits, "Historias de terror y los terrores de historia: La masacre haitiana de 1937 en la República Dominicana," *Estudios Sociales* (April–June 1992): 65–76.

8   The border incidents of 1931 are detailed in FRUS 1931, 1:771–92. U.S. diplomats also helped to resolve "frontier episodes" in February 1932 and April 1933. "Outline of the First Term of the Trujillo Administration," 10 August 1934, 839.00/3797, RG 59, NA; Vega, *Trujillo y Haití*, 1:18, 87–99, 122–33, 167–72.

9   The signing and ratification of the treaty were the occasions for another exchange of visits by the two presidents. Vega, *Trujillo y Haití,* 1:172–270.

10   "Outline of the Sixth Year of the Trujillo Administration," 8 August 1936, 839.00/4050, RG 59, NA.

11   Mateo, *Mito y cultura,* 112–13.

12   Trujillo to Roosevelt, 3 February 1936, OF 138, FDRL.

13   "Outline of Sixth Year," 8 August 1936, 839.00/4050, RG 59, NA.

14   Paterson to Eden, 30 April 1936, FO 371/19788, PRO.

15   Vega, *Trujillo y Haití,* 1:284–89, 304–9.

16   Pike, *FDR's Good Neighbor Policy,* 115, 333.

17   Memo of conversation, Secretary of the Interior Harold Ickes with Hull, 3 February 1936, 839.52 PUERTO RICANS/5, RG 59, NA.

18   Welles to Roosevelt, 13 October 1937, in *Franklin D. Roosevelt and Foreign Affairs* 7:120.

19   Teódulo Pina Chevalier and James J. MacLean, *Datos históricos sobre la frontera domínico-haitiana* (Santo Domingo, 1921).

20   British Minister A. S. Paterson reported that "the provocative speech" Trujillo made at the gathering in Dajabón "appears to have been the signal for the extraordinary massacres of Haytians." Paterson to Eden, 8 November 1937, *British Documents,* 18:60.

21   Vega, *Trujillo y Haití,* 2:275–76, 298–303, 314–15, 319–24, 384–87.

22   Aïda Schoenfeld oral history transcript, 9 February 1982, 54–55, Schoenfeld Papers.

23   Memo of conversation, J. C. McClintock with Paul Rosenfeld, 17 November 1937, 738.39/133, RG 59, NA. Contemporary accounts of the massacre include Reynolds, "Murder in the Tropics," *Collier's* (22 January 1938): 15–16, and Harold Courlander, "Not in the Cables: Massacre in Santo Domingo," *The New Republic* (24 November 1937): 67. Secondary literature on the event includes Derby and Turits, "Historias de terror y los terrores de historia"; Thomas Fiehrer, "Political Violence in the Periphery: The Haitian Massacre of 1937," *Race and Class* (October–December 1990): 1–20; Vega, *Trujillo y Haití,* 1:325–87; R. Michael Malek, "Dominican Republic's General Rafael Trujillo and the Haitian Massacre of 1937: A Case of Subversion in Inter-Caribbean Relations," *SECOLAS Annals: Journal of the Southeastern Conference on Latin American Studies* (March 1980): 137–55; Juan Manuel García, *La matanza de los haitianos: Genocidio de Trujillo, 1937* (Santo Domingo, 1983); and Luis Arias Núñez, *La política exterior en la era de Trujillo* (Santiago, D.R., 1991), 31–126. Pertinent documents are compiled in José Israel Cuello H., *Documentos del conflicto domínico-haitiano de 1937* (Santo Domingo, 1985). For a novel on the subject, see Freddy Prestol Castillo, *El masacre se pasa a pie* (Santo Domingo, 1973).

24 Mary de la Rue to Welles, 22 February 1938, Folder 5, Box 45, Welles Papers, FDRL.

25 Vega, *Trujillo y Haití*, 2:342–47.

26 Memo of conversation, Norweb with Dominican Minister of Justice Julio Ortega Frier, 13 October 1937, 839.5511/unnumbered, RG 59, NA.

27 Welles to Roosevelt, 19 October 1937, in *Franklin D. Roosevelt and Foreign Affairs* 7:121–25.

28 Minister Ferdinand Mayer to Secretary of State, 23 November 1937, 738.39/132, RG 59, NA.

29 President Stenio Vincent to Georges Léger, 3 November 1937, Folder 4, Box 178, Welles Papers, FDRL.

30 Mayer to Secretary of State, 23 November 1937, 738.39/132, RG 59, NA.

31 For photo, see Vega, *Trujillo y Haití*, 1:294; for a description of the "Trujillo Salute," see Norweb to Secretary of State, 30 September 1937, 839.001 TRUJILLO/289, RG 59, NA; for an overview of ideological competition with National Socialism, see Alton Frye, *Nazi Germany and the American Hemisphere, 1933–1941* (New Haven, 1967).

32 Mayer to Secretary of State, 23 November 1937, 738.39/132, RG 59, NA.

33 David G. Haglund, *Latin America and the Transformation of United States Strategic Thought, 1936–1940* (Albuquerque, 1984); Lester Langley, "The World Crisis and the Good Neighbor Policy in Panama, 1936–41," *The Americas* (October 1967): 144–46.

34 Welles to Norweb, 4 November 1937, 738.39/67A, RG 59, NA.

35 Norweb was deeply disappointed to leave the Havana proceedings, and during November 1937 he was distracted by hopes of returning before the conference adjourned. Norweb to Welles, 29 November 1937, Folder 2, Box 43, Welles Papers, FDRL.

36 Dominican Minister Andrés Pastoriza to Ciudad Trujillo, 5 November 1937, caja 7 (4), tomo 232, AGN.

37 *New York Times*, 7 November 1937.

38 Press conference, 9 November 1937, in *Franklin D. Roosevelt and Foreign Affairs*, 7:197.

39 Journal of Walter Woodson, Naval Aide to Roosevelt, 10 November 1937, Ms. 48, Naval War College.

40 Welles to Norweb, 10 November 1937, 738.39/87A, RG 59, NA.

41 *New York Times*, 10 November 1937.

42 Ibid.; Acting Foreign Minister Ortega to Pastoriza, 6 November 1937, caja 7 (5), tomo 245, AGN.

43 Harold Finley, Chargé d'Affaires in Port-au-Prince, to Secretary of State, 4 November 1937, 738.39/68, RG 59, NA.

44    Mayer to Welles, 8 January 1938, Folder 13, Box 46, Welles Papers, FDRL.

45    Welles to Mayer, 10 January 1938, Folder 13, Box 46, Welles Papers, FDRL.

46    In 1937, the Dominican Army had a standing force of three thousand, a reserve force of ten thousand, and eight airplanes (Peguero, "Trujillo and the Military," 230, 239). The relative strengths of the armies are suggested by the orders they placed with the Remington Arms Company on 29 October 1937: Haiti asked for two hundred thousand Springfield cartridges, and the Dominican Republic for seven times as many Springfield and Colt cartridges (Selden Chapin to Welles, 2 November 1937, 738.39/84, RG 59, NA).

47    "Outline of Eighth Year," 7 November, 839.00/4209, RG 59, NA.

48    Norweb to Secretary of State, 8 November 1937, 738.39/74, RG 59, NA.

49    Norweb to Welles, 10 November 1937, Folder 2, Box 43, Welles Papers, FDRL.

50    Memo of conversation, Haitian Foreign Minister Georges Léger with Welles, 10 November 1937, 738.39/83, RG 59, NA.

51    Vincent to Roosevelt, 12 November 1937, in *Franklin D. Roosevelt and Foreign Relations,* 7:213, 227.

52    Memo of conversation, Norweb with Ortega, 15 November 1937, 738.39/98, RG 59, NA.

53    Subsecretary of Foreign Relations Ernesto Bonetti Burgos to Pastoriza, 9 November 1937, caja 7 (5), tomo 245, AGN; memo of conversation, Norweb with Ortega, 15 November 1937, 738.39/98, RG 59, NA.

54    *New York Times,* 15 November 1937.

55    Ortega to Pastoriza, 6 November 1937, caja 7 (5), tomo 245, AGN.

56    Welles to Norweb, 8 November 1937, 738.39/76A, RG 59, NA.

57    Ortega to Pastoriza, 4 November 1937, caja 7 (5), tomo 245, AGN.

58    Norweb to Welles, 9 November 1937, 738.39/81, RG 59, NA.

59    Crassweller, *Trujillo: Caribbean Dictator,* 160–63.

60    Pastoriza to Ortega, 15 November 1937, caja 7 (5), tomo 245, AGN.

61    Ibid.

62    Pastoriza to Ortega, 23 November 1937, and Ortega to Pastoriza, 18 November 1937. Both in caja 7 (5), tomo 245, AGN.

63    Memo of conversation, Hull with Pastoriza, 23 November 1937, 738.39/140; Welles to Norweb, 23 November 1937, 738.39/136A. Both in RG 59, NA.

64    Welles memo of conversation with Pastoriza, 5 November 1937, Folder 6, Box 177, Welles Papers, FDRL.

65    Pastoriza and Manuel de Jesús Troncoso de la Concha to Ortega, 26 November 1937, caja 7 (5), tomo 245, AGN.

66    Welles memo of conversation with Pastoriza and Troncoso, 26 November 1937, Folder 6, Box 175, Welles Papers, FDRL.

67    Pastoriza to Ortega, 18 November 1937, caja 7 (5), tomo 245, AGN.

68  Pastoriza and Troncoso to Ortega, 26 November 1937, caja 7 (5), tomo 245, AGN.

69  Pastoriza and Troncoso to Ortega, 29 November 1937, caja 7 (5), tomo 245, AGN.

70  The meetings were also attended by Pastoriza, Troncoso, Haitian Foreign Minister Georges Léger and Minister to Washington Elie Lescot, Mexican Ambassador Francisco Castillo Nájera, and the Cuban chargé d'affaires.

71  Circular telegram from Hull to all diplomatic missions in the American republics, 14 December 1937, 738.39/200A, RG 59, NA.

72  Pastoriza and Troncoso to Ortega, 9 December 1937, caja 7 (4), tomo 232, AGN.

73  Norweb to Welles, 11 December 1937, Folder 2, Box 43, Welles Papers, FDRL.

74  The Nation (27 November 1937): 577–78.

75  Life (6 December 1937): 73–77.

76  New York Times, 22 December 1937.

77  Paterson to Eden, 24 January 1938, British Documents, 18:304.

78  New York Times, 19 December 1937. Dominican census figures are still cited in calculations of the number of Haitians killed in 1937 (see Vega, Trujillo y Haití, 2:343–45), although there are many reasons why the 1935 count may have underestimated the number of ethnic Haitians living in the Dominican Republic. Individuals of Haitian ethnicity were probably reluctant to be located and identified by their real names, partly out of religious considerations and partly because the Dominican government was already making moves to displace them.

79  Paterson to Eden, 24 January 1938, FO 371/21459, PRO.

80  New York Times, 19 December 1937.

81  New York Times, 27 December 1937.

82  Memo of conversation, Francis White with Haitian Foreign Minister Georges Léger, 13 January 1938, Box 18, White Papers.

83  New York Times, 19 December 1937.

84  New York Times, 21 December 1937.

85  Richberg to Trujillo, 29 January 1937, caja 7 (4), tomo 230, AGN.

86  Welles to NAACP Secretary Walter White, 31 December 1937, Box C-330, Papers of the National Association for the Advancement of Colored People, Library of Congress, Washington, D.C. The NAACP's publication, The Crisis, was silent on the issue, although an article by a Haitian dissident critical of Vincent appeared later (The Crisis [May 1939]: 212).

87  Pastoriza to Ortega, 15 December 1937, caja 7 (5), tomo 232, AGN.

88  Memo of conversation, Welles with Ortega, 10 February 1938, 839.51/4594, RG 59, NA; "Outline of Ninth Year," 27 September 1939, 839.00/4223, RG 59, NA.

89  "Permanent Commission of Washington; Haitian-Dominican Incident — Session of 31 January 1938" and Mayer to Welles, 8 January 1938, Folder 13, Box 46, Welles Papers, FDRL.

90  Paterson to Eden, 24 January 1938, FO 371/21459, PRO.

91  Roosevelt to Trujillo, 5 February 1938, in *Franklin D. Roosevelt and Foreign Relations* 7:240–41.

92  *The Nation* (5 February 1938): 146.

93  *The Nation* (1 January 1938): 730.

94  "Outline of Eighth Year," 7 November 1938, 839.00/4209, RG 59, NA. This report came to different conclusions from Roosevelt's on the efficacy of inter-American mediation: "The diplomatic negotiations attendant upon its settlement also emphasized certain weaknesses in the present treaty machinery for the settlement of controversies between the American states, especially when one party to an international controversy is almost wholly wrong and, therefore, extremely loath to come before the court either of public opinion or of juridical settlement."

95  Secretary of the Legation Eugene Hinkle's report on massacre, 9 September 1938, 839.00/4206, RG 59, NA.

96  Welles memo of conversation with Ortega, 3 February 1938, 839.51/4594, RG 59, NA.

97  Chapin to Duggan, 8 February 1938, 839.00/4167, RG 59, NA.

98  Robert M. Field to Pastoriza, 18 July 1938, caja 7 (5), tomo 245, AGN.

99  Field to Pastoriza, 20 August 1938, caja 7 (5), tomo 245, AGN; Quentin Reynolds "Murder in the Tropics."

100 Atwood report on Trujillo's democratic reforms, 16 December 1937, 839.00/4157; Hinkle report on Dominican Republic as "totalitarian state," 7 July 1938, 839.00/4199. Both in RG 59, NA.

101 *New York Times,* 10 August 1938.

102 Legation dispatch, 8 January 1938, 839.00/4175, RG 59, NA.

103 Norweb to Secretary of State, 17 January 1938, 839.00/4164, RG 59, NA; *New York Times,* 8 April 1938.

104 Norweb to Secretary of State, 17 January 1938, 839.00/4164, RG 59, NA.

105 Welles to Duggan, 8 March 1938, 839.00/4172, RG 59, NA.

106 Norweb to Secretary of State, 18 August 1938, 839.00/4204, RG 59, NA.

107 Norweb to Secretary of State, 29 August 1938, 839.00/4205, RG 59, NA.

108 Chapin to Duggan, 13 September 1938, 839.00/unnumbered, RG 59, NA.

109 Mayer to Secretary of State, 8 April 1938, 701.3938/33, RG 59, NA.

110 Legation report, 19 May 1938, 839.51/4604, RG 59, NA.

111 Norweb to Welles, 6 March 1939, Folder 16, Box 54, Welles Papers, FDRL.

112 "Outline of Ninth Year," 27 September 1939, 839.00/4223, RG 59, NA; Norweb to Welles, 25 March 1939, Folder 16, Box 54, Welles Papers, FDRL.

113   Samuel Eliot Morison to Oswald Garrison Villard, 21 February 1938, Box C-330, NAACP Papers.

114   "Report of Attaché for Intelligence Division, Office of the Chief of Naval Operations," 16 May 1938, 839.00/4185, RG 59, NA.

115   Welles to Roosevelt, 11 April 1938, OF 3186, FDRL.

116   Gellman, *Secret Affairs*, 25–26, 37, 38, 209, 385.

117   Mark Wischnitzer, "The Historical Background of the Settlement of Jewish Refugees in Santo Domingo," *Jewish Social Studies* 4, no. 1 (1942): 42–58. For Roosevelt's policy toward Jewish refugees, see Leo V. Kanawada Jr., *Franklin D. Roosevelt's Diplomacy and American Catholics, Italians, and Jews* (Ann Arbor, 1982), 103–11; David S. Wyman, *Paper Walls: America and the Refugee Crisis, 1938–1941* (Amherst, 1968); and Henry Feingold, *The Politics of Rescue: The Roosevelt Administration and the Holocaust, 1938–1945* (New Brunswick, 1970). For a detailed examination of Trujillo's motives in establishing Sosua, see the following by Hyman J. Kisch: "The Jewish Settlement from Central Europe in the Dominican Republic," Ph.D. diss., Jewish Theological Seminary, 1970; "Rafael Trujillo: Caribbean Cyrus," *Judaism* 29, no. 3 (1980): 368–77. For the context of Jewish agricultural colonies in Latin America, see Judith Laiken Elkin, *Jews in the Latin American Republics* (Chapel Hill, 1980), 125–55; Haim Avni, "Latin America and the Jewish Refugees: Two Encounters, 1935 and 1938," in Avni and Gilbert W. Merkx, eds., *The Jewish Presence in Latin America* (Boston, 1987), 45–68.

118   Dr. Howard Blake to Trujillo, 5 January 1937, 839.52 JEWISH COLONIZATION/ 1, RG 59, NA.

119   Laurence Duggan, Chief of the State Department Latin American Division, analysis of Dominican immigration policy, 29 January 1938, 839.51/4570, RG 59, NA.

120   Chief of Visa Division Avra Warren to Norweb, 29 April and 12 October 1938, 839.55/75 and 87, RG 59, NA.

121   Memo by Hull, 27 July 1938, 839.55/83, RG 59, NA.

122   Memo by Warren, 2 May 1939, 839.55/85, RG 59, NA. The general outline of the legislation had already been decided by Trujillo, reported Minister Norweb: "If the immigration men's recommendations, especially with regard to immigration from Haiti, should jibe with the Generalissimo's views, well and good, and if they did not his views would prevail just the same" (Norweb to Welles, 8 September 1938, Folder 3, Box 47, Welles Papers, FDRL).

123   Legation report, 18 August 1939, 839.5552/2, RG 59, NA. For a detailed study of these efforts, see C. Harvey Gardiner, *La política de inmigración del dictador Trujillo* (Santo Domingo, 1980), 33–92.

124   Memo on Jewish colonization by Welles, 28 November 1938, in *Franklin D. Roosevelt and Foreign Relations*, 8:204.

125    Hinkle report on Jewish immigration offer, 3 December 1938, 840.48 REFU-
GEES/1046, RG 59, NA.
126    "Outline of the Eighth Year," 7 November 1938, 839.00/4209, RG 59, NA.
127    Welles to Roosevelt, 12 January 1939, OF 3186, FDRL.
128    Welles to Roosevelt, 5 January 1939, OF 3186, FDRL.
129    Welles to Roosevelt, 27 February 1939, OF 3186, FDRL.
130    Welles to Roosevelt, 29 April 1939, OF 3186, FDRL.
131    "Minutes of Meeting of the Officers of the Intergovernmental Committee
on Political Refugees," 18 October 1939: 107–8, OF 3186, FDRL.
132    Assistant Secretary of State Adolph Berle to James Rosenberg, 29 September
1939, Myron C. Taylor Papers, FDRL; Legation report, 1 July 1939, 839.55/108,
RG 59, NA.
133    Rosenberg to General Myron C. Taylor, 17 October 1939, Taylor Papers, FDRL.
134    "Minutes of Meeting of the Officers of the Intergovernmental Committee
on Political Refugees," 26 October 1939: 144–45, OF 3186, FDRL.
135    Jewish Telegraphic Agency news dispatch, 27 October 1939, Taylor Papers,
FDRL.
136    Trujillo himself donated the "magnificent" 26,000-acre tract of land at Sosua
on the north coast, once a banana plantation owned by United Fruit. Accounts of the settlement never failed to mention the donation. Rosenberg to
Taylor, 13 February 1940, Taylor Papers, FDRL; also see Gardiner, *La política de
inmigración,* 93–140, 228–37.
137    Clipping from *New York Herald Tribune,* 31 January 1940, Taylor Papers, FDRL.
138    Rosenberg to Trujillo, 17 February 1940, and W. P. Montague, Assignment
Editor of Paramount News, to Rosenberg, 30 December 1940, caja 7 (8),
tomo 279, AGN. Also Paramount News, 20 February 1941, v. 41, no. 51, and
*Sosua: Haven in the Caribbean,* DORSA 1941, Paramount Pictures, Motion Picture Division, NA.
139    Pastoriza to Roberto Despradel, 4 March 1940, caja 7 (8), tomo 279, AGN.
Trujillo's cooperation with the refugee settlement was deemed an "act of
mercy [and] . . . of statesmanship," though somewhat "ironical" in light of
his past record (*The Nation* [25 November 1939]: 569).
140    Roosevelt to Rosenberg, 6 March 1940, PPF 6364, FDRL.
141    Elkin, *Jews in the Latin American Republics,* 146.
142    Interview with Felix Koch, Sosua, Dominican Republic, 12 May 1989. Roseate
views of the settlement are found in Joseph Rosen, "New Neighbors in Sosua,"
*Survey Graphic* (September 1941), and in Julius Moritzen, "Santo Domingo:
A Haven for European Refugees," *Dominican Republic* (March–April 1941):
10–13. The Dominican daily newspaper *Listín Diario* extolled Sosua for the
domestic audience, 24 December 1940. A full-page article and photo spread

included the caption "Note the expression of well-being on all the faces [of the refugees]."

143   Legation report, 15 June 1940, 839.55/119, RG 59, NA.

144   Rosenberg to Pastoriza, 26 June 1940, caja 7 (8), tomo 279, AGN.

145   Rosenberg to Pastoriza, 24 April 1940; DORSA to Siegfried Weil, 2 May 1940. Both in caja 7 (8), tomo 279, AGN.

146   U.S. Minister Robert M. Scotten to Welles, 2 August 1940, Folder 14, Box 64, Welles Papers, FDRL.

147   Article from *New York Herald Tribune,* 16 February 1941, Taylor Papers, FDRL.

148   U.S. Ambassador Ellis O. Briggs, "Impressions of Jewish Refugee Settlement at Sosua, Dominican Republic," 7 August 1944, Embassy at Ciudad Trujillo–1944, vol. 16, RG 84, NA.

149   In fact, Hamilton Fish visited Ciudad Trujillo in 1939 as part of a "Good Will Committee" and subsequently became a vocal, and apparently well-remunerated, booster of Trujillo (*Listín Diario,* 13–22 March 1939). For evidence of payoffs to Fish, see Welles to Roosevelt, 1 July 1942, PPF 6012, FDRL; memo to Secretary of the Treasury Henry Morgenthau from Mr. Gaston, 15 April 1942, *Morgenthau Diaries,* 516:386, FDRL.

150   *New York Times,* 11 February 1940.

SIX    *Gold Braid and Striped Pants: The Culture of Foreign Relations in the Dominican Republic*

1    Some works on the centrality of culture in foreign relations are Johnsuk Chay, ed., *Culture and International Relations* (New York, 1990); Akira Iriye, "Culture and International History," and Michael Hunt, "Ideology," both in Michael J. Hogan and Thomas G. Paterson, eds., *Explaining the History of American Foreign Relations* (Cambridge, 1991); and Amy Kaplan and Donald E. Pease, eds., *Cultures of United States Imperialism* (Durham, 1993).

2    The historiographical literature concerning the organizational roots of foreign relations is vast, but a good survey of the competing theories is Michael J. Hogan and Thomas Paterson, eds., *Explaining the History of American Foreign Relations* (New York, 1991). For Latin American applications of the "bureaucratic" and "corporatist" models, see Jules R. Benjamin, "The Framework of U.S. Relations with Latin America in the 20th Century: An Interpretive Essay," *Diplomatic History* (Spring 1988): 91–112; Howard J. Wiarda, "Toward a Framework for the Study of Political Change in the Iberic-Latin Tradition: The Corporative Model," *World Politics* (January 1973): 206–35. For an application of the bureaucratic model to the Good Neighbor policy, see Ernest R. May, "The 'Bureaucratic Politics' Approach: U.S.-Argentine Relations, 1942–

1947," in Julio Cotler and Richard R. Fagen, eds., *Latin America and the United States: The Changing Political Realities* (Palo Alto 1974), 129–75.

3　Studies on this subject that focus on executive branch policy and territoriality include Donald Warwick, *A Theory of Bureaucracy: Politics, Personality and Organization in the State Department* (Cambridge, 1975); Charles Peters and Michael Nelson, eds., *Culture of Bureaucracy* (New York, 1979); and Francis E. Rourke, *Bureaucracy and Foreign Policy* (Baltimore, 1972).

4　The mirroring of Trujillo's social and governmental circle by the *Carnaval* "Queen, Ambassadors, and her Court" was an annual event in the capital, and the queen's triumphal entrance into the city and the round of parties at its primary social venues were featured prominently in the press. See, for example, *Listín Diario,* 28 March 1932: "El magno desfile y el baile al Gran Protector del Reino [Trujillo] y a las embajadores [de los centros sociales de la república]" and "El baile de anoche en el Club Unión fue una fiesta social distinguida."

5　The role of "good will cruising" is briefly discussed in Donald A. Yerxa, *Admirals and Empire: The U.S. Navy and the Caribbean, 1898–1945* (Columbia, 1993), 86–90; also of interest is Robert L. O'Connell, *Sacred Vessels: The Cult of the Battleship and the Rise of the U.S. Navy* (New York, 1993).

6　Haglund, *Latin America and the Transformation of U.S. Strategic Thought, 1936–1940;* Gerald K. Haines, "Under the Eagle's Wing: The Franklin Roosevelt Administration Forges an American Hemisphere," *Diplomatic History* (Fall 1977): 373–88; Mark Skinner, *Chief of Staff: Prewar Plans and Preparations,* and Stetson Conn and Byron Fairchild, *The Western Hemisphere: The Framework of Hemisphere Defense,* in Kent Roberts Greenfield, ed., *United States Army in World War II* (Washington, 1960), 4:1 and 12:1.

7　Schoenfeld to Welles, 25 November 1935, Folder 9, Box 36, Welles Papers, FDRL.

8　Richard Millett, "The State Department's Navy: A History of the Special Service Squadron, 1920–1940," *American Neptune* (April 1975), 118–38.

9　Robert W. Love Jr., *History of the United States Navy, 1775–1941* (Harrisburg, 1992), xii.

10　The protocol of such occasions had developed into an elaborate code that inscribed the relationship between the ship's commander, the local diplomat (who was the representative of the American president), and the host government. See the chapter "Honors, Distinctions, Salutes, and Ceremonies," especially the "table of honors" for visitors, Articles 230 to 248 of the *Naval Regulations* (Washington, 1927 and 1940), 79–91.

11　David Long, *Gold Braid and Foreign Relations: Diplomatic Activities of U.S. Naval Officers, 1798–1883* (Annapolis, 1988), addresses the diplomatic role of the Navy during the nineteenth century; and Peter D. Karsten, *The Naval Aristocracy: The*

*Golden Age of Annapolis and the Emergence of Modern American Navalism* (New York, 1972) discusses the institutional and social identity of its officer corps.

12   For a general history of the U.S. Marine Corps, see Robert D. Heinl, *Soldiers of the Sea: The United States Marine Corps, 1775–1962* (Annapolis, 1962). Also of great interest on the development of Marine culture and tactics is Craig Cameron, *American Samurai: Myth, Imagination and the Conduct of Battle in the First Marine Division, 1941–1951* (Cambridge, 1994).

13   The transformation of the Marine Corps from a colonial task force to an autonomous "forward base" branch of the military is the backdrop to Hans Schmidt's biography of Smedley Butler: *Maverick Marine: General Smedley Butler and the Contradictions of American Military History* (Lexington, 1987). For Marine training doctrine, see Lieutenant Colonel Henry C. Davis, USMC, "Indoctrination of Latin-American Service," *Marine Corps Gazette* (June 1920): 154–61; First Lieutenant Robert C. Kilmartin, USMC, "Indoctrination in Santo Domingo," *Marine Corps Gazette* (October 1922): 377–86.

14   Lieutenant Colonel Charles J. Miller, USMC, "Diplomatic Spurs: Our Experiences in Santo Domingo," *Marine Corps Gazette*, 3 pts. (February 1935): 43–47; (May 1935): 19–25, 52–59; (August 1935): 35–47. Also see the unattributed article "Santo Domingo after the Marines," *Marine Corps Gazette* (November 1930): 11, 67–69, and Brigadier General George Richards, USMC, "The Monroe Doctrine: Its Application of Today," *United States Naval Institute Proceedings* (October 1932): 1405–31.

15   Rear Admiral Harry S. Knapp, USN, "The Naval Officer in Diplomacy," *United States Naval Institute Proceedings* (March 1927): 309–17; Commander C. C. Baughman, USN, "United States Occupation of the Dominican Republic," *United States Naval Institute Proceedings* (December 1925): 2306–27.

16   Knapp, "The Naval Officer in Diplomacy," 309–10. Knapp was himself a Yale graduate. Similar appraisals of naval diplomacy in the *Proceedings* included Lieutenant Commander G. B. Vroom, USN, "The Place of Naval Officers in International Affairs" (May 1921): 685–700; Lieutenant Leland P. Lovette, USN, "Naval Policy at the Crossroads," which was the Naval Institute's "Prize Article" for 1930 (April 1930): 269–80; and Lieutenant H. A. Rochester, USN, "The Navy's Support of Foreign Policy" (November 1931): 1491–1500.

17   For an exploration of the "mystique" of the U.S. diplomatic ranks, see Robert D. Schulzinger, *The Making of the Diplomatic Mind: The Training, Outlook and Style of the United States Foreign Service, 1908–1931* (Middletown, Conn., 1975); Martin Weil, *A Pretty Good Club: The Founding Fathers of the U.S. Foreign Service* (New York, 1978). For the organizational growth and professionalization of the State Department, see Richard Johnson, *The Administration of United States Foreign Policy* (Austin, 1971); Richard Hume Werking, *The Master Archi-*

tects: *Building the United States Foreign Service, 1890–1913* (Lexington, 1977); and Waldo H. Heinrichs Jr., "Bureaucracy and Professionalism in the Development of American Career Diplomacy," in John Braeman, Robert H. Brenner, and David Brody, eds., *Twentieth-Century American Foreign Policy* (Columbus, 1971).

18  *Uncle Sam—The Good Neighbor,* RKO Radio Pictures (1938), RG 59.18, Motion Picture Division, NA.

19  *Listín Diario,* 15 August 1930.

20  "Report on Leading Personalities" and Galienne to Henderson, 26 May 1930, *British Documents,* 6:270, 362.

21  John Moors Cabot to Susan Hammond, 4 March 1930, Cabot Papers.

22  *Listín Diario,* 21 August 1930.

23  *Listín Diario,* 29 August 1930.

24  Nine countries were represented in the Cuerpo Diplomático in the Dominican Republic during most of the 1930s. This number increased during the Second World War, reaching a high of twenty-seven nations represented at the Dominican Centennial in 1944.

25  Robert McClintock's *Retrospective* of two years in the Dominican Republic, quoting Colonel Richard Cutts, 9 September 1939, 839.00 TRUJILLO/377, RG 59, NA.

26  Nathaniel P. Davis, "American Foreign Service Inspection Report—American Legation, Ciudad Trujillo," 1 February 1937, Foreign Service Inspection Reports, RG 59, NA.

27  Aïda Schoenfeld oral history transcript, 9 February 1982, 47, Schoenfeld Papers.

28  Welles to Norweb, 15 March 1937, Folder 2, Box 43, Welles Papers, FDRL.

29  Norweb to Welles, 30 November 1939, Folder 16, Box 54, Welles Papers, FDRL.

30  *Listín Diario,* 19 October 1932.

31  Schoenfeld to Brown, 31 December 1935, Schoenfeld Papers.

32  Gellman, *Secret Affairs,* 37.

33  Division of Latin American Affairs memos, 25 July, 1 and 11 August 1932, 839.00/3585, 3588, RG 59, NA.

34  Schoenfeld to Rudolf Schoenfeld, 5 February 1936, Schoenfeld Papers.

35  Nathaniel P. Davis, "American Foreign Service Inspection Report—American Legation, Ciudad Trujillo," 1 February 1937, RG 59, NA.

36  "Outline of Seventh Year of the Trujillo Government," 11 September 1937, 839.00/4135, RG 59, NA; Cabot to Hammond, 10 March 1930, Cabot Papers.

37  "Outline of the Ninth Year," 27 September 1939, 839.51/4223, RG 59, NA.

38  Brown to Schoenfeld, 14 August 1933, Schoenfeld Papers.

39  Schoenfeld to Welles, 25 November 1935, Folder 9, Box 36; Norweb to Welles, 21 July 1938, Folder 3, Box 47. Both in Welles Papers, FDRL.

40  Legation dispatch, 26 October 1933, 839.00/3711, RG 59, NA.

41  *Listín Diario*, 20 July 1931.

42  *Listín Diario*, 21 May 1937.

43  Paterson to Eden, 5 February 1936, "Annual Report on Heads of Foreign Missions," FO 371/19788, PRO.

44  Aïda Schoenfeld oral history transcript, 46–54, Schoenfeld Papers.

45  The reference is to *The Private Life of Henry VIII* (1933), in Foreign Office comment on Paterson to Eden, 12 July 1941, FO 371/26040, PRO.

46  Aïda Schoenfeld oral history transcript, 53–54, Schoenfeld Papers.

47  Chargé d'Affaires W. A. Elders to Simon, 15 February 1935, FO 371/18699, PRO.

48  For more on sexual politics, see Derby, "Magic of Modernity," chapter entitled "Gender and State Spectacle."

49  Aïda Schoenfeld oral history transcript, 53–54, Schoenfeld Papers.

50  Legation dispatch, 27 April 1932, 839.00/3878, RG 59, NA.

51  His "excellent" ratings in these areas were emphasized in his military biography, which contained copies and translations of seven favorable efficiency reports, most of them by Thomas Watson. Vega y Pagán, *Military Biography of Trujillo*, 45–56, 163–91.

52  This passage from Nanita, *Trujillo: A Full-Size Portrait*, 25, appeared in slightly different form in the same author's longer *Trujillo: The Biography of a Great Leader* (New York, 1957), 34–35: "Either in uniform or in mufti, he would be an immediate success at any gathering of society in Europe or America."

53  Second Lieutenant Thomas E. Watson to Chief of Staff, Lieutenant Colonel R. H. Dunlop, "Report of Inspection at Azua and Barahona," 22 February 1917, Box 1, Thomas E. Watson Collection, Marine Corps Historical Center, Washington, D.C. (hereafter Watson Papers, MCHC).

54  Certificate of promotion signed by Brigadier General Logan Feland, USMC, "el Jefe del Gobierno Militar," and Secretary of the Interior Police, Colonel B. H. Fuller, USMC, 4 August 1920, Box 1, Watson Papers, MCHC.

55  Lee commendation of Watson, 22 April 1922; Lee report of "Inspection of Training Center, *Policía Nacional Dominicana*, Santiago, D.R.," 29 January 1923; Lee commendation of Watson, 18 March 1924; Watson to Major General Commandant, 15 May 1922 and 16 May 1923. All in Box 1, Watson Papers, MCHC.

56  For a detailed study of the long-term personal relationship between Watson and Trujillo, a book originally titled "Tommy y Rafael," see Bernardo Vega, *Trujillo y las fuerzas armadas norteamericanas* (Santo Domingo, 1992).

57  Sullivan to Watson, 18 September 1930, Box 2, Watson Papers, MCHC.

58  Watson to Myers, 18 December 1930, Box 2, Watson Papers, MCHC.

59  Watson to Cutts, 18 September 1930, Box 2, Watson Papers, MCHC.

60　Cutts to Watson, 17 October 1930, Box 1, Watson Papers, MCHC; *Listín Diario*, 23 October 1930, 20 and 21 January 1931.

61　Goldie, "Report on Leading Personalities," *British Documents*, 7:299.

62　Legation dispatch, 4 November 1930, 839.00 GENERAL CONDITIONS/59, RG 59, NA.

63　Charles Thomsen to Stimson, 11 May 1931, 811.43 FELLOWSHIP OF RECONCILIATION/33, RG 59, NA; Goldie, "Report on Leading Personalities," *British Documents*, 7:299. The compound included "immaculately kept barracks . . . as scrupulously neat as those at an American army post" for the bodyguard, an army battalion, and a "squadron of household cavalry," along with "vine-clad bungalows occupied by government officials and foreign advisers, including the American in charge of the Dominican customs" William Pulliam (E. Alexander Powell, *Aerial Odyssey* [New York, 1936], 53–54).

64　Pulliam to Welles, 28 July 1931, Folder 8, Box 147, Welles Papers, FDRL.

65　Curtis to Stimson, 3 February 1931, copy of letter in Box 2, Watson Papers, MCHC.

66　Watson notes written on menu, 7 October 1930, Box 2, Watson Papers, MCHC. Watson arranged for the military band to play in Parque Colón outside the hotel until "the end of dinner."

67　Watson to Cutts, 2 November 1930, Box 3, Watson Papers, MCHC.

68　Watson to Cutts, 25 November and 20 December 1930, 7 February 1931; Cutts to Watson, 19 December 1930 and 2 March 1931; M. D. Carrel, Ulen and Co., to Watson, 20 February 1931; Carrel to Cutts, 25 February 1931; Watson to Judge Otto Schoenrich, 6 March 1931, Box 3. All in Watson Papers, MCHC.

69　Carrel to Watson, 28 March 1931, Box 3, Watson Papers, MCHC.

70　Carrel to Watson, 20 February 1931, and Watson to Cutts, 28 February 1931, Box 3, Watson Papers, MCHC. Emphasis in original.

71　Watson to Schoenrich, 2 March 1931, Box 3, Watson Papers, MCHC.

72　Watson to Archie V., 25 March 1931, Box 3, Watson Papers, MCHC.

73　Cutts to Watson, 19 December 1930, Box 3, Watson Papers, MCHC.

74　For arms: Watson to Cutts, 12 November and 27 December 1930, 22 May 1931, and Cutts to Watson, 19 November 1930, Box 3, Watson Papers, MCHC. For equipment: Watson to Lieutenant Colonel Seth Williams, USMC, 20 December 1930, and Williams to Watson, 26 December 1930, Box 3, Watson Papers, MCHC. For airplanes: Watson to Cutts, 17 December 1930, Box 3, Watson Papers, MCHC; Watson to Colonel Thomas C. Turner, USMC, Aviation Section, 14 February 1931, and Turner to Watson, 27 February 1931, Thomas C. Turner Collection, MCHC.

75　Watson to Cutts, 28 May 1931, Box 3, Watson Papers, MCHC. Trujillo secretly ordered twenty-five hundred Mausers and two and a half million rounds of ammunition from the Spanish Royal Arms Factory, learned British Minister Goldie. Goldie to the Marquess of Reading, 26 October 1931, *British Documents,* 8:40.

76  Legation dispatch, 23 September 1931, 839.1051/59, RG 59, NA; "Report on Leading Personalities," *British Documents,* 7:299.

77  Watson to Cutts, 9 and 10 March and 28 May 1931, Box 3, Watson Papers, MCHC.

78  *Listín Diario,* 21 March 1931.

79  Watson to Cutts, 28 May 1931, Box 3, Watson Papers, MCHC.

80  Unsigned memo, 21 May 1931, Box 3, Watson Papers, MCHC.

81  Pulliam to Welles, 2 June 1931, Folder 8, Box 147, Welles Papers, FDRL.

82  Roosevelt also exerted himself without success to save Watson's position. Roosevelt to Watson, 18, 21, and 22 July 1931, Box 3, Watson Papers, MCHC; Acting Secretary of State W. R. Castle to Secretary of the Navy Charles Francis Adams, 25 June 1931, EN 3-11(Santo Domingo)/P 16-3(310218), RG 80, NA.

83  Memo of conversation, Scott with Dunn, 29 June 1932, 839.51/3761, RG 59, NA.

84  "Santo Domingo after the Marines," *Marine Corps Gazette* (November 1930): 11, 67.

85  Legation dispatch, 26 April 1933, 839.032 RICHARDS, GEORGE/2, RG 59, NA.

86  Henry L. Roosevelt to Franklin Roosevelt, 13 September 1933, OF 138, FDRL.

87  *New York Times,* 24 September 1937.

88  William T. Stone to Roosevelt, 26 October 1933, OF 138, FDRL.

89  *Baltimore Sun,* 12 November 1933.

90  "Outline of First Term," 10 August 1934, 839.00/3797, RG 59, NA.

91  McLaughlin to Watson, 3 and 5 October 1930, Box 2, Watson Papers, MCHC.

92  Watson telegram to McLaughlin, undated, Box 2; Watson to Cutts, 12 November 1930. Both in Box 3, Watson Papers, MCHC.

93  Watson to Cutts, 17 December 1930 and 2 February 1930; "Plano de la mina 'Priscilla' declarado por Mr. Charles A. McLaughlin," undated, Box 2, Watson Papers, MCHC. McLaughlin held more than four hundred thousand acres in "mineral concessions" for gold mines by 1932, according to Franklin J. Franco, *La era de Trujillo* (Santo Domingo, 1992), 61.

94  Curtis to White, 6 March 1931, 839.01 A/2, RG 59, NA.

95  Crassweller, *Trujillo: Caribbean Dictator,* 173.

96  Lieutenant Colonel Edward L. Barlow, report of conversation with George C. Robertson, Armco International Co., 29 October 1943; Naval Attaché Captain John A. Butler, USMC, Intelligence Report, 27 December 1944. Both contained in General Reference File, Dominican Republic, MCHC.

97   Ornes, *Little Caesar,* 222.

98   *Listín Diario,* 25 June 1930; Brown to Schoenfeld, 4 August 1933. Schoenfeld Papers.

99   C. S. Freeman, Commander Special Service Squadron, to Secretary of the Navy, annual report for fiscal year 1934, 12 July 1934, 778/A9-1(340712), RG 80, NA.

100  Freeman to Secretary of the Navy, annual report for fiscal year 1935, 5 July 1935, 778/A9-1(350705), RG 80, NA.

101  For interdepartmental relations during this period, see Robert G. Albion, *Makers of Naval Policy* (Annapolis, 1945; reprinted 1976), 209–70.

102  G. J. Meyers, Commander Special Service Squadron, to Chief of Naval Operations, supplementary annual report, 8 July 1936, FF8/A9-1(360708), RG 80, NA. Bernardo Vega, in *Nazismo, fascismo y falangismo en la República Dominicana* (Santo Domingo, 1985), interprets the increased naval visitation as a direct response to the visits of German training vessels to Samaná Bay and Ciudad Trujillo, although the Special Service Squadron correspondence indicates that the U.S. Navy was initially more concerned with competition from the Royal Navy.

103  *Listín Diario,* 19 May 1937.

104  Franklin Atwood, Secretary of the Legation, to Selden Chapin, Division of American Republics, 25 May 1937, 811.3310/920, RG 59, NA.

105  *Listín Diario,* 19 May 1937.

106  Atwood to Chapin (see note 104 above).

107  *Listín Diario,* 20 May 1937.

108  Franklin Roosevelt also remembered his visit to Santo Domingo in 1917; and since Joseph Davies had given him a photograph album of Trujillo's public works, FDR too had visual criteria with which to compare the state of development there, even though he politely declined Trujillo's repeated invitations to visit again (Roosevelt to Joseph Davies, sometime in February 1936, OF 138, FDRL). Rear Admiral W. B. Caperton, who commanded the U.S. intervention in the Dominican Republic and was the first military governor there during the occupation, also possessed two bound volumes of photographs combining scenes of the Spanish colonial sites of Santo Domingo and the new buildings and port facilities of Ciudad Trujillo (W. B. Caperton Collection, Ms. Collection 29, Naval War College).

109  Norweb to Welles, 13 and 19 October 1938, Folder 3, Box 47, Welles Papers, FDRL.

110  Rear Admiral Ford A. Todd to Acting Secretary of the Navy William Leahy, 17 October 1938, FF2-6 (8)/P9-1, RG 80, NA. Roosevelt found the sport fishing in Samaná Bay rather poor. For an account of Roosevelt's cruise and his

radio exchange with Trujillo, see Walter Woodson's journal, 30 April–8 May 1938, Ms. 48, Naval War College.

111 R. Emilio Jiménez, "La magna recepción del Benefactor de la Patria en el crucero 'Philadelphia,'" in *Antología poética trujillista* (Santiago, D.R., 1946), 66.

112 Chapin memorandum to Welles, enclosed in Chapin to Commander Louis E. Denfield, USN, 19 April 1939, (SC) A4-5 (3), RG 80, NA. Emphasis in original.

113 Captain J. J. Tavern, Office of Naval Intelligence, Entry 98-F-10-d-#22799, RG 38, NA.

114 Captain R. R. M. Emmet to Chief of Naval Operations, 20 February 1939, A15-2/EM-Trujillo, DR (390201), RG 80, NA.

115 "Outline of the Ninth Year," 27 September 1939, 839.00/4223, RG 59, NA.

116 Minister R. Henry Norweb to Secretary of State, enclosure no. 2, 13 February 1939, A15-2/EM-Trujillo DR (390201), RG 80, NA.

117 For an interesting account of the racial attitudes of the Marines in "the American West Indies" of Haiti and the Dominican Republic, see Harry Franck, *Roaming through the West Indies* (New York, 1920), 106–55.

118 "Report on Leading Personalities in the Dominican Republic," January 1934, *British Documents,* 10:361. With regard to the Dominican elite, "it was the military dress that was accepted, not the man wearing it," said Germán Ornes (*Little Caesar,* 41).

119 Goldie to Reading, 31 August 1931, *British Documents,* 8:9.

120 Pulliam to Welles, 4 July 1936, Folder 13, Box 147, Welles Papers, FDRL.

121 Secretary of State Cordell Hull to Secretary of the Navy Claude Swanson, 9 March 1934, MM1/P15(10)(340309), RG 80, NA. Trujillo also sent the Dominican Republic's highest decoration, the Order of Duarte, to Roosevelt via a proxy. See Oliver Newman to Andres Pastoriza, Dominican Minister to the United States, 8 August 1938, caja 7 (5), tomo 246, AGN. For a visual record of such an award ceremony in the Dominican Republic, including the ritualistic examination of the remains of Columbus, see the film of Nicholas Murray Butler, president of Columbia University and a Trujillo lobbyist, receiving the Order of Duarte ("Santo Domingo," 27 February 1937, Universal News, v. 9, R 541, no. 5, Motion Picture Division, NA).

122 Vega, *Trujillo y las fuerzas armadas norteamericanas,* 233.

123 "Outline of the Ninth Year," 27 September 1939, 839.00/4223, RG 59, NA.

124 Welles memo to Duggan, 8 April 1939, and Duggan memo of conversation with Breckinridge, 28 April 1939, 839.001 TRUJILLO/318 and 321, RG 59, NA.

125 Assistant Secretary of State George Messersmith, memo of conversation with George Djamgaroff, 24 January 1939, 811.91239/16, RG 59, NA.

126 Senator Theodore R. Green to Assistant Secretary of State Adolph A. Berle, 10 April 1939, 839.001 TRUJILLO/320, RG 59, NA.

127  Roosevelt to Senator David Walsh, 25 May 1939, in *Franklin D. Roosevelt and Foreign Affairs,* 15:192; Welles to Green, 8 April 1939, 839.001 TRUJILLO/319, RG 59, NA.

128  *Time* (17 July 1939).

129  Duggan memo of telephone conversation with Norweb, 25 May 1939, 839.001 TRUJILLO/322, RG 59, NA. The Dominican Unknown Soldier's Tomb in the "modern, well-run community" of Ciudad Trujillo became part of the itinerary of visiting naval personnel, as did "the beautiful new Hotel Jaragua . . . complete with outdoor swimming pool, patio and cocktail lounge" ("See You Dad in Ciudad," cruise book of USS *Block Island,* 1953, Naval War College). Trujillo's itinerary was covered in the *New York Times* and *Listín Diario,* 6–10 July 1939, and in *Dominican Republic* magazine (August 1939).

130  "El General Trujillo en Estados Unidos," 6 July 1939, Universal News, v. 11, R 788, Motion Picture Division, NA. Colonel McLaughlin was along on the trip as well, performing his usual duties as a Marine surrogate.

131  Unsigned memo, "Suggested Topics Which the President May Wish to Discuss with General Trujillo," undated, and Hull memo of conversation with Trujillo, 7 July 1939, 839.001 TRUJILLO/350, RG 59, NA; Trujillo to Roosevelt, 26 July 1939, and Roosevelt to Trujillo, 3 August 1939, 839.51/4724, FRUS 1939 5:582–84; *Washington Post,* 6 July 1939.

132  Quoted in Hicks, *Blood in the Streets,* 129.

133  *New York Times,* 24 June, 6, 13, and 14 July 1939.

134  Legation reports, 1 and 29 July, 839.001 TRUJILLO/345 and 353, RG 59, NA; "Outline of the Ninth Year," 27 September 1939, 839.00/4223, RG 59, NA.

135  Chapin memo to Welles and Duggan, 27 January 1940, 839.00 TRUJILLO/405, and Eugene Hinkle memo of telephone conversation with Chapin, 6 February 1940, 839.00 TRUJILLO/410, RG 59, NA.

136  Report of Naval Attaché, Lieutenant John A. Butler, USMC, 1 March 1940, 839.00 TRUJILLO/415 1/2, and Legation dispatch, 21 February 1940, 839.00 TRUJILLO/420, RG 59, NA.

137  Legation dispatch, 29 February 1940, 839.00 TRUJILLO/415, RG 59, NA.

138  Minister of Foreign Relations Arturo Despradel to Hull, 2 March 1940, caja 8, tomo 282, AGN.

139  Record of staff conversations between Representatives of the Government of the Dominican Republic [Trujillo; Minister to the U.S. Andrés Pastoriza; McLaughlin] and the United States of America [U.S. Minister Robert Scotten; Commander Rufus King, USN; Lt. Colonel Arthur R. Harris, USA; Capt. John A. Butler, USMC], 17 August 1940, War Plans Division [WPD] 4318, RG 165, NA.

140  Edward O. Guerrant, *Roosevelt's Good Neighbor Policy* (Albuquerque, 1950), 155.

141  Quoted in John Lewis Gaddis, *Strategies of Containment* (Cambridge, 1981), 1.

142  War Plans Division memo for Assistant Chief of Staff, General George V. Strong, WPD 4115-38, RG 165, NA.

143  Remarks by General Marshall at luncheon for him given by Trujillo, 24 September 1940, caja 8, tomo 288, AGN.

144  Warren to Hull, 31 July 1942, with enclosed sheets of photographs and captions, 839.463/9, RG 59, NA.

145  *Listín Diario*, 5 July 1942.

146  See, for example, Warren to Bonsal, 5 October 1942, 839.00/10-542, and Warren's report on the Fourth of July celebrations for 1943, which included a "field day program" presented by the Sosua refugees (9 July 1943, 839.461/4, RG 59, NA).

147  Ambassador Avra Warren to Philip Bonsal, Chief of the Division of American Republics, 5 October 1942, 839.00/10-542, RG 59, NA.

148  Ibid.

149  Spruille Braden, *Diplomats and Demagogues: The Memoirs of Spruille Braden* (New Rochelle, N.Y., 1971), 320.

150  Ellis O. Briggs, *Farewell to Foggy Bottom: The Recollections of a Career Diplomat* (New York, 1964), 222–23.

151  Briggs to Hull, 28 July 1944, 839.24/7-2844, RG 59, NA.

152  Briggs memo of conversation with Trujillo, 25 October 1944, 839.00/20-443, RG 59, NA.

153  Braden, *Diplomats and Demagogues,* 268–69.

154  Briggs, *Farewell to Foggy Bottom,* 223–24.

155  Bernardo Vega, ed., *Los Estados Unidos y Trujillo, año 1945: Colección de documentos del Departamento de Estado y de las fuerzas armadas norteamericanas* (Santo Domingo, 1982). See especially Vega's synopsis of "the power struggle between *trujillista* and *anti-trujillista* North American diplomats" (pp. 18–22).

156  *Revista Militar* (February 1942): 2, 83–84.

157  Constantine M. Perkins, Naval Academy Class of 1881, "The Isle of Boozodoo, Island Where My Dreams Come True," 6 April 1921, 16870-693, RG 38, NA. The drinking culture of the occupation is also reflected in Military Police reports of incidents involving drunken soldiers, in the Marines' magazine *Santo Domingo Leatherneck,* and in the causes of death for several of the casualties suffered during the occupation.

158  Watson to Archie V., 25 March 1931, Box 3, Watson Papers, MCHC.

159  Robert Blake Jr., memoir of Colonel Robert Blake, Box 1, Robert Blake Collection, MCHC.

160  As consul in Cap Haitien, Warren had helped to salvage the career of the Marine commander of the Haitian Gendarmerie, General Freddy Wise, when the high commissioner, General William Russell, "tried to have him cashiered" because "their two wives were mortal enemies and Freddy was a

drunk." Warren intervened "to save him because one of his drunken fits took place at my house and I pulled him out of it" (Warren to Bonsal, 5 October 1942, 839.00/10-542, RG 59, NA). Unlike other chiefs of mission in the Dominican Republic, Warren seems to have mingled easily in military company and enjoyed close personal relations with high-ranking officers.

161    Admiral Milton Miles photo album of visit to Dominican Republic, February 1953, Ms. Collection 24, Naval War College.

162    Weekly embassy report, 29 May 1953, 739.00(W), RG 59, NA.

163    Norweb to Welles, 30 November 1939, Folder 16, Box 54, Welles Papers, FDRL.

164    The link continued to be expressed by an ever wider stream of U.S. Navy vessels to Ciudad Trujillo. Twenty-eight vessels visited in the month of February 1957, thirty in February 1958 (12 February 1957 and 12 February 1958, 739.00[W], RG 59, NA). Trujillo reciprocated by sending three Dominican Navy craft to the Armed Forces Day celebrations in Hampton Roads, Virginia, in 1957 (21 May 1957, 739.00[W], RG 59, NA).

165    The metaphor of "statecraft as stagecraft" is Derby's ("Magic of Modernity"). In his 1955 speech opening the Fair of Peace and Fraternity of the Free World, a Dominican version of the World's Fair that Trujillo had visited in New York on his first trip to the United States, Trujillo outlined the elements of Dominican sovereignty that he had achieved. These included financial autonomy, military organization, and international status: "I received a nation with diplomatic relations with only a small number of countries . . . and today it is a nation which, practicing the principles of solidarity, acts on the level of foreign affairs with the conviction that the frontiers of worthy people end only where liberty ends" (Crassweller, *Trujillo: Caribbean Dictator,* 296).

166    For more on food and Dominican nationalism, see Lauren H. Derby, "Gringo Chickens with Worms," in *Close Encounters of Empire: Writing the Cultural History of U.S.-Latin American Relations,* ed. Gilbert M. Joseph, Catherine C. LeGrand, and Ricardo D. Salvatore (Durham, 1998), 451–93.

167    *Listín Diario,* 20 May 1937.

SEVEN    *Fortress America, Fortaleza Trujillo: The Hull-Trujillo Treaty and the Second World War*

1    For the history of hemisphere defense and war preparedness in Latin America, see John Child, *Unequal Alliance: The Inter-American Military System 1938–1978* (Boulder, 1980); Gordon Connell-Smith, *The Inter-American System* (London, 1966); John Lloyd Mecham, *The United States and Inter-American Security, 1889–1960* (Austin, 1961); William L. Langer and S. Everett Gleason, *The Challenge to Isolation, 1937–1940* (New York, 1952); and William L. Langer, *The Undeclared War, 1940–1941* (New York, 1953).

2   For Lend-Lease, see Leon Martel, *Lend-Lease, Loans, and the Coming of the Cold War: A Study of the Implementation of Foreign Policy* (Boulder, 1979), and Warren F. Kimball, *The Most Unsordid Act: Lend-Lease, 1939–1941* (Baltimore, 1969). For the Export-Import Bank, see Frederick C. Adams, *Economic Diplomacy: The Export-Import Bank and American Foreign Policy, 1934–39* (Columbia, 1976). For cultural initiatives, see J. Manuel Espinosa, *Inter-American Beginnings of United States Cultural Diplomacy, 1936–1948* (Washington, 1976).

3   Roosevelt used the phrase at a press conference in January 1940; quoted in Green, *Containment of Latin America*, 35.

4   William L. Langer and S. Everett Gleason, *The Challenge to Isolation: The World Crisis of 1937–1940 and American Foreign Policy* (New York, 1952), 2:623.

5   Lieutenant Colonel Arthur R. Harris, USA, "Memorandum for the Assistant Chief of Staff, War Plans Division," 6 September 1940, WPD 4115-38, RG 165, NA.

6   Memo of conversation, Francis White with Cordell Hull, 7 November 1940, Box 19, White Papers.

7   Despradel to Hull, 7 August 1934, 839.51/4195, FRUS 1934 (Washington, 1952), 5:199–200.

8   For U.S. economic policy in Haiti, see Paul H. Douglas, "Occupied Haiti," and Arthur C. Millspaugh, "Haiti under American Control, 1915–1930," in Drake, *Money Doctors*, 26–58.

9   Memo of conversation, Phillips with Davies and Brache, 19 February 1935, 839.51/4270, RG 59, NA.

10  Welles to Wilson, 19 March 1935, 839.51/4293, RG 59, NA.

11  J. F. McGurk memo, "Violations and Contemplated Violations of the Convention of 1924," 21 March 1935, 839.51/4293, RG 59, NA.

12  Memo of conversation, Welles with Brache, 20 March 1935, 839.516/51, RG 59, NA.

13  Memo of conversation, Welles with Brache, 22 March 1935, 839.51/4285, RG 59, NA.

14  James Gantenbein memo, "The Fiscal Situation in the Dominican Republic," 4 April 1935, FW 839.51/4280, RG 59, NA.

15  Gantenbein memo on Dominican finances, 8 May 1935, 839.51/4280, RG 59, NA.

16  White to Hull, 11 July 1935, Box 21, White Papers.

17  White to Hull, 8 August 1935, 839.51/4317, RG 59, NA. White had his own conflict of interest with Davies and Brache. Even while he was adamantly supporting the convention that the Dominican representatives wanted to abrogate, he was angling to sell his house on Massachusetts Avenue to the Dominican government for use as a legation. He wrote to Davies, asking him

to put in a "good word" with Brache on the subject. White to Davies, 2 April 1935, Box 21, White Papers.

18  Pulliam to Welles, 10 August 1935, 839.51/4318, RG 59, NA.

19  Memo of conversation, White with Burke, 14 February 1936, Box 17, White Papers.

20  Memo of conversation, White with Pastoriza, 9 March 1936, Box 17, White Papers.

21  Memo of conversation, Dominican Minister Andrés Pastoriza with Welles, 4 May 1936, 839.51/4387A, RG 59, NA.

22  Memo of conversation, White with Seth Richardson, 9 July 1936; memo of conversation, White with Richardson, 28 July 1936. Both in Box 17, White Papers.

23  Schoenfeld to Hull, 24 January 1936, 839.51/4348, RG 59, NA; Schoenfeld to Hull, 16 March 1936, 839.51/4366, RG 59, NA.

24  The three-masted yacht Sea Cloud, called "the most luxurious yacht in the world," was later purchased by Trujillo from Davies and his wife, Marjorie Meriweather Post (La Nación, 13 October 1955). Trujillo renamed it Angelita, for his daughter, and it bore his assassinated body away from the Dominican Republic in 1961. The vessel, now bearing the original name Sea Cloud, still plies the Caribbean as an exclusive cruise ship and calls at Dominican ports.

25  Memo of conversation, McGurk with Roswell Tripp, 5 May 1936, 839.516/63, RG 59, NA; Schoenfeld to Hull, 22 May 1936, 839.516/65, RG 59, NA.

26  Welles to Schoenfeld, 11 June 1936, Folder 10, Box 36, Welles Papers, FDRL.

27  Memo of conversation, White with Beebe, 3 September 1936, Box 17, White Papers; FBPC Annual Report 1936, 348–50; Clark to bondholders, 15 December 1936, Box 20, White Papers.

28  Vega, Trujillo y el control financiero, 276.

29  Pastoriza to Davies, 1 February 1937, caja 7 (4), tomo 230, AGN.

30  Hull to Pastoriza, 10 February 1937, 839.51/4489A, FRUS 1937 (Washington, 1954), 5:440–42.

31  Chapin to Duggan, 6 April 1937, FW 839.51/4509, RG 59, NA.

32  Memo by Chapin, 15 February 1937, 839.51/4487.5, and memo of conversation, Hull with Pastoriza and Max Henríquez Ureña, 11 February 1937, FRUS 1937, 5:442.

33  Welles to Schoenfeld, 11 June 1936, Folder 10, Box 36, Welles Papers, FDRL.

34  Minister R. Henry Norweb to Hull, 28 February 1938, 839.51/4588, FRUS 1937, 5:493–94.

35  Pulliam to Schoenfeld, 13 April 1938, Schoenfeld Papers.

36  Dominican Foreign Minister Julio Ortega Frier memo on Convention of 1924, 4 May 1938, 839.51/4607; Pastoriza to Welles, 10 May 1938, 839.51/4603; Pastoriza to Welles, 27 June 1938, 839.51/4612.5. All in RG 59, NA.

37  Pastoriza to Welles, 10 May 1938, 839.51/4603, and Ortega memo, 4 May 1938, 839.51/4607, RG 59, NA.

38  Welles to Pastoriza, 19 May 1938, 839.51/4607, RG 59, NA.

39  Chargé d'Affaires Eugene Hinkle to Hull, 6 June 1938, 839.51/4610, FRUS 1938 (Washington, 1955), 5:496.

40  Memo of conversation, Welles with Pastoriza and Arturo Despradel, 24 June 1938, FW 839.51/4624, RG 59, NA.

41  Norweb to Hull, 18 September 1939, 839.51/4740, RG 59, NA.

42  Clark to Herbert Feis, 15 April 1937, Box 20, White Papers. Clark had never been optimistic about help from the State Department; in an address to the Bond Club in January 1935, he told his audience not to be optimistic if "the Department of State tells you that it will exercise its unofficial good offices." And he went on to define the phrase: "Unofficial good offices consists roughly in the American Ambassador or Minister or Chargé d'Affaires going to the Foreign Office and after smoking a cigar or drinking a cocktail, saying 'Now, Mr. Minister, we have an American citizen named X and he seems to think he has been wronged. We don't know much about the facts. He says so and so but we would be very glad if you would look into this and see whether or not something might not be done.' This is what they call unofficial good offices." Clark address at the Bond Club, 16 January 1935, Box 20, White Papers.

43  White to DDuggan, 14 July 1938, Box 18, White Papers.

44  Memo of conversation, Welles with Miguel López Pumarejo, 25 July 1938, 710.H AGENDA/81, RG 59, NA; Feis to Spruille Braden, 18 March 1939, Box 11, Papers of Herbert Feis, Library of Congress.

45  Memo of conversation, Feis with White, 3 May 1938, Box 18, White Papers.

46  Feis to Braden, 15 May 1939, Box 11, Feis Papers.

47  In this stance Welles had the support of the Johnson Act of 1934, which forbade government loans to nations that had defaulted on their foreign debts. Green, *Containment,* 20.

48  Castle to White, 19 November 1938, Box 21, White Papers. Reuben Clark, also irritated by the Good Neighbor policy, launched a particularly impolitic letter to the editor of *Foreign Affairs:* "There is so much deceit and hypocrisy in the All-America bogey—this 'one for all and all for one' hysteria—that I have trouble keeping my temper and tongue" (Clark to Hamilton Fish Armstrong, Box 21, White Papers).

49  Gellman, *Good Neighbor Diplomacy,* 160–61.

50  Memo of conversation, White with Feis, 23 June 1939, Box 19, White Papers.

51  *New York Times,* 28 October 1939.

52  *Chicago Tribune,* 31 October 1939, in Box 21, White Papers. Reuben Clark responded with an article in the *American Journal of International Law,* listing ten permanent settlements and six temporary ones that had been negotiated by

the FBPC as of 1939, resulting in a total of $104 million in interest payments. See J. Reuben Clark, "Collecting on Defaulted Foreign Dollar Bonds," *American Journal of International Law* (January 1940): 2. The FBPC had also been criticized by the Securities and Exchange Commission after hearings conducted by Judge James Landis between 1935 and 1937 showed a conflict of interest between the council and the bond-issue houses, which were important contributors to the FBPC budget. Securities and Exchange Commission, *Report on the Study and Functions of Protective and Reorganization Committees* (Washington, 1937), 632–722.

53   Frederick Delano to Roosevelt, 17 November 1939, and Welles to Roosevelt, 22 December 1939, OF 3505, FDRL.

54   Steward, *Trade and Hemisphere,* 171–73.

55   Memo of conversation, White with Norweb, 19 March 1940, Box 19, White Papers.

56   Pastoriza to Hull, 25 June 1940, 839.51/4808, FRUS 1940 (Washington, 1959), 5:798–800.

57   Gellman, *Good Neighbor Diplomacy,* 15; Duggan to Welles, 1 July 1940, 839.51/4819, RG 59, NA.

58   Memo of conversation, Welles with Lancaster, 7 May 1940, 839.001 TRUJILLO/425, RG 59, NA; "Dominican Government Finances," 8 August 1940, 839.51/4856, RG 59, NA.

59   Draft of Pan-American Day speech, 14 April 1939, OF 480, FDRL.

60   *New York Times,* 4 April 1939.

61   *New York Times,* 25 April 1939.

62   Norweb to Hull, 23 February 1940, 839.51/4781, RG 59, NA.

63   Ornes, *Little Caesar,* 272.

64   Roosevelt to Welles, 17 March 1938, 811.3339/38, RG 59, NA.

65   Commander J. W. Whitfield to Chief of Naval Operations, 25 March 1938, (SC) A4-5(3)/EF 63, RG 80, NA.

66   Rear Admiral Ford A. Todd to Chief of Naval Operations, 17 October 1938, 811.3339/52, RG 59, NA; Admiral William D. Leahy to Secretary of State, 12 October 1938, (SC) A4-5 (3), RG 80, NA.

67   Paterson to Foreign Minister Viscount Halifax, 20 February 1939, FO 371/22768, PRO.

68   Todd to Chief of Naval Operations, 25 October 1938, A4-5(3)/EF 69, RG 80, NA.

69   Paterson to Eden, 2 May 1936, FO 371/19788, PRO.

70   "Outline of the Eighth Year of the Trujillo Regime," 7 November 1938, 839.00/4209, RG 59, NA.

71   First Secretary Robert Mills McClintock, "Outline of the Ninth Year of the Trujillo Regime," 27 September 1939, 839.00/4223, RG 59, NA; Naval Attaché,

Captain John A. Butler, USMC, report on "German Activities in the Dominican Republic," 5 April 1940, C-10-e/23005, RG 38, NA.

72   Todd to Chief of Naval Operations, translation of "Civic Primer" enclosed, 17 October 1938, 811.3339/52, RG 59, NA.

73   "Outline of the First Term," 10 August 1934, 839.00/3797, RG 59, NA.

74   For more on Flor de Oro and Porfirio Rubirosa, the first of her seven husbands, see the chapter "Gender and State Spectacle" in Derby, "Magic of Modernity."

75   Vega, *Nazismo,* 342.

76   Photos of Despradel and Rohrecke presenting credentials accompany the detailed text of these events in Vega, *Nazismo,* 81–82.

77   Paterson to Eden, "Report on Heads of Foreign Missions," 19 December 1941, FO 371/30546, PRO.

78   Vega, *Nazismo,* 155.

79   Paterson to Eden, "Report on Heads of Foreign Missions," 19 December 1941, FO 371/30546, PRO.

80   Thomas A. Bailey and Paul B. Ryan, *Hitler vs. Roosevelt: The Undeclared Naval War* (New York, 1979).

81   *New York Times,* 3 October 1939.

82   *New York Times,* 16 October 1939.

83   Adolph A. Berle memo exchange with Willard Barber and Duggan, 2 November and 5 December 1939, 839.001 TRUJILLO/unnumbered, RG 59, NA. Other reports of Dominican collaboration with German subs originated in Haiti, and persisted during the war. See, for example, the report of a sub rendezvous witnessed by Haitian fishermen: Lieutenant Colonel Thomas Young, Military Attaché in Haiti, 20 July 1942, C-10-e/23005-H, RG ,8, NA.

84   Legation report, 5 December 1939, 839.00N/17, RG 59, NA; "Outline of Ninth Year," 27 September, 839.00/4223, RG 59, NA.

85   Chargé d'Affaires Eugene Hinkle, 23 February 1940, 839.51/4781, RG 59, NA.

86   Paterson to Eden, 30 December 1940, FO 371/26045, and Paterson to Eden, 9 September 1942, FO 371/30563, PRO.

87   *Listín Diario,* February 1941.

88   Paterson to Eden, "Report on Heads of Foreign Missions," 19 December 1941, FO 371/30546, PRO.

89   Paterson to Eden, 30 December 1940, FO 371/26045, and Paterson to Eden, 9 September 1942, FO 371/30563, PRO.

90   Paterson to Eden, 19 March 1941, FO 371/26045, PRO.

91   "Outline of the Ninth Year," 27 September 1939, 839.00/4223; 6 February 1940, 839.001 TRUJILLO/410; 21 February 1940, 839.001 TRUJILLO/420. All in RG 59, NA. Norweb had requested a "fine brass-bound permanent naval attaché . . . a young marine officer" to install in the new legation building, know-

ing it would make his job easier (Norweb to Welles, 7 August 1939, Folder 16, Box 54, Welles Papers, FDRL). But he doubted the potential of a military attaché, because Trujillo was "such a leatherneck himself that no West Pointer would ever be invited here to counsel the stepchildren of the Marines" (Norweb to Welles, 6 August 1938, Folder 3, Box 47, Welles Papers, FDRL).

92    Representative Robert W. Kean to White, 12 February 1940, and White to Kean, 13 February 1940, Box 21, White Papers. Senator Hugh Butler was the most outspoken critic of the Roosevelt administration's foreign aid. See Marks, *Wind over Sand,* 233.

93    Memo from Finley, 29 March 1940, 839.51/4785, RG 59, NA.

94    Collado to Duggan and Welles, 5 June 1940, 839.51/4802, RG 59, NA.

95    Pastoriza to Hull, 4 December 1939, 839.51/5022, RG 59, NA.

96    Joint Planning Committee report, 5 December 1941, WPD 4115-66, RG 165, NA.

97    Biography of Lieutenant General Pedro A. del Valle, USMC, Pedro A. del Valle Collection, PC 1483, Folder 1, MCHC.

98    Vega, *Trujillo y las fuerzas armadas norteamericanas,* 227, 242, 255–56, 260, 269–70, 276–77. Del Valle again visited Trujillo in 1946, sympathizing with Trujillo's problems with "those boys" in the State Department. Watson to Trujillo, 14 May 1946, Watson Papers, MCHC. Also see Vega, *Trujillo y las fuerzas armadas norteamericanas,* 299, 302–3.

99    Memorandum for the Assistant Chief of Staff, War Plans Division, by Lieutenant Colonel Norman Randolph, 1 July 1940, WPD 4115-24, RG 165, NA.

100   Scotten to Hull, 21 June 1940, 810.10 DEFENSE/181.5, FRUS 1940, 5:103–4. Scotten himself had sounded the theme of "effective cooperation between our two peace-loving nations within the framework of continental solidarity for defense of the Americas" upon presenting his credentials in June 1940. His speech was published in *Dominican Republic* magazine (July 1940).

101   *Listín Diario,* 27 June 1940.

102   The Havana Conference, especially the roles played by the Dominican delegation and Cordell Hull, was also well publicized in the Dominican press. For instance, see *Listín Diario,* 15 and 30 July 1940.

103   Record of staff conversations between Representatives of the Government of the Dominican Republic [Trujillo; Minister to the United States Andrés Pastoriza; McLaughlin] and the United States of America [U.S. Minister Robert Scotten; Cdr. Rufus King, USN; Lt. Colonel Arthur R. Harris, USA; Capt. John A. Butler, USMC], 17 August 1940, WPD 4318, RG 165, NA.

104   *New York Times,* 16 August 1940; Scotten to Hull, 17 August 1940, 839.001 TRUJILLO/437, RG 59, NA.

105   Ibid.

106   Record of staff conversations between Representatives of the Government of

the Dominican Republic and the United States of America, 17 August 1940, WPD 4318, RG 165, NA.

107 Lieutenant Colonel Harris, memo on staff conversations, 6 September 1940, WPD 4115-38, RG 165, NA.

108 The doctor arrived with the visiting USS *Dixie,* which stayed in the capital for nearly a week and took part in the usual round of entertainments (Hull to Trujillo, 10 June 1940, 839.001 TRUJILLO/427A; Hull to Scotten, 28 June 1940, 839.001 TRUJILLO/433A; Hull to Scotten, 6 July 1940, 839.001 TRUJILLO/435.5A. All in RG 59, NA). Trujillo was often ill during 1940; Scotten found him "sick, nervous and restless . . . in very bad shape" in July and suffering from "chronic malaria" in October (Scotten to Welles, 1 July and 11 October 1940, Folder 14, Box 64, Welles Papers, FDRL).

109 Duggan to Finley, 15 July 1940, 839.51/4820, RG 59, NA; 23 July 1940, Welles to Scotten, 839.51/4823, FRUS 1940, 5:800.

110 Welles to Scotten, 14 August 1940, Folder 14, Box 64, Welles Papers, FDRL.

111 Welles to Scotten, 10 August 1940, 839.51/4824A, and Scotten to Hull, 6 August 1940, 839.51/4828, RG 59, NA.

112 Scotten to Hull, 21 August 1940, 839.51/4832, RG 59, NA; Hull to Scotten, 24 August 1940, 839.51/4832, FRUS 1940, 5:804–6.

113 Hull to Scotten, 26 August 1940, 839.51/4838, FRUS 1940, 5:807–8.

114 *Listín Diario,* 24 and 30 August, 3 September 1940.

115 Memo of conversation, Hull with Trujillo and Pastoriza, 21 September 1940, 839.51/4892, FRUS 1940, 5:829.

116 Scotten to Hull, 24 September 1940, 839.51/4902.5, and 22 September 1940, 839.407/10, RG 59, NA.

117 Department of State press release, 24 September 1940. The U.S.-Dominican Convention of 1940 is printed in the Department of State Treaty Series, no. 965.

118 Scotten to Hull, 20 October 1940, 839.407/12, RG 59, NA.

119 Scotten to Hull, 21 October 1940, 839.51/4934, RG 59, NA.

120 Scotten to Hull, 4 November 1940, 839.001 TRUJILLO/463, RG 59, NA.

121 Clipping contained in 17 October 1940, 839.51/4929, RG 59, NA.

122 Clipping contained in 23 October 1940, 839.51/4936, RG 59, NA.

123 Clippings sent to Francis White, 14 November 1940, 839.51/4951, and 25 November 1940, 839.51/4950.5, RG 59, NA.

124 *New York Times,* 30 September 1940.

125 Emilio Rodríguez Demorizi, *Trujillo y Cordell Hull: Un ejemplo de política panamericanista* (Ciudad Trujillo, 1956).

126 Murray Jacoby article in *Cooperación,* August 1943, contained in 839.00 TRUJILLO/32, RG 59, NA; Mateo, *Mito y cultura,* 37–38.

127  Memo of conversation, White with Frank Vedder, 13 November 1940, Box 19, White Papers.

128  Pastoriza to Hull, 5 September 1940, 839.51/4875, RG 59, NA.

129  Hull to Scotten, 17 December 1940, 839.51/4937, RG 59, NA; New York Times, 22 and 23 December 1940.

130  New York Times, 7 September 1940.

131  Department of State Bulletin (12 October 1940): 291–94.

132  Scotten to Hull, 18 October 1940, 810.20 DEFENSE/270 7/12, RG 59, NA.

133  White to Senate Foreign Relations Committee, 29 October 1940, Box 20, White Papers; letter from White, 20 October 1940, 839.51/4921.5, RG 59, NA; Hull to Roosevelt, 18 July 1940, OF 25e, FDRL; Duggan to Hull, 10 October 1940, 839.51A/478, RG 59, NA; White to Hull, 15 October 1940, Box 20, White Papers.

134  William Grafton Rogers to Hugh Wilson, 28 October 1940, 839.51/4937.5, RG 59, NA.

135  Memo of conversation, White with Finley, 24 September 1940, Box 19, White Papers.

136  Memo of conversation, White with Duggan, 25 September 1940, Box 19, White Papers.

137  Memo of conversation, White with Arthur Burke, 26 September 1940, Box 19, White Papers.

138  Memo of conversation, White with Schoepplere, 26 September 1940, Box 19, White Papers.

139  Memo of conversation, White with Renchard, 29 October 1940, Box 19, White Papers.

140  Memo of conversation, White with Wilson, Duggan, Hackworth, and others, 7 November 1940, Box 19, White Papers.

141  Ibid. See also memo of conversation, White with Finley, 6 November 1940, 839.51/4950, RG 59, NA.

142  Listín Diario had called the convention "a thorn profoundly fixed in the living flesh of the national dignity." Newspaper clipping appended to Legation dispatch, 13 November 1937, 839.51/4551, RG 59, NA.

143  On a Proposed Convention with the Dominican Republic Relating to Customs Revenue: Hearings before the Committee on Foreign Relations, U.S. Senate, 76th Congress, 3d session, 27 November 1940. For White's protest against "the annulment of the Receivership," see White to the Senate Foreign Relations Committee, 29 October 1940, Box 20, White Papers.

144  Hearings, 27 November 1940.

145  Hearings, 4 December 1940. Clark had written earlier that bondholders were often "aged people" who "write from hospitals, infirmaries, county poor houses, and bare houses" (Clark, "Collecting," 4).

146  *Hearings,* 4 December 1940.

147  White memo of testimony, 4 December 1940, Box 19, White Papers; memo by Finley, 4 December 1940, 839.51/4979, RG 59, NA.

148  *Congressional Record* (14 February 1941): 1025; Philip Bonsal to Welles, 12 February 1941, 839.51A/495.5, RG 59, NA.

149  *Congressional Record* (14 February 1941): 1026.

150  Scotten to Hull, 15 February 1941, 839.51/5027, RG 59, NA.

151  Letter to FBPC, 4 April 1941, 839.51/5062, RG 59, NA.

152  Clark to White, 2 April 1941, Box 1, White Papers.

153  Munro to White, 25 September 1941, Box 21, White Papers.

154  White to Munro, 29 September 1941, Box 21, White Papers.

155  Despradel to Hull, 19 June 1934, 839.51/4158, RG 59, NA.

156  José Antonio Osorio Lizarazo, *The Birth and Growth of Anti-Trujillism in America* (Madrid, 1958).

157  Kimball, *Unsordid Act,* 243–46.

158  Orme Wilson, Liaison Officer, to Colonel Matthew Ridgway, 11 February 1941, WPD 4318-2, RG 165, NA; Brigadier General E. Reybold to Brigadier General L. T. Gerow, 14 June 1941, and Gerow to Reybold, undated reply, WPD 4318-4, RG 165, NA; Gerow to Defense Aid Director, 11 December 1941, WPD 4318-6, RG 165, NA; Secretary of the Navy Frank Knox to Commandant, USMC, 14 August 1941, EF63/L11-3(22)(410813), RG 80, NA; Captain Paul Hendren to Moore Lynn, Division of Defense Aid, 25 October 1941, (410911), RG 80, NA; and Commandant, USMC, to Chief of Naval Operations, 11 May 1942 (420511), RG 80, NA.

159  *Listín Diario,* 9 and 12 December 1941.

160  For a detailed account of these sinkings and other U-boat attacks in the Caribbean, with several pages of photos, see Vega, *Nazismo,* 227–41.

161  The Naval Aviation Mission was proposed to Trujillo and accepted by him within days of Pearl Harbor. Gerow memo, 18 December 1941, WPD 4318-7, RG 165, NA.

162  Roorda, "The Cult of the Airplane," 269–310.

163  Lieutenant Colonel R. C. Smith, memo to the Assistant Chief of Staff, War Plans Division, 21 May 1941, and Orme Wilson, Liaison Officer, memo to Chief, Liaison Branch, War Department, 13 June 1941. Both these and related documents are in WPD 4318-3, RG 165, NA.

164  Chargé d'Affaires Edward P. Lawton to Hull, with clippings from *La Nación,* 11 May 1942, 839.00/4318, RG 59, NA.

165  Warren to Secretary of State, 18 August 1942, 839.001 T., R./548, RG 59, NA.

166  Lieutenant General Frank M. Andrews memo to General Van Voorhis, 30 April 1941; Andrews to Trujillo, 26 August 1942; Trujillo to Andrews, 31 Au-

gust 1942. All in Box 7, Personal Correspondence File, Papers of Frank Maxwell Andrews, Library of Congress.

167    Warren to Hull, 8 and 26 January 1944, 839.7962/49 and 50, RG 59, NA.

168    Warren to Hull, 7 January 1944, 839.415/75, RG 59, NA; draft program of First Centennial Celebration of the Dominican Republic, enclosed with Warren to Hull, 8 February 1944, 839.415/121, RG 59, NA.

169    Photo of ceremony, 5 April 1943, Folder O, Box 175, Office of War Information, "Photos of Notable Personalities," RG 208-PU, NA.

170    See the photo and accompanying news copy of the award ceremony, filed by the Office of War Information, 27 October 1943, Folder Z, Box 138, RG 208-PU, Still Photography, NA. The *New York World-Telegram* announced the awards with a photo of Montez, 25 October 1943.

171    Gellman, *Good Neighbor Diplomacy*, 176–80; idem, *Secret Affairs*, 302–21.

172    "Minutes of the Meetings of the Coordination Committee for the Dominican Republic," vol. 16, 1944, RG 84, NA.

173    Ambassador Ellis O. Briggs to Hull, 28 July 1944, 839.24/7-2844, RG 59, NA.

174    Briggs to Hull, 5 July 1944, 839.00/7-544, RG 59, NA.

175    Briggs to Hull, 28 July 1944, 839.24/7-2844, RG 59, NA.

176    Briggs to Secretary of State, 21 July 1944, with *La Nación* clippings enclosed, 839.20111/7-2144, RG 59, NA.

177    Briggs to Secretary of State, 5 September 1944, with clipping from the *Star and Herald* (Panama), 24 August 1944, 839.00/5-544, RG 59, NA.

178    Cabot to Norman Armour, Division of American Republic Affairs, 12 September 1944, 839.00/9-544, RG 59, NA.

179    Daniel P. Hagdorn, *Central American and Caribbean Air Forces* (London, 1993), 97.

180    Chargé d'Affaires Robert Newbegin to Secretary of State Edward Stettinius, 13 April 1945, Embassy in Ciudad Trujillo–1945, Box 150, RG 84, NA.

181    *Washington Times,* 14 February 1945.

182    Vega, *Los Estados Unidos y Trujillo, año 1945,* 234.

183    Peña Batlle made an important speech on the subject in the border town of Elías Piña in November 1942, and in 1946 he published a book on the subject, *Historia de la cuestión fronteriza.* Also see Vega, *Nazismo,* 40; Mateo, *Mito y cultura,* 163–82.

184    *Time* (5 and 19 November 1945).

185    Vega, *Los Estados Unidos y Trujillo, año 1945,* 273–74.

186    *Washington Post,* 23 November 1945.

187    Assistant Secretary Spruille Braden, aide-mémoire, 28 December 1945, 839.24/11-2945, RG 59, NA. See also Chester J. Pach, "The Containment of U.S. Military Aid to Latin America, 1944–1949," *Diplomatic History* (Summer 1982): 225–44.

188  Vega, *Los Estados Unidos y Trujillo, año 1945*, 28.

189  Chargé d'Affaires Andrew Wardlaw, "Attempts to Link the Name of President Trujillo and Former Secretary of State Hull," 20 November 1945, Box 150, 1945, RG 84, NA.

190  Hagedorn, *Central American and Caribbean Air Forces*, 98–100; Daniel P. Hegadorn and John Dienst, *North American F-51 Mustangs in Latin American Air Force Service* (Arlington, Tex., 1985), 2–4.

191  Charles D. Ameringer, *The Caribbean Legion: Patriots, Politicians, Soldiers of Fortune, 1946–1950* (State College, 1995).

192  Pach, "Containment of U.S. Military Aid," 237–39.

193  Vega, *Trujillo y las fuerzas armadas norteamericanas*, 307.

194  For example: Dominican Ambassador to the United States Joaquín Salazar's attack on Braden at Pan-American Society lunch, 9 May 1955, Weekly Embassy Reports, 739.00(W), RG 59, NA. Braden had intervened to prevent Trujillo from changing the name of the town of Dajabón, focal point of the Haitian massacre, to "Franklin D. Roosevelt" in 1945. In 1953, Trujillo commemorated a monument with a "bronze plaque . . . in derogation of Messrs. Braden and Briggs" on Avenida George Washington near the Trujillo-Hull Monument (Ambassador William T. Pheiffer to Secretary of State John Foster Dulles, 21 September and 5 December 1953, 739.00/9-2153 and 12-533, RG 59, NA). See also the exchange of letters between Braden, Briggs, Assistant Secretary of State John Moors Cabot, and Deputy Assistant Secretary of State Robert Woodward on Trujillo's defamations: 26 October 1953 to 5 January 1954, Box 24, Spruille Braden Papers, Columbia University Library, New York. Thanks to Victoria Allison for the Braden Papers citations.

195  Embassy report, "The Personality and Current Policies of Generalísimo Trujillo," 27 January 1953, 739.11/1-2753, RG 59, NA.

196  Briggs to Secretary of State, 5 September 1944, 839.00/5-544, RG 59, NA.


EIGHT    *The Good Neighbor Policy and Dictatorship*

1  Bernardo Vega, *Un interludio de tolerancia: El acuerdo de Trujillo con los comunistas en 1946* (Santo Domingo, 1987).

2  Hall, "Sugar and Power," 57–67.

3  Rear Admiral Harry S. Knapp, "The Naval Officer in Diplomacy," *United States Naval Institute Proceedings* (March 1927): 317.

4  Schoenfeld to Welles, 4 September 1936, Folder 10, Box 36, Welles Papers, FDRL.

5  Norweb to Welles, 14 July 1938, Folder 3, Box 47, Welles Papers, FDRL.

6  "The United States Military Government in the Dominican Republic, 1916–1922: A Case History," U.S. Army School for Military Government and Ad-

ministration, New York, 2d Section, Group V, 14 August 1943, Hoover Institution on War, Revolution, and Peace, Stanford University, Palo Alto, Calif.

7   Vega, *Trujillo y las fuerzas armadas norteamericanas,* 268, 277, 316–18, 322–23, 330.

8   Lieutenant Colonel Henry C. Davis, USMC, "Indoctrination of Latin-American Service," *Marine Corps Gazette* (June 1920): 155.

9   Ibid.

10  Ellis Briggs, oral history, quoted in Michael L. Krenn, *The Chains of Interdependence: U.S. Policy toward Central America, 1945–1954* (Armonk, N.Y., 1996), 103.

11  Diederich, *Trujillo: The Death of the Goat.*

12  *Navy Times,* 22 May 1995.

Primary Sources

UNPUBLISHED

Archivo General de la Nación, Santo Domingo, Dominican Republic
 Records of the Dominican Legation in the United States

Franklin D. Roosevelt Presidential Library, Hyde Park, N.Y.
 President's Personal File
 Official File
 Sumner Welles Papers
 Myron C. Taylor Papers
 Henry Morgenthau Diaries
 Adolph A. Berle Papers

Herbert Hoover Presidential Library, West Branch, Iowa
 Hoover Presidential Papers—Foreign Affairs
 Henry L. Stimson Diaries

Library of Congress, Manuscripts Branch, Washington, D.C.
 Papers of Herbert Feis
 Papers of Cordell Hull
 Papers of Frank Maxwell Andrews
 Papers of the NAACP
 Papers of Norman Davis
 Papers of Samuel Guy Inman

Marine Corps Historical Center, Washington, D.C.
 Thomas E. Watson Collection

James K. Noble Collection
Thomas C. Turner Collection
Robert Blake Collection
Roy Geiger Collection
Pedro A. del Valle Collection

Milton Eisenhower Library, Johns Hopkins University, Baltimore, Md.
Francis White Papers

National Archives, Washington, D.C.
Record Groups:
38 (Navy Department, Naval Intelligence Division)
59 (General Records of the State Department, Decimal File and Inspection Reports)
80 (General Records of the Navy Department)
84 (Department of State Foreign Service Posts)
165 (War Department, War Plans Division)
Still Photography Division
Motion Picture Division

Naval War College, Newport, R.I.
Milton Miles Collection
Walter Woodson Collection
W. B. Caperton Collection

Organization of American States, Washington, D.C.
Columbus Memorial Lighthouse Collection

Pioneer Business Records Service, Brooklyn, N.Y.
Records of the Foreign Bondholders Protective Council

Public Record Office, Kew, England
British Foreign Office Series 140, 371

Private Collection
Papers of H. F. Arthur Schoenfeld

Sterling Memorial Library, Yale University, New Haven, Conn.
John Moors Cabot Papers
Thomas Thacher Papers

Universidad Autónoma de Santo Domingo, Dominican Republic
Archivo Tulio Cestero

PUBLISHED

*Government Documents*

*Album de oro de la Republica Dominicana: Por la unión y confraternidad entre los pueblos de la América Latina, 1936.* Havana: Sindicato de Artes Gráficas de la Habana, 1936.
*Boletin de Relaciones Exteriores.* Santo Domingo/Ciudad Trujillo: 1934–41.
Bourne, Kenneth, and D. Cameron Watt, general eds. *British Documents on Foreign Affairs: Reports and Papers from the Foreign Office Confidential Print.* Part II, Series D, Latin America, 1914–39, vols. 6–20. Bethesda, Md.: University Publications of America, 1989–92.
Cuello H., José Israel, ed. *Documentos del conflicto dominico-haitiano de 1937.* Santo Domingo: Ediciones Taller, 1985.
Department of Commerce: Bureau of Foreign and Domestic Commerce. *Living Conditions and Costs in the Dominican Republic.* Special Circular no. 391, Division of Regional Information, 25 April 1938.
Department of State: *Papers Relating to the Foreign Relations of the United States.* Washington: Government Printing Office: *1922* (1938), *1923* (1938), *1924* (1939), *1929* (1944), *1930* (1945), *1931* (1946), *1932* (1948), *1933* (1950), *1934* (1951), *1935* (1953), *1936* (1953), *1937* (1954), *1938* (1955), *1939* (1956), *1940* (1959), *1941* (1962), *1942* (1962), *1943* (1965), *1944* (1967), *1945* (1969).
Department of the Treasury: U.S. Register of the Treasury, Bureau of the Census, Foreign Commerce and Navigation of the United States, 1870–1924. Washington, D.C.: Government Printing Office.
*Gaceta Oficial.* Santo Domingo/Ciudad Trujillo: 1930–1945.
*Hearings before a Select Committee on Haiti and Santo Domingo: Inquiry into the Occupation and Administration of Haiti and Santo Domingo,* 2 vols., 67th Congress, 1st and 2d sessions, 1921 and 1922.
*Hearings before the Committee on Foreign Affairs, U.S. House of Representatives: Christopher Columbus Memorial Lighthouse at Santo Domingo,* 70th Congress, 2d session, 1929.
*Hearings before the Committee on Finance, U.S. Senate: Sale of Foreign Bonds or Securities in the United States, pursuant to Senate Resolution 19,* 72d Congress, 1st session, 1933.
*Hearings before the Committee on Foreign Relations, U.S. Senate: On a Proposed Convention with the Dominican Republic Relating to Customs Revenue,* 76th Congress, 3d session, 1940.
*Franklin D. Roosevelt and Foreign Affairs,* 2d series, 14 (New York: Clearwater Publishing, 1979 and 1983).
*Public Papers and Addresses of Franklin D. Roosevelt,* vols. 2–8, 1933–45. New York: Macmillan, 1938 and 1941.
Trujillo Molina, Rafael L. *Discursos, mensajes y proclamas,* vols. 1–6, 1930–45. Santiago: Editorial El Diario, n.d.

*Newspapers and Periodicals*

Dominican Republic
  *La Información*
  *La Opinión*
  *Listín Diario*
  *Revista Militar*

United States
  *Baltimore Sun*
  *Dominican Republic*
  *Life*
  *Marine Corps Gazette*
  *The Nation*
  *Newsweek*
  *New York Herald Tribune*
  *New York Times*
  *Time*
  *United States Naval Institute Proceedings*
  *Washington Post*
  *Washington Times*

*Books, Articles, and Pamphlets*

Balaguer, Joaquín. *El tratado Trujillo-Hull y la liberación financiera de la República Domi-nicana*. Bogotá: Consorcio Editorial, 1941.

Baughman, Commander C. C., USN. "United States Occupation of the Dominican Republic." *United States Naval Institute Proceedings* (December 1925): 2306–27.

Besault, Lawrence de. *President Trujillo: His Work and the Dominican Republic*. Wash-ington, D.C.: Washington Publishing Co., 1936.

Blake, Lieutenant Colonel Robert, USMC. "Campaigning around the Caribbean." *Marine Corps Gazette* (June 1938): 8.

Bonetti Burgos, Ernesto. *Bandera de la raza*. Ciudad Trujillo: Publicaciones de la Secretaria de Estado de Relaciones Exteriores, 1936.

Castro H., Julio César. *Paralelo (Mussolini-Trujillo)*. Santo Domingo: Talleres del Ejér-cito, 1933.

Castro Noboa, H. B. de. *Antología poética trujillista*. Santiago, D.R.: Editorial El Diario, 1946.

Clark, J. Reuben. "Collecting on Defaulted Foreign Dollar Bonds." *American Journal of International Law* (January 1940): 1–10.

Comité Ejecutivo Permanente del Faro de Colón. *El Faro a Colón*. Ciudad Trujillo: Imprenta Dominicana, C. por A., 1950.

Comité Nóbel del Parlamento Noruego. *Memorial dirijido al Comité Nóbel del Parlamento Noruego en que se propone al generalísimo doctor Rafael Leonidas Trujillo Molina, presidente de la República Dominicana, como candidato al premio Nóbel de la Paz correspondiente al año 1936.* Santo Domingo: Universidad de Santo Domingo, Imprenta Listín Diario, 1936.

Contin, Juan M. *Por qué Trujillo es el lema y el emblema de la patria.* Ciudad Trujillo: n.p., 1938.

Courlander, Harold. "Not in the Cables: Massacre in Santo Domingo." *The New Republic* (24 November 1937): 67.

Cruz Alvarez, Arquímedes. *Rafael Leonidas Trujillo. Notas biográficas.* Santo Domingo: Cromos, 1930.

Davis, Lieutenant Colonel Henry C., USMC. "Indoctrination of Latin-American Service." *Marine Corps Gazette* (June 1920): 154–61.

Dulles, Allen W. "The Protection of American Foreign Bondholders." *Foreign Affairs* (April 1932): 3–13.

Espaillat, Rafael A. "Conferencia dictada en el ejército nacional." Ciudad Trujillo: Talleres del Ejército, 1934.

———. *Trujillo: The Last Caesar.* Chicago: Henry Regnery, 1963.

Fellowes, Lieutenant Edward A., USMC. "Training Native Troops in Santo Domingo." *Marine Corps Gazette* (December 1923): 215–33.

Fernández Mato, Ramón. *Trujillo: O la trasfiguración dominicana.* Santo Domingo: Veritas, 1945.

Franck, Harry. *Roaming through the West Indies.* New York: Blue Ribbon Books, 1920.

Gantenbein, James W. *The Columbus Lighthouse.* Washington, D.C.: Pan American Union, 1936.

———. *Financial Questions in Foreign Policy.* New York: Octagon Books, 1939.

Garrido, Victor. *La conquista de la gloria.* Ciudad Trujillo: Publicaciones del Partido Dominicano, Editora Montalvo, 1940.

Gruening, Ernest. "The Dictatorship in Santo Domingo: A 'Joint Concern.'" *The Nation* (23 May 1934): 583–85.

Hernández Franco, T. *El cuarto año de gobierno del presidente Trujillo.* Santiago, D.R.: Imprenta La Información, 1934.

———. *Los dos años de gobierno del presidente Trujillo.* Santiago, D.R.: Imprenta La Información, 1932.

Heureaux, Ulises. *Rafael Leonidas Trujillo Molina.* Santo Domingo: Cromos, 1933.

Jiménes Grullón, Juan Isidro. *Una gestapo en América: Vida, tortura, agonía y muerte de presos políticos bajo la tiranía de Trujillo.* Santo Domingo: Editora Alfa y Omega, 1981 (originally 1945).

Johnson, Commander Lucius W. *Report on Relief Work in the Santo Domingo Disaster.* Washington, D.C.: Government Printing Office, 1930.

Kilmartin, First Lieutenant Robert C., USMC. "Indoctrination in Santo Domingo." *Marine Corps Gazette* (October 1922): 377–86.

Knapp, Rear Admiral Harry S., USN. "The Naval Officer in Diplomacy." *United States Naval Institute Proceedings* (March 1927): 309–17.

Loughran, Elizabeth W., and the Latin America Committee. *The United States and the Dominican Republic: A Report of the Latin America Committee.* Washington, D.C.: Catholic Association for International Peace, 1936.

Lovette, Lieutenant Leland P., USN. "Naval Policy at the Crossroads." *United States Naval Institute Proceedings* (April 1930): 269–80.

Mejía Ricart, Gustavo Adolfo. *El significado histórico del 23 de febrero del 1930.* Ciudad Trujillo: Impresora Listín Diario, 1940.

Miller, Lieutenant Colonel Charles J., USMC. "Diplomatic Spurs: Our Experiences in Santo Domingo." *Marine Corps Gazette*, 3 pts. (February 1935): 43–47; (May 1935): 19–25, 52–59; (August 1935): 35–47.

Mota, Fabio A. *Neo-socialismo dominanismo*: aspectos de la obra aspiritual del presidente Trujillo. Ciudad Trujillo: Editorial Caribes, 1936.

Murray-Jacoby, H. "The Diplomacy of President Trujillo." *Cooperación* (August 1943): 7–18.

Nanita, Abelardo René. *Trujillo.* Ciudad Trujillo: Impresora Dominicana, 1951.

——. *Trujillo: The Biography of a Great Leader.* New York: Vantage Press, 1957.

——. *Trujillo de cuerpo entero.* Santiago, D.R.: El Diario, 1939.

——. *Trujillo: A Full-Size Portrait,* trans. M. A. Moore. Santiago, D.R.: El Diario, 1939.

Partido Revolucionario Dominicano. *La historia del hombre que se proclama igual a Dios.* Mexico City: n.p., 1944.

Pérez Leyba, Salvador A. *El Generalísimo Trujillo Molina, la Convención Domínico-Americana y la política de "Buen Vecino."* Ciudad Trujillo: Imprenta Listín Diario, 1935.

Pina Chevalier, Teódulo. *Día de San Rafael.* Ciudad Trujillo: Imprenta Luis Sánchez Andujar, 1933.

Powell, E. Alexander. *Aerial Odyssey.* New York: Macmillan, 1936.

Renolds, Quentin. "Murder in the Tropics." *Collier's* (22 January 1938): 15–16.

Richards, Brigadier General George, USMC. "The Monroe Doctrine: Its Application of Today." *United States Naval Institute Proceedings* (October 1932): 1405–31.

Rochester, Lieutenant H. A., USN. "The Navy's Support of Foreign Policy." *United States Naval Institute Proceedings* (November 1931): 1491–1500.

Sánchez Lustrino, Gilberto. *Trujillo, el constructor de una nacionalidad.* Ciudad Trujillo: Cultural, 1938.

Schoenrich, Otto. *Santo Domingo: A Country with a Future.* New York: Macmillan, 1918.

Sinks, Alfred H. "Trujillo, Caribbean Dictator." *American Mercury* (October 1940): 164–71.

Thomsen, Charles A. "Dictatorship in the Dominican Republic." *Foreign Policy Reports* (15 March 1936): 30–40.

Trujillo, Rafael L. *Cartilla cívica para el pueblo dominicano.* Santiago, D.R.: Impresora La Información, 1933.

——. *La nueva patria dominicana.* Santo Domingo: 1934.

——. *La nueva patria dominicana: Suplemento.* Santo Domingo: 1935.

Villard, Oswald Garrison. "Santo Domingo, 1937." *The Nation* (20 March 1937): 323–24.

Vroom, Lieutenant Commander G. B., USN. "The Place of Naval Officers in International Affairs." *United States Naval Institute Proceedings* (May 1921): 685–700.

White, John W. *The Dominican Republic To-Day.* Ciudad Trujillo: Editorial La Nación, 1945.

——. *The Land Columbus Loved.* Ciudad Trujillo: Editora Montalvo, 1945.

## Secondary Sources

PUBLISHED

Adams, Frederick C. *Economic Diplomacy: The Export-Import Bank and American Foreign Policy, 1934–39.* Columbia: University of Missouri Press, 1976.

Albion, Robert Greenhalgh. *Makers of Naval Policy.* Annapolis: Naval Institute Press, 1945; reprinted 1976.

Albion, Robert Greenhalgh, and Jennie Barnes Pope. *Sea Lanes in Wartime: The American Experience, 1775–1942.* New York: W. W. Norton, 1942.

Ameringer, Charles D. *The Caribbean Legion: Patriots, Politicians, Soldiers of Fortune, 1946–1950.* State College: Pennsylvania State University Press, 1995.

Arias Núñez, Luis. *La política exterior en la era de Trujillo.* Santiago, D.R.: Pontificia Universidad Católica Madre y Maestra, 1991.

Atkins, G. Pope, and Larman C. Wilson. *The United States and the Trujillo Regime.* New Brunswick: Rutgers University Press, 1972.

Bailey, Thomas A., and Paul B. Ryan. *Hitler vs. Roosevelt: The Undeclared Naval War.* New York: Free Press, 1979.

Balaguer, Joaquín. *Memorias de un cortesano de la "era de Trujillo."* Santo Domingo, D.R.: Editora Corripio, 1988.

Baylen, J. O. "American Intervention in Nicaragua, 1909–33: An Appraisal of Objectives and Results." *Southwest Social Science Quarterly* 35 (1954): 128–54.

Bell, Ian. *The Dominican Republic.* Boulder: Westview Press, 1981.

Bemis, Samuel Flagg. *The Latin American Policy of the United States.* New York: Harcourt, Brace & Co., 1943.

Betances, Emilio. *State and Society in the Dominican Republic.* Boulder: Westview Press, 1995.

Bhabha, Homi. "Of Mimicry and Man: The Ambivalence of Colonial Discourse." In Annette Michelson et al., eds., *October: The First Decade, 1976–1986* (Cambridge: MIT Press, 1987): 317–25.

Black, George. *The Good Neighbor: How the United States Wrote the History of Central America and the Caribbean.* New York: Pantheon Books, 1988.

Black, Jan Knippers. *The Dominican Republic: Politics and Development in an Unsovereign State.* London: Unwin Hyman, 1986.

Bosch, Juan. *Las dictaduras dominicanas.* Santo Domingo: Editora Alfa y Omega, 1988.

———. *La fortuna de Trujillo.* Santo Domingo: Editora Alfa y Omega, 1985.

———. *Trujillo: Causas de una tiranía sin ejemplo.* Caracas: Librería Las Novedades, 1959.

Braden, Spruille. *Diplomats and Demagogues: The Memoirs of Spruille Braden.* New Rochelle, N.Y.: Arlington House, 1971.

Braden, Spruille, and Ellis O. Briggs. *Our Inter-American Policy.* Washington, D.C.: Government Printing Office, 1971.

Briggs, Ellis O. *Farewell to Foggy Bottom: The Recollections of a Career Diplomat.* New York: David McKay, 1964.

Burns, James MacGregor. *Roosevelt: The Lion and the Fox.* New York: Harcourt, Brace & World, 1956.

Cabot, John Moors. *First Line of Defense: Forty Years' Experience of a Career Diplomat.* Washington, D.C.: School of Foreign Service, Georgetown University, 1979.

Calder, Bruce. *The Impact of Intervention: The Dominican Republic during the U.S. Occupation of 1916–24.* Austin: University of Texas Press, 1984.

Calhoun, Frederick. *Power and Principle: Armed Intervention in Wilsonian Foreign Policy.* Kent, Ohio: Kent State University Press, 1986.

Cameron, Craig. *American Samurai: Myth, Imagination and the Conduct of Battle in the First Marine Division, 1941–51.* New York: Cambridge University Press, 1994.

Cassá, Roberto. *Capitalismo y dictadura.* Santo Domingo: Universidad Autónoma de Santo Domingo, 1982.

———. *Historia social y económica de la República Dominicana,* 2 vols. Santo Domingo: Editora Alfa y Omega, 1981.

Castor, Suzy. *Migración y relaciones internationales: El caso haitiano dominicano.* Santo Domingo: Editora Universitaria, 1987.

Challener, Richard D. *Admirals, Generals, and American Foreign Policy.* Princeton: Princeton University Press, 1973.

Child, John. "From 'Color' to 'Rainbow': U.S. Strategic Planning for Latin America, 1919–1945." *Journal of Interamerican Studies and World Affairs* (May 1979): 233–59.

————. *Unequal Alliance: The Inter-American Military System 1938–1978.* Boulder: Westview Press, 1980.

Cobbs, Elizabeth. *The Rich Neighbor Policy: Rockefeller and Kaiser in Brazil.* New Haven: Yale University Press, 1991.

Collin, Richard H. "The 1904 Detroit Compact: U.S. Naval Diplomacy and Dominican Revolutions." *The Historian* (May 1990): 432–52.

————. *Theodore Roosevelt, Culture, Diplomacy, and Expansion: A New View of American Imperialism.* Baton Rouge: Louisiana State University Press, 1985.

————. *Theodore Roosevelt's Caribbean: The Panama Canal, the Monroe Doctrine, and the Latin American Context.* Baton Rouge: Louisiana State University Press, 1990.

Connell-Smith, Gordon. *The Inter-American System.* London: Oxford University Press, 1966.

Cordero Michel, José R. *Análisis de la era de Trujillo,* 5th ed. Santo Domingo: Editora Universitaria, 1987.

Crassweller, Robert D. *Trujillo: The Life and Times of a Caribbean Dictator.* New York: Macmillan, 1966.

Cronon, E. David. "Interpreting the New Good Neighbor Policy: The Cuban Crisis of 1933." *Hispanic American Historical Review* (November 1959): 538–67.

Curry, Earl R. *Hoover's Dominican Diplomacy and the Origins of the Good Neighbor Policy.* New York: Garland Publishing, 1979.

Dallek, Robert. *Franklin D. Roosevelt and American Foreign Policy, 1932–45.* New York: Oxford University Press, 1979.

DeConde, Alexander. *Hoover's Latin American Policy.* Palo Alto: Stanford University Press, 1951.

Delpar, Helen. *The Enormous Vogue of Things Mexican: Cultural Relations between the United States and Mexico, 1920–1935.* Tuscaloosa: University of Alabama Press, 1992.

Derby, Lauren H. "Haitians, Magic and Money: *Raza* and Society in the Haitian-Dominican Borderlands, 1900–1937." *Comparative Studies in Society and History* (July 1994): 488–526.

Derby, Lauren H., and Richard Turits. "Historias de terror y los terrores de historia: La masacre haitiana de 1937 en la República Dominicana." *Estudios Sociales* (April–June 1992): 65–76.

Díaz Ordóñez, Virgilio. *La era de Trujillo, 25 años de historia dominicana: La política exterior de Trujillo,* 3 vols. Ciudad Trujillo: Impresora Dominicana, 1955.

Diederich, Bernard. *Trujillo: The Death of the Goat.* Boston: Little, Brown & Co., 1978.

Dozer, Donald F. *Are We Good Neighbors?* Gainesville: University Press of Florida, 1961.

Drake, Paul, ed. *Money Doctors, Foreign Debts, and Economic Reforms in Latin America from the 1890s to the Present.* Wilmington, Del.: Scholarly Resources, 1994.

Elkin, Judith Laiken. *Jews in the Latin American Republics.* Chapel Hill: University of North Carolina Press, 1980.

Enloe, Cynthia. *Bananas, Beaches, and Bases: Making Feminist Sense of International Politics.* London: Pandora, 1989.

Espaillat, Arturo R. *The Last Caesar.* Chicago: Henry Regnery, 1963.

Espinosa, J. Manuel. *Inter-American Beginnings of United States Cultural Diplomacy, 1936–1948.* Washington, D.C.: Government Printing Office, 1976.

Feis, Herbert. *1933: Characters in Crisis.* Boston: Little, Brown & Co., 1966.

Fejes, Fred. *Imperialism, Media, and the Good Neighbor.* Norwood, N.J.: Ablex Publishing, 1986.

Ferguson, James. *The Dominican Republic: Beyond the Lighthouse.* New York: Monthly Review Press, 1992.

Ferrell, Robert H. *American Diplomacy in the Great Depression: Hoover-Stimson Foreign Policy, 1929–1933.* New Haven: Yale University Press, 1957.

Fiehrer, Thomas. "Political Violence in the Periphery: The Haitian Massacre of 1937." *Race and Class* (October–December 1990): 1–20.

Fielding, Raymond. *The March of Time, 1935–1951.* New York: Oxford University Press, 1978.

Franco, Franklin J. *La era de Trujillo.* Santo Domingo: Fundación Cultural Dominicana, 1992.

Franks, Julie. "The Gauilleros of the East: Social Banditry as Political Practice in the Dominican Sugar Region, 1900–24." *Journal of Historical Sociology* (Spring 1995): 158–81.

Friedel, Frank. *Franklin D. Roosevelt: A Rendezvous with Destiny.* Boston: Little, Brown, 1990.

Frye, Alton. *Nazi Germany and the American Hemisphere, 1933–1941.* New Haven: Yale University Press, 1967.

Fuller, Captain Stephen M., USMC, and Graham Cosmas. *The Marines in the Dominican Republic.* Washington, D.C.: Government Printing Office, 1974.

Galíndez Suárez, Jesús. *La era de Trujillo: Un estudio casuístico de dictadura latinoamericana.* Santiago de Chile: Editorial del Pacífico, 1956. English edition: *The Era of Trujillo, Dominican Dictator,* ed. Russell H. Fitzgibbon. Tucson: University of Arizona Press, 1973.

Gallegos, Gerardo. *Trujillo: Cara y cruz de una dictadura.* Madrid: Ediciones Iberoamericanas, 1968.

García, Juan Manuel. *La matanza de los haitianos: Genocidio de Trujillo, 1937.* Santo Domingo: Editora Alfa y Omega, 1983.

García Bonnelly, Juan Ulises. *La era de Trujillo, 25 años de historia dominicana: Las obras públicas en la era de Trujillo,* 20 vols. Ciudad Trujillo: Impresora Dominicana, 1955.

Gardiner, C. Harvey. *La política de inmigración del dictador Trujillo.* Santo Domingo: Universidad Nacional Henríquez Ureña, 1980.

Gardner, Lloyd C. *Economic Aspects of New Deal Diplomacy.* Madison: University of Wisconsin Press, 1956.

Gellman, Irwin F. *Good Neighbor Diplomacy: United States Policies in Latin America, 1933–1945.* Baltimore: Johns Hopkins University Press, 1979.

————. *Roosevelt and Batista: Good Neighbor Diplomacy in Cuba, 1933–1945.* Albuquerque: University of New Mexico Press, 1973.

————. *Secret Affairs: Franklin Roosevelt, Cordell Hull, and Sumner Welles.* Baltimore: Johns Hopkins University Press, 1995.

Georges, Eugenia. *The Making of a Transnational Community: Migration, Development, and Cultural Change in the Dominican Republic.* New York: Columbia University Press, 1990.

Gilderhus, Mark. *Pan American Visions: Woodrow Wilson and the Western Hemisphere, 1913–1921.* Tucson: University of Arizona Press, 1986.

Gimbernand, Jacinto. *Trujillo: Un estudio de su dictadura.* Santo Domingo: Publicaciones América, 1985.

Goldwert, Marvin. *The Constabulary in the Dominican Republic and Nicaragua: Progeny of United States Intervention.* Gainesville: University Press of Florida, 1962.

Green, David. *The Containment of Latin America.* Chicago: Quadrangle Books, 1971.

Greenfield, Kent Roberts, ed. *United States Army in World War II.* Washington, D.C.: Government Printing Office, 1960. Vol. 1: Stetson Conn and Byron Fairchild, *The Western Hemisphere: The Framework of Hemisphere Defense.* Vol. 4: Mark Skinner Watson, *Chief of Staff: Prewar Plans and Preparations.*

Grieb, Kenneth J. "American Involvement in the Rise of Jorge Ubico." *Caribbean Studies* (April 1970): 5–21.

————. *Guatemalan Caudillo: The Regime of Jorge Ubico, Guatemala, 1931–1944.* Athens: Ohio University Press, 1979.

————. "The U.S. and General Jorge Ubico's Retention of Power." *Revista de Historia de América* 38 (1971): 119–35.

————. "The U.S. and the Rise of General Maximiliano Hernández Martínez." *Journal of Latin American Studies* (November 1971): 151–72.

————. "Warren G. Harding and the Dominican Republic: U.S. Withdrawal, 1921–1923." *Journal of Interamerican Studies* (July 1969): 425–40.

Grow, Michael. *The Good Neighbor Policy and Authoritarianism in Paraguay: United States Economic Expansion and Great-Power Rivalry in Latin America during World War II.* Lawrence: Regents Press of Kansas, 1981.

Guerrant, Edward O. *Roosevelt's Good Neighbor Policy.* Albuquerque: University of New Mexico Press, 1950.

Hagedorn, Daniel P. *Central American and Caribbean Air Forces.* London: Air-Britain, 1993.

Hagedorn, Daniel P., and John Dienst. *North American F-51 Mustangs in Latin American Air Force Service*. Arlington, Tex.: Aerofax, 1985.

Haglund, David G. *Latin America and the Transformation of U.S. Strategic Thought, 1936–1940*. Albuquerque: University of New Mexico Press, 1984.

Haines, Gerald K. "Under the Eagle's Wing: The Franklin Roosevelt Administration Forges an American Hemisphere." *Diplomatic History* (Winter 1977): 373–88.

Hamill, Hugh. *Caudillos: Dictators in Spanish America*. Norman: University of Oklahoma Press, 1992.

————. *Dictatorship in Spanish America*. New York: Knopf, 1965.

Hanson, Gail. "Ordered Liberty: Sumner Welles and the Crowder-Welles Connection in the Caribbean." *Diplomatic History* (Summer 1994): 311–32.

Hartlyn, Jonathan. "The Dominican Republic: The Legacy of Intermittent Engagement." In Abraham F. Lowenthal, ed., *Exporting Democracy: The United States and Latin America*. Baltimore: Johns Hopkins University Press, 1991.

Healy, David F. *Drive to Hegemony: The United States in the Caribbean, 1898–1917*. Madison: University of Wisconsin Press, 1988.

————. *Gunboat Diplomacy in the Wilson Era: The U.S. Navy in Haiti, 1915–1916*. Madison: University of Wisconsin Press, 1976.

Heinl, Robert D. *Soldiers of the Sea: The United States Marine Corps, 1775–1962*. Annapolis: U.S. Naval Institute Press, 1962.

Heinrichs, Waldo H. Jr. "Bureaucracy and Professionalism in the Development of American Career Diplomacy." In John Braeman, Robert H. Brenner, and David Brody, eds., *Twentieth-Century American Foreign Policy*. Columbus: Ohio State University Press, 1971.

Hicks, Albert C. *Blood in the Streets: The Life and Rule of Trujillo*. New York: Creative Age Press, 1946.

Hodgson, Godfrey. *The Colonel: The Life and Wars of Henry Stimson, 1867–1950*. New York: Knopf, 1991.

Hoetink, Harry. *The Dominican People, 1850–1900: Notes for a Historical Sociology*, trans. Stephen K. Ault. Baltimore: Johns Hopkins University Press, 1982.

Hull, Cordell. *The Memoirs of Cordell Hull*. New York: Macmillan, 1948.

Inman, Samuel Guy. *Through Santo Domingo and Haiti: A Cruise with the Marines*. New York: Committee on Cooperation in Latin America, 1919.

Jablon, Howard. *Crossroads of Decision: The State Department and Foreign Policy, 1933–37*. Lexington: University Press of Kentucky, 1983.

Johnson, Richard. *The Administration of United States Foreign Policy*. Austin: University of Texas Press, 1971.

Josephson, Matthew. *Empire of the Air: Juan Trippe and the Struggle for World Airways*. New York: Harcourt, Brace, 1944.

Juárez, Joseph Robert. "United States Withdrawal from Santo Domingo." *Hispanic American Historical Review* (Spring, 1962): 152–90.

Kanawada, Leo V. Jr. *Franklin D. Roosevelt's Diplomacy and American Catholics, Italians, and Jews*. Ann Arbor: University of Michigan Press, 1982.

Karsten, Peter D. *The Naval Aristocracy: The Golden Age of Annapolis and the Emergence of Modern American Navalism*. New York: Free Press, 1972.

Kimball, Warren F. *The Juggler: Franklin Roosevelt as Wartime Statesman*. Princeton: Princeton University Press, 1991.

———. *The Most Unsordid Act: Lend-Lease, 1939-1941*. Baltimore: Johns Hopkins University Press, 1969.

Kisch, Hyman J. "Rafael Trujillo: Caribbean Cyrus." *Judaism* 29, no. 3 (1980): 368-77.

Knight, Melvin. *The Americans in Santo Domingo*. New York: Vanguard Press, 1928.

Koppes, Clayton R., and Gregory Black. *Hollywood Goes to War: How Politics, Profits, and Propaganda Shaped World War II Movies*. Berkeley: University of California Press, 1990.

Krehm, William. *Democracies and Tyrannies of the Caribbean*. Westport, Conn.: Lawrence Hill, 1984.

Krenn, Michael L. *The Chains of Interdependence: U.S. Policy toward Central America, 1945-1954*. Armonk, N.Y.: M. E. Sharpe, 1996.

Labourt, José. *Trujillo: Seguiré a caballo*. Santo Domingo: Ediciones de Taller, 1984.

Langer, William L. *The Undeclared War, 1940-1941*. New York: Harper, 1953.

Langer, William L., and S. Everett Gleason. *The Challenge to Isolation: The World Crisis of 1937-1940 and American Foreign Policy*. New York: Harper, 1952.

Langley, Lester D. *America and the Americas: The United States in the Western Hemisphere*. Athens: University of Georgia Press, 1989.

———. *The Banana Wars: An Inner History of American Empire, 1900-34*. Lexington: University Press of Kentucky, 1983.

———. "Negotiating New Treaties with Panama, 1936." *Hispanic American Historical Review* (May 1968): 220-33.

———. *Struggle for the American Mediterranean: United States-European Rivalry in the Gulf-Caribbean, 1776-1904*. Athens: University of Georgia Press, 1976.

———. "The World Crisis and the Good Neighbor Policy in Panama, 1936-41." *The Americas* 24 (1967): 144-46.

LeGrand, Catherine. "Informal Resistance on a Dominican Sugar Estate: The Ozama Plantation during the Trujillo Regime." *Hispanic American Historical Review* (Fall 1995): 555-96.

Levine, Robert M. *Tropical Diaspora: The Jewish Experience in Cuba*. Gainesville: University Press of Florida, 1993.

Lieuwen, Edwin. *Arms and Politics in Latin America*. New York: Praeger, 1961.

Logan, Rayford W. *Haiti and the Dominican Republic*. New York: Oxford University Press, 1968.

Long, David. *Gold Braid and Foreign Relations: Diplomatic Activities of U.S. Naval Officers, 1798-1883*. Annapolis: U.S. Naval Institute Press, 1988.

Love, Robert W. Jr. *History of the United States Navy, 1775–1941*. Harrisburg: Stackpole Books, 1992.

Malek, R. Michael. "Dominican Republic's General Rafael Trujillo and the Haitian Massacre of 1937: A Case of Subversion in Inter-Caribbean Relations." *SECOLAS Annals: Journal of the Southeastern Conference on Latin American Studies* (March 1980): 137–55.

Maney, Patrick J. *The Roosevelt Presence: A Biography of Franklin Delano Roosevelt*. New York: Twayne Publishers, 1992.

Marks, Frederick W. *Wind over Sand: The Diplomacy of FDR*. Athens: University of Georgia Press, 1988.

Martel, Leon. *Lend-Lease, Loans, and the Coming of the Cold War: A Study of the Implementation of Foreign Policy*. Boulder: Westview Press, 1979.

Martínez-Fernández, Luis. "Caudillos, Annexationism, and the Rivalry between Empires in the Dominican Republic, 1844–1874." *Diplomatic History* (Fall 1993): 571–97.

Mateo, Andrés L. *Mito y cultura en la era de Trujillo*. Santo Domingo: Librería La Trinitaria and Instituto del Libro, 1993.

May, Ernest R. "The 'Bureaucratic Politics' Approach: U.S.-Argentine Relations, 1942–1947." In Julio Cotler and Richard R. Fagen, eds., *Latin America and the United States: The Changing Political Realities*. Palo Alto: Stanford University Press, 1974.

McClintock, Anne. *Imperial Leather: Race, Gender, and Sexuality in the Colonial Conquest*. New York: Routledge, 1995.

McCullough, David G. *The Path between the Seas: The Creation of the Panama Canal, 1870–1914*. New York: Simon & Schuster, 1977.

Mecham, John Lloyd. *The United States and Inter-American Security, 1889–1960*. Austin: University of Texas Press, 1961.

Mencía Lister, Rafael. *Trujillo y su época*. Santo Domingo: Taller, 1992.

Millett, Allan R. *Semper Fidelis: The History of the United States Marine Corps*. New York: Macmillan, 1980.

Millett, Richard. *Guardians of the Dynasty: A History of the U.S.-Created Guardia Nacional de Nicaragua and the Somoza Family*. Maryknoll, N.Y.: Orbis Books, 1977.

———. "The State Department's Navy: A History of the Special Service Squadron, 1920–1940." *American Neptune* (April 1975): 118–38.

Millett, Richard, and G. Dale Gaddy. "Administering the Protectorates: The U.S. Occupation of Haiti and the Dominican Republic." *Revista/Review Interamericana* (Fall 1976): 383–402.

Millett, Richard, and Marvin Soloman. "The Court Martial of Lieutenant Rafael L. Trujillo." *Revista/Review Interamericana* (Fall 1972): 396–404.

Morison, Elting E. *Turmoil and Tradition: The Life and Times of Henry L. Stimson*. Boston: Houghton Mifflin, 1960.

Munro, Dana G. "The American Withdrawal from Haiti, 1929–34." *Hispanic American Historical Review* (Winter 1969): 1–26.

―――. *Intervention and Dollar Diplomacy in the Caribbean, 1900–1921*. Princeton: Princeton University Press, 1964.

―――. *The United States and the Caribbean Republics, 1921–1933*. Princeton: Princeton University Press, 1974.

Musicant, Ivan. *The Banana Wars: A History of United States Military Intervention in Latin America from the Spanish-American War to the Invasion of Panama*. New York: Macmillan, 1990.

Myers, William Starr. *The Foreign Policies of Herbert Hoover, 1929–1933*. New York: Charles Scribner's Sons, 1940.

Nash, George H. *The Life of Herbert Hoover*, 2 vols. New York: W. W. Norton, 1983 and 1988.

Ninkovich, Frank A. *The Diplomacy of Ideas: U.S. Foreign Policy and Cultural Relations, 1938–1950*. Cambridge: Cambridge University Press, 1981.

Nunn, Frederick M. *The Time of the Generals: Latin American Professional Militarism in World Perspective*. Lincoln: University of Nebraska Press, 1992.

O'Connell, Robert L. *Sacred Vessels: The Cult of the Battleship and the Rise of the U.S. Navy*. New York: Oxford University Press, 1993.

Ornes, Germán E. *Trujillo: Little Caesar of the Caribbean*. New York: Thomas Nelson & Sons, 1958.

Osorio Lizarazo, José Antonio. *Birth and Growth of Anti-Trujillism in America*. Madrid: n.p., 1958.

Pach, Chester J. Jr. *Arming the Free World: The Origins of the United States Military Assistance Program, 1945–1950*. Chapel Hill: University of North Carolina Press, 1991.

―――. "The Containment of U.S. Military Aid to Latin America, 1944–49." *Diplomatic History* (Summer 1982): 225–44.

Pérez, Louis A. Jr. *Army Politics in Cuba, 1898–1958*. Pittsburgh: University of Pittsburgh Press, 1976.

Pérez, Manuel Ramón. *Décimas sobre la era de Trujillo*. Ciudad Trujillo: Editora Mont Alvo, 1955.

Pérez Sánchez, José. "La prensa durante los primeros años de Trujillo." *Eme Eme* (July–August 1973).

Perkins, Dexter. *The United States and Latin America*. Baton Rouge: Louisiana State University Press, 1961.

Perkins, Whitney. *Constraint of Empire: The U.S. and Caribbean Interventions*. Westport, Conn.: Greenwood Press, 1981.

Phillips, William. *Ventures in Diplomacy*. Boston: Beacon Press, 1952.

Pike, Fredrick B. *FDR's Good Neighbor Policy: Sixty Years of Generally Gentle Chaos*. Austin: University of Texas Press, 1995.

————. *The United States and Latin America: Myths and Stereotypes of Civilization and Nature*. Austin: University of Texas Press, 1992.

Plummer, Brenda. *Haiti and the United States: The Psychological Moment*. Athens: University of Georgia Press, 1992.

Pratt, Julius. *Cordell Hull, 1933–1944*, 2 vols. New York: Cooper Square Publishers, 1964.

Prestol Castor, Freddy. *El masacre se pasa a pie*. Santo Domingo: Ediciones Taller, 1973.

Pulley, Raymond. "The U.S. and the Dominican Republic, 1933–1940: The High Price of Caribbean Stability." *Caribbean Studies* (October 1965): 22–31.

Quirk, Robert E. *An Affair of Honor: Woodrow Wilson and the Occupation of Veracruz*. Lexington: University Press of Kentucky, 1962.

Rabe, Stephen G. "Inter-American Military Cooperation, 1944–1951." *World Affairs* (Fall 1974): 132–49.

Richard, Alfred Charles. *The Hispanic Image on the Silver Screen: An Interpretive Filmography from Silents into Sound*. Westport, Conn.: Greenwood Press, 1992.

Rivera Cuesta, Marcos. *Las fuerzas armadas y la política dominicana*. Santo Domingo: Talleres de Artes Gráficas, 1986.

Rodman, Selden. *Quisqueya: A History of the Dominican Republic*. Seattle: University of Washington Press, 1964.

Rodríguez Demorizi, Emilio. *Trujillo y Cordell Hull: Un ejemplo de política panamericanista*. Ciudad Trujillo: Editora del Caribe, C. por A., 1956.

Rouquié, Alain. *Military and the State in Latin America*, trans. and ed. Paul E. Sigmund. Berkeley: University of California Press, 1987.

Rourke, Francis E. *Bureaucracy and Foreign Policy*. Baltimore: Johns Hopkins University Press, 1972.

Schmidt, Hans. *Maverick Marine: General Smedley Butler and the Contradictions of American Military History*. Lexington: University Press of Kentucky, 1987.

————. *The U.S. Occupation of Haiti, 1915–34*. New Brunswick: Rutgers University Press, 1973.

Schoonover, Thomas D. *The United States in Central America, 1869–1911: Episodes of Social Imperialism and Imperial Rivalry in the World System*. Durham: Duke University Press, 1991.

Schulzinger, Robert D. *The Making of the Diplomatic Mind: The Training, Outlook and Style of the United States Foreign Service, 1908–1931*. Middletown, Conn.: Wesleyan University Press, 1975.

Smith, Robert F. *The United States and Revolutionary Nationalism in Mexico, 1916–1932*. Chicago: University of Chicago Press, 1972.

Steward, Dick. *Trade and Hemisphere: The Good Neighbor Policy and Reciprocal Trade*. Columbia: University of Missouri Press, 1975.

Tejera R. Ramón A. *El vuelo panamericano pro Faro a Colón.* Santo Domingo: Collección Quinto Centenario, 1992.

Vega, Bernardo. *Control y represión en la dictadura trujillista.* Santo Domingo: Fundación Cultural Dominicana, 1986.

——. *Unos desafectos y otros en desgracia: Sufrimientos bajo la dictadura trujillista.* Santo Domingo: Fundación Cultural Dominicana, 1985.

——. *Los Estados Unidos y Trujillo, 1930.* 2 vols. Santo Domingo: Fundación Cultural Dominicana, 1986.

——. *Los Estados Unidos y Trujillo, año 1945.* Santo Domingo: Fundación Cultural Dominicana, 1982.

——. *Un interludio de tolerancia: El acuerdo de Trujillo con los comunistas en 1946.* Santo Domingo: Fundación Cultural Dominicana, 1987.

——. *Nazismo, fascismo y falangismo en la República Dominicana.* Santo Domingo: Fundación Cultural Dominicana, 1985.

——. *El 23 de febrero, o la más anunciada revolución de América.* Santo Domingo: Fundación Cultural Dominicana, 1989.

——. *Trujillo y el control financiero norteamericano.* Santo Domingo: Fundación Cultural Dominicana, 1990.

——. *Trujillo y las fuerzas armadas norteamericanas.* Santo Domingo: Fundación Cultural Dominicana, 1992.

——. *Trujillo y Haití, 1930–1937.* 2 vols. Santo Domingo: Fundación Cultural Dominicana, 1988 and 1995.

——. *Los Trujillos se escriben.* Santo Domingo: Fundación Cultural Dominicana, 1985.

——. *La vida cotidiana dominicana: A través del archivo particular del Generalísimo.* Santo Domingo: Fundación Cultural Dominicana, 1986.

Vega y Pagán, Ernesto. *Military Biography of Generalísimo R. L. Trujillo M.* Ciudad Trujillo: Editorial Atenas, 1956.

——. *Síntesis histórica de la Guardia Dominicana.* Ciudad Trujillo: Editorial Atenas, 1953.

Ward, Geoffrey C. *A First-Class Temperament: The Emergence of Franklin Roosevelt.* New York: Harper & Row, 1989.

Warwick, Donald. *A Theory of Bureaucracy: Politics, Personality and Organization in the State Department.* Cambridge: Harvard University Press, 1975.

Weil, Martin. *A Pretty Good Club: The Founding Fathers of the U.S. Foreign Service.* New York: W. W. Norton, 1978.

Welles, Sumner. *Naboth's Vineyard: The Dominican Republic, 1844–1924,* 2 vols. New York: Savile Books, [1928] 1966.

Werking, Richard Hume. *The Master Architects: Building the United States Foreign Service, 1890–1913.* Lexington: University Press of Kentucky, 1977.

Weston, Rubin Francis. *Racism in U.S. Imperialism: The Influence of Racial Assumptions on American Foreign Policy, 1893–1946*. Columbia: University of Missouri Press, 1972.

Whitaker, Arthur P. *The Western Hemisphere Idea: Its Rise and Decline*. Ithaca: Cornell University Press, 1954.

White, Graham. *FDR and the Press*. Chicago: University of Chicago Press, 1979.

Wiarda, Howard J. *Dictatorship and Development: The Methods of Control in Trujillo's Dominican Republic*. Gainesville: University Press of Florida, 1968.

———. *The Dominican Republic: Nation in Transition*. New York: Praeger, 1969.

———. "Dominican Dictatorship Revisited: The Caudillo Tradition and the Regimes of Trujillo and Balaguer." *Revista/Review Interamericana* (Fall 1977): 417–35.

Wiarda, Howard J., and Michael J. Kryzanek. *The Dominican Republic: A Caribbean Crucible*. Boulder: Westview Press, 1982.

Wilson, Joan Hoff. *Herbert Hoover, Forgotten Progressive*. Boston: Little, Brown, 1975.

Wischnitzer, Mark. "The Historical Background of the Settlement of Jewish Refugees in Santo Domingo." *Jewish Social Studies* 4, no. 1 (1942): 42–58.

Wood, Bryce. *The Dismantling of the Good Neighbor Policy*. Austin: University of Texas Press, 1985.

———. *The Making of the Good Neighbor Policy*. New York: Columbia University Press, 1961.

Woods, Randall Bennett. *The Roosevelt Foreign Policy Establishment and the "Good Neighbor": The United States and Argentina, 1941–1945*. Lawrence: University of Kansas Press, 1979.

Yerxa, Donald A. *Admirals and Empire: The United States Navy and the Caribbean, 1898–1945*. Columbia: University of South Carolina Press, 1993.

### UNPUBLISHED

Derby, Lauren. "The Magic of Modernity: Dictatorship and Civic Culture in the Dominican Republic, 1916–1962." Ph.D. diss., University of Chicago, 1998.

Franks, Julie. "Transforming Property: Landholding of Political Rights in the Dominican Sugar Region, 1880–1930." Ph.D. diss., State University of New York–Stony Brook, 1997.

Hall, Michael. "Sugar and Power: Eisenhower, Kennedy, and the Trujillos, 1958–1962." Ph.D. diss., Ohio University, 1996.

Kisch, Hyman J. "The Jewish Settlement from Central Europe in the Dominican Republic." Ph.D. diss., Jewish Theological Seminary, 1970.

MacMichael, David C. "The U.S. and the Dominican Republic, 1871–1940: A Cycle in Caribbean Diplomacy." Ph.D. diss., University of Oregon, 1964.

McHale, James. "The New Deal and the Origins of Foreign Public Lending." Ph.D. diss., University of Wisconsin–Madison, 1971.

Muto, Paul H. "The Illusory Promise: The Dominican Republic and the Process of Economic Development, 1900–1930." Ph.D. diss., University of Washington–Seattle, 1976.

Peguero, Valentina. "Trujillo and the Military: Organization, Modernization and Control of the Dominican Armed Forces, 1916–1961." Ph.D. diss., Columbia University, 1993.

"The United States Military Government in the Dominican Republic, 1916–1922: A Case History." United States Army School for Military Government and Administration, New York, 2d section, Group V, 14 August 1943. Hoover Institution on War, Revolution and Peace, Stanford University, Palo Alto, Calif.

Veeser, Cyrus. "Remapping the Caribbean: Private Investment and U.S. Intervention in the Dominican Republic, 1890–1908." Ph.D. diss., Columbia University, 1997.

# INDEX

Acosta y Lara, Horacio, 115
Adams, Charles Francis, 53, 74
Adams, John Quincy, 23
Advisory Committee on Political
    Refugees, 144
Agricultural Adjustment Act, 89
Alfonseca, José, 36, 40
All America Cable Company, 101
American Bridge Company, 103
American Colony, 18–19, 43–44, 55, 86,
    92, 102–4,115, 123, 150, 157–59, 168,
    172, 185–87, 206, 212, 235–38
Andrews, Frank Maxwell, 221–23
Argentina, 25, 155, 160, 184, 186, 226,
    228
Arias, Desiderio, 16
Arielismo, 25
Associated Press, 20, 101, 111, 114, 138
Associated Telephone and Telegraph,
    103
Atwood, Franklin, 135–36
Axis powers, 2, 184, 203–8, 220

Babcock, Orville E., 11
Báez, Buenaventura, 9–10
Báez, Mauricio, 232

Baker, Newton, 74
Barletta, Amadeo, 122–26
Batista, Fulgencio, 178–79, 209
Bazil, Osvaldo, 104
Bencosme, Sergio, 106–7, 232
Bennett, W. Tapley, 222
Berle, Adolf, 145, 206
Besault, Laurence de, 111
Betancourt, Rómulo, 232, 241
Beverly, James, 54
Bhabha, Homi, 118
Bickers, William, 42, 48
Blaine, James G., 24
Blake, Howard, 143
Blake, Robert, 173, 188
*Blondie Goes Latin,* 28
Boca Chica Beach, 110, 172
Bogotá Conference. *See* Pan-American
    Conferences
*Boletín de Relaciones Exteriores,* 85, 121
Bonetti Burgos, Ernesto, 93
Borah, William, 49
Borno, Louis, 129
Bosch, Juan, 95
Bowman, Isaiah, 144
Brache, Elías, 68, 124

Brache, Rafael, 51, 68, 102, 104, 123–24, 194–96, 238

Braden, Spruille, 186–87, 226–29, 234

Brazil, 25, 29, 200

Breckinridge, James, 176, 178

Brett, George H., 222–23

Briggs, Ellis O., 182–87, 223–29, 241

Brookings Institution, 67

Brown, Heywood, 180

Brown, James E., 78

Buenos Aires Peace Conference. See Pan-American Conferences

Burke, Arthur, 214

Butler, John A., 181, 209

Butler, Nicholas Murray, 112

Cabot, John Moors, 34–61, 156, 175, 189, 224

Cáceres, Ramón, 14–15

Caffery, Jefferson, 76, 80, 86, 169

Calixte, Démosthène, 136

Caracas, 104, 106

Caribbean Defense Command, 222–23

Caribbean Legion, 232

Carrel, M. D., 167

Case, J. Herbert, 75

Castillo Nájera, Francisco, 138

Cayo Confites (Cuba), 232

Central Intelligence Agency, 240–42

Cestero, Tulio, 47, 59, 115, 122

Chapin, Selden, 175, 198–99

Chaplin, Charlie, 206–7

Chenery, William, 141

Chevalier, André, 183

Cibao Valley (Dominican Republic), 16, 31, 47, 90, 95, 159

Ciudad Trujillo. See Santo Domingo

Clark, J. Reuben, 74–75, 81–84, 103, 200, 217; Memorandum on the Monroe Doctrine, 74–75

Cold War, 5, 193, 230–34, 242

Collins, James A., 221

Colombia, 200–1

Columbia University, 38, 112

Columbus, Christopher, 112–18; Columbus Memorial Lighthouse 26, 114–17, 221

Connally, Thomas, 225

Convention of Conciliation, 138–40

Convention of 1924, 19, 34, 64–87, 177, 180, 193–202, 210–19

Coolidge, Calvin, 26–27, 34

Costa Rica, 227, 233

Cotton, Joseph, 37–50

Crassweller, Robert, 170

Cuba, 6, 9–13, 32, 49, 89, 104, 130, 155, 186, 192, 208, 227, 232–3, 239; Cuban Revolution of 1898, 24; Cuban Revolution of 1933, 79, 171; mediation of Haitian massacre, 135–38; Platt Amendment, 24; U.S. Army occupation, 18

Cuban-American Sugar Company, 51

Culebra (Puerto Rico), 181

Curtis, Charles, 54

Curtis, Charles B., 31–59, 68, 76, 91, 101, 156–57, 165–68

Cutts, Richard M., 21–22, 45, 50, 56–57, 157, 166–67, 236

Dajabón (Dominican Republic), 131

Davies, Joseph E., 3, 76–87, 105, 111–12, 122, 141, 194–97

Davis, Henry C., 241

Dawes, Charles, 79

Dawes Commission, 27, 34, 213

de Alba, Pedro, 116

de Lara, Ramón, 96

del Rio, Dolores, 29

del Valle, Pedro A., 208–9

Deschamps, Enrique, 47

Despradel, Arturo, 181, 205, 209

Despradel, Roberto, 83, 205, 217

Dessalines, Jean-Jacques, 8

Destroyers-for-Bases, 214

Díaz, Simón, 37

Dictatorship, 87, 175, 230–43; in the Caribbean region, 4, 32–33, 227; Good Neighbor policy toward, 124–26, 146–48, 192–93, 203–10, 224–29; in Latin America, 127–28, 228–29; and public opinion, 61–62, 109

Diplomatic Corps, 91, 149–91, 204–7, 212

Djamgaroff, George, 114, 116

Dollar diplomacy, 14–15, 27, 73

Dominican Armed Forces, 233–34; Air Force, 71, 224; Coast Guard, 205; National Army, 22, 32–42, 49–57, 127, 134, 138, 150, 156, 156–91; National Guard, 18–22, 102; Navy, 82, 166

Dominican Chamber of Commerce, 110–11, 167

Dominican Emergency Law, 66–87

Dominican-German Scientific Institute, 204

Dominican lobby, 3, 105, 110–14, 122, 216, 227, 235–38

Dominican National Police. See Dominican Armed Forces: National Guard

Dominican Republic: border with Haiti, 129–31; business climate, 103; Constitution, 33–35; foreign debt, 11–15, 63–87, 195–202, 210–19; guerrilla fighters, 18, 165; identification with Trujillo, 97–99; independence of, 9–10; infrastructural development, 12, 59, 173–74; nationalism, 129, 237; political parties, 47, 52 (see also Partido Dominicano); Revolution of 1930, 30–47, 58, 80, 83, 91, 225; social classes, 15, 43–44, 90–91,

149, 155–64, 187–88; strategic value, 11, 192–93, 208–10; U.S. Marine occupation of, 2, 16–22, 25–26, 33, 51, 95, 117, 164–65, 188, 209, 217, 219, 239–41; War of Restoration, 11

Dominican Republic Settlement Association, 145–46

Dominican Tobacco Company, 123

Drago Doctrine, 65–66

Duarte, Juan Pablo, 9, 98

Duggan, Laurence, 114, 116, 144, 214–15

Duggan, Stephen, 114

Dulles, John Foster, 189

Dunn, William E., 78, 107

Eisenhower, Dwight, 228; administration of, 242

Estrella Ureña, Rafael, 31, 36–44, 91, 104–5, 155, 157

Estrella, José, 90

Evian Conference, 143–45

Exiles, 48, 54, 102–6, 186, 218, 227, 231–32

Export-Import Bank, 192, 202, 208, 211, 213, 217

Federal Bureau of Investigation, 54, 105

Federal Trade Commission, 72–73

Feis, Herbert, 73, 200–1, 208

Fiallo, Fabio, 100

Field, Robert M., 141

Finley, Harold, 216

Fish, Hamilton, 113–14, 138, 147, 178, 180

Flanagan, William Jr., 242

Florida, 10, 23

Flying Down to Rio, 28–30

Forbes Commission, 27, 50

Foreign Bondholders Protective Council, 72–89, 103, 111, 193–202, 208–19

*Foreign Policy Reports,* 102–4
Fortaleza Ozama, 20, 36, 40, 47, 83, 92,
    173, 219
Fortaleza Trujillo. *See* Fortaleza Ozama
Foster, Henry Clay, 110
France, 13; Caribbean colonization,
    7–9, 190
Freeman, C. S., 171

Galienne, W. H., 37–40, 46, 51, 122, 155
Galíndez, Jesús de, 106, 232, 241
Gann, Edward E., 54
Gantenbein, James, 82, 195
García Godoy, Emilio, 225–27
Gellman, Irwin, 128
General Electric, 75
General Motors, 75, 123
General Receivership of Dominican
    Customs, 14, 34, 64–89, 193–202,
    210–19
Germany, 13, 178, 194, 203–8
Gleave, J. L., 115
Gondra Treaty, 27, 138–40
Good Neighbor policy, 1–4; alliances
    with dictators, 154–55; and anti-
    Semitism, 147–48; and defense of
    the hemisphere, 192–230 *passim;*
    Hoover administration version, 27–
    28, 61–62; and lack of institutional
    coordination, 149–91, 224–25, 234–
    43; and Latin American debt, 63–87;
    and mediation, 133–43; and Monroe
    Doctrine, 122–26; origins of, 22–30;
    and publicity, 90–128, 146–48; and
    racism, 147–48, 241; and recognition
    policy, 48–54; Roosevelt administra-
    tion version, 27–30, 88–89, 107–10,
    117, 125–26, 192–93
Göring, Hermann, 207
Grant, Ulysses S., 11

Grau San Martín, Ramón, 241
Great Britain, 9, 190
Great Depression, 62–67
*Great Dictator, The,* 206–7
Green, Theodore, 113–14, 178–79, 216
Gruening, Ernest, 124–25
Guantánamo Bay, 242
Guaranty Trust, 196, 214
Guatemala, 32, 227, 232–33, 240
Guillaume Sam, Vilbrun, 16
Gunboat diplomacy, 22, 27, 151, 242

Hackworth, Green, 199, 215–16
Haina Military Academy, 19–21, 164,
    174, 184, 240
Haiti, 112, 192, 208, 221, 225, 228, 239;
    border with Dominican Republic,
    129–31; colonial history, 7–8; con-
    flict with the Dominican Republic,
    10–11, 129, 132–33, 147, 190, 227, 233,
    242; debt settlement, 194–95; Garde
    d'Haiti, 18, 136, 209; Haitian Revo-
    lution, 8–9; U.S. Marine occupation,
    16–17, 25–27, 34, 67, 129, 153. *See also*
    Haitian massacre
Haitian massacre, 4, 114, 120, 126–48,
    180, 205, 226
Haitian National Guard. *See* Haiti:
    Garde d'Haiti
Harding, Warren G., 18, 26, 34, 76
Harris, Arthur, 209–10
Harvard University, 38–39, 79, 82, 183
Havana Conferences. *See* Pan-American
    Conferences
Havana Radio Conference, 133
Havana, 6, 38, 79, 104–5, 186, 209
Henríquez y Carvajal, Francisco, 16
Heureaux, Ulisis, 11–15, 48, 55, 65, 197
Hispaniola. *See* Dominican Republic;
    Haiti

Hitler, Adolf, 127, 138, 204–7
Holidays: Civic Reviews, 95–96; Dominican Centennial, 185, 221; Dominican Independence Day, 40, 95–96; Fourth of July, 159, 183, 185; Restoration Day, 54, 95–96, 209, 221; Washington's Birthday, 159
Honduras, 32, 228
Hoover, Herbert, 26; administration of, 1–2, 22, 102, 105, 217–18; background, 70; Good Neighbor policy, 28, 61–64; "good will" tour of Latin America, 34; Latin American debt policy, 63–72; reaction to Dominican Revolution of 1930, 32–53; as secretary of commerce, 34
House, Edward, 25
Hughes, Charles Evans, 19
Hughes-Peynado Plan, 19–20, 65, 68. See also Welles, Sumner: Convention of 1924
Hull, Cordell, 92, 119–20, 137, 143–44, 181, 238; and Avenida Cordell Hull, 212–13; and Latin American debts, 74–75, 78–87, 194–216; meetings with Trujillo, 179–80; and Mussolini, 123–24; and publicity, 106–9; and reciprocity treaties, 89; retirement of, 224; as symbol of Good Neighbor policy, 212–13, 226–27. See also Hull-Trujillo Treaty
Hull-Trujillo Treaty (Convention of 1940), 4, 182, 210–19, 227–28; Trujillo-Hull Treaty Monument, 212–13, 221

Ickes, Harold, 131, 201
Inman, Samuel Guy, 74, 143
Institute of International Education, 114

Inter-American Bank, 202
Inter-American Commission of Women, 141
Inter-American Defense Board, 189, 208
Interdepartmental Committee on Cooperation with the American Republics, 201–2
Intergovernmental Committee on Political Refugees, 143–45
Italy, 122–27, 203–8

Jackson, Andrew, 24
Jefferson, Thomas, 23
Jewish refugees, 143–48
J. G. White Company, 167
Jiménez, Juan Isidro, 16
Johns Hopkins University, 144, 183
Johnson Amendment to Securities Act of 1933, 72–73, 77
Johnson, Andrew, 11
Johnson, Hiram, 66
Johnston, Leland, 240–41
Joint Army and Navy Planning Committee, 208
Jones, Jesse, 201–2

Kellogg, Frank, 33–34
Kennedy administration, 242
Kerr, David R., 187–88
Kilbourne, Edwin I., 103
King, Rufus, 209–10
King, William, 113
Kirchway, Freda, 145
Knapp, Harry S., 16–17, 153–54, 235–36
Knowles, Horace, 18
Knox, Frank, 192

L'Ouverture, Toussaint, 8–9
La Guardia, Fiorello, 180

La Jaragua Hotel, 189, 213
La Romana (Dominican Republic), 17
La Vega (Dominican Republic), 97
Latin America: and Great Depression,
    62–67; military strength of, 32; U.S.
    policy toward, 3–5, 16–32; U.S. trade
    with, 26. *See also* Dictatorship: in
    Latin America
League of Nations, 26, 119
Lee, Harry, 18–20, 165
Léger, Georges, 132–35
Lend-Lease Act, 5, 192, 208, 219–24,
    227
Lescot, Elie, 136
Lima Conference. *See* Pan-American
    Conferences
Logroño, Arturo, 124, 130, 162, 205
London Economic and Monetary
    Conference, 72
London Naval Conference, 38
Lovatón, Lina, 163
Luce, Henry, 106
Luperón (Dominican Republic), 232
Luperón, Gregorio, 11

Maccario, Antonio, 123–24
Machado, Gerardo, 43, 49
MacLean, James J., 21
Magazines: *Collier's*, 141–42; *Cosmo-
    politan*, 100; *The Dominican Republic*,
    103, 110; *Fortune*, 114; *Life*, 114,
    138; *Marine Corps Gazette*, 241; *The
    Nation*, 111, 113, 124, 138–40, 145,
    223; *Revista Militar*, 22, 187; *Time*,
    106, 179, 226
*March of Time*, 106–9, 111, 137, 207
Marshall, George C., 178, 182, 189, 228
Martínez Reyna, Virgilio, 52
Martínez Trujillo, María, 163
Martinique, 205
Mayer, Ferdinand, 132–34, 140–42

McAdoo, William, 26
McClintock, Robert Mills, 144
McGurk, Joseph F., 86, 124, 175, 186,
    195, 224–25
McKinley, William, 24
McLaughlin, Alma, 170
McLaughlin, Charles, 169–70, 181, 203,
    209
Mella, Ramón, 9
Merritt, Matthew, 113
Mexico, 6, 10, 160, 194; mediation of
    Haitian massacre, 135–38; Marine
    occupation of Veracruz, 17
Michelena, Oscar, 91–93, 99–100,
    104–6, 123, 162
Michelena, Santiago, 91
Michelena, Teté, 162
Miles, Milton, 189, 228
Military Assistance Program, 228
Mona Passage, 11, 192
Monroe Doctrine, 13, 23–25, 88, 122–26
Montecristi (Dominican Republic), 131
Montevideo Conference. *See* Pan-
    American Conferences
Montez, María, 29, 222
Moore, Walton, 112, 116
Morales, Angel, 47–48, 51, 101–6, 111
Morganthau, Henry, 194, 201–2, 214
Morrow, Dwight, 75, 77
Mouton, Robert, 113
Munich Conference, 173
Munro, Dana, 48, 202, 217
Murphy, Gerald, 232, 241
Murray-Jacoby, H., 112
Mussolini, Benito, 122–27, 203–5
Myers, G. J., 172
Myers, J. T., 165

Nanita, Abelardo, 89, 125, 165
National City Bank, 14, 51, 214, 217
National Negro Congress, 140

New York, 9, 38, 63, 104, 180
Newman, Oliver, 78, 80, 111
Newspapers: *Baltimore Sun,* 101, 167;
  *Boston Herald,* 42; *Chicago Daily News,*
  166; *La Opinión* (Santo Domingo),
  90, 93, 95, 99; *Listín Diario* (Santo
  Domingo), 52–53, 95, 99, 119, 155,
  160, 172, 183, 209; *London Times,*
  84; *New York Herald Tribune,* 84,
  105, 145; *New York Times,* 42, 50, 98,
  123, 134–35, 139, 147–48, 212; *New
  York World-Telegram,* 180; *Wall Street
  Journal,* 84; *Washington Herald,* 111;
  *Washington Post,* 139, 180, 226
Nicaragua, 10, 32, 34, 67, 151, 153, 228
Nigua Prison, 113
Nobel Peace Prize, 118, 120, 130
Norweb, R. Henry, 119, 132–35, 141–
  42, 157–58, 173, 179, 190, 199, 202,
  218–19, 237

O'Neill, Eugene, *The Emperor Jones,*
  28–30
Order of Duarte, 112, 121, 206, 222
Organization of American States, 120,
  231–32, 242
Ornes, Germán: *Trujillo, Little Caesar of
  the Caribbean,* 239
Ortega Frier, Julio, 130, 132, 135, 198–
  99, 205
Osorio Lizarazo, José Antonio, 218

Panama Conference. *See* Pan-American
  Conferences
Panama: Declaration of, 214; Canal,
  4, 11, 25, 29, 192, 211; Canal Zone,
  13, 38; Railroad, 11, 13; Republic of,
  11–13, 222–23
Panama-Pacific International Exposition, 25
Pan American Airways, 28, 34, 101, 103,

167–68, 191, 209, 220 Pan-American
  Aviation Day, 221
Pan-American Conferences: Bogotá
  (1948), 231; Buenos Aires (1936),
  39, 104, 107, 119–20, 134–35, 199;
  Havana (1928), 27; Havana (1940),
  29, 181, 209–10; Lima (1938), 29,
  120; Montevideo (1933), 74–75, 80,
  85, 115, 119, 122; Panama (1939), 29,
  214; Santiago, Chile (1923), 27, 115
Pan-American Day, 28, 88, 119, 203,
  221–22
Pan-Americanism, 22–30, 128, 192–93,
  228
Pan-American Pact, 25–26
Pan-American Union, 26, 114–16,
  120–21, 140, 179
Partido Dominicano, 93–94, 97, 99–
  100, 103–4, 133, 204
Partido Trujillista. *See* Partido Domini-
  cano
Pastoriza, Andrés, 103, 107–8, 131–38,
  147, 197, 202, 209, 218, 238
Paterson, Alexander, 123, 125, 139–40,
  161, 205–7
Pearl Harbor, 220
Pearson, Drew, 59–62, 69, 101–2, 167
Pellerano Alfau, Arturo J., 52, 99
Peña Batlle, Manuel Arturo, 185, 226
Perkins, Constantine M., 188
Perón, Eva, 186
Perón, Juan, 186, 226
Petri, E. H., 57–58
Peurifoy, John, 240
Peynado, Francisco, 19–20, 65
Peynado, Jacinto, 96, 107, 120, 130,
  141–42
Philip, Hoffman, 139
Philippines, 18, 49, 89
Phillips, William, 76–77
Pico Duarte, 98

Piña Chevalier, Teódulo, 21, 183
Pittman, Key, 80
Platt Amendment, 24, 194
Polk, James K., 24
Porta, Mario, 205–7
Port-au-Prince, 14, 104, 130
Porter, Charles, 232
Porter, Cole, 28
Porter, David Dixon, 11
Post, Marjorie Meriweather, 112
Posvar, Lester, 101–2
Puerto Plata, 42–43, 48, 170
Puerto Rico, 6, 9, 166, 239; Dominican
  exiles in, 54; immigration 130–31;
  U.S. Army occupation of, 18
Pulliam, Muriel, 86
Pulliam, William, 68–69, 86, 100, 102,
  115–16, 168, 178, 198

Radio City Music Hall, 107–8
Randolph, Norman, 208
Reconstruction Finance Corporation,
  73, 201
Reynolds, Quentin, 141–42, 147
Reynolds, Robert, 112–13
Ricart, Alfredo, 92, 103
Richards, George, 120, 168–69
Richberg, Donald, 139
Rivers: Higuamo, 103; Ozama, 7, 55,
  57, 98, 107, 116, 172, 176; Yaque del
  Norte, 98; Yuna, 98
Robeson, Paul, 30
Robison, Samuel S., 19–20
Rockefeller, Nelson, 185–86, 222–25
Roebling, John A., 98
Rogers Act, 153–54
Rohrecke, Hans Felix, 204–7
Roosevelt Corollary to the Monroe
  Doctrine, 13, 65, 75
Roosevelt, Eleanor, 121, 167–68
Roosevelt, Franklin, 38, 118, 120–22,

174, 204, 222; administration of,
  1–3, 22, 104–5; affinity for Marine
  Corps, 169; death, 224; Good Neigh-
  bor policy, 27–30, 88–89, 107–10,
  117, 125–26, 192–93, 234, 238; Latin
  American debt policy, 72–87, 194–
  202, 211–14; and mediation of Hai-
  tian massacre, 132–42; meeting with
  Trujillo, 179–80; policy toward dic-
  tatorships, 182, 230–43; refugee
  policy of, 143–48; relationship with
  Welles, 79
Roosevelt, Henry Latrobe, 169–70
Roosevelt, James, 121, 198
Roosevelt, Theodore Jr., 54, 56, 59,
  166–68
Roosevelt, Theodore, 13–14, 65
Rosenberg, James, 145–46
Rosso, Augusto, 124
Rowe, Leo, 115–16
Rubirosa, Porfirio, 205
Russell, William, 16

Saarinen, Eliel, 115
Saavedra Lamas, Carlos, 74, 119
Saint Domingue. See Haiti
Samaná Bay (Dominican Republic), 11,
  53, 121, 174, 203–5
San Cristóbal (Dominican Republic),
  21, 44, 97, 132
San Domingo Improvement Company,
  12, 14
San Francisco (California), 25
San Juan (Puerto Rico), 104–5, 204
San Pedro de Macorís (Dominican
  Republic), 17, 103, 121
San Zenón hurricane, 55–59, 67, 71,
  115, 165–66, 174, 190
Sánchez, José del Rosario, 9
Santana, Pedro, 9–10

Santiago (Dominican Republic), 16, 31, 36–37, 43–44, 90, 95, 131, 160
Santiago Conference. *See* Pan-American Conferences
Santo Domingo, 3, 14, 26, 67, 105, 110, 115–17, 130, 141, 203, 233, 241; aviation facilities, 220–21; Dominican Revolution of 1930, 35–43; founding of, 6; renamed Ciudad Trujillo, 59, 97–98, 107; U.S. Marine control of, 16–21; social life in, 155–64, 182–89; U.S. Navy visits to, 52, 149–54, 170–82. *See also* San Zenón hurricane
Santo Domingo Country Club, 20, 91, 157–60, 168, 178, 191
Schoenfeld, Aïda, 86, 161–65
Schoenfeld, H. F. Arthur, 76–86, 91–93, 97–98, 117, 123–24, 151, 157–63, 198
Schoenrich, Otto, 167
Scott, Winthrop, 45, 62
Scotten, Robert McGregor, 206–14, 220–21
*Semana Patriótica*, 17–18
Sheffield, James, 77
Ships: *Arend* (Dutch cruiser) 57; HMS *Danae*, 57; USS *Grebe*, 56–57; USS *Langley*, 204; USS *Memphis*, 16, 121–22, 191; USS *Mugford*, 203; USS *Omaha*, 172; USS *Philadelphia*, 173–74, 204; *Presidente Trujillo* (presidential yacht), 107, 112, 177; *Presidente Trujillo* (merchant vessel), 220; USS *Raleigh*, 170; USS *Sacramento*, 52–53, 170; *San Rafael* (merchant vessel), 220; *Schlesien* (German battleship), 203; *Sea Cloud* (yacht), 111–12, 197; USS *Tennessee*, 26; USS *Texas*, 177–78, 203; HMS *Wistaria*, 39–40
Silva Vildosola, Carlos, 61

Smith, Joe W., 222–23, 240
Smoot-Hawley Tariff, 64
Somoza, Anastasio, 151, 179
Sosua refugee settlement, 128, 143–48
Soviet Union, 197, 204
Spain, 155; cession of Florida, 10, 23; colonialism of, 6–9, 191; Spanish-American War, 11; Spanish Civil War, 144
Special Service Squadron, 20, 26, 32, 38, 53–54, 154, 171–72, 188, 209, 242. *See also* U.S. Navy: "good will" visits
Stalin, Joseph, 197, 230
Standard Oil, 75, 222
Standing Liaison Committee (Navy, State, and War Departments), 175–76, 208
Steamship lines, 191; Bull Insular Line, 100; Clyde Line, 12; German Horn Line, 100, 204; New York and Port Rico Steamship Company, 100
Stimson, Henry, 27, 32, 35, 38–39, 49, 54, 61, 64–72
Sugar, 6–9; Boca Chica estate, 21; Consuelo estate, 103, 220; production in the Dominican Republic, 12, 14, 17, 55, 103, 218, 233, 238; Sugar Act of 1765, 9; Sugar Act of 1934, 89; U.S. quota on, 89; workers, 130–31
Sullivan, William B., 56–58
Sumner, Charles, 11, 78
Swanson, Claude, 169, 179

Taft, William Howard, 15
Tainos, 6
Todd, Ford A., 173–74
Townsend, Mathilde, 79, 86
Transcontinental Treaty, 23
Troncoso, Jesús María, 221
Troncoso de la Concha, Manuel de Jesús, 130, 137–38, 142

Trujillo, Bienvenida, 163
Trujillo, Flor de Oro, 205, 222
Trujillo, Héctor, 93, 170
Trujillo, Rafael: background, 21, 131; censorship by, 80, 99–102; consolidation of power, 90–99; domination of culture and society, 149–52, 155–91 passim; efforts to obtain loans, 68–87, 196–97; elections of, 47–48, 105, 220; era of, 55, 98, 116, 191, 232–33; foreign policy apparatus, 238–39; inaugurations of, 54–55, 59, 156; Las Caobas estate, 189; love life, 162–63; Marine Corps training, 21–22, 240; monopolies, 93; and Mussolini, 122–26; Order of, 222; personalism, 59, 94–99, 233; postwar policy of, 230–42; publicity, 110–22; recognition of by United States, 48–54; regime of, 1–5; relationship with U.S. military representatives, 56–59, 69, 149–52, 164–82, 187–91, 209, 219–22, 238–41; seizure of power, 31–62; visits to the United States, 178–82, 189, 216–17, 233; and wardrobe, 163–65, 189; wartime policy of, 194–230 passim
Trujillo, Ramfis, 161
Trujillo, Virgilio, 143
Truman, Harry S., 225–28
Tugwell, Rexford Guy, 223

Uncle Sam, The Good Neighbor, 108–9, 154
U.S. Air Force, 241
U.S. Congress, 242; House of Representatives Subcommittee on Naval Affairs, 203; Senate Foreign Relations Committee, 34, 80, 215–16, 225
U.S. Marine Corps, 45; Avenida USMC, 176–78, 203; competition with State

Department, 150–55, 164–76, 178–82, 234–40; culture of, 150, 188; hurricane assistance in Santo Domingo, 54–59, 165–66, 176; Marine Air Corps, 56; training of Dominican National Guard, 18–22, 102, 106–7. See also Dominican Republic: U.S. Marine occupation of
U.S. Navy, 11, 15; Atlantic Fleet, 181; Commission on Navy Yards and Navy Stations, 53; Fleet Problem Twenty, 204; "good will" visits, 150–55, 170–91, 203, 207–8, 228, 235, 242; Naval Aviation Mission, 220; Naval Intelligence Division, 142–43; Naval War College, 235; Western Hemisphere Group, 242. See also Special Service Squadron
U.S. State Department, 3, 18, 207; budget, 159; competition for direction of U.S. foreign policy, 150–55, 164–76, 178–82, 234–40; Division of American Republics, 108, 172–75, 186, 208, 225; Division of Latin American Affairs, 48, 75, 169; Foreign Service, 151–54, 175, 186, 240; loan policy, 63–67, 193–202; nonintervention policy of, 39–46, 60–61, 105, 108–9; Office of Inter-American Affairs, 29, 185, 192; policy toward Trujillo regime, 54–62, 151–52, 224–29; professionalization of, 151–54; Protocol Division, 120; recognition policy, 48–54; representation in the Dominican Republic, 14, 159–60, 221–22; Visa Division, 183
U.S. War Department, 89, 189; Bureau of Insular Affairs, 14, 54; Military Assistance Program, 228–29, 234; Military Mission to the Dominican

Republic, 223–24, 234; War Plans
Division, 182
Ulen and Company, 167
Upshur, William, 176–78

Vandenburg, Arthur, 215–16, 225
Vargas, Getulio, 29
Vásquez, Horacio, 20–22, 31–45, 49, 54,
79, 103, 129, 155
Vedder, Frank, 213
Velásquez, Federico, 47–48, 102, 104
Venezuela, 227, 232–33
Veracruz (Mexico), 17
Verdi, Giuseppe, *Aïda,* 161
Versailles Peace Conference, 26
Vicini Burgos, Juan B., 20
Vidal, Rafael, 83
Villard, Oswald Garrison, 111, 113
Vincent, Stenio, 120, 130–42, 163
Virgin Islands, 56

Wadsworth, Eliot, 68; and Wadsworth
Commission, 166
Waldorf Astoria Hotel, 216–17
Wall Street, 63–64, 75
Walsh, David, 138, 178
Warren, Avra, 182–88, 221–23
Washington Treaty (1923), 49–50
Washington, D.C., 24, 178–80, 188–89,
236, 240
Washington, George, 23, 117–18, 121;
and Avenida George Washington,
174, 177–78, 183, 221
Watson, Thomas E., 57, 164–69, 178,
209, 240

Welles, Sumner, 3, 75–76, 110, 157–
58, 210, 218; anti-Semitism of, 143;
background, 78–79; and Convention
of 1924, 19–20, 65, 79–80, 166; and
Haitian massacre, 132–42; *Naboth's
Vineyard,* 78, 102; opposition to
Trujillo regime, 60, 82–87, 101–5,
174–78, 194–202, 213, 218, 226–28,
240; resignation of, 222; support for
Columbus Lighthouse, 115–16
Westendorp Company, 12–13
Wheeler, J. E., 115
White, Francis, 48–50, 74–75, 195–96,
199–202, 214–19
White, Walter, 139
Williams, Gregon, 169
Williams, Yancey S., 172–73
Wilson, Edwin, 77, 80, 86
Wilson, Hugh, 211–15
Wilson, Woodrow, 38; and intervention
in Haiti and the Dominican Repub-
lic, 15–18; Pan-American policy of,
25–26
Windward Passage, 11, 192
World Peace Fair (Ciudad Trujillo,
1955), 233
World's Fair (New York, 1939), 116–17,
125
World War I, 2, 17, 65
World War II, 4, 29, 116, 127, 132, 149,
155, 179–82, 192–93, 202–30, 242
Wright, Frank Lloyd, 115

Young, Evan, 33–35
Yugoslavia, 200

Eric Paul Roorda is Assistant Professor in the Department
of History at Bellarmine College.

Library of Congress Cataloging-in-Publication Data
Roorda, Eric Paul.
The dictator next door : the good neighbor policy and the
Trujillo regime in the Dominican Republic, 1930–1945 /
Eric Paul Roorda.
p.   cm. — (American encounters/global interactions)
Includes bibliographical references (p.   –   ) and index.
ISBN 0-8223-2234-X (alk. paper). —
ISBN 0-8223-2123-8 (pbk. : alk. paper)
1. United States—Foreign relations—Dominican Republic.
2. Dominican Republic—Foreign relations—United States.
3. Dominican Republic—History—1930–1961.   4. Trujillo
Molina, Rafael Leónidas, 1891–1961.   I. Title.   II. Series.
E183.8.D6R59   1998
327.7307293—dc21   98-12100   CIP